DATE DUE

DE 3 '88			
DE 19 '88			
MAY 3 '89			
FEB 19 '91			
MAR 0 8 '91			
MAY APR 1 0 '91			
DEC 1 0 '92			
RT'D DEC 0 7 '92			
MAY 1 0 '97			
GAYLORD			PRINTED IN U.S.A.

EXILE AND RETURN

EXILE AND RETURN

The Struggle for a Jewish Homeland

Martin Gilbert

J. B. Lippincott Company

Philadelphia and New York

U.S. Library of Congress Cataloging in Publication Data

Gilbert, Martin, birth date
 Exile and return.

 Bibliography: p.
 Includes index.

 1. Zionism—History. 2. Palestine—History—
1917-1948. I. Title.
DS149.G5225   1978   956.94'001   78-9780
ISBN-0-397-01249-7

Dedicated to the Memory of
Carmella Yadin

Contents

List of Maps   *xi*
List of Illustrations   *xiii*
Preface   *xv*

Part One: Israel Dispersed
An Historical Survey

1 Israel Dispersed   *3*
2 Medieval Persecutions, Flight and Hope   *13*
3 Sixty Years of Ferment, *1815-1875*   *26*
4 The Russian Cauldron, *1875-1891*   *35*
5 'A Great and Beautiful Cause', *1891-1897*   *44*
6 'A Flag and an Idea', *1898-1905*   *52*
7 'Jerusalem Must be the Only Ultimate Goal', *1906-1914* *66*

Part Two: From National Home to Sovereign State
A Documentary Study

8 Zionism and the First Two Years of War, *1914-1916*   *79*
9 The Evolution of the Balfour Declaration, *1917*   *92*
10 Hopes and Promises, *1917-1919*   *109*
11 'A National Idea of a Commanding Character', *1919-1921* *119*
12 The Palestine Mandate Secured, *1921-1922*   *135*
13 Persecutions, Riots and Refugees, *1923-1933*   *149*
14 'Formidable in Action . . . Strong in Restraint', *1933-1937* *160*
15 Jewish Hopes and Arab Pressures, *1937*   *178*
16 Jewish Hopes and British Appeasement, *1938*   *195*
17 'The Violation of the Pledge', *January-June 1939*   *216*
18 Towards the Abyss, *July-December 1939*   *236*
19 Beyond the Abyss, *1939-1942*   *252*

CONTENTS

20 Holocaust, Resistance and Flight   *258*
21 Closing the Door, 'Justice' and Revolt, *1945-1946*   *272*
   Epilogue: The Coming of Jewish Statehood, *1947-1948*   *297*

   Careers after 1948   *310*
   List of Archival Sources   *312*
   Bibliography   *325*
   Index   *333*

List of Maps

Map 1   The First Jewish Dispersions   *page 4*
Map 2   The 'Western' Diaspora in Roman Times   8
Map 3   Jewish Medieval Expulsions   10
Map 4   The Black Death Riots, 1347-1350   14
Map 5   The Expulsion of the Jews from Spain, Portugal, Sicily and
     Sardinia, 1492-1497   16
Map 6   The Jews of Palestine Under Byzantine and Muslim Rule   18
Map 7   The Ukrainian Massacres, 1648-1650   23
Map 8   The 'Hep! Hep!' Riots of 1819   30
Map 9   The Jewish Pale of Settlement in Russia   37
Map 10   The Anti-Jewish Pogroms in Tsarist Russia   63
Map 11   Jewish Farms and Villages in Palestine by 1914   67
Map 12   Arab Attacks on Jewish Settlements before 1914   75
Map 13   Britain's Promise to the Arabs, 1915   88
Map 14   The Sykes-Picot Agreement, 1916   90
Map 15   The British Advance into Palestine, 1917   94
Map 16   Britain and the Palestine Mandate   147
Map 17   The Peel Commission Plan, 1937   181
Map 18   The Proposed Jewish State: A Territorial Comparison   183
Map 19   Concentration Camps in Germany by 1938   213
Map 20   Routes of the 'Illegal' Immigrants Before the War   224
Map 21   Jewish and Arab Immigration into Palestine Between the Wars   231
Map 22   Restrictions on Jewish Land Purchase, 1940   248
Map 23   The Fate of the Jews of Russia, 1941-1945   254
Map 24   The Concentration Camps   263
Map 25   Jewish Revolts Against the Nazis, 1942-1945   266
Map 26   The Jewish Death Toll, 1939-1945   271
Map 27   Routes of the 'Illegal' Immigrants, 1945-1948   277
Map 28   The United Nations Partition Plan of November 1947   305

List of Illustrations

1 Theodor Herzl with his fellow Zionist leaders, Jerusalem, 2 November 1898, waiting to greet the Kaiser.
2 Chaim Weizmann and the Emir Feisal, near Akaba, 4 June 1918.
3 Churchill on Mount Scopus, 29 March 1921.
4 General Allenby, Lord Balfour and Sir Herbert Samuel at the opening of the Hebrew University, Jerusalem, 1 April 1925.
5 Sir Mark Sykes, a supporter of both Zionist and Arab aspirations.
6 Arthur Ruppin, pioneer of the Kibbutz movement.
7 'Jews are not wanted here': a sign photographed in Germany in 1935.
8 A synagogue in the Sudetenland destroyed during the *Kristallnacht*, 18 November 1938.
9 A protest by Jerusalem Jews against the 1939 White Paper.
10 Watched by the Nazis, Jewish refugees leave Memel, 25 March 1939.
11 A ship with 'illegal' Jewish immigrants approaches the shores of Palestine after a perilous journey from the Black Sea.
12 The Zionist Congress, at Geneva, hears the news of the Nazi-Soviet Pact, 24 August 1939. David Ben-Gurion is seated between Moshe Sharett (far left) and Chaim Weizmann.
13 The Mufti of Jerusalem greeted by a senior Nazi official in Berlin, 1941.
14 Jewish refugees from Transnistria reach Palestine by rail from Turkey, July 1944.
15 Golda Meir on hunger strike, in protest against the British refusal to allow Jewish refugees to travel to Palestine through Italian ports in April 1946.
16 Jews being taken off the *Exodus*, before being forcibly transferred to another ship and returned to Europe, July 1947.

Preface

SINCE the establishment of the State of Israel in 1948, there has been a continuing debate about the nature, the evolution, and the aims of Zionism. This book seeks to answer some of the most frequently asked questions of this debate. Part One, Israel Dispersed, provides a background survey to the troubled and often tragic history of the Jews from ancient times to the evolution of Zionism in the nineteenth century, and traces the perennial desire of the Jews to return to the Land of Israel. Part Two, From National Home to Sovereign State, examines the political and diplomatic activities of the Zionists, their supporters and their opponents during the years 1914 to 1948, when the ideal of return was transformed into a reality, against enormous odds.

The documentary study of Part Two spans the First World War, the Balfour Declaration, and the twenty-five years of Britain's Palestine Mandate. It is dominated by Jewish immigration, by Arab protests and revolt, by the growth of European persecutions, and by British policy towards the Middle East, reaching its climax in the Second World War, with the Nazi Holocaust of European Jewry, and culminating in the fate of the survivors.

Binding these episodes together, and providing a central theme for the British politicians and officials whose job was to formulate policy, was the Jewish determination to rebuild the Jewish homeland – a determination so strong that neither superior power, nor the continued pressures of malice and hatred, could undermine it, or keep the Jews from statehood.

The specific source for each of the documents quoted in Part Two is given in the List of Archival Sources, and my thanks are due to those archivists and librarians who have given me access to previously unpublished materials. I should like to thank in particular the curators and staffs of the Bodleian Library, Oxford; the British Library, London; the Central Zionist Archive, Jerusalem; Churchill College, Cambridge; Durham University; the Foreign Office Library and Records, London; the Imperial War Museum, London; the India Office Library and Records, London; the Public Record Office, Kew; St Antony's College Middle East Centre, Oxford; the State Archives, Jerusalem; the Weizmann Archive, Rehovot; the Wiener Library, London, and the Yad Vashem Holocaust Memorial and Archive, Jerusalem.

I should also like to thank the owners of collections in private hands, who gave me permission to consult the papers of Leopold Amery, Lewis Harcourt, Venetia Montagu, Harry Sacher, T. E. Lawrence and Josiah Wedgwood.

I am deeply grateful to those historians on whose expertise and historical researches I have drawn in both Part One and Part Two of this book. I have gained particular benefit from the recent researches and publications of Reuben Ainsztein, Dan Bahat, Yehuda Bauer, Isaiah Friedman, Elie Kedourie, Joshua Sherman, Fritz Stern, David Vital and Ronald Zweig, each of whom has put in their debt all those who study the subjects on which they have made such substantial contributions to historical knowledge. Their historical works, together with the contemporary pamphlets, editions of speeches, books, memoirs and diaries which I have used, are listed in the bibliography.

My thanks must also go to all those groups and institutions who asked me to lecture on the historical origins of the State of Israel, on aspects of Zionism, and on British policy towards the Jews; it was as a result of collecting material for these lectures that this book evolved. My thanks are therefore due to the '45 Aid Society; the Anglo-Israel Association; the Federation of Women Zionists of Great Britain and Ireland; the Hebrew University of Jerusalem, and the London Friends of the Hebrew University (the Herbert Samuel lecture); the Institute of Jewish Affairs; the Jewish Book Council; Kibbutz Hazorea; the Leo Baeck (London) Lodge of the Bnai Brith; St Antony's College Middle East Centre, Oxford; the Oxford Centre for Postgraduate Hebrew Studies (the Sacks lecture); the Rainbow Group; Tel Aviv University; the Van Leer Foundation, Jerusalem; the West London Synagogue, and the Zionist Federation of Great Britain and Ireland, each of whom provided stimulating audiences and helpful critics. I am also grateful to Hugo Gryn and Arthur Lourie, who not only scrutinized aspects of the book itself, but by their friendship gave me much support.

My special thanks must go to Judy Holdsworth, who undertook the typing of the manuscript; to Penny Houghton and Larry Arnn, who read the proofs; to Rosemary Pettit who scrutinized the typescript; to T. A. Bicknell, who drew the maps; and to Linda Osband who saw the book through the Press.

This book could not have been written without the devoted help and criticism of my wife, for whose superb encouragement there can be no adequate acknowledgement.

I should like to thank all those archives and individuals who gave me access to their photographic collections, and whose photographs are used in this book: The Central Zionist Archive, Jerusalem, (plates 1, 3, 9, 12 and 13); the Hagannah Archive, Tel Aviv, (plate 14); the Keren Hayesod Archive, Jerusalem, (plates 15 and 16); Mrs Hannah Ruppin, (plate 5); Mr Hanna Safieh, (plate 4); the Weizmann archive, Rehovot, (plate 2); the Wiener Library, London, (plates 7, 8 and 10) and the Yad Vashem archive, Jerusalem, (plate 11). The photograph of Sir Mark Sykes is reproduced by permission of Cassels Ltd, Publishers, London.

PART ONE
Israel Dispersed
An Historical Survey

I

Israel Dispersed

THE Jews were living in Canaan three thousand years ago. They were first parted from their land in 722 BC with the Assyrian conquest of the northern Jewish kingdom of Samaria, and the deportation of thousands of Israelites east-wards to Mesopotamia. The Bible gives the number of captives as 27,290. Less than 150 years later the Babylonians conquered the southern Jewish kingdom of Judaea, together with its capital, Jerusalem. The Temple of Solomon, the holiest site of Judaism, was destroyed, and the Jews were once more taken eastwards, as slaves and captives, to the river Euphrates.

The Bible records the lament of these early exiles: 'By the waters of Babylon, there we sat down and wept. Yea, we sat down and wept, as we remembered Zion.' From that moment, Jewish existence was threatened in every decade, both for those who continued to live in the Land of Israel, and for those in exile who sought a secure haven in the ever-increasing circles of the dispersion. For many, no real haven could be found, and in each generation they would repeat the lament of the Psalmist:

> How shall we sing the Lord's song
> In a strange land?

Fifty years after the Babylonian destruction of the Temple, some Jews were allowed to return to Jerusalem. Others remained in exile, sometimes, as in Babylon itself, winning wide measures of self-government. Some, in search of a decent livelihood, pushed out even further eastwards to the shores of the Caspian Sea, some northwards to the Black Sea, some south-east to the Persian Gulf. In every port and village that was prepared to accept them, Jews formed small com-munities, and through their synagogue services and Holy Days, preserved their Judaism both as a religious faith, and as a way of life.

From the towns and villages of these first dispersions, the Jews travelled throughout the known world. From the Land of Israel, too, they ventured in search of a livelihood to all the ports and market towns of the civilized world, first to those of Egypt and of the Persian Empire, then to Alexander's Macedonian domains, then to the scattered City States of ancient Greece, and to the maritime emporia of ancient Carthage.

3

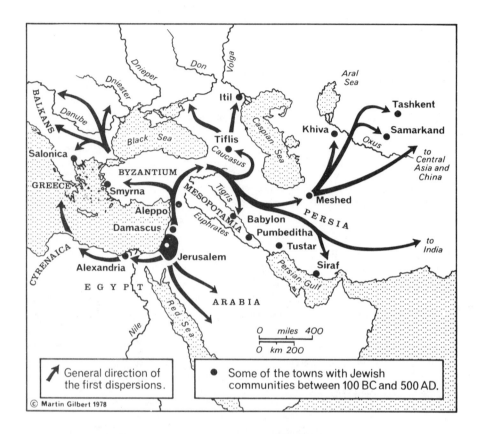

In the legend:
General direction of the first dispersions.

Some of the towns with Jewish communities between 100 BC and 500 AD.

© Martin Gilbert 1978

In the age of Greek supremacy, Jews were to be seen in their new homes all along the Mediterranean coast of Spain, France and North Africa. Westwards, they settled in the islands of Djerba, Majorca, Sardinia, Sicily and Malta. Eastwards their efforts took them to the furthermost shores of the Black Sea. Everywhere their small but vibrant communities, their close family life, their love of learning within the family, their schools, their prayers, their sabbath, their Holy Days and their Bible, gave them a unity and an inner strength despite the vast distances of their dispersal.

In Jerusalem itself, the Temple had been rebuilt by a growing Jewish community. Indeed, throughout these early years of the dispersion, the Temple served as a beacon to re-kindle the faith, and was a point of regular pilgrimage. On each of the three pilgrim festivals, the Passover, Tabernacles, and the Feast of Weeks, Jews flocked to Jerusalem to celebrate. In 40 AD the Jewish philosopher, Philo of Alexandria, noted: 'Countless multitudes from countless cities come to the Temple at every festival, some by land, and others by sea, from east and west

4

and north and south.' Twenty-six years later the Jewish historian Josephus recorded that, when the Roman Governor of Syria entered the town of Lydda, he had found it deserted, 'for the whole multitude were gone up to Jerusalem for the feast of the Tabernacles'.

From the earliest times, the desire of the Jews to maintain their traditions and culture was a difficult and even dangerous one. Not only the challenge of trade and frequent economic hardships, but renewed persecution and expulsion, continued in every generation to drive the Jews to the most distant regions of the known world. Following the eclipse of Egypt, Greece and Carthage, the Syrian armies conquered the Land of Israel, but in 168 BC were driven out by a Jewish revolt led by Judah Maccabee, and for a hundred years the Jews were again independent. But in 63 BC their land was conquered again, this time by Roman troops, and the Jewish homeland was once again ruled by strangers. Some Jews followed in the wake of the Roman armies, trading precariously but tenaciously as merchants, across the Alps to the Rhine, and across the Carparthians to the Danube. As the authority of Rome spread outwards, a few Jewish families would stop to live and trade in each of the forts, and at each of the river crossings, along the many new roads of the growing Roman Empire.

Despite the military power of Rome, Jewish independence was not easily destroyed. In 66 AD the Jews of Judaea rose in revolt, holding out in several towns and fortresses for more than four years. But, the power of Rome was formidable, and in 70 AD the Temple was destroyed. Three years later, in 73 AD the defenders of the fortress of Masada, the last stronghold to hold out, chose suicide rather than surrender.

Before their suicide, the leader of the Jews on Masada, Eleazar, told his followers, as the historian Josephus recorded: 'I cannot but esteem it as a favour that God hath granted us, that it is still in our power to die bravely, and in a state of freedom, which hath not been the case with others who were conquered unexpectedly.' Eleazar added:

As for those that were already dead in the war, it is reasonable that we should esteem them blessed, for they are dead in defending, and not in betraying their liberty.

But as to the multitude of those that are now under the Romans, who would not pity their condition? And who would not make haste to die, before he would suffer the same miseries with them?

Eleazar also told his colleagues of the fate of the Jews at Roman hands. 'Some of them have been put upon the rack', he reported, 'and tortured with fire and whippings, and so died. Some have been half-devoured by wild beasts, and yet have been preserved alive to be devoured by them a second time, in order to afford laughter and sport to our enemies. . . .'

The Roman vengeance was indeed terrible. Tens of thousands of Jews were killed, many villages razed to the ground, and thousands of Jews sold into slavery, some even pitted against wild animals in the arena, as 'sport' for their captors. The destruction of the Temple was to remain a traumatic memory for succeeding generations of Jews, who looked back on it with fear and trepidation.

In 115 AD it was the Jews of the Diaspora who rose in revolt, fighting against the Romans in Mesopotamia, Egypt, Cyprus, and along the north African coast. As the revolt spread, the Jews of Judaea also took part in it; but within two years it had been crushed. The Moorish commander Lucius Quietus, having suppressed the Mesopotamian rebels, was sent by the Romans to Judaea and the Galilee, where he re-imposed the Roman rule with marked severity; and, having done so, set up an idol on the Temple Mount as an act of deliberate provocation.

Even so, the powers of Jewish resistance were not entirely destroyed, and in 132 AD the Jews of Judaea, Samaria and the Galilee rose in revolt once more, under the leadership of Simeon bar Kokhba. The Roman governor was defeated, Jerusalem regained, and fierce battles fought as Roman reinforcements advanced ruthlessly from the coastal plain. For three and a half years the Jews resisted, but one by one their forts were captured, and their villages burnt to the ground. Once more, thousands of Jews were sent as slaves to all the slave markets of the Roman world. In the Galilee, Jewish olive plantations were destroyed. Elsewhere Jewish farms were confiscated, or laid waste.

The suppression of Bar Kokhba's revolt was completed by 135 AD. The persecution that followed was a time of suffering. Many learned men were murdered. All synagogues and prayer meetings were forbidden. No Jew was allowed to live in Jerusalem; indeed, Jews were only permitted to enter the city once a year, on the fast of the ninth of Av, to weep over the ruins of the Temple. The Romans even changed the name of Judaea, hoping to eliminate all Jewish memories and links: henceforth it was to be known as Syria Palaestina: thus 'Palestine' came into being.

The memory of these cruel events was to be a central theme of Jewish history and survival. Here began the tradition of martyrdom. A contemporary Jewish sage in Babylonia caught the spirit of lament when he wrote:

> Why are you being led out to be decapitated?
> Because I circumcised my son.
> Why are you being led out to be burnt?
> Because I read the Torah.
> Why are you being led out to be crucified?
> Because I ate unleavened bread.

By 150 AD, despite the ferocity of Roman persecution, the Jews were living scattered, but with their faith intact, in a vast region stretching from the Straits of Gibraltar to the borders of India; from the Black Sea to the Red Sea; from the river Loire to the river Indus. Those who were allowed by the Romans to remain in the Land of Israel, although refused entry to Jerusalem, set up communities both in the coastal plain and in the Galilee; at Jabneh, on the coastal plain south of Jaffa, scholars and rabbis gathered after the fall of Jerusalem, and for nearly a century Jabneh remained a centre of rabbinical scholarship.

Numbering at least three millions, the Jews of the Roman Empire constituted more than 5 per cent of the Empire's population, and followed a wide variety of occupations. In Mesopotamia they were farmers; in Egypt, traders; in Italy, weavers, garment-makers and even actors. Everywhere they were as much at ease farming as trading. Everywhere they guarded their Hebrew alphabet and language, and their devotion to one God. Each Passover they recounted the story of their flight from Egypt, from slavery to freedom, and prayed with fervour: 'Next year in Jerusalem'. Each Day of Atonement, in meditation and fasting, they sought forgiveness for their sins. In their daily prayers they sought peace 'for us, and for all Israel'. The ethical code of the Bible and its history of their wanderings, the warnings of the Prophets and their belief in a messianic redemption, gave them a unity which no dispersal or persecution could destroy, and forged a link with the land of their Patriarchs which no distance could break. In Palestine itself, the archaeological evidence from biblical times shows much rebuilding of synagogues, at Bet Alfa in the Jezreel valley, at Hammat-Gader in the shadow of the Golan heights, at Jericho in the Jordan valley, and on the Mediterranean at both Ashkelon and Gaza.

During these early years of the Christian era, Jewish life flourished, particularly in Babylonia. It was at the academies of Sura and Pumbeditha that the Babylonian Talmud was compiled; its wisdom and precepts were to guide Jews all over the world in all subsequent generations, providing them with a comprehensive law by which to live their daily lives, and preserve their customs and their faith. But while the Jews of Babylonia flourished both in number and spirit, westwards, with the fall of the Roman Empire, the Jews of Byzantium faced a fanatical Christianity which demanded conversion, or expulsion, sometimes even conversion or death, and treated them as aliens, as enemies, and as a people with' no rights to a fair trial or a quiet life. Only fifty-four years after the completion of the Babylonian Talmud, the Emperor Justinian brought all the power of Byzantium against the conduct of Jewish worship.

Each change in the political structure of Europe, of Asia, of Africa put the Jews at risk. Such changes were frequent, sudden, violent, and widespread, bringing death and dispersal to hundreds of Jewish communities throughout the inhabited world in each of the nineteen centuries that followed the collapse of the Roman Empire.

With the sudden and whirlwind conquest by Islam in the seventh and eighth centuries, those Jews who lived in a wide arc of lands from Spain to India found once more a new master. In places the Jews welcomed Muslim rule. Having been cruelly persecuted by the Christians, both the Jews of Caesarea, in Palestine, and

Towns (modern names) with Jewish communities from Roman times.

0 miles 200

0 km 200

© Martin Gilbert 1978

the Jews of Toledo in Spain, opened the gates of their cities to the Muslim invader.

With the Arab conquest of Palestine between 636 and 641 AD, the Jews of Palestine recovered from the hardships imposed by Byzantine rule, and were active as weavers, growers of cereal, and fishermen. Not only were there active Jewish communities in the Galilee, at Jerusalem, in the Jordan valley on both sides of the river, and in the Gulf of Elath on the Red Sea; but many Jews returned to Palestine from other lands under Muslim rule. One of the leading Jewish families in tenth century Jerusalem came from one of the extremities of the Muslim world, Fez, in Morocco: one of their number, Solomon ben Judah, was head of the rabbinical academies in both Jerusalem and Ramla, and maintained relations with the Jewish communities of Damascus, Aleppo, Tyre, and even Seville in Spain.

Within the Muslim world, at certain times, the Jews found positions of authority, and the chance of prosperity. Both Mosul and Azerbaijan had Jewish

Governors. At Tustar in Persia, a Jewish carpet industry flourished. At the port of Siraf, on the Persian Gulf, a Jewish Governor ruled. In Egypt, one Jew became Minister of Taxation and Finance, while another became Inspector of the Affairs of State. Protected by such successful figures, the Jewish community could take its full part in the life of the State. Wherever their rulers allowed them to live unmolested, the Jews brought prosperity, skills and talents to the life of the State.

Yet even under Islam, the scale of tolerance could quickly turn, and with grim results. To the Muslim, the Jew was always a 'dhimmi', or second-class citizen, and anti-Jewish violence could have terrible results, particularly when one of the more fanatical Muslim sects was in the ascendant. One such sect, the Almohades, came to prominence in 1033, when more than six thousand Jews were massacred at Fez in Morocco. In 1066 a further five thousand Jews were killed in the city of Granada, in Muslim Spain. Even under more tolerant Muslim rule, the Jews in every town and village of the Muslim world, including Palestine, had to take second place under the Muslims. Yet in many such towns their ancestors had been living there for many centuries before Islam's conquests.

The Jews of Arab lands learnt to accept their permanent lowly status, in return for the right to lead humbler lives relatively unmolested. In Muslim-ruled Spain, Jewish culture blossomed into a 'golden age'. Philosophy, literature, poetry, trade and commerce, costume and architecture made those years memorable in Jewish history. Jewish physicians and diplomats were prominent and, with the first Christian conquests, Jews acted as mediators between the two warring communities. As Christianity spread, however, the status of the Jews of Spain worsened; for the Church was often unwilling to allow the Jew even second-class citizenship.

The Jews of Byzantium were, in the end, no less fortunate. Forced to flee by Byzantine persecution, they had come to rest in northern Europe. At first they were protected by the local rulers, and even granted privileges in certain towns, living for five hundred years after the fall of the Roman Empire in relative peace along the Rhine, the Moselle, the Danube and the Main. But in the eleventh century they met, along each of these German rivers, the fierce persecutions of the first Crusaders.

The religious bigotry of the eleventh century expressed itself in violence and slaughter. Within the course of a few years it left thousands of Jews dead, and drove thousands more eastwards. As they were driven towards the marshes and swamplands of eastern Europe, these Jews of Germany, or of 'Ashkenaz', as they themselves called it, still clung to their houses of study, to their sages, to their religious regulations, and even to their local Germanic dialect, Yiddish, by which they were to be known, recognized and even pilloried for nearly a thousand years.

Uprooted by Crusader persecutions, the Jews of Ashkenaz travelled from

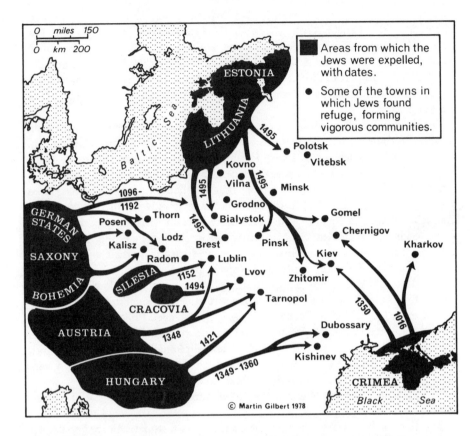

Areas from which the Jews were expelled, with dates.

Some of the towns in which Jews found refuge, forming vigorous communities.

© Martin Gilbert 1978

town to town, first eastwards, some westwards again, some to the Baltic, some to the Danube, content whenever they were unmolested, glad whenever a town opened its gates to them, yet repeatedly and suddenly thrown out time and time again by the whim of a local lord, or converted to Christianity under the threat of death, or murdered by a mob incited against them. The map of Europe was criss-crossed by the expulsion of Jews from country after country: from the Crimea in the eleventh century, from Silesia in the twelfth, from England in the thirteenth, from France and Hungary in the fourteenth, from Austria, Bavaria, Saxony and Lithuania in the fifteenth.

The map of these expulsions has no pattern: it is a chaos of tragic uprootings, of bloodlettings, of torture, of homes abandoned, of hope suppressed. For the Jews of Ashkenaz no century was free from the furious zeal of those who had the desire, and the power, to drive them out. But the very intensity and frequency of medieval persecution seemed to strengthen the bonds of Jewishness and spirituality. In every town in the Rhine valley and northern France, houses of study taught the Torah. The aspiration of learning and education became widespread. Learned rabbis and sages were highly regarded by Jews throughout northern Europe, their wisdom studied, their words pondered. One of the greatest Jewish scholars of all time, Rashi, flourished at Troyes towards the end of the eleventh century.

Throughout the Middle Ages the homeless wandering Jew was a feature of Christian Europe. One of the greatest of all Jewish philosophers, Maimonides, was born in Spain in the twelfth century, but was forced to leave his birthplace, Cordova, when it was seized by a fanatical and barbaric Muslim conqueror. He went first to live in Fez, in Morocco; then he travelled to Egypt, where he became personal physician to the Caliph. Yet the influence of Maimonides was not confined to the towns in which he lived; like Rashi before him, and like many of the Jewish sages in the centuries to come, his personal contribution to Judaism in one corner of the dispersal benefited the whole Jewish world.

The Crusader conquests in the eastern Mediterranean posed a grave threat to the Jews of that whole area. Reaching Beirut, the Crusaders showed what would be the fate of the Jews of Palestine when all thirty-five Jewish families living in the city were massacred. At Haifa, the Jews joined the Muslims in the port's defence. But the Crusaders swept all before them, and thousands of Jews were murdered in the Galilee, on the coastal plain, in Samaria, and Judaea. Many of those who were not murdered were either sold into slavery in Europe, or ransomed to the Jewish community in Egypt.

Even during the harsh years of Crusader rule, the Jews looked to the land of Israel with a special longing. The Spanish-born Jew, Judah Halevi, expressed this longing when he wrote, of Jerusalem:

> Beautiful heights,
> Joy of the world,
> City of a great king,
> For you my soul yearns,
> From the lands of the west.
>
> My pity collects and is roused
> When I remember the past:
> Your story in exile,
> Your temple destroyed.
>
> I shall cherish your stones and kiss them,
> And your earth will be sweeter
> Than honey to my taste.

In 1140 Halevi himself set out from Spain for the Land of Israel. According to legend, he was approaching the walls of Jerusalem when an Arab – or, some said, a Crusader horseman – trampled him to death. As he lay dying he is said to have recited one of his own poems: 'Zion, shall I not seek thee?'

From 1099 to 1187 the Crusaders were sovereign in Jerusalem. They drove the Jews from the Jewish quarter of the city, and brought in Christian Arab tribes from east of the river Jordan to settle in the Jewish homes and alleyways which they had so brutally cleared out. But the Jewish love of the Land of Israel could not be blotted out so easily, and in 1210, when Crusader rule ended, more than 300 rabbis from Flanders and Provence travelled to Palestine to help build up again the Jewish communities which had been decimated by Crusader massacres and expulsions.

In 1267 the Spanish-born scholar and philosopher, Nahmanides, who had been born in Gerona, near the Pyrenees, was forced to flee from Spain because of his successful biblical disputation with Christian theologians. He travelled to Palestine, arriving there only seven years after a further tragedy, the Tartar invasion from central Asia, in which thousands of Jews and Christians had been murdered, and Jerusalem devastated once more. From Jerusalem, Nahmanides wrote to one of his sons who had remained in Spain, that the city 'has no master, and he that wishes may take possession of its ruins'. Nahmanides, a man of courage and vision, set to work to help restore the shattered community, explaining to his son:

We have procured, from Shechem, Scrolls of the Law, which had been carried thither from Jerusalem at the time of the Tartar invasion. Thus we shall organize a synagogue, and shall be able to pray here.

Men flock from Damascus, Aleppo, and from all parts to Jerusalem to behold the Place of the Sanctuary, and to mourn over it. May you, my son and your brothers, and the whole of our family, see the salvation of Jerusalem.

2

Medieval Persecutions, Flight and Hope

DURING the thirteenth century the Jews were ferociously persecuted in Morocco and Tunisia, two main centres of the once tolerant Muslim world. In the fourteenth century they were likewise persecuted throughout Christian Europe, where they were blamed, totally without cause, for the spread of the Black Death. Under torture, individual Jews were forced to confess to deliberately spreading the disease. Between December 1347 and June 1350 anti-Jewish riots took place wherever the Black Death struck. More than 300 Jewish communities were attacked, from Valencia in Spain to Breslau on the Oder; from Antwerp on the river Scheldt to Mantua on the river Po.

The Jews were not passive in the face of these repeated onslaughts, and Jewish self-defence was a noted feature in several communities: Cologne, Mainz and Frankfurt among them. In some towns the Church protected the Jews from the mob. But the slaughter was nonetheless terrible: in Strasbourg alone, in February 1349, two thousand Jews were burnt to death on a massive scaffold set up in the Jewish cemetery. A few were spared death by accepting baptism, but even some of these were murdered four months later, when the Black Death actually reached the city.

Throughout central Europe a stereotype of the Jew, even more vicious than earlier stereotypes, gained wide circulation. Following the Black Death killings, the Jew was portrayed as a spreader of disease, and as a sinister force of corruption and destruction. This crude image was to survive and flourish for six centuries, making it easy for those who wished to do so to rouse simple-minded people against the Jews in many lands.

Following the Black Death riots, even more Jews fled eastwards, joining those who had fled across the Oder at the time of the Crusader massacres three hundred years before. At first they were welcomed in these eastern lands: in 1364 Casimir the Great of Poland issued the first of a series of charters to protect the Jews within his realm. 'If the Jew enters the House of a Christian', one of these charters decreed, 'no one has a right to cause him any injury or unpleasantness.' Twenty-four years later Grand Duke Vitovt of Lithuania granted privileges to the Jews who came to live in Brest-Litovsk, one of the towns under his rule.

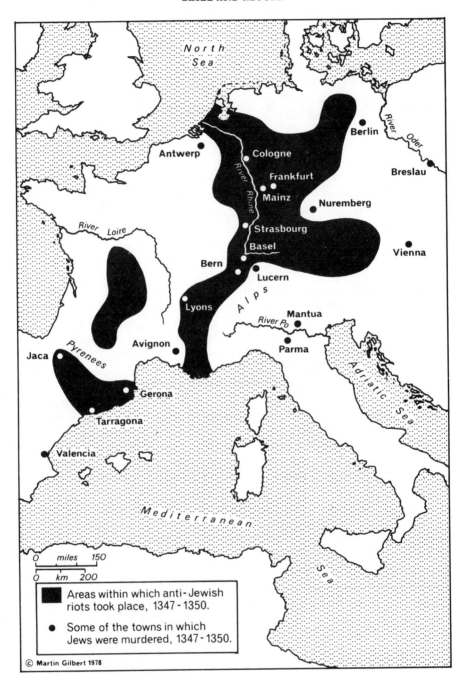

North
Sea

Berlin

River Oder

Antwerp

Cologne

Breslau

Frankfurt

River Rhine

Mainz

Nuremberg

River Loire

Strasbourg

Vienna

Basel

Bern

Lucern

Alps

Lyons

Mantua

River Po

Avignon

Parma

Jaca

Pyrenees

Adriatic Sea

Gerona

Tarragona

Valencia

Mediterranean

Sea

0   miles   150

0   km   200

◼ Areas within which anti-Jewish
   riots took place, 1347 - 1350.

● Some of the towns in which
   Jews were murdered, 1347 - 1350.

© Martin Gilbert 1978

Further south, in Galicia, the Jews were granted full autonomy in their communal affairs.

The Jews who gathered in eastern Europe formed large and closely-knit communities. Keeping Yiddish as their daily language, they treasured their religious heritage, prized the virtues of education, of study and of charity, rejoiced with each Sabbath in their God and his works, and kept their close family life as the central guardian of their heritage.

To the west, another tragedy was looming. For the Jews of Spain and Portugal, the mild rule of Islam had been replaced by the harsh rule of Christian kings. In the face of Christian intolerance, the achievements of five generations of Jewish philosophers, scholars and statesmen of Spain now counted for nothing. In 1355 more than 12,000 Jews were massacred by the mob in Toledo. In the Spanish Cortes, the Jewish question provoked deep hostility: the Jews, the Cortes declared in 1371, were 'evil and rash men, enemies of God and of all of Christianity', who caused 'numerous evils and sow corruption with impunity'. In a vicious satire, the Royal Chancellor, Lopez de Ayala, portrayed the Jews as bloodsuckers:

> Here come the Jews all alike
> And present their detailed writing,
> To drink the blood of the poor people
> Promising jewels and gifts to the courtiers.

In 1373 anti-Jewish riots broke out in Lisbon. Five years later, in Seville Archdeacon Ferrant Martínez preached from the pulpit that any Christian who killed or harmed a Jew would be causing no displeasure to the king or queen. These sermons were repeated for thirteen years. The Jews, Martínez declared, should be expelled from the towns and villages, and their synagogues demolished. The venom of anti-semitism was successful: on 6 June 1391 the Jewish quarter of Seville was attacked by the mob. Every Jew had but a single choice, immediate conversion, or instant death. Agitators, trained by Martínez, travelled from town to town, and the mob took up the cry: 'Death or holy water for the Jews!' As the destruction of Jewish property spread northwards to Barcelona and the Pyrennees, Lopez de Ayala noted: 'The eagerness to plunder the Jews grew greater each day.'

As the anti-Jewish violence spread throughout Spain, 50,000 Jews were massacred on the island of Majorca alone, and 1391 was remembered as 'the year of persecutions and oppression'. In the new century, tens of thousands of Jews sought to save their lives by conversion to Christianity. In Tortosa, in 1412, the Jews were forced to 'defend' their religion in a public disputation, and the town's records give witness to 3,000 conversions within two years. But popular anti-Jewish feeling was not assuaged by such contrived spectacles, and further

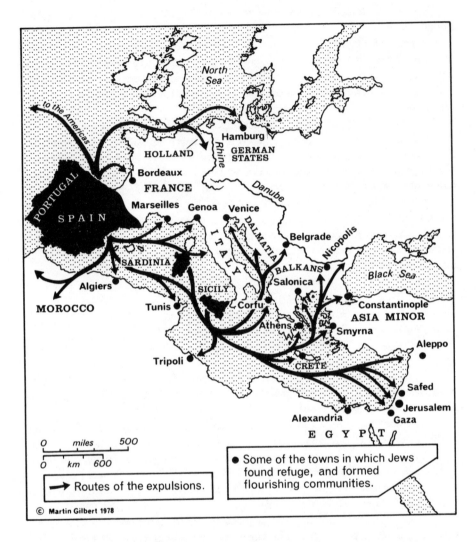

Some of the towns in which Jews found refuge, and formed flourishing communities.

Routes of the expulsions.

© Martin Gilbert 1978

vicious riots in Lisbon in 1449 and 1482 were an ominous hint of what was to come: the complete expulsion of the Jews from Portugal and Spain.

Yet, to the last year of Jewish life in Spain, Jewish creativity continued. In 1482 a Hebrew printing press, one of the earliest printing presses in Europe, had been set up in the Spanish city of Guadalajara, while five years later one was set up in Faro, in southern Portugal, and two years later in Lisbon, the Portuguese capital. But in 1492 the Jews were expelled *en masse* from Spain, and in 1497 from Portugal. More than 50,000 accepted Christianity, and were allowed to remain, many of them as 'secret' Jews, hiding their faith from all but their most intimate family circle.

More than 160,000 Jews were forced to leave Spain and Portugal altogether. These 'Sephardi' Jews – the Jews of Spain, or Sepharad – scattered in all directions. The havens they sought in their dispersal were to become the central points of a new Jewish renaissance in the next century. More than 25,000 reached Holland; 20,000 found a home in Morocco; 10,000 in France and 10,000 in Italy. Some 5,000 made the perilous journey to the newly-discovered land across the Atlantic Ocean, America. But the largest single group, 90,000 in all, went to the thriving cities and towns of the Ottoman Empire: to Algiers, to Alexandria, to Damascus, to Smyrna, to Salonica, to Constantinople, and to the urban and rural centres of Palestine. Many of those who went to Palestine settled in the Galilee: in 1495 they were reported in Safed trading in fruit and vegetables, cheese, oil and spices; and within a century Safed had become a centre of Jewish mysticism and rabbinical learning.

The Jews of Spain who reached Palestine found there a small but vigorous Jewish community, which had maintained itself, despite many difficulties, since the defeat of the Crusaders and the Muslim reconquest. It was under the tolerant rule of the Mamluk sultans of Egypt that the return of the Jews had gathered momentum: in 1322 a Jewish geographer from Florence, Ashtory Ha-Parhi, had settled in the Jezreel valley, where he wrote a book on the topography of Palestine, while the Jews of Safed, Ramla and Gaza were even recommended by Christian travellers as ideal guides. Thus Jacques of Verona, a Christian monk who visited the Holy Land in 1335, not only noted the long-established Jewish community at the foot of Mount Zion, in Jerusalem, but wrote:

A pilgrim who wished to visit ancient forts and towns in the Holy Land would have been unable to locate these without a good guide who knew the Land well or without one of the Jews who lived there. The Jews were able to recount the history of these places since this knowledge had been handed down from their forefathers and wise men.

So when I journeyed overseas I often requested and managed to obtain an excellent guide among the Jews who lived there.

The fifteenth century had seen no diminution of the Jewish presence in Palestine. Jews continued to return, typified by Elijah of Ferrara, an Italian rabbi who became spiritual head of the Jerusalem Jewish community in 1438, and by another Italian Jew, Obadiah of Bertinoro, also a famous rabbinical scholar, who settled in Jerusalem in 1488. As for Christian observers, they continued to be impressed by the Jews of the Holy Land. In 1486 a distinguished pilgrim, the Dean of Mainz Cathedral, Bernhard von Breidenbach, noted that the Jews of both Jerusalem and Hebron 'will treat you in full fidelity – more so than anyone else in those countries of the unbelievers'. But Muslim rule had become harsh and

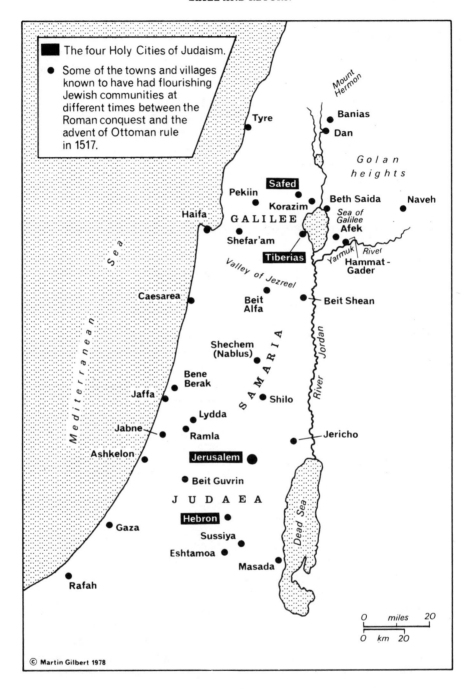

The four Holy Cities of Judaism.

● Some of the towns and villages known to have had flourishing Jewish communities at different times between the Roman conquest and the advent of Ottoman rule in 1517.

Mount Hermon

Tyre

Banias

Dan

Golan heights

Pekiin

Safed

Korazim

Beth Saida

Naveh

Haifa

GALILEE

Sea of Galilee

Afek

Shefar'am

Valley of Jezreel

Tiberias

Yarmuk River

Hammat - Gader

Caesarea

Beit Alfa

Beit Shean

River Jordan

Shechem (Nablus)

SAMARIA

Bene Berak

Jaffa

Shilo

Lydda

Jabne

Ramla

Jericho

Ashkelon

Jerusalem

Beit Guvrin

J U D A E A

Dead Sea

Hebron

Gaza

Sussiya

Eshtamoa

Masada

Rafah

Mediterranean Sea

0   miles   20

0   km   20

© Martin Gilbert 1978

18

intolerant: in 1491 a pilgrim from Bohemia, Martin Kabtanik, recorded, in his book *Journey to Jerusalem*, how:

There are not many Christians but there are many Jews, and these the Moslems persecute in various ways. Christians and Jews go about in Jerusalem in clothes considered fit only for wandering beggars.

The Moslems know that the Jews think and even say that this is the Holy Land which has been promised to them and that those Jews who dwell there are regarded as holy by Jews elsewhere, because, in spite of all the troubles and sorrows inflicted on them by the Moslems, they refuse to leave the Land.

It was in the very year that Kabtanik's book was published that the Jews were expelled from Spain. Twenty-five years later the conquest of Palestine by the Ottoman Turks provided a new tolerance, and a new impetus to Jewish life. By 1530 as many as 10,000 Jews lived in the area around the Galilee town of Safed, trading in fruits and vegetables, cheeses, spices, and olive oil. Others were prominent in the weaving trade. In Jerusalem, the Jewish community built four fine synagogues, which were to see 400 years of continuous worship, until their destruction in 1948.

Christian visitors to the Holy Land noted the new Jewish prosperity during the early years of Ottoman rule. In 1574 a French doctor from Le Mans, P. Belon, visited the Galilee. In his observations on his visit he wrote:

We look around Lake Tiberias and see the villages of Beth Saida and Korazim. Today Jews are living in these villages and they have built up again all the places around the lake, started fishing industries and have once again made the earth fruitful, where once it was desolate.

In the four hundred years after their expulsion from Spain, from 1500 to 1900, the life of the Jews of western Europe and America was to be full of hope for long-term security, for acceptance of their particular customs and qualities, and for opportunies to serve the State within whose borders they had come to live. Their achievements, in whatever careers were open to them, were remarkable. Yet even with the growth of modern Europe and the New World, medieval superstitions still brought pain and suffering to the Jews. In some parts of South America the Inquisition sought out Jews with a bitter hatred, giving all 'secret' Jews whom it caught the choice between death or 'true' conversion. In Lima in 1570, in Mexico City in 1574, and in Cartagena in 1610, Jews were burnt at the stake for refusing conversion.

In Italy, a country of many small and warring States, the Jews, after nearly two thousand years of continuous existence and of wide cultural achievements, culminating in the first Hebrew printed book, produced at Reggio in 1475, sank deeper and deeper into the mire of Catholic intolerance, and were picked out decade-by-decade as the victims of an intense religious fanaticism. In 1415 Pope Benedict XIII had ordered the censorship of the Talmud; in 1427 the shipowners of Venice and Ancona had been forbidden, by Papal Edict, to take on board any Jews wishing to go to the Land of Israel; in 1475 the Jews of Trent had been falsely accused of murdering a Christian boy in order to use his blood. Nor did the new century bring any improvement. In 1516 the Jews of Venice were forced to live in a few narrow streets of the town, known as the 'Ghetto', giving a new, and ominous word to Jewish history, and later to other oppressed minorities who lived in towns, but were not allowed to merge fully into urban life.

In 1550 the Jews of Genoa were expelled; in 1556 'secret' Jews were burnt at the stake in Ancona; in 1569 the Jews were expelled from the Papal States, and in 1597 from Milan.

For Christian Europe, the sixteenth century was one of religious ferment, with the 'theses' of Martin Luther setting the course for the Protestant reformation. In 1543 Luther published a pamphlet entitled *Of the Jews and Their Lies*. Its tone gives a clear flavour of the antisemitic literature that circulated in Christian religious circles at that time. 'Let me give you my honest advice,' Luther wrote, and he continued:

First, their synagogues or churches should be set on fire, and whatever does not burn up should be covered or spread over with dirt so that no one may ever be able to see a cinder or stone of it. And this ought to be done for the honour of God and of Christianity in order that God may see that we are Christians, and that we have not wittingly tolerated or approved of such public lying, cursing and blaspheming of His Son and His Christians. . . .

Secondly, their homes should likewise be broken down and destroyed. For they perpetrate the same things there that they do in their synagogues. For this reason they ought to be put under one roof or in a stable, like gypsies, in order that they may realize that they are not masters in our land, as they boast, but miserable captives, as they complain of us incessantly before God with bitter wailing.

Thirdly, they should be deprived of their prayerbooks and Talmuds in which such idolatry, lies, cursing, and blasphemy are taught.

Fourthly, their rabbis must be forbidden under threat of death to teach any more. . . .

Fifthly, passport and travelling privileges should be absolutely forbidden to the Jews. For they have no business in the rural districts since they are not nobles, nor officials, nor merchants, nor the like. Let them stay at home.

Sixthly, they ought to be stopped from usury. All their cash and valuables of silver and gold ought to be taken from them and put aside for safekeeping. For this reason, as said before, everything that they possess they stole and robbed from us through their usury, for they have no other means of support. . . .

Seventhly, let the young and strong Jews and Jewesses be given the flail, the ax, the hoe, the spade, the distaff, and spindle, and let them earn their bread by the sweat of their noses as is enjoined upon Adam's children. For it is not proper that they should want us cursed *Goyyim* to work in the sweat of our brow and that they, pious crew, idle away their days at the fireside in laziness, feasting and display. And in addition to this, they boast impiously that they have become masters of the

Christians at our expense. We ought to drive the rascally lazy bones out of our system.

If, however, we are afraid that they might harm us personally, or our wives, children, servants, cattle, etc., when they serve us or work for us – since it is surely to be presumed that such noble lords of the world and poisonous bitter worms are not accustomed to any work and would very unwillingly humble themselves to such a degree among the cursed *Goyyim* – then let us apply the same cleverness [expulsion] as the other nations, such as France, Spain, Bohemia, etc., and settle with them for that which they have extorted usuriously from us, and after having divided it up fairly let us drive them out of the country for all time.

Luther's pamphlet ended with an appeal to all princes and nobles with Jews in their domains to act 'so that you and we may all be free of this insufferable devilish burden – the Jews'.

Less than twenty years after Luther's anti-Jewish diatribe, a Turkish Sultan, Suleiman I, made it possible for a large number of Jews to return to the Holy Land, under the benevolent Muslim rule of the Ottomans. In 1561 Suleiman gave Tiberias, one of the four Jewish holy cities, to a former 'secret' Jew from Portugal, Don Joseph Nasi, who rebuilt the city and the villages around it. Jews from Italy, and from elsewhere in the Mediterranean area, came to settle there, attracted by the wool and silk industries which Nasi promoted. When, a hundred years later, the city fell into ruins, many Jews remained in the nearby villages of the Galilee, farming, fishing and trading. Elsewhere in the Holy Land in the sixteenth century, the tolerance of Turkish rule enabled several Jewish communities to maintain their cultural and spiritual unity: in Jerusalem, in Hebron, and in Gaza, Jewish life was also upheld with vigour. In Safed, in 1563, a Jewish printing press was established: the first outside Europe. In Hebron, the revival of Jewish life was particularly marked: in 1518, three years after the start of Ottoman rule, the prosperous Jewish community there had been plundered, many Jews killed, and the survivors forced to flee. But in 1540 the community was restored, the Jewish quarter rebuilt, Spanish Jews made welcome, and a tradition of religious discussion, laws and philosophy evolved under several famous teachers, among them Elijah de Vides, who had come from the Galilee, and whose major work, on the Jewish moral code, was printed in Venice in 1579.

Ottoman rule gave the Jews a chance of a relatively unmolested existence throughout the sixteenth and seventeenth centuries. Throughout the seventeenth century also, one Christian power enabled the Jews to flourish, trade and live at peace with their neighbours; this was Holland. As the Dutch established their colonies in North and South America, in the Caribbean, in Africa and in the East Indies, numerous strong Jewish communities were established in these regions, and flourished. Protected by the flag and power of Holland, enterprising Jewish traders from Amsterdam brought prosperity both to their own communities and to Holland. By 1640 their trade and commerce spread to every corner of the globe; west to America, southward to the west coast of Africa and to Cape Town, eastwards to the Persian Gulf, to Mauritius, to India and Ceylon, to the Dutch East Indies, and even to remote Formosa, off the coast of China.

But, as happened so often in the history of the Jewish dispersal, no golden age in one part of the world seemed possible without a black age elsewhere. In 1648, while the Jews of Holland were at their most successful and most peaceful, the Jews of Poland, Lithuania, White Russia and the Ukraine – those who had found safety there more than three hundred years before from the Christian persecutions of Germany and Central Europe – were assailed by a violence and a hatred without parallel since Roman times. In two years, more than 100,000 Jews were murdered. Many thousands were tortured. Some chose conversion to Christianity in order to save their lives. Some were seized by the Tartars and sold into slavery thousands of miles away, across the deserts of central Asia. Many were murdered while fleeing. Tens of thousands of Jewish homes were set aflame, and more than three hundred communities were completely destroyed.

Several thousand Jews, who were forced to flee from their homes, found safety by distant flight, to Holland, to the Balkans, and even back to the Germany from which their forebears had fled only a few centuries before. Strasbourg, the scene of the horrific mass murder of 1349, now, three centuries later, accepted the refugees, and gave them the chance to become active, prosperous citizens. Thousands of other victims of the Ukrainian violence sought to rebuild their lives in the same region, along the same rivers. But in the next fifty years, the wave of anti-Jewish hatred spread eastwards, to the lands newly conquered by Moscow, where Jews fell under the rule of yet another overlord intolerant of their presence.

The Jews of eastern Europe slowly rebuilt their shattered homes. They were filled, also, with a deep spiritual longing. At first it took the form of a search for some quick source of help and light, a self-proclaimed messiah, Shabtai Zevi. The flame of this messianic movement spread as quickly as the flame of disaster had done. Not only in eastern Europe, but in the Balkans, in Italy, in France, in Morocco, in Holland, in the Ottoman Empire, in Egypt, and in the Land of Israel itself, the new messianic claim seized hold of the imagination, both of Sephardi and Ashkenazi Jews whose future seemed insecure. Even in England, where the Jews had only recently returned nearly four hundred years after their expulsion, wagers were held as to when the new 'Messiah' would be crowned King of the Jews in Jerusalem, and thousands of Jews throughout Europe were seized by the hope that Zevi would lead them back to the Holy Land, and to a Jewish kingdom.

Tricked by the Turkish Sultan, Zevi accepted conversion to Islam, and the flame of his movement quickly passed. But it left behind it many sparks of longing, and it was not long before that longing received a further and horrific impetus. In 1734 the first of a new series of vicious outbreaks of Jew-hatred took place in the same regions which had been tormented by the Cossacks a century

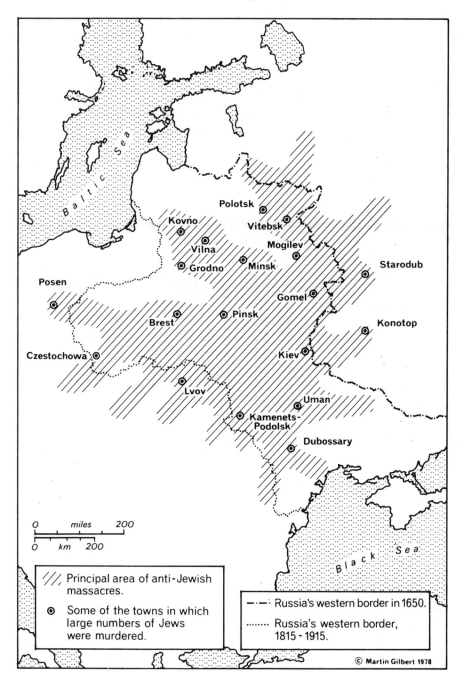

Polotsk

Kovno
Vitebsk

Vilna
Mogilev

Grodno Minsk
Starodub

Posen

Gomel

Brest Pinsk
Konotop

Czestochowa
Kiev

Lvov

Uman

Kamenets-
Podolsk

Dubossary

```
0        miles      200

0         km        200
```

Black Sea

Baltic Sea

/// Principal area of anti-Jewish
    massacres.

⊙   Some of the towns in which
    large numbers of Jews
    were murdered.

—·—· Russia's western border in 1650.

.... Russia's western border,
         1815 - 1915.

© Martin Gilbert 1978

before. These were the Haidamak persecutions, in which Christian monks glorified the murder of Jews, and spoke of the confiscation of Jewish property as an act of piety. Propaganda by Russian Orthodox priests intensified the popular hatred of the Jew.

In 1734, 1750, and again in 1768, the massacre of Jews spread once more through the Ukraine. In 1768, in the town of Uman, the Jews defended themselves tenaciously, but most of them, including their women and children, were brutally murdered in the synagogue. Some, agreeing to pay a ransom, were brutally murdered after they had paid it. This slaughter of innocents, the destruction of synagogues, the burning of homes, not only failed to shake, but strengthened, the deep Jewish sense of community and spirituality. For in the wake of the Haidamak massacres, eastern European Jewry was swept by a deep, lasting, and spiritually uplifting revolution, Hassidism. Once more, Jewish creativity had found a remarkable focus.

Hassidism was a religious movement that appealed to the Jewish masses. It embodied a belief in the need to rejoice in religion, and to do so with song and dance, with zeal and study. Devoted to their charismatic leaders, the Hassids were a closely knit group whose enthusiasm spread rapidly, not only across the map of eastern Europe, but even westwards across the Carpathians. Henceforth, the Hassidic leaders, and the dynasties which they founded, sought through prayer and study a direct and intimate link between man and God. Above all, the Hassids believed that joy – *simhah* – was the prime factor in Jewish life, and the key element in divine worship.

Love of the Land of Israel played a major part in the Hassidic philosophy, so much so that in 1777 a group of several hundred Hassids, old and young, set off from Russia for Palestine, then under Turkish rule. Two years earlier, the Turks had imposed a heavy 'head-tax' on all Jews, while in 1720 the Ashkenazi synagogue in Jerusalem had been seized by local Arabs, and the scrolls of the law destroyed. But the Hassids were undeterred, and, together with many non-Hassidic Jews, they made the hazardous journey, led by one of their best-known learned men, the forty-three-year-old Menahem Mendel of Vitebsk. The Hassids settled in the Galilee, joining the thriving Jewish community of those whose ancestors had come from Spain and Portugal more than 250 years before.

From the first mystic teachings of their leader, the Ba'al Shem Tov, to their mid-twentieth-century communities in Israel, Britain and the United States, the Hassids were an inspiring example of how religious faith can flourish despite some of the most prolonged, and in the end some of the most evil, persecutions devised by man.

As the Russian Empire spread westwards, in 1771, 1791 and 1815, not only the Hassids, but more than five million Jews, came under the rule of Tsarist intolerance and exclusion.

Parallel with the mounting misfortunes of the Jews of Russia, and almost unnoticed by Europe, the strength and confidence of the Jews of the United States had grown with every decade, for they were able to share the challenges of a society which accepted them both as Jews, as patriots, and as equal citizens. As early as 1654 Jews had settled in the then Dutch port of New Amsterdam, later New York, and within fifty years there was a steady flourishing of Jewish life; the first synagogues were founded in New York in 1730 and in Philadelphia twelve years later, while in 1761 an American Jew, Joseph Ottolenghi, was elected a member of the Georgia State Assembly.

The opening year of the nineteenth century found the Jews of the United States moving steadily westwards, as far as Ohio by 1817; while in every walk of life Jews participated on an equal footing with non-Jews. In 1816 a Jew, Salamon, from Philadelphia, was appointed cashier of the Bank of the United States at Lexington, while overseas, another Jew, Mordecai M. Noah, served as United States Consul in Tunis from 1813 to 1816.

For the Jews of western Europe, the nineteenth century also opened hopefully. Under the influence of the French revolution and of Napoleon, the Jews of Frankfurt, Mainz, Venice and Rome found the restrictions on their dwelling places lifted, and the gates of the Ghetto torn down. In 1807 the Jews of Westphalia were granted full emancipation by Napoleon's brother Jerome, while four years later the Jews of Hamburg, Mecklenburg, Lubeck and Bremen were all granted full civil rights.

Even towards the Land of Israel Napoleon seemed to offer, albeit briefly, a new hope for a Jewish return when, in 1799, he advanced from Egypt towards Constantinople. In May 1799, when his armies, having captured Haifa, were being besieged at Acre by the Turks and the British, the official French newspaper reported from Paris that one of Napoleon's aims was 'to give back to the Jews their Jerusalem'. The newspaper also noted that: 'Bonaparte has caused a proclamation to be issued, in which he invites all the Jews of Asia and Africa to come and range themselves under his flags, in order to re-establish Jerusalem as of old.'

3
Sixty Years of Ferment
1815-1875

IN 1815, the year of Napoleon's final defeat and exile, the poet Byron expressed the understanding of the non-Jew towards Jewish suffering, when he wrote, in *Hebrew Melodies*:

> Tribes of the wandering foot and weary breast,
> How shall ye flee away and be at rest!
> The wild dove hath her nest, the fox his cave,
> Mankind their country – Israel but the grave!

Yet the sympathies which this poem expressed were, in Byron's case, short-lived. As the Jews knew, outside support could be cut off with often bewildering rapidity; true friends, who understood the Jewish character in all its complexities, were few. Byron's own attitude was a clear example of this, for only eight years after writing *Hebrew Melodies*, he published his satirical *Age of Bronze*, in which he strongly opposed Jewish emancipation, and denounced in scathing terms the alleged Jewish support for Turkish tyranny and opposition to the Greek struggle for independence. For the Jews of Greece, however, the choice was not a simple one between tyranny and freedom. Under Christian rule they had suffered terribly in Greece, but with the coming of the Ottoman Turks in 1453, they had been left in relative peace, and their religious, cultural and communal life had flourished.

It was therefore not surprising that the Jews of Greece, protected for more than 350 years by the Ottoman Turks, should have shown loyalty to their Ottoman rulers during the Greek revolt of 1821. Their loyalty certainly cost them a great deal. In every town where the Greek rebels were successful, and the Ottoman forces defeated, Jews were murdered with savage zeal. In the Peloponnese, 5,000 Jews were massacred – men, women and children. It was to be sixty years before the communities that remained were granted legal status by the Greeks.

Even under Muslim rule, the Jewish condition worsened as the nineteenth century progressed. In the Persian town of Meshed, in March 1839, a fanatical Muslim mob, incited by a false rumour, burst into the century-old Jewish quarter, burned the synagogue and destroyed the scrolls of the Law. A massacre seemed imminent, and was only averted by the revival of one of the curses of medieval society, the forcible conversion of the whole Jewish community to Islam. Thus the Jews of Meshed officially ceased to exist, becoming Jadid al-Islam, or New Muslims. In secret, they managed to preserve their Judaism, even making the Muslim pilgrimage to Mecca and Medina in order to keep up the appearance of their enforced new faith.

Slowly, in search of a place where they could openly return to Judaism, small groups of 'secret' Jews from Meshed migrated to central Asia, to India, to Britain, and to Palestine. Those who remained in Meshed had to lead a precarious double-life. It was only a century later, after the creation of the State of Israel, that the majority of them were able to abandon Islam, and go, as a restored Jewish community, to the Jewish state. One such 'secret' Jew was Mordekhai Zar, who had been born in Meshed in 1914, and who became Deputy Speaker of the Israeli Parliament in 1969, exactly 130 years after that day of tribulation in the life of a remote and vulnerable Jewish community.

In February 1840, less than a year after the forcible conversions in Meshed, a second blow struck the Jews who lived under Muslim rule. In the city of Damascus, the Jews were falsely accused of murdering a Christian monk and his Muslim servant. According to the accusation, the blood of the two victims had been used to make the Passover bread. A Jewish barber was arrested at random, and tortured until he 'confessed'. The names he gave led to more arrests. Two of those arrested died under torture. A third converted to Islam to save his life. More Jews were arrested, including children; and the torture continued.

Alarmed by the fate of Damascus Jewry, the Jews of France, Britain and the United States intervened. Non-Jews also joined mass meetings of protest in London, Paris, and New York. These pressures succeeded; those Jewish prisoners who were still alive were released, and the Sultan issued an edict forbidding the trial of Jews on the 'blood-libel' charge. But the Damascus Affair, like the events in Meshed a year before, were grim reminders of the precarious nature of Jewish life, even in the lands of Islam.

The European and American concern over the Damascus persecutions did not alleviate for long the plight of the Jews who lived under Muslim rule elsewhere. Throughout the 1860s the Jews of Libya were subjected to punitive taxation. In 1864, in the Moroccan cities of Marrakesh and Fez, as many as five hundred Jews were killed by the Muslim mob, and a further eighteen were killed in Tunis in 1869. These torments drove the Jews of Arab lands to seek havens elsewhere. Some chose Palestine, and the more benevolent rule of the Turkish Sultan. In November 1843 a British Christian missionary, then in Jerusalem, had recorded the arrival in the city of 150 Jews from Algiers, and he noted: 'There is now a large number of Jews here from the coast of Africa, who are about to form themselves into a separate congregation.'

Jew and non-Jew alike had been shocked by the Damascus affair, which had reinforced the idea that the Jews should have somewhere to go where they could be their own masters, free from the whims and tyrannies of those who had a hatred of the Jewish faith and culture. Among those who had protested against the Damascus tortures was a British Jew, Moses Montefiore, who, after a successful business career, had come to devote his life to the cause of his persecuted fellow-Jews wherever they might be. On 11 June 1842, a grandson of the Duke of Marlborough, Colonel Charles Churchill, wrote to Montefiore that, in his view, the Jews ought to promote the regeneration of Palestine and the eastern Mediterranean region. Were they to do so, they would, Churchill believed, 'end by obtaining the sovereignty of at least Palestine'.

Charles Churchill felt strongly that the Jews should resume what he described to Montefiore as their 'existence as a people'. Four years after his letter, in 1845, a fellow Englishman, George Gawler, published a pamphlet urging the establishment of Jewish colonies in Palestine as 'the most sober and sensible remedy for the miseries of Asiatic Turkey'. Gawler, who had fought in 1815 at the battle of Waterloo, and had later become the first Governor of South Australia, published a second pamphlet, in 1847, on the need for the emancipation of the Jews, and two years later he accompanied Montefiore to Palestine.

It was Gawler who pressed Montefiore to set up Jewish agricultural villages in Palestine. Nor were he and Churchill alone among British non-Jews in advocating a Jewish return to the Land of Israel. In 1847 a British peer, Lord Lindsay, on his return from Palestine, wrote in his account of his travels:

The Jewish race, so wonderfully preserved, may yet have another stage of national existence opened to them, may once more obtain possession of their native land . . . .

The soil of Palestine still enjoys her sabbaths, and only waits for the return of her banished children, and the application of industry, commensurate with her agricultural capabilities, to burst once more into universal luxuriance, and be all that she ever was in the days of Solomon.

The efforts of Sir Moses Montefiore to encourage Jewish villages in Palestine were rewarded with success in 1856, when he received an edict from the Sultan allowing the Jews to buy land there. Montefiore took immediate advantage of this, buying agricultural land both at Jaffa and Jerusalem, and later extending his land-purchases to the Galilee, at Tiberias and Safed. George Gawler continued to support Montefiore's efforts, and remained a firm advocate of the right of the Jews to be masters in their own house. On 10 August 1860 he wrote in the *Jewish Chronicle*:

I should be truly rejoiced to see in Palestine a strong guard of Jews established in flourishing agricultural settlements and ready to hold their own upon the mountains of Israel against all aggressors.

I can wish for nothing more glorious in this life than to have my share in helping them to do so.

28

In the United States and western Europe, the nineteenth century brought a new dimension to Jewish history, and with the spread of liberalism and democracy, the Jew was increasingly able to play a positive, and an equal part in political, economic and even social life. In 1810, a Jew, Mayer Moses, had been elected to the Charleston Legislature, and in 1832 the Jews of Canada had been granted full civil rights including the right to sit in the Canadian Parliament, and to hold public office.

As early as 1848, a Jew had entered the French Cabinet, and with each succeeding decade, individual Jews reached Ministerial office elsewhere in western Europe; in Holland in 1860, in Italy in 1870, in Britain in 1909, in Denmark in 1911. A baptised Jew, Benjamin Disraeli, had already, in 1868, become Prime Minister in Britain. By 1870, almost all the universities of western Europe had opened their doors to Jewish students. The medical professions admitted Jewish doctors. Jewish lawyers and journalists worked on equal terms with their non-Jewish colleagues. Jews even found themselves granted the social honours and titles previously reserved for the old aristocracies. In 1885 a Jew received a peerage in Britain; the new Lord was Nathaniel Rothschild, a great grandson of the Frankfurt founder of the dynasty, Mayer Amschel Rothschild.

For the Jews of Germany, the forty-five years since the defeat of Napoleon in 1815 had been full of uncertainty. There were many Germans who argued that, with the evolution of the 'German-Christian State', it was the duty of the Jews to renounce both their religion and their racial origins, and to find in assimilation, and even in Christianity, their true future as German citizens. Many Jews were converted to Christianity, and among the growing number of assimilated Jews were to be found some of the most famous German 'Jews', including the poet Heine, and Karl Marx.

In 1819, however, a virulent outbreak of mob violence, the 'Hep! Hep!' riots, had shown the depth of popular German anti-semitism. Throughout Germany, Jews were made the scapegoats for the economic distress that had followed in the wake of the Napoleonic wars. There was bitterness against the success of individual Jewish bankers and financiers. Romantic and Nationalist writers found a ready audience for anti-semitic songs and slogans in the beer-cellars and student societies. Then, on 2 August 1819, the Jews of Würzburg fled from their homes as German students smashed windows and looted shops. The riots spread quickly, throughout the Rhineland and Bavaria, into East Prussia, and beyond the German States to Austria, Poland and Denmark.

The 'Hep! Hep!' riots confirmed the assimilationist Jews in their view of the need for assimilation. One Jewish newspaper explained that it had decided not to react unduly against the riots, lest this 'weaken our co-religionists' love for our Christian fellow citizens'. Yet the cry of 'Hep! Hep!' was heard again in Germany eleven years later, during the 1830 revolution, with the result that

Towns affected by the 'Hep! Hep!' riots, 1819.

Rural areas affected: the States of Bavaria, Baden, Hesse and Wuerttenberg.

© Martin Gilbert 1978

tens of thousands of German Jews decided to seek a new life free from fear, in the distant United States; German-born Jews were among the earliest members of the Chicago Jewish community, founded in 1841.

Following the second 'Hep! Hep!' riots of 1830, violent anti-semitism faded in Germany, and the local Jews, by commerce, by patriotism, and by partial assimilation, were able to achieve a leading place in German trade and banking, in industry and science, in the arts and literature, and in journalism. Their success was symbolized by the triumphant financial success of the Rothschilds, whose founder, Mayer Amschel Rothschild, had died in Frankfurt-on-Main in 1812, and whose sons carried his banking business and his success to England, France, Austria and Italy. Yet success itself was not always a guarantee of safety; the Rothschild banking houses had been one of the particular targets of the rioters in 1819.

German anti-semitism was never far from the surface of daily life, stimulated by hatred of successful Jews, and suspicion of assimilated Jews, whose patriotism to Germany was still doubted. Anti-semitic remarks and writings came openly from philosophers and historians, politicians and pamphleteers, who believed it to be their duty to single out for criticism the Jews in their midst.

The story of Gerson Bleichröder, a German Jewish banker, provides an example of how even emancipation could provide no escape from antisemitic feeling. As Bismarck's personal banker, he received a title in 1866, the Iron Cross in 1871, and was made a member of the hereditary German nobility in 1872. As an international financier, he received further decorations from Bavaria, Austria, Russia, France and Brazil. But German society looked with hostility upon his social success, and Bismarck's friendship with this wealthy, loyal Jew was described by one senior Prussian diplomat as 'novel and offensive'. The German attitude to Jews was such that even a direct appeal from the Chief Rabbi of Metz to Bleichröder in 1871 could not halt the brutal mass expulsion, in mid-winter, of thousands of Polish-born Jews, men, women and children, from the newly conquered city of Metz. The German Government's aim, officially explained at the time, was 'to Germanize Lorraine', and to remove 'those elements that were contrary to the German spirit'.

Bismarck's own son Herbert, hating his father's close link with Bleichröder, wrote to a friend in 1881: 'I look on the filthy Jew as an evil in himself.' Six years later the young Bismarck, then State Secretary, opposed the entry of Jews into the German Foreign Office on the grounds that they always became 'pushy' when placed in high positions. As the Jews succeeded in more and more professions, German anti-semitism grew. Yet Bleichröder himself, desperate though he was to become accepted by German society, and active though he was in enhancing the finances of German power, never forgot the plight of Jews elsewhere. In May 1867 he appealed direct to Bismarck on behalf of the Jews of Jassy, in Moldavia, against whom the Rumanians had turned with savage persecution. For more than a decade he used his influence to seek to win equal rights of citizenship for Rumanian Jewry; a campaign which achieved a measure of success at the Vienna Congress of 1878. On 1 July 1878 the Congress, by its Article 44, demanded of Rumania that, in return for recognition of its independence, it extended equal rights to all within its borders, including the Jews.

But even this success, while won through all the weight of German diplomacy, could not mask the deeper German antisemitism. There were many things decided at Vienna 'that did not please me', the German Emperor told a friend three months later: 'for instance, the emancipation of the Jews in Rumania; but I was sick and was not allowed to do or say anything'. Nor did the Rumanians themselves intend to honour their pledge. Four days after the signature of Article 44, The Times reported that a leading Rumanian newspaper had declared that the Jews would not have equal rights, 'and we will use force rather than submit to the conditions imposed on us'. This was indeed so: for Rumanian anti-semitism continued to receive official backing from the State.

31

Bleichröder continued his efforts on behalf of Jews elsewhere. In his contacts with senior Tsarist officials after 1880, he repeatedly raised the question of the ill-treatment of Russian Jews; he sent money to destitute Jews in Arab lands, as far away as Morocco and Baghdad; and in 1882 he provided a substantial sum of money for the Alliance Israélite school in Jerusalem.

Although many German Jews bore in patience whatever anti-semitism they encountered, and denied that there was any danger to them personally in the conversation or writings of anti-semites, there was another response, by a German Jew, Rabbi Kalischer, who denied that there was safety in assimilation. Living in the German town of Thorn, on the German-Polish border, Kalischer argued that spiritual redemption could only come for the Jews after their physical return to the Land of Israel.

Pointing out that all European nations were struggling to achieve independence, Kalischer rebuked his fellow-Jews for failing to have a similar objective. In 1860 he supported a society, set up that year in Frankfurt-on-Oder with the aim of promoting a return of the Jews to Jerusalem. The society published his book, *Derishat Ziyon (Zion's Greetings)*, in which he pressed, as the essential first stage of Jewish redemption, a return of the Jews to the land of their fathers, not to live on charity, but through manual work and agriculture; not dependent for security on the Turks, but defending themselves by their own Jewish guards, specially trained for the task.

Kalischer travelled throughout Europe, seeking to win Jewish support for his scheme. One of the first to support it was another German Jew, Moses Hess, a philosopher and writer whose political sympathies had at first been with the new Communist ideology of Karl Marx, whom Hess had helped and befriended. As a young man, Hess had believed that the Jews had already accomplished their historic mission, and should therefore assimilate. But, like many assimilationist Jews, he had been shocked by the Damascus affair in 1840, and later by personal anti-semitic experiences, and he came to believe that the Jews must do everything possible not only to preserve their nationality in the Diaspora, but also to seek their political and social restoration in Palestine.

In 1862, Hess published his book *Rome and Jerusalem*, in which he acknowledged his debt to Rabbi Kalischer, and urged the setting up, in Palestine, of what he called 'Jewish societies of agriculture, industry and trade in accordance with Mosaic, i.e., socialist, principles'. In the introduction to *Rome and Jerusalem* Hess explained, in a moving statement, his, and German Jewry's predicament:

Here I stand once more, after 20 years of estrangement, in the midst of my people; I participate in its holy days of joy and mourning, its memories and hope, its spiritual struggles in its own house and with the civilized people among which it lives, but with which, despite 2,000 years of living and striving together, it cannot organically coalesce.

A thought which I had stifled forever within my heart is again vividly present with me; the thought of my nationality, inseparable from the inheritance of my ancestors, the Holy Land and the eternal city, the birthplace of belief in the divine unity of life and in the future brotherhood of all men.

This thought, buried alive, had for years throbbed in my sealed heart, demanding outlet. But I lacked the energy necessary for the transition, from a path apparently so remote from Judaism as mine was, to that new path which appeared before me in the hazy distance and only in its general outlines.

The vision which Rabbi Kalischer and Moses Hess expounded with such fervour did not perish. One of the first to turn it into practical reality was a Jew from Strasbourg, Charles Netter, who, after living as a businessman in Lille, Moscow and London, had settled in Paris in 1851, and begun a life of concern for Jewish disabilities. In 1860 he had been one of the founders of the Alliance Israélite Universelle, an organization set up to provide practical work and training for Jews in distress anywhere in the world.

Netter was quickly attracted to the idea of extending the work of the Alliance to Palestine, and in 1867 he suggested helping Jews from Persia to escape their life of poverty and persecution by setting up agricultural settlements in Palestine. After a visit there in 1868, Netter wrote with enthusiasm of Palestine as a place where Jews could go in order to escape from hostility elsewhere, and be trained in agricultural pursuits. Netter's enthusiasm had a practical result; in 1869 he went to Constantinople where, like Sir Moses Montefiore before him, he obtained the approval of the Sultan for his scheme.

A year later, in 1870, as a result of Netter's efforts, a Jewish Agricultural School was founded near Jaffa. Known as Mikveh Israel (The Hope of Israel), it was an important step on the road to fulfilling Kalischer's vision of Jewish agricultural self-sufficiency. Kalischer himself thought of leaving Germany to settle there but, at the age of seventy-five, was unable to make the journey.

Elsewhere in Palestine, Sir Moses Montefiore had continued his philanthropic and constructive work year by year, and in 1860 the Montefiore Houses, the first residential houses to be built outside Jerusalem's city walls, had been opened as a shelter for poor Jews, complete with their own windmill, to enable them to be less dependent on outside charity. Four years later, a girls' school had been founded inside the Old City by a member of the Rothschild family, Evelina de Rothschild, and by 1870 there were 9,000 Jews in Jerusalem, amounting to half the city's population.

The idea of a return of the Jews to Palestine, although given its main intellectual impetus by two German Jews, Kalischer and Hess, had also found a spiritual mentor in Rabbi Judah Alkalai, a Sephardic Jew. Born in 1798 at Semlin, near Belgrade, Rabbi Alkalai had, like so many Jews in Europe, been deeply disturbed by the Damascus affair, and argued that Jewish redemption could only come in the wake of human action. Even the growing controversy between orthodox and reform Judaism could be resolved, Alkalai believed, through Jewish 'national' unity. But God would wait for man to take the first steps. Such was Alkalai's message, and in 1874 he, himself, aged seventy-six, moved to Jerusalem, where he pressed for spoken Hebrew as the Jewish language of everyday life, and for the organization of world Jewry as a national force.

In the same year as Rabbi Alkalai's move to Jerusalem, a British explorer, Charles Warren, published a book entitled, boldly, *The Land of Promise*. In his book he envisaged a Palestine with as many as fifteen million inhabitants. In order to reach this goal Warren advocated widespread Jewish rural settlement. In a second book, *Underground Jerusalem*, published a year later, in 1875, Warren wrote that for the time being Palestine would have to be governed on behalf of the Jews by someone else, 'allowing the Jew gradually to find his way into its army, its law, and its diplomatic service, and gradually to superintend the farming operations, and work himself on the farms'. But after only twenty years of such activity, Warren believed, the Jewish principality 'might stand by itself, as a separate kingdom guaranteed by the Great Powers'.

4

The Russian Cauldron
1875-1891

EMANCIPATION brought to European Jewry, for the first time in more then a thousand years, the myriad opportunities of equal rights and full citizenship. It made the Jew feel less of an alien, encouraging his participation, and even his assimilation, into the societies of the west. Many Jewish families abandoned their Jewish identity entirely and, by intermarriage, brought their Jewish heritage to an end. No such temptation presented itself to the vast mass of Russian Jewry. For them, each decade of the nineteenth century brought further hardship, conjuring up the image of past troubles rather than the hope of any future easement.

With the defeat of Napoleon in 1815, more than five million Jews had found themselves within the newly enlarged frontiers of Tsarist Russia, and their numbers grew rapidly. Yet year by year their legal and economic situation had worsened. In 1824, more than 20,000 Jews had been expelled from the frontier provinces of Vitebsk and Mogilev, and forced to live elsewhere, deprived of their livelihood. In 1827, a law had been passed forcing some Jewish boys from the Lithuanian and Ukrainian provinces to do between twelve and twenty-five years military service. In 1835 the laws restricting Jewish residence to the 'Pale of Settlement', Russia's twenty-five western provinces, had been strengthened.

A year later, in 1836, a strict censorship of Jewish books had been imposed, and Jewish books had been burnt in the Tsar's capital, St Petersburg. In 1844 the Jewish Community Councils had been abolished; hitherto they had served as self-governing bodies for each of the Jewish communities, with powers to raise taxation, to resolve community disputes, and to represent the community in the local authorities.

Whereas, in western Europe, the Jew was being allowed to participate in the societies of which he sought to be a part, in Russia he was excluded. Anti-semitism flourished. So too did legal discrimination. In 1845 Tsar Nicholas conceived the idea of dividing the Jews into two categories, the 'useful' and the 'non-useful'. In the 'useful' category were to be wealthy merchants, craftsmen and farmers, whose rights would be respected. The 'non-useful' would include the small tradesmen, the poor, the pedlars and the unemployed, on whom military service would be imposed. The Jews of western Europe protested against this discrimination, and in 1846 Sir Moses Montefiore travelled specially from Britain to Russia to argue against the law. His efforts were in vain. Not only was the law imposed in 1851 but, four years later, with the coming of the Crimean War, the number of Jews liable to military service was tripled, and Jewish children throughout the Pale were kidnapped by special 'snatchers' and sent to army barracks hundreds, and even thousands of miles, from their homes. But even in the army discrimination was ever present, and Jews, however long or brave their service record, were not admitted to officer's rank.

The division of Jews into 'useful' and 'non-useful' continued after 1855, under the new Tsar, Alexander II. 'Useful' Jews were allowed to live anywhere in Russia, even outside the Pale, in St Petersburg and Moscow, or in the cities of the Volga and Ural regions. In 1861 the category of 'useful' was extended to university graduates, and in 1865 it was granted to medical orderlies, midwives, and certified craftsmen. Jews began also to distinguish themselves in journalism, law, medicine, science, literature and the arts; and individual Jews began to flourish as bankers, railroad 'kings', industrialists and exporters. But their success both in the world of culture and of business provoked an immediate hostile reaction. Jews, it was alleged, were an alien element within the Russian state, a disruptive force that sought to take over and to destroy the mainsprings of Russian life. Such accusations were spread publicly in books and newspapers, and violent outbursts against the Jews quickly followed. In 1871 a mob burst in upon the Jewish quarter of Odessa, looting and burning. In 1878 the blood-libel charge was revived, this time against the Jews of Kutais, in the Caucasus.

In March 1881 Tsar Alexander II was assassinated by socialist revolutionaries, who called on the people of Russia to overthrow the Tsarist regime. The Government struggled to maintain law and order. Quickly, the Jews were singled out as a scapegoat. It was put about, with official connivance, that the ills of Russia stemmed from Jewish power and corruption. One more, as at Odessa ten years earlier, angry mobs burst into Jewish streets, looting Jewish shops, burning Jewish property, and even killing those who sought to resist them. Many towns felt the ferocity of these attacks, which began at Elizavetgrad on 15 April 1881, spreading quickly to more than thirty of the surrounding villages and townlets. In May, Jews were attacked in four more provinces of the Pale, and by the end of 1881 more than two hundred Jewish communities had suffered looting, burning and devastation which left 100,000 Jews without their means of livelihood, and 20,000 without homes.

In the wake of these persecutions, small groups of Russian Jews gathered together to discuss what was to be done. Some argued in favour of emigration to the United States of America, and even in favour of a petition to Congress for a specifically Jewish territory that might eventually become one of the States of the Union. Others argued in favour of Jewish settlement in Palestine. This latter possibility was also much discussed by the quarter of a million Jews of Rumania,

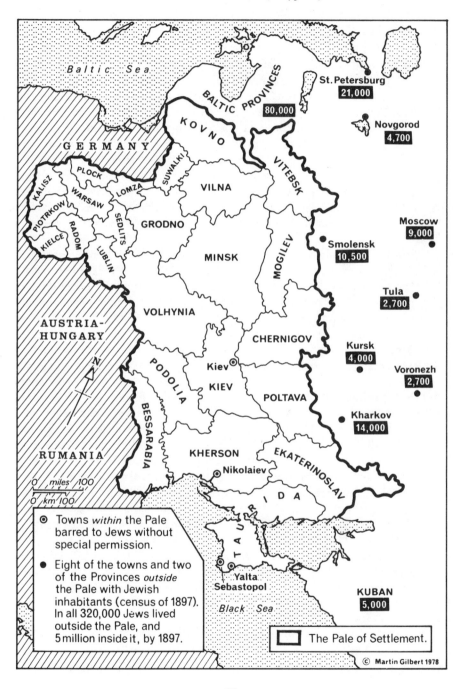

Baltic Sea

GERMANY

BALTIC PROVINCES
80,000

St. Petersburg
21,000

KOVNO

Novgorod
4,700

PLOCK
KALISZ
WARSAW
PIOTRKOW
KIELCE
RADOM
SEDLITS
LOMZA
SUWALKI
LUBLIN

VILNA

VITEBSK

GRODNO

Moscow
9,000

MINSK

MOGILEV

Smolensk
10,500

AUSTRIA-HUNGARY

VOLHYNIA

Tula
2,700

PODOLIA

CHERNIGOV

Kiev

KIEV

Kursk
4,000

Voronezh
2,700

POLTAVA

BESSARABIA

Kharkov
14,000

KHERSON

EKATERINOSLAV

RUMANIA

Nikolaiev

0 miles 100
0 km 100

TAURIDA

⊙ Towns *within* the Pale barred to Jews without special permission.

● Eight of the towns and two of the Provinces *outside* the Pale with Jewish inhabitants (census of 1897). In all 320,000 Jews lived outside the Pale, and 5 million inside it, by 1897.

Yalta
Sebastopol

Black Sea

KUBAN
5,000

☐ The Pale of Settlement.

© Martin Gilbert 1978

37

whose persecution had continued, despite the decisions of the Congress of Vienna, and whose status in fact remained that laid down by the Rumanian legal decision of 1877, which stated that 'the Jews do not have a country of their own and therefore do not belong to any State'.

The Jews of Rumania had appealed for funds to help them go to Palestine, both to the Alliance Israélite Universelle in Paris and to the Board of Deputies of British Jews in London, but the response was meagre. Then, on 20 December 1881, the representatives of thirty-two local Rumanian groups met at Focsani. For three days the fifty-one delegates discussed the Jewish need to 'regain national honour' and to re-awaken in Jewish hearts those 'holy feelings which the sheer weight of pain, want, and poverty had put to sleep for thousands of years'. It was finally decided that, as a first step, a hundred families should leave for Palestine in the following year. Thus was born the first positive action of what was to become a great movement of Jews from both Rumania and Russia, the 'Lovers of Zion'.

In Russia, two groups of families, fourteen in all, one group from Kremenchug and the other from Kharkov, had determined, at the end of 1881, to set out for Palestine as soon as possible. Their leader, Zalman David Levontin, himself only twenty-six, left for Palestine in January 1882 to study the problems with which his settlers would be faced. 'As for me,' he wrote to a friend, 'I have found it *necessary* to leave our country and go to the Holy Land, or in other words, to move from words to deeds.' During his journey, Levontin appealed for funds in the Jewish press, an appeal that was answered by one of his own uncles. Land was purchased on the coastal plain, at Rishon le-Zion, and in August 1882 Levontin and the other families set off for Palestine. That same month the first group of Rumanian Jews, 288 people in all, left Europe for their newly purchased land, Samarin, just south of Haifa. By the end of 1882 Lovers of Zion groups had sprung up all over southern Russia and Rumania, determined to join, or to support, further groups of would-be settlers in the Land of Israel.

The Lovers of Zion were not alone in urging Russian Jews to go to Palestine, rather than to America. On 21 January 1882 a fast had been held throughout Russia in memory of the victims of the pogroms. During the fast, a twenty-year-old Jewish student from Kharkov, Israel Belkind, had invited a few of his friends to his home, to discuss what to do. They too had decided to go to Palestine, rather than to America, and to build there what they called 'a political centre for the Jewish people'. For the name of their movement they chose the word BILU, from the Hebrew initials of the biblical exhortation: 'House of Jacob, come you, and let us go'; within only a few months their membership reached 500.

One of the earliest members of BILU was the twenty-three-year-old Ze'ev Dubnow. At first he too, like so many young Russian Jews, had believed in the need for Jews to assimilate into the societies in which they were born. But, like

THE RUSSIAN CAULDRON, 1875-1891

many of his contemporaries, he had been so shaken by the intensity of anti-semitic feelings revealed by the pogroms of 1881 that he joined BILU without hesitation and, in a moving declaration, expressed the feelings of all those who looked to BILU as an opportunity for Jewish dignity:

> The aim of our journey is rich in plans. We want to conquer Palestine and return to the Jews the political independence stolen from them two thousand years ago. And if it is willed, it is no dream. We must establish agricultural settlements, factories and industry. We must develop industry and put it into Jewish hands. And above all, we must give young people military training and provide them with weapons.
>
> Then will the glorious day come, as prophesied by Isaiah in his promise of the restoration of Israel. With their weapons in their hands, the Jews will declare that they are the masters of their ancient homeland.

Dubnow was among the first group of pioneers who, setting off from Odessa under Israel Belkind's leadership, reached Jaffa on 6 July 1882. They were welcomed to Palestine by Charles Netter, who encouraged their idealism, and gave them work at the Mikveh Israel agricultural school, which he had founded twelve years before. Netter, however, died later that same year, and the BILU pioneers found themselves without a patron, forced to hire themselves out as labourers, and without the resources to set up their own community. Nevertheless, by persevering, they did manage to purchase some 800 acres of land in the Judaean foothills and, in December 1884, less than three years after their first dream of action, they began to build up their own settlement, Gederah.

The pogroms which had stirred so much anguish and activity in Russia did not end in April 1881, but continued for another year with unabated ferocity. In Minsk, a fifth of the city was destroyed by fire. In Korets, a thousand buildings were destroyed and thirty-nine Jews murdered. The conscience of Christian Europe was shocked by these excesses. In February 1882, at a protest meeting in London, the British Catholic leader, Cardinal Manning, declared, about the Jewish people:

> Russia and England are of yesterday, as compared with the imperishable people, which, with an inextinguishable life and immutable traditions, and faith in God and in the laws of God, scattered, as it is, all over the world, passed through the fires unscathed, trampled into the dust and yet never combining with the dust into which it is trampled, lives still, a witness and a warning to us all.

The pogroms continued; since Crusader times, Easter had been a dread time for European Jews, and at Balta, during Easter 1882, which coincided with Passover, six hundred Ukrainian peasants, incited by their priests to an intense hatred of the 'killers of Christ', burst into the Jewish quarter. Nine Jews were killed, more than twenty girls were raped, several hundred shops looted, and nearly a thousand houses destroyed. In May, the pogrom came again to Odessa, where there was massive looting throughout of Jewish shops and houses.

Both the Lovers of Zion and the BILU pioneers, equally shaken by the virulence of the pogroms, continued to advocate a return of the Jews to Palestine, not simply to gaze on Zion, or to weep at the Wailing Wall, or to be buried on the Mount of Olives, but to build up the land by their own efforts, by agriculture and manual labour, by draining the swamps and transforming them into fields and farms. One strong supporter of all they sought to do was an Englishman, a non-Jew, Laurence Oliphant. In 1879 Oliphant had tried to negotiate with the Sultan for land east of the Jordan, which Jews could cultivate. Following the pogroms of 1881 and 1882, Oliphant travelled throughout Eastern Europe, urging those who wished to flee to go, not to America, but to Palestine. His appearance was almost messianic. 'Providence has delivered the wand of our nation's leadership into your hands,' five members of the Lovers of Zion wrote to him from Nikolaiev, 'and with your possession of it a new era in the history of the Jews with all its suffering begins'. On 12 May 1882, in London, the *Jewish Chronicle* printed Oliphant's emphatic advice that the Jews should choose Palestine 'in preference to America', where , he warned, 'Judaism, scattered and dispersed in all parts, threatens to disappear.'

In May 1882 new restrictive laws were introduced by the Tsarist authorities, directed solely against the Jews. These 'May Laws' forbade Jews to live in hundreds of villages, in which for more than three hundred years they had farmed and traded, with the result that half a million Jews were forced to leave their homes, and move, their livelihood lost, into the already crowded towns of the Pale. At the same time, a further quarter of a million Jews were uprooted from the western border areas of Russia, and likewise forced to move into the towns.

Poverty and destitution followed in the wake of these expulsions. In Vilna, for example, more than 22 per cent of all the Jews in the city were in receipt of poor relief from the community; while, in Odessa, four hundred dinners a day were provided at cheap eating houses, more than 150 of them entirely without charge.

What was to be the future of the Jews of Russia? In 1882 a Jewish doctor from Odessa, Leon Pinsker, sought to answer this question. Like Moses Hess before him, Pinsker had begun his adult life as an assimilationist. He had been one of the first Jews allowed to study at Odessa University. Having graduated from the Law Faculty there, he discovered that, as a Jew, he had no chance of actually practising as a lawyer. Instead, he turned to medicine, still hoping to be accepted in Russian society. He became a regular contributor to a weekly magazine which urged Jews to speak Russian, as opposed to Yiddish, and advocated Jewish familiarization with Russian culture. The Odessa pogrom of 1871 led him to abandon his literary efforts. Ten years later, the pogroms of 1881, and a close study of Jewish history led him to the conclusion that the universal hatred of Jews, not only in Russia, but throughout Europe, was such that even humanitarian rights would be denied them whenever danger threatened.

In 1882 Pinsker travelled to Italy, Austria, France, Germany and London. Everywhere he went, he discussed with Jewish leaders his view that what the Jews needed was a national centre. Many of those whom he met were sceptical, and argued that America provided an adequate haven. But a leading British Jew, Arthur Cohen, a Member of Parliament, encouraged Pinsker to put his views in writing, and so he wrote his book, *Auto-Emancipation*, in which he argued that anti-semitism was inevitable wherever the Jews were a minority; that they could only be a majority if they had a homeland of their own.

In his book, Pinsker wrote of how:

We do not count as a nation among the other nations, and we have no voice in the council of the peoples, even in affairs that concern ourselves. Our fatherland is an alien country, our unity dispersion, our solidarity the general hostility to us, our weapon humility, our defence flight, our originality adaptability, our future tomorrow. What a contemptible role for a people that once had its Maccabees.

The impact of Pinsker's book was immediate, its message seemingly underlined by a further outbreak of anti-Jewish mob violence in June 1884, this time in Kunavina, where seven Jews were killed. Five months later, in November 1884, the Lovers of Zion met in conference at Kattowitz, in Upper Silesia. It was the week after Sir Moses Montefiore's hundredth birthday. Of the thirty-two delegates, twenty-two were from Russia, six from Germany, two from England, and one each from France and Rumania. Pinsker, who was elected chairman, spoke of the need for the Jews to return to work on the land. The Russian-born writer and journalist, Nahum Sokolow, put forward specific proposals for industrial development in Palestine. A British Jew, Zerah Barnett, who had twice been to Palestine, first in 1871 to help found the Mea Shearim quarter outside the walls of Jerusalem, and again in 1878 to help found the Jewish village of Petah Tikvah, spoke, as the delegate from London, of the hardships facing the settlers.

The Kattowitz Conference allocated money for two projects already existing in Palestine, for Petah Tikvah itself, and for the newly established settlement of Yesud ha-Ma'alah, struggling to survive in the desolate swamplands of the Huleh marsh. Two committees were formed, one in Odessa and one in Warsaw, while the son of Rabbi Kalischer announced that he was giving the Lovers of Zion the plot of land which he had bought near Rachel's Tomb, on the road between Jerusalem and Bethlehem. The conference ended by arranging for the establishment of Lovers of Zion societies throughout Russia, and also outside Russia, in London, Paris, Berlin, Belgrade and even New York.

In May 1885 the focus of Jewish attention switched momentarily but forcefully to the Arab world, following a savage anti-Jewish outbreak in the Moroccan town of Demnate. The Jewish press in Europe gave wide coverage to this pogrom within the Muslim world. Sir Moses Montefiore, ever vigilant in the cause of Jewish rights, mounted a solemn protest.

Following the Demnate massacre, a young Russian Jewish boy, not yet eleven years old, wrote to one of his teachers of the need to 'rescue our exiled, oppressed brethren who are scattered in all corners of the world and have no place where to put up their tents'. For the sake of these Jews, the schoolboy added, it was essential 'to establish a place to which we can flee for help'. As the boy saw it, the thanks of the Jews must go to Moses Montefiore and Baron Edmond de Rothschild. The Lovers of Zion must be supported, for it was a Society 'which understands what lies before it and sees the evil threatening us'. In America, the young boy believed, although it was a land 'where enlightenment prevails', the Jews would be 'beaten'; they would be beaten also in Africa, and particularly in Morocco; in addition, he was convinced, 'we will not be pitied'. His letter ended:

> Let us carry our banner TO ZION AND RETURN TO OUR FIRST MOTHER UPON WHOSE KNEES WE WERE BORN. – For why should we look to the Kings of Europe for compassion that they should take pity upon us and give us a resting place? In vain! All have decided: THE JEW MUST DIE, but England will nevertheless have mercy upon us. In conclusion to Zion! – Jews – to Zion! let us go.

The writer of this letter was Chaim Weizmann, then just about to set off from his home in the tiny village of Motol to secondary school in Pinsk. His youthful anguish and aspirations foreshadowed a lifetime devoted to the cause of Zion, and to a Jewish homeland in Palestine.

Sir Moses Montefiore died on 28 July 1885, three months before his 101st birthday. Since his first visit to Jerusalem in 1827, he had been looked up to by persecuted Jews all over the world as their 'champion'. In the two decades following Montefiore's death, steady progress was made in Palestine towards the realization of his ideal. The pioneers there faced terrible hardships: disease, swampland, a primitive local agriculture, brigands, isolation and poverty. But two years before Montefiore's death, the thirty-six-year-old Baron Edmond de Rothschild, who had been born in Paris, had been drawn actively into the task of giving financial help to all the struggling settlements in Palestine: hence the young Weizmann's praise. In 1887 Baron Edmond visited the settlements himself, demanding of those whom he helped that they use Hebrew as their spoken language, that they preserve the Jewish religious traditions, that they maintain modest living standards, and that they do their own manual labour. In return, he provided funds both for agricultural development, and for the founding of a prosperous wine industry. 'The Baron', as he was known to the settlers, also bought large parcels of land throughout Palestine for future Jewish agricultural development.

By 1890, the number of Russian-born Jews who had settled in Palestine reached 50,000. In Jerusalem alone the Jews numbered more than 25,000, out of a total population in the city of only 40,000. The Arabs, a majority in the sparsely populated countryside, watched with alarm this influx of newcomers from Russia, and on 24 June 1891 the leading Muslims of Jerusalem telegraphed to the Turkish authorities in Constantinople 'praying they the entry of such Jews should be prohibited, as, not only was the labour market over-stocked, but also the Muslims themselves would be greatly the sufferers, as, the European Jews being skilled in all different kinds of trades, the Muslims could not compete against them'.

As a result of this protest all Jewish immigration was forbidden by the Turks in July 1891, but, after a short while, the ban was not enforced. That same year a Christian priest, Hugh Callan, asked, in his *History of Jerusalem*: 'What is to be her future? Shall the Russians rule through their Greek Church (as they like to), or shall the Jews possess her? This at least is sure: while, the rest are strangers, the Jews are still the only patriots there.'

5

'A Great and Beautiful Cause'
1891-1897

BETWEEN 1881 and 1914 more than two million Russian Jews left Russia in search of a secure home, an unmolested daily life, and the chance of education and self-advancement. More than half a million of these refugees went to Britain, France and western Europe. Eighty thousand went to Palestine. But the vast mass, more than two million, crossed the Atlantic to the Argentine, to Canada, and to what they called in Yiddish, the *goldene medina* – the 'golden realm' – the United States.

Myriad opportunities opened up for the Jews who reached the United States, opportunities denied them entirely in Russia and eastern Europe. Settling throughout the United States – from Boston, New York and Philadelphia, to Chicago and St Louis, and across to San Francisco on the Pacific Ocean, the Jews from Russia strove hard to succeed. Many flourished as 'custom pedlars', or small businessmen. They established many of America's leading chain stores and emporia. They were pioneers of trade union activity, and they built up comprehensive self-help organizations, using their own new wealth to help their less fortunate fellow-Jews.

In New York, the Jews were more than a million strong by 1910. Jewish theatres, hospitals, schools and newspapers, all flourished, and the rich vigour of the Yiddish language, and of Yiddish literature, found yet another home, thousands of miles from both its origins and its wanderings. In 1900 a non-Jewish observer wrote, of the Jews of the Manhattan slum: 'Ignorant they are, but with a thirst for knowledge that surmounts any barrier.' Thus was fulfilled, by the opening decades of the twentieth century, the call expressed by the New York Jewess Emma Lazarus, in 1883, and inscribed on the Statue of Liberty:

> Give me your tired, your poor,
> Your huddled masses yearning to be free,
> The wretched refuse of your teeming shore,
> Send these, the homeless, tempest-tost to me.
> I lift my lamp beside the golden door!

The Jews of the United States multiplied and flourished, their creative genius released from centuries of uncertainty and persecution in eastern Europe.

Businessmen and inventors, judges and lawyers, doctors and surgeons, writers and artists, philosophers and rabbis, found in America wide spheres of action and achievement.

In western Europe there was an equally remarkable flowering of the Jewish genius in the years before the First World War, when Jewish self-help, Jewish community organization, and Jewish participation in national, political, cultural and scientific life reached new dimensions of activity and success. In Germany, Austria-Hungary, Britain, France and Italy, individual Jews contributed to the wealth and achievements of their respective societies, often as pioneers in science and medicine, in philosophy and the arts. Yet, despite their desire to be full and loyal citizens in the lands of their birth, many Jews felt that they were never fully accepted into the societies in which they lived.

In Russia, the day of the assimilationists had been brief. In 1886 a Tsarist law had limited the number of Jewish students in both schools and universities within the Pale to 10 per cent even though, in many towns, they formed more than 50 per cent of the population. At Easter 1891, which again coincided with the Passover celebrations, more than 20,000 Jews were suddenly ordered to leave Moscow for ever, cut off in the most cruel way from their homes and livelihood. When one senior official proposed a less harsh policy towards the Jews, the Tsar himself noted on the proposal: 'But we must not forget that it was the Jews who crucified our Lord and spilled his priceless blood.'

In one effort to find a haven for Russian Jewry, an Austrian Baron, Maurice de Hirsch, a Jew who had grown rich as one of Europe's great railway builders, gave £8 million to the formation of a Jewish Colonization Association, which bought land in the Argentine. More than 1,000 Jewish families had reached these distant farms by 1894. They were small in comparison to the total number of Russian Jews, nor were they as numerous as the number reaching Palestine under the auspices of the Lovers of Zion. Yet these Argentine settlements could not satisfy those for whom Palestine was not merely a haven, but the true centre of Jewish political and spiritual regeneration.

In 1891 the dreams and activities of the Lovers of Zion were shaken by a fierce criticism. It came from one of the most brilliant Russian Jewish writers of his time, Ahad Ha'am, who, after his first visit to Palestine, argued that Palestine must become more than a series of settlements. What was needed, he argued, was a 'spiritual centre'. High moral standards were therefore essential. Work and modesty, the frugal and humble life, were an indispensable part of any return to Zion.

Ahad Ha'am wrote of the difficulties which he believed were being ignored: the barrenness of much of the soil, the hostility of the local Arabs who could not be expected to 'yield their place easily', and the power of the Turkish authorities to obstruct settlement. Yet he wrote also of the old vision, infused with a new spiritual content. While emigration to America was still the only way to

45

provide the solution to the Jews' economic problem, he wrote, there was, in addition:

... the need to create for ourselves a fixed centre through the settlement of a great mass of our people in one territory on an agricultural basis, so that both the Jews and their enemies may know that there is somewhere in the world a place where, though it may be too small to contain the whole people, a Jew can lift up his head like a man, can get his living from the soil by the sweat of his brow, and can create his own conditions of life in his own national spirit.

If there was to be any hope of solving that aspect of the question, Ahad Ha'am added, 'it is to be found only in Palestine'.

Ahad Ha'am visited Palestine again in 1893. Once more he was critical, this time of Jewish agricultural work based on the Chalukah, or charity, system, and of the poor state of Hebrew education. The Chalukah money, coming from Jews in Europe and America, bred lethargy and scorn towards those who urged work and skill as the means of building up Jewish farms, schools and communities. Ahad Ha'am also contrasted the passivity of the Jews praying at the Wailing Wall, at the fast to commemorate the destruction of the Temple in 70 AD, and the bravery of their forebears. 'It seemed to me,' he wrote, as though we were surrounded by the shades of our heroic ancestors, who gave their lives on this spot and on this night for their country and their nationality, and that they were gazing in amazement on these their descendants, seated by their glorious graves with *books* in their hands.'

From Palestine, Ahad Ha'am travelled to Paris and London. 'As for the English Jews,' he wrote in his diary, 'and the hopes I had that they would do something for the Jewish cause – I blush for shame and will say nothing.' While in England Ahad Ha'am was overcome with doubts about the Jewish fate, writing pessimistically in his diary: 'Is there really a bright future in store for us? Or is this only the last ray of light?'

In September 1893, while Ahad Ha'am was in London, a young Jewish journalist from Vienna was on holiday near Vienna. His name was Theodor Herzl, and he was arguing at a friend's house about the Jewish future, putting forward an argument for assimilation. 'Ever heard of Charles Darwin?' Herzl asked his friend. 'He puts forward the theory that the species adapts itself. We shall do the same. By living with the Gentiles, by imitating their ways, by being forced into the political and economic currents and influences which determine their lives, we shall become like them.' Once the Jews were like the Gentiles, Herzl believed, they would be free of the Jewish problem. 'Here is our Fatherland,' Herzl's friend concluded. Yes, Herzl agreed, 'In our Austrian Fatherland.'

Leaving his friend's house that evening, Herzl passed a group of hooligans who shouted at him: 'Pig of a Jew.' Herzl was shaken; it was certainly not him personally they were abusing, he thought. 'They don't know me at all. It was my

Jewish nose and my Jewish beard they were sneering at. So much for all my fine thoughts about time and liberalism solving this problem.'

Herzl's subsequent awakening was swift and dramatic. While in Paris to report the trial of Captain Dreyfus, he was shaken by the strength of French hostility, not merely towards one Jewish army officer, but towards all Jews. On 2 June 1895 he went to see Baron Maurice de Hirsch to unfold a new scheme: the need for all Jews, even the wealthy and the contented, to work towards the goal of a Jewish state in Palestine. 'I had no intention of becoming involved in Jewish affairs.' Herzl told Hirsch, 'but the alarming growth of anti-semitism has made me change my mind,' and he went on: 'For nearly two thousand years we have been dispersed all over the world and without a State of our own. This has led to much tragedy and degradation. If we had our own political centre again we could begin to solve our problem.'

Hirsch listened politely, but replied sceptically to Herzl's vision: 'The rich Jews will give you nothing. They're hard. They harden their hearts to the sufferings of the poor.' Undeterred, Herzl appealed to the Vienna Rothschilds, headed by Baron Albert Rothschild. On 18 June 1895 he sent the Rothschilds a letter in which he wrote with darkest pessimism of the Jews' fate in Europe. 'Improvement', he insisted, 'is out of the question,' and he added:

If someone were to ask me how I know this, I should tell him that I also know where a stone rolling down an incline finally arrives – namely, at the very bottom. Only ignoramuses or madmen do not take the laws of nature into account.

Therefore we must finally end up at the bottom, rock bottom. What appearance this will have, what form this will take, I cannot surmise. Will it be a revolutionary expropriation from below or a reactionary confiscation from above? Will they chase us away? Will they kill us?

I have a fair idea that it will take all these forms, and others. In one of the countries, probably France, there will come a social revolution whose first victims will needs be the big bankers and the Jews.

Anyone who has, like myself, lived in this country for a few years as a disinterested and detached observer can no longer have any doubts about this.

In Russia there will simply be a confiscation from above. In Germany they will make emergency laws as soon as the Kaiser can no longer manage the Reichstag. In Austria people will let themselves be intimidated by the Viennese rabble and deliver up the Jews. There, you see, the mob can achieve anything once it rears up. It does not know this yet, but the leaders will teach it.

So they will chase us out of these countries, and in the countries where we take refuge they will kill us.

Herzl's answer was 'a Jewish exodus' to Palestine. But Albert Rothschild did not even reply.

On June 20, only two days after Herzl had delivered his letter to the Rothschilds, another letter was being written 500 miles to the east, in the Russian town of Pinsk, where more than 20,000 Jews made up three-quarters of the town's total population. The writer was the twenty-year-old Chaim Weizmann, then a student. His letter, a private one written to a friend, expressed his distaste at the sight of the condition and morale of Russian Jewry. The Jews of Pinsk, he wrote, made 'a vile, repulsive impression', and he went on to explain:

... instead of people, one comes across creatures devoid of personality, with no interests, no desires, no demands, who are pleased or displeased for some reason or other known to no-one, not even to themselves.

Hundreds of Jews push on and hurry about the streets of our town, with anxious faces marked by great suffering, but they seem to do it unconsciously, as if they were in a daze.

Three months later, Weizmann wrote again from Pinsk. The 'only decent and educated people', he declared, were those whom he called the 'Palestinians', the members of the local Lovers of Zion society. But as for the majority of the Jews, he wrote: 'There is a depressed, dull state of mind everywhere; people expect something, some sort of miracle, and look vacantly into the future.'

That same month, when Karl Lueger's anti-semitic party triumphed in the municipal elections in Vienna, Theodor Herzl noted in his diary: 'The mood among the Jews is one of despair.' Herzl, however, persevered in his belief that he could persuade both Jews and Gentiles to support the idea of a Jewish State in Palestine. He made contact with the Sultan of Turkey, sought to influence the German Kaiser, wrote an outspoken letter to Bismarck, pressed his arguments vigorously with the leading Jews of western Europe and even wrote, on 15 November 1896, to the Grand Duke Vladimir of Russia, an uncle of the Tsar, seeking to enlist his support in what he described as 'the solution of a question as old as Christianity, a great and beautiful cause, designed to delight the noblest hearts. It is the return of the Jews to Palestine!'

Some of those to whom Herzl had expounded his ideas considered him insane. One Jewish friend advised him to see a psychiatrist. But he found one distinguished and respected ally in Max Nordau, another Jewish newspaper correspondent living in Paris in the 1890s, who told him: 'If you are insane, we are insane together. Count on me!' Nordau, who had been born in Hungary, was well-known as a lifelong opponent of aristocratic corruption and monarchical oppression. In his much publicized and controversial book, *The Conventional Lies of our Civilization*, written in 1884, when he was thirty-five, he had condemned not only contemporary society, but also the hatred of Jews, which he portrayed as a symptom of national degeneration. For most of his life Nordau had lived in Paris, earning his living as a newspaper correspondent for both a Berlin and a Budapest newspaper; while in Paris he, like Herzl, had witnessed the new wave of anti-semitism. From the moment the two men met, Nordau had encouraged Herzl in his endeavours, endeavours which reached a culmination in February

1896 when Herzl published his book *The Jewish State*. In it he declared bluntly: 'Palestine is our ever-memorable historic home. The very name of Palestine would attract our people with a force of marvellous potency.'

In *The Jewish State*, Herzl pointed to the part played by anti-semitism in bringing the Jews to their existing desperate situation. 'We have honestly endeavoured', he wrote, 'to merge ourselves in the social life of surrounding communities and to preserve only the faith of our fathers. We are not permitted to do so. In vain we are loyal patriots. . . .' And he added:

We might perhaps be able to merge ourselves entirely into surrounding races, if these were to leave us in peace for a space of two generations. But they will not leave us in peace. For a little period they manage to tolerate us, and then their hostility breaks out again and again. The world is provoked somehow by our prosperity, because it has for many centuries been accustomed to consider us as the most contemptible among the poverty-stricken. In its ignorance and narrowness of heart, it fails to observe that prosperity weakens our Judaism and extinguishes our peculiarities. It is only pressure that forces us back to the parent stem; it is only hatred encompassing us that makes us strangers once more.

The Jews, Herzl wrote, were 'one people – our enemies have made us one'. It was the distress of the Jews that bound them together, and 'thus united, we suddenly discover our strength. Yes, we are strong enough to form a State, and, indeed, a model State. We possess all human and material resources necessary for the purpose.'

The Jewish State was a handbook of practical action. In it Herzl described some of the detailed work needed to set up such a State in Palestine. Much of his book dealt with specific details of emigration, land-purchase, house-building, the labour laws, the proposed nature of manual work, commerce, the industry, the education, the welfare, and the social life of the new State.

Once the Jews were 'fixed in their own land', Herzl wrote, it would no longer be possible to scatter them all over the world. 'The Diaspora cannot take place again,' he added, 'unless the civilization of the whole earth shall collapse,' and he went on to proclaim:

Here it is, fellow Jews! Neither fable nor deception! Every man may test its reality for himself, for every man will carry over with him a portion of the Promised Land – one in his head, another in his arms, another in his acquired possessions. . . .

But we must first bring enlightenment to men's minds. The idea must make its way into the most distant, miserable holes where our people dwell. They will awaken from gloomy brooding, for into their lives will come a new significance.

'The Maccabeans will rise again,' Herzl proclaimed in his closing sentences. 'We shall live at last as free men on our own soil, and die peacefully in our own homes.'

Following the publication of Herzl's book, a ferment of argument and antici-
pation was unleashed among the Jews of Europe. Many western Jews were totally
opposed to the idea of a Jewish State. On 18 March 1897 Herzl recorded in his
diary a meeting with the Chief Rabbi of Vienna, Moritz Güdemann, who spoke
to Herzl 'about the "mission of Jewry", which consists in being dispersed
throughout the world'. This mission, Herzl commented, 'is talked about by all
those who are doing well in their present places of residence – but they are the
only ones'. Yet, even for the fragmentary process of piecemeal settlement in
Palestine, Herzl's carefully defined proposal for full, and rapid statehood was a
revelation not all of them could fully comprehend. For Ahad Ha'am, the real
need was not for a political centre at all, but for a centre of spiritual regeneration,
and even this he did not expect to see for many years; on 29 July 1897 he wrote
to a friend: 'I am already held by many to be a pessimist who sees and pro-
phesies nothing but evil; so what good would come of what I have to say?'
Herzl, however, was an optimist, and he persevered until, on the morning of
Sunday, 29 August 1897, the first Zionist Congress opened in Basle.

More than two hundred delegates gathered at Basle, at least a quarter of them
from Russia. The scepticism of the Lovers of Zion had been overcome. Even
Ahad Ha'am, although not a delegate, was present at the Congress, and allowed
himself to be a part of the official photograph. There were Jews from Palestine,
Jews from Arab lands, Jews from Britain, and even a Jewess from New York,
Rosa Sonnenschein, the editor of the *American Jewess*. In all, Jews from twenty-
four different states and territories had gathered together.

Herzl, as President of the Congress, spoke with fervour to an audience which,
however sceptical some of them might have been in the months leading up to
the meeting, were now caught up in the future which he envisaged. 'We have
an important task before us,' he told them. 'We have met here to lay the foundation stone of the house that will some day shelter the Jewish people.' It was not
to be a secretive or chance affair. 'We have to aim', he insisted, 'at securing legal,
international guarantees for our work.' Nor would the delegates merely disperse
once their deliberations were over. 'At this Congress', Herzl declared, 'we bring
to the Jewish people an organization it did not possess before.'

Herzl's aim was to enable an outcast people to act with dignity. The Jews, he
explained, were no longer to 'steal into the land of their future'. Instead, they
would negotiate their return openly, by a legal agreement with the Great Powers.
That agreement, Herzl insisted, 'must be based on rights and not on toleration'.
Once the negotiations were successfully completed, he envisaged, not the
existing pace of piecemeal settlement – 'infiltration' he called it – but 'the settlement of Jewish masses on a large scale'.

During his speech Herzl focussed almost entirely on the positive aspects of
Zionism, which was, he said, 'a civilized, law-abiding, humane movement
towards the ancient good of our people'. It was Max Nordau, the Congress

Vice-President, who stressed the material and moral misery of the Jews in the dispersal. In eastern Europe, North Africa and Asia, he said, where as many as nine-tenths of world Jewry were living, 'there the misery of the Jews is to be understood literally. It is a daily distress of the body, anxious for every day that follows, a tortured fight for bare existence.' But there was also, he said, the misery of the western Jew, the emancipated, half-assimilated Jew, a misery that took the form 'of perpetual injury to self-respect and honour, and of a brutal suppression of the striving for spiritual satisfaction'. And Nordau continued:

The emancipated Jew is insecure in his relations with his fellow beings, timid with strangers, even suspicious of the secret feelings of his friends. His best powers are exhausted in the suppression, or at least the difficult concealment, of his own real character. For he fears that this character might be recognised as Jewish, and he never has the satisfaction of showing himself as he is in all his thoughts and sentiments. He becomes an inner cripple.

The Zionist Congress ended by adopting the Basle Programme, which Nordau had drafted, and which began with the blunt sentence: 'The task of Zionism is to secure for the Jewish people in Palestine a publicly recognized, legally secured homeland.' To fulfil this task, the Congress decided formally to:

1. Encourage the systematic settlement of Palestine with Jewish agricultural workers, labourers and artisans.
2. Organize and unite the Jewish people by the creation of groups in various countries whose object would be to foster the aims of the movement. These groups were to be organized in accordance with the laws of their respective countries.
3. Dedicate itself to strengthening Jewish consciousness and national feeling.
4. Organize political efforts so as to obtain the support of the various Governments of the world for the aims of Zionism.

Herzl, while aware of all the work still to be done, the raising of funds, the negotiations with the Great Powers, and the struggle for wider Jewish support, was elated by what had been achieved. On 3 September 1897, on his return to Vienna, he wrote in his diary:

Were I to sum up the Basel Congress in a word – which I shall guard against pronouncing publicly – it would be this: At Basel I founded the Jewish State.
If I said this out loud today, I would be answered by universal laughter. Perhaps in five years, and certainly in fifty, everyone will know it.

'The foundation of a State', Herzl added, 'lies in the will of a people for a State. . . .'

6

'A Flag and an Idea'
1898-1905

ZIONISM, with its call for a Jewish revival in Palestine, made an immediate impact on Russian Jewry. But, at the same time, many Russian Jews were attracted to a different cause, that of revolutionary socialism involving, not an escape from Tsarist tyranny, but the destruction of Tsarism itself. On 7 October 1897, only five and a half weeks after the opening of the first Zionist Congress in Basle, a secret convention opened in Vilna of a new Jewish organization, the Bund, dedicated to the coming of a Russian socialist government. In March 1898 the Bund was formally admitted to the Russian Social Democratic Labour Party, as an autonomous body; henceforth it was to play a major part in the emergence of Russian revolutionary socialism, while attracting many Jews by its demand for equal political and civil rights for Russian Jews.

Henceforth the Zionists had to meet the challenge of the Bundists, whose appeal to a persecuted people was, like theirs, a strong one.

The second Zionist Congress opened, again at Basle, on 28 August 1898. Among those present was the twenty-three-year-old Chaim Weizmann, who had been studying chemistry at Fribourg University, in Switzerland, only fifty miles from Basle. The number of delegates had doubled at the second Congress; there were more than 400. But the debates were bitter, and Herzl found himself mediating among many diverse and often strongly contrasting opinions. In September the young Weizmann returned to Pinsk. He was not impressed by the state of Zionism that he found there, writing to some friends: 'Propaganda is not yet being conducted as it should. A great shortage of speakers is felt. One ought to take advantage of these fiery times. . . .'

For Herzl, every opportunity was one of which he intended to take advantage, for a sense of impending success had seized hold of his imagination. To ten thousand Jews who gathered to hear him speak in the East End of London he declared, on 3 October 1898: 'I fervently believe the time is very close when the Jewish people will be very definitely on the march.'

Later that month, Herzl visited Palestine, timing his visit to coincide with that of the German Kaiser, William II, with whom he had already spoken in Constantinople. On November 2, in Jerusalem, the Kaiser received a Jewish deputation, which presented him with an album of photographs of the Jewish settlements in Palestine. As a result of his two audiences with the Kaiser, Herzl, as President of the World Zionist Organization, was accorded a recognition which gave Jewish Zionist aspirations a status inconceivable even a decade before. But this new found status seemed in no way even a prelude to statehood, for while the Kaiser had expressed interest in the Jewish agricultural experiments, he added, in his talk with Herzl on November 2, that these must be conducted 'in a spirit of absolute respect for the Sultan's sovereignty', while Herzl recorded in his diary a joke circulating in Vienna after the Kaiser's visit, that 'this Zionism is a wonderful thing. What a pity it has to be carried out by Jews.'

At times, Herzl despaired of keeping his followers united. 'Days of despondency,' he noted on 11 February 1899. 'The tempo of the movement is slowing down. The catchwords are wearing out.' But anti-semitism and Jew hatred was in no way fading. Indeed, in 1899, it gained a new literary force with the publication of Houston Stewart Chamberlain's book, *The Foundations of the Nineteenth Century*. Chamberlain had been born in Britain in 1855, had been educated in France, and had chosen to live in Germany, where he married the daughter of Richard Wagner. In his book he developed the theory of the 'blond' Nordic race, the originators, in his view, of all that was noble in western civilization. All that was bad, Chamberlain asserted, came from racial mixing, and particularly from any 'Nordic' intermarriages with Jews, who were, he declared, a 'mongrel' people incapable of creativity, the universal corruptors. According to Chamberlain, King David, the Prophets, and Jesus, were not Jews at all, but of Germanic origin.

Houston Stewart Chamberlain's ideas won acclaim in Germany. The Kaiser was one of his supporters, and his book was later to influence the most vicious anti-semite of all, Adolf Hitler, with whom Houston Chamberlain came to be on terms of personal friendship. In the same year that *The Foundations of the Nineteenth Century* was published, a book was published in Cairo, entitled *The Talmud Jew*, whose author, August Rohlings, likewise portrayed the Jew as a disruptive force in world history. These books fed existing prejudices, gave them a false legitimacy, and cloaked evil in spurious science. Also in 1899, another blood-libel accusation was made against the Jews, this time in Bohemia inside the Austro-Hungarian Empire.

These anti-Jewish accusations, even where localized, affected Jews all over the world. Whether in Meshed or Damascus, in Russia or Bohemia, the charge levelled against one group of Jews threatened the peaceful existence of Jews elsewhere, and therefore bound them together in sympathy. For hostile non-Jews like Houston Stewart Chamberlain or August Rohlings, this cohesion of the Jews was proof of some Jewish 'conspiracy' which had to be crushed. For the Jews themselves, cohesion was their only chance of physical as well as spiritual survival. As a Jewish doctor in Manchester, George Dulberg, wrote to the *Jewish Chronicle* on 31 August 1900:

Judaism is not a religion merely like Catholicism or Protestantism; it is a brother-hood, a race if you like, and that it will remain as long as there are two Jews left in the whole world.

Say what you will, no matter how an English Jew or a German Jew may love or feel for his English or German neighbour, he will have a greater love, a greater sympathy for another Jew, even if that other Jew may come from the other end of the world.

Amid the pressures and distress caused by anti-semitism, the Jews struggled to find some way of creating a normal life in which their existence would not be so frequently questioned and threatened by those among whom they lived. On 26 September 1901, during the Jewish New Year, Chaim Weizmann wrote to Vera Khatzman, the girl who was later to be his wife: 'I wish that you may become a representative of the new generation which will come to take the place of the shattered company of Jewish workers of today.' His letter continued:

May your pure bright soul be filled with love for your people, a suffering people, an enslaved people, unjustly persecuted, a people brutally rejected by its own sons, and yet a giant people concealing in itself a divine strength, great and wonderful creative power, wisdom, character, and the germ of a world conscience.

May Israel rise – poor, oppressed, abused Israel, forgotten by its own sons.

May the young shoots now appearing on the old time-worn trunk grow into a mighty tree in the shade of which the Wandering Jew may seek repose.

May its sons and daughters return and apply their strength to healing the sores that have appeared in the body of an ancient people which yet harbours so much youthful fervour. . . .

Weizmann's letter ended: 'Israel is awaiting its children – and they are coming, they are returning, and may the coming years be a festival of re-union, a festival of the return of him who has been lost.'

The ideas which Weizmann expressed so poignantly in his letters to Vera Khatzman were echoed by young Jews throughout Europe, for whom Zionism now seemed to offer the chance of a life of dignity and independence. In 1901, the twenty-three-year-old Ezekiel Wortsmann wrote, in a Yiddish pamphlet entitled 'What Do the Zionists Want?', published in London: 'We consider ourselves as strangers everywhere, even where we have been given complete civil rights, because we want to have a home of our own.' Wortsmann also argued that it was not enough to 'revive a people' in Palestine; it was also essential 'to revive its national tongue', the Hebrew language.

Already, in Palestine itself, largely as a result of the pioneering work of the Russian-born Eliezer Ben Yehuda, Hebrew was becoming more and more accepted as the common language among the Jews, while Ben Yehuda himself was working with enormous energy to compile a Hebrew dictionary which would incorporate new words, based on old forms, but enabling the biblical language to be of use in every possible contingency of modern life.

54

Although the Jews were a minority in Palestine, they formed compact and active communities, struggling, experimenting, and growing; and, despite the dull hand of the Turkish bureaucracy, they lived their daily life with a sense of dignity and independence. The Jews who arrived to join them were welcomed as if returning home. But for the Jews who fled from Russia to western Europe, another attitude awaited them; often they were 'aliens', and even at times, in the popular parlance, 'undesirable aliens'.

In Britain, a Royal Commission on Alien Immigration had been set up in 1902 to examine the whole question of the influx of Jews from Russia. Many of the non-Jewish witnesses spoke angrily of the life and activities of the Jewish immigrants. Alderman James Silver, former editor of the *East London Observer*, told the Commissioners of how the 'foreign colony' had spread eastwards and southwards, pushing out 'Britishers' to such an extent that 'the feeling entertained towards them as a body by the British people compelled to live there is bitter'. The Jewish characteristic was 'to deal with, to negotiate with, and to herd with people of his own race'. Even worse, the Jewish trader not only worked 'unceasingly', but was 'satisfied with a smaller profit', so that, the Alderman protested, 'I regret to say many British people prefer to go to the cheapest market rather than support people of their own race.'

The Commissioners were told of how every Jewish activity provoked the hostility of the local inhabitants. Rubbish collection was costing the community more, 'owing to the dirty habits of the foreigners'. The Jews 'did not trouble in the slightest degree to learn the language of the country of their adoption'. According to Councillor Lewis, the heart of the Englishman failed when he saw 'hordes of these wretched people – unclean, unkempt, speaking a foreign language, and half-barbarians – come tramping along our main streets in charge of some interpreter'. Worst of all, in Alderman Silver's view:

Every house seems to vomit forth people. No decent, self-respecting Englishman would live under such conditions, and it is the contempt and disgust excited in him at seeing people live under such circumstances that feeds the feeling of indignation existing in East London at the unrestricted influx of these foreigners. . . .

Doubtless in point of morality they are as virtuous as we are, but the conditions under which they exist – for they cannot be said to live – are indecent and disgusting, and excite feelings of loathing.

On 7 July 1902 the Royal Commission examined Theodor Herzl, who, in a powerful exposition of the Jewish case, told the Commissioners that the reason why Jews flocked to Britain and America was 'a desire for the freedom of life and soul which the Jew cannot under present conditions know in eastern Europe'. The Commissioners must remember, Herzl continued, that this 'self-imposed sentence of exile is not with Jews as with those of other nationalists, for a term of years – with the Jews it is a life sentence'. On arrival in his place of exile, the Jews

55

often found themselves still as aliens, provoking the very anti-semitism from which they had fled. Intermarriage was no solution for, as Herzl put it, 'when the world came to appreciate the Jew at his true worth to a sufficient extent as to desire intermarriage with him, then the world would probably recognize his value as a separate entity, and give us our right to exist as a separate people, according us our rightful place among the peoples of the world'.

Herzl then expressed to the Commissioners what he described as the 'main principle' of Zionism:

. . . the solution of the Jewish difficulty is the recognition of Jews as a people, and the finding by them of a legally recognized home, to which Jews in those parts of the world in which they are oppressed would naturally migrate, for they would arrive there as citizens just because they are Jews, and not as aliens.

This would mean the diverting of the stream of emigration from this country and from America, where so soon as they form a perceptible number they become a trouble and a burden to a land where the true interest would be served by accommodating as many as possible.

Given to Jews their rightful position as a people, I am convinced they would develop a distinct Jewish cult – national characteristics and national aspirations – which would make for the progress of mankind.

Wherever Jewish refugees went, Herzl argued, they created anti-semitism. But he was convinced that this problem would not arise, 'if a home be found them which will be legally recognized as Jewish'. The Commissioners were sceptical. suggesting once more that the remedy might lie in assimilation. But Herzl answered this from his own past, telling the Commissioners:

I myself was an assimilated Jew, and I speak from experience. I think the Jews have rather a tendency to assimilate, they have a natural tendency to assimilate; but there comes the moment when they are in a very good way on the road to assimilation, and then just at that moment comes anti-Semitism.

The whole of history has taught us that never have Jews been in a happier condition than they were in Spain before events which led up to the Inquisition and Expulsion of the fifteenth century; they were to Spain all they could be, and they had all they could have.

Herzl's argument was central to Zionism: even in countries where the Jews had at first been welcomed, had flourished, and had proved to be loyal patriots, the moment nearly always came when they were turned against, solely because they were Jews. In Russia, in towns where Jews had lived for nearly eight hundred years, the Jew was now, as Herzl expressed it, 'the scapegoat, the whipping boy; and one day he tries no longer to be a scapegoat, and he seeks other skies'. Even in Britain, Herzl believed, it was possible that massive Jewish immigration would eventually stir up strong anti-semitic feelings.

In what way, the Commissioners asked Herzl, were the Jews really a 'nation' as such. A nation, Herzl replied, was any group of men 'held together by a common enemy'. And what, he was asked, would the 'common enemy' be as far as the Jews were concerned, to which he answered, in two words: 'The anti-semite.'

Herzl was then asked, why not continue to send the Jews to the Argentine? After all, the Baron de Hirsch had provided substantial finances for Jewish colonies there. No, Herzl replied, that plan had been a failure, 'because when you want a great settlement, you must have a flag and an idea. You cannot make those things only with money.'

Continuing, Herzl expressed the essence of Zionism when he told the Commissioners:

With money you cannot make a general movement of a great mass of people. You must give them an ideal. You must put into them the belief in their future, and then you will be able to take out of them the devotion to the hardest labour imaginable.

I will give you an example. Argentina has a very good soil, and the conditions for agricultural labour are much better than in Palestine, but in Palestine they work with enthusiasm and they succeed. I am not speaking of the artificially made colonies, but self-helping colonies, which have that great national idea.

For the Jews of Russia, one of the most cruel forms of discrimination was the exclusion of Jewish children and students from the full rights of education. This exclusion spurred the development of a central feature of Zionism, the need for educational opportunities, in which Jews would be as free as anyone else to develop their own creative skills. But on 8 June 1901, in yet a further blow to the Jews of Russia, the Tsarist Ministry of Education had directed that the existing 10 per cent quota for Jewish university students should not be calculated for the overall student body, but separately for each faculty, thus greatly reducing the number of Jews in those faculties, like Law and Medicine, which Jewish students favoured.

In order to free Jewish education from its dependence upon hostile governments, the Zionists put forward the idea of a Jewish university in Palestine. More than a thousand years earlier, the academies of Sura and Pumbeditha had been the last fully autonomous Jewish intellectual centres, yet even they had been subject to Mesopotamian overlordship. Since then, in Europe, North Africa and Asia, every Jewish school was at the mercy of local laws, often hostile to Jewish learning, while the numerical restriction of Jewish students in almost all places of learning effectively denied a higher education to many Jews who wished to pursue their studies.

As the restrictions on Jewish education in Russia grew more severe, the desire for specifically Jewish studies, whether religious, historical or literary, gave added power to the idea of an autonomous Jewish university in Palestine. On 3 May 1902 Herzl himself set out some of the arguments, and some of the appeal of such a university, in a letter to the Turkish Sultan, Abdul Hamid, to whom he wrote: 'The Jewish University should bring together all the scholarly qualities of the best universities, technical schools, and schools of agriculture. The institution will offer nothing unless it is of the very first rank. Only then can it render real service to scholarship, to the students, and to the country.'

The idea of a Jewish university, and all that such a university implied, quickly became an integral part of Zionist thinking. During a conference of Russian Zionists which opened in Minsk on 4 September 1902, Ahad Ha'am stressed the links between Zionism as a movement for national revival, and the cultural needs of the Jewish people; both, he believed, could be given a new focus in Palestine. Among the resolutions which were passed in Minsk, was one which expressed the sympathy of the Conference with the idea of a Jewish university. At a further Zionist Congress held in Vienna at the end of October 1902, Chaim Weizmann joined with the twenty-four-year-old Martin Buber in a motion aimed at facilitating 'a Jewish University in Palestine'. The mood of the Conference was such that the phrase '*only* in Palestine' was insisted upon, following which, Weizmann was appointed head of a small office in Geneva, devoted to the task of advancing the university project.

The difficulties in the way of these plans were substantial: land, funds, people, were all lacking; dissension within the Zionist movement, even on this issue, reflected the diverse backgrounds and differing needs of the leaders. Herzl himself had come, since May, to favour setting up the university in western Europe rather than in Palestine. On 6 November 1902 Weizmann wrote from Geneva to a friend:

Confidentially, we are confronted with a serious crisis in all fields of Zionism. All the more, therefore, does an act such as the establishment of a Jewish University seem absolutely necessary to me. We must create new generations that are less corroded by the Exile.

Inside Russia, persecution strengthened the Jewish sense of identity. But in western Europe the lure of assimilation was great. For the Zionists, however, assimilation was an even greater evil than persecution, for with it came the threat of the extinction of Judaism altogether. On 23 March 1903, when the British Zionist Leopold Greenberg appeared before the Royal Commission on Alien Immigration, he pointed out that if the Jew was 'content to become submerged, to assimilate in the country to which he migrates, he would become quickly lost in the general population, and hence in a generation or two would become English or American as the case may be'. But asked to comment on the merits of such a result, Greenberg stated emphatically: 'Assimilation must be detrimental to the Jews, because it must tend to submerge the Jewish nation.' For the persecuted Jew, Greenberg explained, 'anything like general assimilation would for him be but a transference from the frying pan into the fire'.

A massive increase in persecution inside Russia now dominated Jewish concerns. Since the time of the first Zionist Conference in 1897, a Russian anti-semite, Pavolaki Krushevan, had been publishing a newspaper in Kishinev in which, with vicious regularity, he warned the Christians of Bessarabia not to allow themselves to be exploited by the Jews. In February 1903 Krushevan began to circulate yet another blood-libel charge against the Jews: in the town of Dubossary, he alleged, a Christian child had already been murdered so that its blood could be used in the coming Passover. The Passover came two months later, on 19 April 1903. That night, and throughout the following day, an anti-Jewish mob was on the rampage in Kishinev. The garrison of more than five thousand Tsarist troops stood idly by as the pogrom spread, while agents of the Ministry of the Interior were directly involved in rousing the mob. When the pogrom was over, forty-nine Jews had been killed and 500 injured. In addition, more than 2,000 families had been left homeless. 700 houses looted and destroyed, and 600 businesses totally ruined.

The Kishinev pogrom stirred Jewish and non-Jewish opinion throughout western Europe and the United States, just as the Elizavetgrad pogrom had done twenty years before. But, despite international protests, the pogroms continued throughout 1903, and Jews were murdered in Kiev, in the Caucasus and in Moscow. In June, a Tsarist law forbade all Zionist meetings on Russian soil, while yet another anti-semitic publication, the *Protocols of the Elders of Zion*, began to be widely circulated, imputing to the Jews a world-wide conspiracy whose aim was to destroy the existing states of Europe, and to dominate the world.

In the face of repeated attacks, the Jews of Russia were not without a few resources of their own and, during 1903, a Jewish self-defence group sprang up in Odessa, the scene of almost continuous anti-semitic outbreaks. One of the initiators of the Odessa self-defence group was the twenty-three-year-old Vladimir Jabotinsky who, in the wake of the Kishinev pogrom, had immersed himself in Zionist activity, and become an outspoken opponent of those who argued that the answer to persecution was assimilation: the denial, and eventual disappearance, of Judaism itself.

Less than four months after the Kishinev pogrom, on 5 August 1903, Herzl took the courageous step of going to Russia himself, to plead direct with the Minister of the Interior, Plehve, whose agents had been so active in stirring up anti-Jewish feeling during the course of the pogrom. His visit was not entirely in vain; hailed by the Jews of Vilna as the 'King of the Jews', he met in St Petersburg unexpected sympathy for Zionism, provided, as Plehve himself stressed at their first interview on August 8, that 'it worked towards emigration'. Plehve went so far as to agree to Herzl's request for an 'effective intervention' from Russia with the Sultan of Turkey, in favour of a Charter for Jewish colonization in Palestine.

On August 12 Plehve sent Herzl a letter in which he stated bluntly:

So long as Zionism consisted of wanting to create an independent state in Palestine and undertook to organize the emigration from Russia of a certain number of its Jewish subjects, the Russian Government could be completely favourable to it. But once this principal Zionist objective is abandoned, to be replaced by straight propaganda for a Jewish national entity in Russia, it is obvious that the Government can in no way tolerate this new direction taken by Zionism. It would only create groups of individuals quite alien and even hostile to the patriotic sentiments which are the strength of every state.

That is why confidence can be placed in Zionism only on condition that it returns to its former programme of action. If it did so, it would be able to count on moral and material support from the day when certain of its practical measures would help to reduce the size of the Jewish population in Russia. This support could take the form of protecting the Zionist emissaries to the Ottoman Government, of facilitating the work of the emigration societies, and even of providing for the needs of these societies, obviously from sources other than the state budget, by means of a tax levied on the Jews.

It was his hope, Plehve added, that as Jewish emigration from Russia increased, the position of Russia's remaining Jews would improve. Indeed, at their second meeting, on August 13, Plehve went so far as to assure Herzl that what would suit the Russian Government best would be the 'creation of an independent Jewish State, capable of absorbing several million Jews'.

On August 14, the day after Herzl's second discussion with Plehve, the British Colonial Secretary, Joseph Chamberlain, made an offer to the Zionists which was to cause much heart-searching and dissension: he offered, through L. J. Greenberg, to consider the possibility of setting up an autonomous Jewish Colony in British East Africa. The sixth Zionist Congress met at Basle on August 22. Herzl, who had returned from Russia, supported Chamberlain's offer of what came to be known as the Uganda scheme. Many of the Russian delegates were so angered by what they saw as the abandonment of Palestine that they walked out of the hall. Herzl argued forcefully that Uganda could provide a homeland for at least a short time; but he had not abandoned either his vision, or his efforts, of the past six years, and, at the final session on August 28, he declaimed with passion the biblical injunction: 'If I forget thee, O Jerusalem, let my right hand forget her cunning.'

The Russian pogroms continued; at Gomel in September 1903 there were more deaths. Two months later the Russian Zionists, meeting at Kharkov, formally rejected the Uganda scheme, and sent a delegation to Vienna to demand of Herzl face-to-face that in future he would propose no other Jewish settlement than that in Palestine. The deputation reached Vienna on 31 December 1903, by which time Chamberlain's offer had in fact been postponed, partly on account of what the Colonial Office described as 'local' African feeling. But Uganda had held little attraction for the bulk of poorer Jews, even in England. Those who supported it, like the novelist Israel Zangwill, had never been in the mainstream of Zionist activity. Nor had its emergence deflected the growing efforts to build more and more on the existing work and settlements in Palestine itself. At the beginning of December a Jewish mining engineer, Moses Novomeysky, then living in Irkutsk in Siberia, had raised 600 roubles towards a Jewish university in Palestine. Thanking him for his gift, Chaim Weizmann wrote from Geneva on 4 December 1903: 'We greet you as another fighter for the great design to establish a true Spiritual Centre for the Jewish people in Palestine.'

It was this concept of the 'great design' in every aspect of Zionist work that gave the Jews a new sense of purpose, of dignity, and of hope, as they contemplated the possibility of a Jewish government in Palestine. On 24 December 1903 a London rabbi, Dayan Asher Feldman, wrote in the *Jewish Chronicle*:

Zionism has become a strong factor in East End life. It has rallied round it the intellectual forces of East End Jewry. The national ideal – the ideal of the Jewish spirit – has taken a strong hold upon the greater bulk of the Jewish population. It has attracted the flower of Jewish youth.

The ideal has given rise to numerous associations, nearly every one of which has its literary programme, its lectures and debates, its reading parties and Hebrew talks, whilst some have started, on a very modest scale, reading rooms and circulating libraries.

The floating of the Uganda scheme had intensified the Zionist debate within Jewish circles, and focussed Jewish aspirations even more firmly on Palestine. On 11 April 1904 Herzl, then a dying man, was able to persuade the Zionist General Council that he had remained faithful to his original ideal of a return to the Land of Israel. The Uganda scheme had also stirred up feeling in non-Jewish circles, creating the very anti-semitism of which Herzl had warned the Royal Commission on Alien Immigration, nearly two years before. In a debate in the House of Commons on 20 June 1904, one Member of Parliament, Cathcart Watson, warned of how the Africans of Uganda had been 'seething with indignation' at the prospect of Russian or Rumanian Jewish settlers. 'Such an Empire within our Empire', he warned, 'was nothing short of suicidal madness.' Another MP, the Irish nationalist Haviland Burke, declared:

. . . a Jew was a Jew all the world over. Wherever they went the Jews remained a distinct race; and he believed that the institution of a Jewish community in East Africa or anywhere else, would mean trouble in the near future.

He believed that the Jewish race, for one reason or another, had been at the bottom of all our troubles in South Africa, and that they owned great English newspapers as absolutely as if those newspapers were edited by a Rabbi and printed in a synagogue.

It was against the public interest of this country to do anything to strengthen the forces of Judaism as against christianity, or even, he would say boldly, as against paganism. . . .

Five days after this debate, Chaim Weizmann received a verbatim account of it in Geneva. It was clear from the debate itself, he wrote to Vera Khatzman, 'that the government is not even thinking of offering the Jews autonomy. All it will give, if it gives anything at all, is earth for the grave.'

On 3 July 1904 Theodor Herzl died. 'What a heavy load has fallen on our shoulders!' Weizmann wrote to Vera Khatzman five days later. 'Terrible times have befallen us, but ours is such a feeble generation.' Nor did the terrible times have any respite, for 1905 saw a harsh continuation of the trials of Russian Jewry and, as the year advanced, Jewish rights were further curtailed, hampering the daily life and work of hundreds of thousands of professional and working men. Hundreds of incidents, small in themselves, contributed to the Jewish sense of isolation. During the year, the stock exchange in Kursk forbade the participation of Jewish stockbrokers. The Bessarabian Horticultural Society barred Jewish horticulturalists, despite their important contribution hitherto to market gardening throughout the province. In Odessa, the shoemakers' association refused to let the hundreds of Jewish shoemakers participate in their work. Jewish students from the Baltic town of Libau, brought by their teachers to Moscow on a scientific expedition, were refused entry into the city solely because they were Jews.

In February 1905 a pogrom broke out in the Crimean town of Theodosiya; in April the Jews of Melitopol were attacked by the local mob; in May there was a pogrom in Zhitomir. Far from being spontaneous outbreaks of anti-Jewish violence, these pogroms were increasingly co-ordinated by a new anti-semitic organization, the Union of the Russian People, whose secret fighting units, known as the Black Hundreds, travelled from town to town to incite hatred against Jewish shopkeepers and merchants.

The seventh Zionist Congress opened in Basle on 27 July 1905. Among the speakers was the Russian-born Boris Schatz, who proposed the establishment of an art school in Jerusalem, in order to foster a Jewish 'national' style of arts and crafts. His idea was accepted with alacrity; a year later the school itself was in existence. As for Zangwill and the 'Territorialists', this conference saw their complete withdrawal from the Zionist organization. Other 'territorial' solutions were likewise treated with disdain; a Dutch newspaper suggestion that Surinam would provide a Jewish haven provoked bitter scorn, all the more so because Zangwill gave it his support.

Often instigated by the Black Hundreds, attacks on Jews continued throughout Russia during the autumn and winter of 1905. In August nineteen Jews were killed, and fifty-six seriously injured in a further outbreak of violence in Kishinev. In October, 300 Jews were massacred in Odessa, and 120 in Ekaterinoslav. But,

Baltic Sea

St.Petersburg

LITHUANIA

Dusyata

GERMANY

Lodz

Warsaw

Bialystok

Minsk

Moscow

Czestochowa

Sedlits

Brest-
Litovsk

Mogilev

Gomel

Starodub

Nyezhin

AUSTRIA-
HUNGARY

Kiev

Konotop

Pereyaslav

Smyela

Balta

UKRAINE

Kharkov

RUMANIA

Ananayev

Kremenchug

Focsani

Kishinev

Elizavetgrad

Odessa

Nikolaiev

Ekaterinoslav

Melitopol

Rostov-
on-Don

Simferopol

CRIMEA

Black Sea

Caucasus

miles 100

km 100

The Jewish Pale of Settlement.

Pogroms.

© Martin Gilbert 1978

Kutais

63

at the same time, despite Russian police hostility, groups of Jews still banded together to form self-defence organizations. One such group, in Poltava, succeeded in saving many lives during a pogrom there in November. Among its founder members was the twenty one year old Izhak Shimshelevich, who hid some of his group's weapons in his home. Seven months later the police discovered the arms cache, exiled his father to Siberia – where he was forced to remain for sixteen years – and imprisoned his brother, his sister, and his aunt. Izhak Shimshelevich escaped, and within a year had emigrated to Palestine: forty-five years later, as Izhak Ben-Zvi, he became the second President of the State of Israel.

By the end of 1905 more than eight hundred Jews had been murdered in Russia. More than 60 towns and 600 villages had shared in this orgy of killing and looting. It was a time of distress for Jews everywhere. On 27 September 1905, Chaim Weizmann had written to Vera Khatzman from Geneva of the life of his generation of Jews: 'the bitter struggle for survival', as he described it, 'the longing to do everything possible for the cause, the struggle against one's own impotence, the desire to extend one's full potential, and more'. As for the Jewish future, he wrote:

Extraordinary things seldom occur, and I have lost faith in miracles. I have ceased to hope that we, our generation, shall live to see days that are any brighter than those we are now living through. Our fate is to prepare better days for our children, if not for our grandchildren.

Nevertheless I am certain that were we to survey the present from a vantage point of 30 years, we would say: it was hard, very hard, but it was a good, full life, lived to the utmost. It was a time when we lived and fought not only for ourselves, but for life in the future!

One British non-Jew who sympathized with the plight of Russian Jewry was a thirty-one-year-old Liberal Member of Parliament, Winston Churchill. He was present, with Weizmann, on 10 December 1905 at what the *Jewish Chronicle* described as 'one of the most remarkable meetings that Manchester Jewry has ever witnessed'. On the previous day, Churchill had been offered his first Government post, that of Under-Secretary at the Colonial Office. During the course of his speech he told an audience of several thousand that they had met to protest 'against the appalling massacres and detestable atrocities recently committed in the Empire of Russia'. Churchill then declared:

The numbers of victims had been enormous, many thousands of weak and defenceless people had suffered terribly, old people alike with little children and feeble women who were incapable of offering resistance, and could not rely at all on the forces of law and the regulations of order.

That those outrages were not spontaneous but rather in the nature of a deliberate plan combined to create a picture so terrible that one could hardly distinguish it in its grim reality, even amid the darkness of Russia.

They had met there to express, in no uncertain terms, how deeply moved the whole British nation were at such atrocious deeds.

7

'Jerusalem Must be the Only Ultimate Goal'
1906-1914

DURING 1906 there were yet more pogroms in Russia, for the fifth consecutive year. On 14 June a pogrom broke out in Bialystok, and within forty-eight hours eighty Jews had been murdered. On 22 June Chaim Weizmann wrote to Vera Khatzman from Manchester:

> The terrible news emerging daily from Russia, the menacing sword suspended over all our people in general and our dear ones in particular, the stifling atmosphere of decay and ignorance prevailing here – all this makes life unbearable sometimes, and on occasion one's power of resistance refuses to function. When will it all be over? When shall we have a single calm day, a single happy hour?

> Looking back one grows afraid; looking ahead, heavy, so heavy, I am eternally obsessed with the feeling that something unpleasant, destructive, is about to happen. I tremble before every postal delivery!

In August thirty Jews were killed during a pogrom in Sedlits, and when the third conference of Russian Zionists opened at Helsingfors on 4 December 1906, the mood was one of urgency and determination. The conference produced the Helsingfors Programme, of which Vladimir Jabotinsky was one of the architects, and which laid down that settlement in Palestine should not have to wait until the Jews had obtained some form of diplomatic rights or protection there, but should proceed uninterrupted, and at a greater pace. The Helsingfors Programme also urged the Zionists to 'strengthen Diaspora Jewry and provide it with new cultural, material and political means in its struggle for the creation of a sound national life in the Land of Israel'.

Fierce anti-Jewish riots in Rumania in 1907 gave a further impetus to immigration to Palestine, and in the ten years between 1904 and 1914 more than 25,000 Jews reached the Land of Israel. This brought the total Jewish population to nearly 100,000, almost a fifth of the local Arab population; both peoples lived side by side in a land as yet sparsely populated, largely barren, and capable, with proper care, of sustaining a much larger population.

In those same ten years, more than a million Jews reached the United States from Russia alone. Yet despite the continuing appeal of the United States, the materially more difficult choice, Palestine, still excited those for whom it was not simply a question of somewhere to go, but of a return to the historic home of the

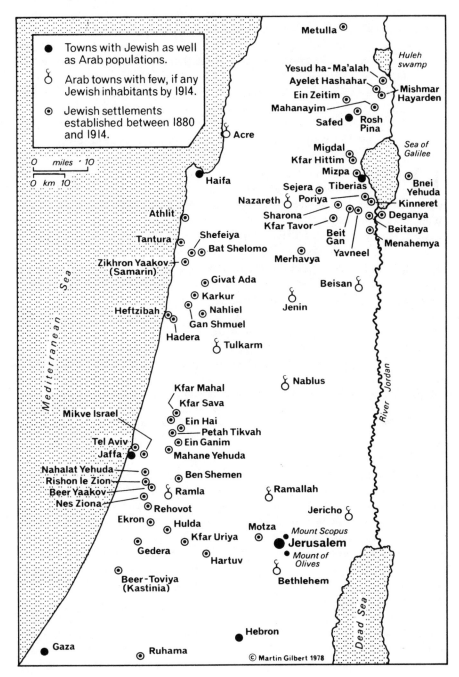

Towns with Jewish as well as Arab populations.

Arab towns with few, if any Jewish inhabitants by 1914.

Jewish settlements established between 1880 and 1914.

0 miles 10
0 km 10

Metulla

Huleh swamp

Yesud ha-Ma'alah
Ayelet Hashahar
Ein Zeitim
Mishmar Hayarden
Mahanayim
Safed Rosh Pina

Sea of Galilee

Acre

Migdal
Kfar Hittim
Mizpa
Haifa

Sejera Tiberias
Nazareth Poriya
Sharona
Kfar Tavor
Beit Gan
Yavneel

Bnei Yehuda
Kinneret
Deganya
Beitanya
Menahemya

Athlit

Tantura
Shefeiya
Bat Shelomo
Zikhron Yaakov (Samarin)
Merhavya

Givat Ada
Karkur
Nahliel
Gan Shmuel
Hadera
Heftzibah

Beisan

Jenin

Tulkarm

Mediterranean Sea

River Jordan

Kfar Mahal
Kfar Sava
Mikve Israel
Ein Hai
Petah Tikvah
Ein Ganim
Mahane Yehuda
Tel Aviv
Jaffa
Nahalat Yehuda
Rishon le Zion
Beer Yaakov
Nes Ziona
Rehovot
Ekron
Hulda
Gedera
Kfar Uriya
Hartuv
Beer-Toviya (Kastinia)

Nablus

Ben Shemen
Ramla
Ramallah

Jericho

Motza
Mount Scopus
Jerusalem
Mount of Olives
Bethlehem

Dead Sea

Hebron

Gaza Ruhama

© Martin Gilbert 1978

Jewish people, to which individual Jews turned in each generation, and in whose life they had always played a part, despite at times frightening persecutions from both Christians and Muslims alike. In Jerusalem the Jewish population had reached 40,000 by 1905, and constituted more than two-thirds of the city's total population. Two years later a British traveller, Miss Freer, noted in her book *Inner Jerusalem*: 'We are so accustomed to think of the modern Jew as a recent immigrant to Palestine that it is somewhat surprising to find that Jerusalem is virtually a Jewish city.'

On 16 November 1907 the British Consul in Jerusalem, E. C. Blech, sent a full report on the Jews of Palestine to his immediate superior, the British Ambassador in Constantinople. 'At Jaffa', he wrote, 'the Jewish population has in ten years risen from 1,000 to between 10 and 20,000 and represents about one third of the inhabitants of that port.' Throughout Palestine, he estimated, there were now 100,000 Jews, out of a total population of between 400,00 and 450,000. Even so, Blech believed, the future of the Zionist ideal was a remote one, perhaps unobtainable, for, as he wrote: 'I think it may safely be said that none but the highly religious and enthusiastic section have much faith in the establishment within a near future of a Jewish state in Palestine.' His report continued:

The more sober-minded turn from the visionary fulfilment of prophecies to the actual facts of the vast immigration of Jews now being conducted with apparent success into the Argentine Republic, Canada and the United States. It has been asserted to me that New York has a Jewish population approaching a million.

Palestine, with its scanty soil, flinty rocks and inadequate water supply can hardly support under existing circumstances much more than double its present population; and there is but slight foundation for the apprehensions of a prominent Turkish official here who, when I mentioned to him recently that there were said to be nearly twelve million Jews in the world, exclaimed 'Good Lord! they are not all coming to Palestine, are they?'

Among the Jews who were in Jerusalem during 1907 was a thirty-year-old German lawyer, Arthur Ruppin. He had been sent to Palestine by the Zionist organizations to report on the situation of the Jews throughout the country, and, as a result of what he saw, he decided to accept, for two years, the newly established post of director of the Palestine Zionist Organization. 'Either I shall find a suitable field of work in Palestine,' he wrote in his diary on 31 December 1907, 'and then my life's task will be the creation of an autonomous Jewish community there, or I shall become convinced that this idea is impracticable and live my life out as a lawyer in Berlin. . . .'

In Christian Europe, anti-semitism continued to flourish in certain quarters, fomented by individual writers and journalists who devoted themselves to Jew hatred. Since 1888, in Vienna, the journalist Ernst Vergani had edited a newspaper, the *Deutsche Volksblatt*, which expressed the most virulent of anti-semitic accusations. Vergani gave special prominence to police court stories involving sexual charges against Jews. In particular, he tried to create the image of the promiscuous, evil-minded Jew, who sought to lure and abuse Christian girls.

Vergani also accused the Jews of controlling the Viennese Press, and of using this control to urge disarmament, thus weakening Austria-Hungary, and making it a prey for Marxists who – in the pay, he alleged, of Jewish millionaire bankers – would then take over the State.

The images which anti-semites like Vergani sought to create gained a certain credence among the ignorant and the malicious. It was also inevitable that the reiterated stories of Jewish cowardice, of the Jew as a peddler of pornography, and of the Jew as a corrupting influence in the Press and the universities, should provide a disturbing undercurrent for daily Jewish life, not only in Vienna, but in every city where such ideas could find an outlet.

As anti-semitism continued to smoulder in the civilized milieu of western Europe, the hopes for some form of Uganda scheme had still not died within the Jewish communities outside Palestine. Israel Zangwill, for example, now canvassed the possibility of forming a Jewish territory somewhere in Siberia, or in Manchuria. Nor was this debate confined to Jews alone. In Britain, the Under-Secretary of State for the Colonies, Winston Churchill, who had recently visited East Africa, was among those who were asked to give their opinion. Churchill was already familiar both with the plight of the Jews, and with their aspirations. Having been asked about the Uganda scheme, he replied, on 30 January 1908, in a letter to Alderman Moser of Bradford:

I am in full sympathy with the historical traditional aspirations of the Jews. The restoration to them of a centre of true racial and political integrity would be a tremendous event in the history of the world. Whether the wide effort of the Jewish race should be concentrated upon Palestine to the exclusion of all other temporary solutions, or whether in the meanwhile some other outlet of relief and place of unification should be provided for the bitter need of those who suffer from day to day, are questions on which I could scarcely presume to express any opinion.

But my visit to East Africa has made me acquainted with many difficulties which seem to lie in the path in that country, and this fact necessarily increases my sympathy with your efforts to reach what must be your ultimate goal.

Jerusalem must be the only ultimate goal. *When* it will be achieved it is vain to prophesy: but that it *will* some day be achieved is one of the few certainties of the future. And the establishment of a strong, free Jewish state astride of the bridge between Europe and Africa, flanking the land roads to the East, would not be only an immense advantage to the British Empire, but a notable step towards the harmonious disposition of the world among its peoples.

In February 1908 the eighteen year old Adolf Hitler arrived in Vienna from provincial Austria. For five years Hitler observed the Jews of the city with a growing hatred which he was later to describe in his book *Mein Kampf*. Influenced by Ernst Vergani's paper, the *Deutsche Volksblatt*, Hitler began to look closely at the Jews of Vienna, particularly those from eastern Europe. 'The odour of those people in caftans often used to make me feel ill,' he recalled, and he went on to ask: 'Was there any shady undertaking, any form of foulness, especially in cultural life, in which at least one Jew did not participate?' Hitler's hatred soon turned towards the 175,000 Jews of Vienna, even though they formed less than 9 per cent of the city's total population. As he wrote in his book:

Wherever I went, I now saw Jews, and the more I saw, the more clearly did I perceive how apart they were from the rest of humanity. In particular, the inner city and the districts north of the Danube canal were swarming with a population which even outwardly had no resemblance to the Germans.

It was not only the Jews against whom Hitler turned while he was in Vienna. As he wrote in *Mein Kampf*:

The racial conglomeration which ruled the imperial capital was repugnant to me. Equally repugnant was the whole national hotch-potch of Czechs, Hungarians, Ruthenians, Serbs, Croats etc – and in the midst of it all that eternal fission-fungus of humanity, Jews and again Jews.

Thus Hitler absorbed, reflected and intensified that same Viennese anti-semitism which scarcely ten years earlier had helped to drive Herzl forward into Zionism. Indeed, the anti-semitic speeches of the Mayor, Karl Lueger, spanned that whole decade, and were read by both men. But Hitler went further even than Lueger, for he refused to accept Lueger's argument that, if a Jew converted to Christianity, he was no longer a Jew but became acceptable. Hitler believed, as Ernst Vergani insisted week after week in the *Deutsche Volksblatt*, that a Jew was always a Jew, whether he was a converted Jew, an assimilated Jew, a Zionist or a religious Jew. Indeed, Hitler was angered by what he regarded as the 'fictitious conflict' between the Liberal Jews of Vienna, and their Zionist critics, believing, as he wrote, that 'there was no real rift in their internal solidarity'.

Hitler was convinced that there existed an inner Jewish solidarity, which sought to hide itself behind a mask of divided counsels; he considered this as proof of what he called 'the moral mildew of the chosen race', whose true aim was not to have a State of their own, but to dominate the whole world. He therefore wrote with contempt in *Mein Kampf* of those Jews who, as he put it, 'disparaged their own nation, mocked at its greatness, reviled its history and dragged the names of its most illustrious men in the gutter'.

While Hitler was nurturing his anti-semitic fantasies in Vienna, the Jews themselves were continuing to seek, in Palestine, a new life and new opportunities denied them in so many other lands. Since 1891, under the initial inspiration of Zerah Barnett, the Jews of Jaffa had begun to buy land outside the town in order

70

to establish small but entirely Jewish quarters; on 11 April 1909, following an appeal by Arthur Ruppin to the Jewish National Fund headquarters in Cologne, the first housing plots were allocated for the first entirely Jewish town, Tel Aviv, located on the sand dunes north of Jaffa. That same autumn, seven Jewish farmers established the first all-Jewish co-operative farm in Palestine, at Deganya, on the southern shore of the Sea of Galilee. On 10 December 1909, in a letter to the Zionist organization in Berlin, Ruppin, whose brainchild the co-operative had been, explained that, as the farmers had no money, they would be granted credit to develop the farm, but, in return, would be paid 'a high percentage of the profits', and could choose their own manager.

Within a few months of the founding of the co-operative farm at Deganya, another Jewish farmer, the Rumanian-born Aaron Aaronsohn, set up a small agricultural experimental station at Athlit, just south of Haifa. Like Ruppin, Aaronsohn was determined to see the economy of Palestine restored and developed, and had enlisted the help of several leading American Jews in this task. But his decision to use Arab labour upset many Zionists, who did not wish to become dependent upon Arab labour, but to develop, as Ruppin was doing, a Jewish agricultural and labouring class.

Not only Palestinian agriculture, but also industry, seemed to offer the prospect of Jewish involvement. During 1910 Novomeysky, the Russian Jewish mining engineer, visited Palestine to examine the country's industrial potential. He had already, while in Berlin four years before, become convinced that the Dead Sea could provide a source of valuable chemicals for industrial use, and his enquiries on the spot confirmed his views. Returning to Berlin, he helped to establish a Palestine Industrial Syndicate, and encouraged the Zionists in their hope of creating not merely farms and towns, but the industrial capacity for true self-help and economic independence.

For many of those Jews who looked to Palestine as the scene of a future autonomous Jewish homeland, an essential feature of their work was the use of Hebrew as a common language for all Jews; at that time, in the different Jewish communities, Russian, Rumanian, Arabic, French, German, Yiddish, Spanish and many other languages were the language of daily life, with Hebrew serving only as the language of prayer. In 1910 the cause of the Hebrew language as the vehicle of contemporary Jewish life and culture was further advanced by the publication in Palestine of the first volume of Ben Yehuda's Hebrew dictionary.

In Russia it was not only the Zionists who had won recruits as a result of the new pogroms. Like the Zionists, the Bundists had also gained strength, and had organized a number of large and effective self-defence groups in the towns where Jews were most under attack. But the wider political movement of which they were a part was not united, and, with the split of the Russian Social Democratic Labour Party into two factions, Bolshevik and Menshevik, the Bundists had supported the Mensheviks. At the same time, many individual Jews had joined Lenin's Bolshevik banner, and took an increasingly important part in Bolshevik ideology and organization.

In Russia, the pogroms of 1906 had given way to an upsurge of anti-semitic literature and abuse. In the Duma, anti-semites denounced the Jews, and all things Jewish. In 1908 the anti-semitic deputies denounced the Jewish soldiers in the Tsar's army as an element 'which corrupts the army in time of peace and is extremely unreliable in time of war'. In 1910 a bill aimed at abolishing the Pale of Settlement was defeated, and, in an immediate reaction, several thousand Jews who had managed to find work and houses outside the Pale were forced back to it. In the spring of 1910 more than a thousand families were expelled from the city of Kiev, which, although within the area of the Pale, was not a part of it. Children, invalids, and old people were all ruthlessly evicted. The numerical restrictions on Jewish school and university attendance were rigidly enforced. Some educational institutions, in an excess of zeal beyond even the legal requirements, went so far as to exclude Jewish students altogether. In March 1911 a further law took away the right of Jews, who had been forced to leave secondary schools on account of the restrictions, to receive a testimonial of education from their former school.

Jewish cultural institutions in Russia were likewise under constant hostile pressure from the Tsarist authorities, and in 1911 the Jewish Literary Society, a sponsor of public lectures and libraries, and maintaining 120 branches throughout the Pale, was forced to close. But the most severe blow of all came on 21 July 1911, when the police arrested a thirty-seven-year-old Russian Jew, Mendel Beilis, and accused him of the ritual murder of a twelve-year-old Christian boy, Andrei Yushinsky.

For more than two years, Beilis was kept in prison without trial. In his memoirs he wrote of the torments of those two years, poised, as he put it, between hope and despair:

The days were dragging along. When was my trial to take place? There were days when I felt that I was perilously near to insanity. On such occasions I would look in amazement at my guard, at myself, and would think, is all this reality?

Am I the man lying here on the cold and filthy floor, among these creeping reptiles – is this the same Mendel Beilis who used to be a man of consequence, dressed like other humans and living a peaceful like with his wife and children? I experienced moral tortures of a kind hardly possible to bear or even to describe. . . .

In the prison itself the morality from typhoid fever was about six or seven men per day. This was in no way surprising in view of the extraordinary filth, the disgusting food, the unheated rooms (not infrequently during the frosts I used to find my hand frozen to the ice on the wall).

The Beilis trial opened in Kiev on 25 September 1913. For two years the blood-libel charge had given all Russian anti-semites a renewed opportunity to accuse the Jews of barbaric practices, and to publicize still further the *Protocols of the Elders of Zion*, with its wild imputation of a Jewish world conspiracy aimed at undermining and destroying Christian society. During the trial the Bund organized a protest strike which was observed by 20,000 Jewish workers. The trial also led to widespread protests throughout western Europe and the United States. Beilis himself was ably defended, and the insistence by a Catholic priest at the trial that ritual murder was a part of Jewish religion was successfully challenged in court by the Rabbi of Moscow.

On 28 October 1913 Beilis was declared not guilty. Russian Jewry was over-joyed. As for Beilis himself, he decided to leave Russia altogether, and on 16 February 1914 he reached Palestine. On his arrival, he and his five children were met by Jewish schoolchildren carrying flags and flowers. 'The Land of Israel', he later recalled in his memoirs, 'had an invigorating effect upon me; it gave me new life and hope. Nature itself, the life of the people, inspired me with vigor and the desire to live.' In Jerusalem, the Arabs allowed him to visit the Al Aksa mosque, on the grounds that he was one of the 'great Jewish heroes'. He settled in Tel Aviv where, he wrote, 'for the first time, I began to appreciate what the true Jewish life is. I saw for the first time a race of proud, uncringing Jews, who lived openly and unafraid.'

Although Beilis had been acquitted of the blood-libel, the charge against him, and through him against the Jews, had gained a wide currency. Nor did it cease to circulate after his release. 'There are many people here who believe in it,' Chaim Weizmann wrote from Manchester to a friend on 24 October 1913, 'because it is plausible to believe things of a people who is generally considered as different and as inferior. The anti-semitic touch and note is felt everywhere.' A British writer, Stephen Graham, in an article published in the *English Review* sixteen months after Beilis had been judged innocent, declared:

A Christian boy had been found done to death in a horrible fashion: his veins cut in a special way with knives, forty wounds in his body – the position of the wounds having evidently some sort of mystic significance. Beilis was innocent – though he was certainly involved in the murder. Someone was guilty, a madman or a Jew; and, indeed, the probability is that a Jew did actually commit the crime. Whether it was for ritual purposes or not is another matter. Most people would agree that it was a great mistake on the part of the Russian Government to fight the Jews on the count of the murder of a Christian child.

If among illiterate and savage Jews that dwell in the remoter parts of the Pale there should exist dark sects in whose rites child-sacrifice, Moloch worship, and the like, are practised, – it is merely a curiosity among religions of contemporary Europe. But the great quarrel of Russians with Jews is not on that ground. They would willingly spare an accidental Christian child now and then. No; it is with the Jewish business spirit, and in his enmity towards Christianity and the 'unprofitable' Christian life that the Russian has his quarrel. . . .

One of the most interesting phenomena of the time has been the persecution of the brilliant anti-Semitic pamphleteer Rozanof. . . .

During the trial Rozanof came forward and contributed to the *Novoe Vremya* and other papers a most substantial account of the ritual practices of the Jews. Credit must be given him for extraordinary research. He had gone into the depths of black magic as propounded in almost inaccessible volumes on occultism, and had come back with a circumstantial case against secret sects of the Jews. He explained the heiroglyphics of the wounds of Yushinsky. . . .

Graham's article typified the crude anti-Jewish ideas of some educated men, and showed how, even in England, as Herzl had feared, anti-semitism could find its champions. At the same time, Zionism was growing in England. On 26 February 1913, during the period between Beilis's arrest and his trial, L. J. Greenberg, who had become a director of the recently formed Anglo-Palestine Company, wrote to the Foreign Office:

Our object is not financial gain. We seek the concessions we are urging in Palestine for a triple object.

We desire to find for Jews who are forced to migrate from countries in which they are badly treated a home in which they will be welcomed as a much needed labour-force, where they can be assured of human rights during their lives, and can see a prospect of good and useful citizenship for their children.

In the next place, we are anxious to form in Palestine a Jewish nucleus, so as to ensure for the future the maintenance of Jewish ideals and Jewish traditions.

In the last place, we are anxious to see the land with which our people have been historically associated raised from its position of degradation and desolation to the worthy place it should and can occupy.

Greenberg's aspirations were echoed by those Jews who had already taken up residence in Palestine, and who were seeking to put them into practice. 'We want to create in Palestine a Jewish community with its own culture,' Arthur Ruppin wrote in his diary on 1 January 1914. And he added: 'To do this, the Jewish population will have to be in the majority and its economic circumstances will have to be sound. . . . We will therefore have to acquire the greater part of land land in Palestine and direct our immigrants into agriculture.'

Ruppin knew the difficulties, and even dangers, of this task. For in Palestine itself, Arab hostility to the Jews had already on several occasions shown itself in violence. On 25 November 1913 Ruppin had received a telegram from the Galilee: 'Moshe Barsky, Deganiah, murdered Saturday. Yesterday worker Joseph Salzmann, Kinneret, murdered.' Barsky, a boy of eighteen, had come to Deganiah from Russia. On learning of his death, Barsky's father, who was still in Russia, urged his younger son to go out to Palestine in Moshe's place, and he did so. News of this soon spread, encouraging others to go.

All the reports from Palestine during 1914 showed the growing attraction of

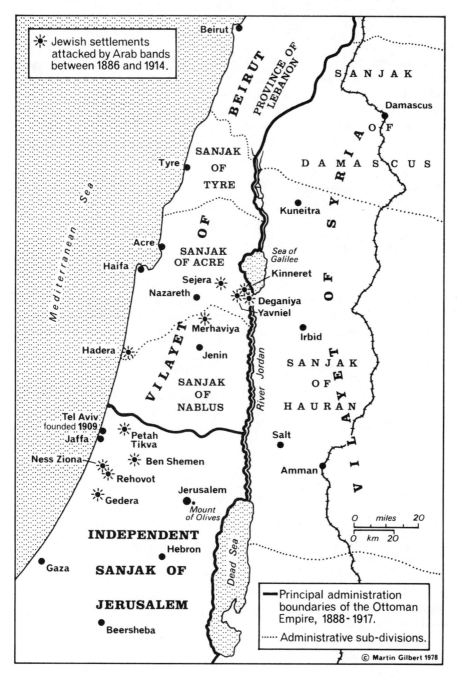

Jewish settlements attacked by Arab bands between 1886 and 1914.

Principal administration boundaries of the Ottoman Empire, 1888- 1917.

.... Administrative sub-divisions.

© Martin Gilbert 1978

Palestine for the Jews, despite the difficulties in clearing swamps and marsh and stony fields. Nor could the attacks of small Arab bands act as a deterrent. For the appeal of Palestine was not a material one.

On 15 March 1914 the British Consul in Jerusalem, P. J. C. McGregor, reported to his Ambassador in Constantinople, that the 'nationalist spirit' was showing itself 'with increased vigour' in the Zionist schools. At the same time, restrictions on Jewish immigration and land purchase had disappeared, McGregor reported, owing to the 'complacent attitude' of the Turkish authorities. This was indeed so; only six days before McGregor's report, the Zionists had achieved a success of major importance to their aspirations, particularly in the realm of education, for on 9 March, Arthur Ruppin was able to write in his diary: 'Today I succeeded in buying from Sir John Gray Hill his large and magnificently situated property on Mount Scopus, thus acquiring the first piece of ground for the Jewish university in Jerusalem.'

With this purchase, the Jewish desire for an autonomous, self-governing university, freed from the restrictions which were imposed on Jews in so many lands, came a step closer to its realization. Much of the money needed to buy the land from its British owner had been sent by tens of thousands of poor Russian Jews to the Odessa headquarters of the Lovers of Zion.

The contrast between the slow but hopeful work in Palestine, and Jewish disabilities elsewhere, remained a stark one. In Rumania, further anti-semitic outbursts in 1914 sent a shudder of fear through the Rumanian Jewish community, and provoked international concern. On 15 May 1914, a former British Prime Minister, A. J. Balfour – to whom Chaim Weizmann had already explained the basic tenets of Zionism – issued a public statement urging the Rumanian Government to play its part in the civilization of eastern Europe. Balfour's statement urged the Rumanians to grant the Jews 'civil rights', and noted that the Rumanian Jews 'may pay taxes to a Government which does not count him as a citizen: he must fight for a Nation to which he is not permitted to belong, by law he is a stranger in the land of his birth, and while he bears all the burdens of citizenship, he may not enjoy its commonest privileges.'

In this perceptive statement, a non-Jew showed clearly the reasons why, by 1914, the Zionist Jews had become convinced that the Jewish future lay in Jewish self-government, and why, only eighteen years after Herzl had published his *Jewish State*, the vision of Palestine had become, for many Jews, a positive and necessary objective worthy of the most strenuous and devoted efforts.

PART TWO

From National Home to Sovereign State

A Documentary Study

8

Zionism and the
First Two Years of War
1914-1916

WITH the outbreak of war in Europe in August 1914, the five million Jews of Tsarist Russia found themselves 'allied' to the more liberal governments of Britain and France. That such an alliance might help the Zionist cause was envisaged by Chaim Weizmann when he wrote to the Russian-born Zionist Shmarya Levin on September 8 that he was 'preoccupied' with the question of 'the unification of Jewry', or of such part of it as might present definite demands 'at a future peace conference'. These demands, Weizmann explained, would involve 'both the Palestine question and the question of the legal status of Russian Jewry'. But, he added, the news from the east was not encouraging: 'In Russia – expulsions, restrictions, drafting by lot; in Poland – boycott; all as in the past.'

During September 1914 the German armies moved forward into Russian Poland, while the Russian army had crossed the borders of Austrian Galicia. In both areas, the Jews formed almost a majority of the local population. On September 14 Weizmann wrote again, to Ahad Ha'am: 'When one remembers that between these terrible millstones our nation, too, is being ground to dust, and that our hopes, "successes", everything, everything has perhaps collapsed, my blood runs cold, and my heart sinks.'

Yet Weizmann still felt, as he told Ahad Ha'am, that something might now be done, 'in favour of the Russian Jews, and possibly of Palestine too', while the fate of all European nations, and even Turkey, was in the balance. A few days later, Weizmann met Vladimir Jabotinsky, who had just returned from Belgium where he was acting as a war correspondent for a Russian newspaper, and who told Weizmann 'that all our hopes of improving the lot of Russian Jewry are *absolutely in vain*'.

It was another Russian-born Jew, the electrical engineer Pinhas Rutenberg, who, early in September 1914, believing that Britain would be victorious, was convinced that, if a Jewish force could be raised to fight with the allied armies, there would be a better chance of the Jews being given a voice at the post-war Peace Conference, and might lead to the restoration of a Jewish State in Palestine. Rutenberg was in London on September 28, where he saw both Weizmann and

Ahad Ha'am. The same idea was also mooted, only a few weeks later, by Vladimir Jabotinsky.

Pondering the effect which the war might have on Zionist aspirations, Weizmann wrote to Shmarya Levin on October 18 that, if the Germans were victorious 'all Jewish hopes – including the Zionist – must fall'. If the Jews could count on any help, he believed, 'it is only from England and America'. In the event of Turkey entering the war, and being defeated, he hoped 'that in that case Palestine will come under English influence, and England will understand the Zionists better than anyone else'. Weizmann's letter continued:

Unfortunately, the world now belongs to the guns. But as soon as the situation clarifies, we could with a clear conscience point out to both France and England the abnormal and cruel position of the Jews who have soldiers in all armies, who fight everywhere and are recognized nowhere.

We can draw their attention to the positive achievements and potentialities of the Jews and to our desire and ability to create from all the suffering, dispersed Jews a force which could serve progress and civilisation. We could show the interest of all those nations now fighting for small nations in securing for the Jewish nation also the right to exist. We shall be understood now in England, and in France, and in America. Only a few rich and assimilated Jews, both here and in other countries, will not want to understand us.

The force of our moral claim must be self-evident, and the political conditions for the realization of our ideal will be favourable. It is necessary to prepare for such a time, and preparations can be successfully begun only when the roar of the guns has somewhat quietened down. . . .

Wherever the Jews lived, Weizmann told Levin, it was 'everywhere as citizens of a second class'. In Palestine it would be different, and he went on to explain:

We – given more or less good conditions – could easily move a million Jews into P. within the next 50-60 years and England would have a very effective and strong barrier, we would have a country and would relieve *some* pressure in Russia, relieve some in the States and here and before everything else we would cease to be *morally the homeless*, however small our home may be.

Weizmann hoped for a victory, not only over the Germans, but over the German anti-Zionist Jews who had long been the object of his scorn. He remembered, also, the much-repeated phrase of the German historian, von Treitschke, often on the tongue of anti-semites, *Die Juden sind unser Unglück* – 'the Jews are our misfortune'. The war, he told Levin, was 'the struggle of the pagan Siegfried against the spirit of the Bible, and the Bible will win'. As for the Jews of Russia, he wrote:

Those 350,000 Jews at present fighting in the ranks of the Russian army, a few months after the trial of Beilis, present the best and the most vivid example of the eternal Jewish fairness and justice – of the eternal spirit of the Bible – indestructible and fearing neither 19-inch guns nor Treitschke's philosophical pronouncements.

On the following day, October 19, Weizmann wrote to Zangwill, setting out his hopes for the future. 'Now, when the general reckoning comes,' he wrote, 'is a time to put forward our claim for the establishment of an organized autonomous Jewish community in Palestine'. His letter continued:

Nobody doubts our intellectual achievements, nobody can doubt now, that we are capable of great physical efforts, that would all the mental, moral and physical forces of Jewry be concentrated on one aim – the building up of a Jewish community – this community would certainly not lag behind and stand comparison with any modern highly civilized state.

There are only a few Jews who may doubt it, the bulk of the Jewish people and the non-Jewish world has no such doubts. That being established we are a force, a progressive constructive potential force going to waste, because split, atomized and disorganized, and therefore lost to the coming better world.

As the war zones of eastern Europe were extended across Poland, Galicia and the Bukovina, the Jews were caught up in a ferocious battle. But, unlike the other civilians for whom the war also meant foreign armies, looting and burning, the Jews suffered from the added cruel burden that they were singled out by the local population as the scapegoat. At the beginning of October, the Jews in Britain had received a harrowing account of Jewish suffering from the war zone itself. On October 22 Weizmann wrote to Ahad Ha'am:

In Poland there is a total pogrom carried out by both Poles and Russians. There are pogroms in Vilna, Grodno, Byelostok. All the soldiers are being assured that were it not for the Yids – traitors – the Prussian army would have been utterly routed. What's going to happen? One is so terrified and horror-stricken by all this that one cannot find rest anywhere.

On the morning of 29 October 1914 two Turkish warships, commanded by a German Admiral, bombarded the Russian Black Sea ports of Odessa, Nikolaiev and Sebastopol. Three days later, on 31 October 1914, all British warships in the eastern Mediterranean were instructed by a signal from the Admiralty in London: 'Commence hostilities at once against Turkey.' By this telegram Britain, already at war for nearly three months with both Germany and Austria-Hungary, drew upon herself a third combatant, and was soon committed to the military defeat, and possible territorial fragmentation, of the Ottoman Empire.

The coming of war between the Allies and Turkey was, for the Zionists, a cause of immediate alarm. Suddenly it seemed as if the Zionist experiment itself might become caught up in the ebb and flow of war in the Near East. Weizmann, despite his earlier hopes as far as Russian Jewry and the war were concerned, wrote pessimistically to Ahad Ha'am on October 30: 'And so it has happened.

Turkey has also gone to war and our poor beloved Palestine and all that has been created there by years of strenuous work is now in danger.' He was worried, also, for personal reasons, as one of his brothers and his three sisters, were all in Palestine. On November 2 he wrote to a friend in the Hague: 'The recent developments in Turkey fill me with anxiety. Our colonies, our institutions – everything may be swept away now.'

Two particular dangers threatened the Jews of Palestine now that Turkey was at war with both Russia and Britain: first, the fact that most of the settlers were still legally Russian subjects, and second, the direct British links with several Zionist companies, such as the Anglo-Palestine Company, which was incorporated in England. Writing in his diary on 25 December 1914, Arthur Ruppin described the worsening situation of Palestinian Jewry:

On Thursday, 17 December, 500 Russian Jews were suddenly rounded up by the *kaimakam* in Jaffa and deported to Egypt by sea. In vain I lodged a complaint with the *kaimakam* about this measure: I had no success whatever in getting it cancelled, and at the harbour that evening I had to watch whole families with their hurriedly collected belongings – old people, mothers with babies – being driven on to the boat in infinite disorder.

That one *kaimakam* is able to destroy the work of many years in a single day made me realize on what weak foundations all our efforts at settlement rest.

The question of what would be the future of Palestine, if Britain were to defeat the Turks, was the subject of a memorandum, dated 22 January 1915, by a Liberal Cabinet Minister, Herbert Samuel, himself a Jew, who considered the possibility of a predominantly Jewish role in Palestine's future government. Samuel's initial comments were cautionary ones, and bore directly on the question of the Arab presence, and Arab attitudes. In his memorandum, Samuel wrote:

If the attempt were made to place the 400,000 or 500,000 Mohammedans of Arab race under a Government which rested upon the support of 90,000 or 100,000 Jewish inhabitants, there can be no assurance that such a Government, even if established by the authority of the Powers, would be able to command obedience.

The dream of a Jewish State, prosperous, progressive, and the home of a brilliant civilization, might vanish in a series of squalid conflicts with the Arab population. And even if a State so constituted did succeed in avoiding or repressing internal disorder, it is doubtful whether it would be strong enough to protect itself from external aggression from the turbulent elements around it.

Samuel added sombrely: 'To attempt to realise the aspiration of a Jewish State a century too soon might throw back its actual realisation for many centuries more.'

By the end of February 1915 there was much excitement in Whitehall at the prospect of the imminent defeat of the Turks at the Dardanelles, where a massive

British naval attack was planned for March 18. Several Cabinet Ministers saw what they imagined would be the British conquest of Turkey as an opportunity for the partition of the Ottoman Empire. Herbert Samuel now wrote a second, less pessimistic memorandum, in which he pressed for some form of British protectorate over Palestine, in the interest of future Jewish settlement. Other Ministers had different views, as Asquith wrote to a friend on March 13, five days before the attack at the Dardanelles was to begin:

H. Samuel has written an almost dithyrambic memorandum urging that in the carving up of the Turks' Asiatic dominions, we should take Palestine, into which the scattered Jews cd in time swarm back from all the quarters of the globe, and in due course obtain Home Rule. (What an attractive community!)

Curiously enough, the only other partisan of this proposal is Lloyd George, who, I need not say, does not care a damn for the Jews or their past or their future, but who thinks it would be an outrage to let the Christian Holy Places – Bethlehem, Mount of Olives, Jerusalem &c – pass into the possession or under the protectorate of 'Agnostic Atheistic France'! Isn't it singular that the same conclusions shd be capable of being come to by such different roads?

Kitchener, who 'surveyed' Palestine when he was a young Engineer, has a very poor opinion of the place, wh even Samuel admits to be not larger than Wales, much of it barren mountains, & part of it waterless &, what is more to the point, without a single decent harbour. So he (K) is all for Alexandretta, and leaving the Jews & the Holy Places to look after themselves.

The future of Palestine had now become an object of intense British interest. On March 16, only two days before the British naval attack on the Dardanelles, General Sir Edmund Barrow, the Military Secretary at the India Office, who had fought in the Egyptian campaign of 1882, proposed officially that 'in the eventuality of an early peace' with Turkey, Palestine should be 'neutralized', and then administered as an 'autonomous province' of the Turkish Empire, 'by an International Commission or Corporation under the protection of the allied Powers'. A similar arrangement already existed, he pointed out, for Shanghai, 'though of course on a much smaller scale'. Barrow's memorandum continued:

The abolition of direct Turkish rule in Palestine is also a political consummation which will appeal to many, both Christian and Jew, but which would inevitably create dissension among the Powers unless they were all equally interested in the new dispensation. Any attempt to acquire a special privileged position by one would be resented by the rest of the Powers and would speedily lead to that Armageddon in the Valley of Esdraelon which has terrified the imagination of the world for ages past.

Within the British Cabinet, one Jewish Minister, Edwin Montagu, set himself up as a fierce opponent of Zionist aspirations. He, too, wrote a memorandum on March 16, but its tone was of the utmost scorn towards any Jewish national entity; it would, he wrote, be 'a disastrous policy' to attempt to set up 'under British Protectorate a Jewish State'.

There was, Montagu argued, 'no Jewish race now as a homogeneous whole,' and he added:

It is quite obvious that the Jews in Great Britain are as remote from the Jews in Morocco or the black Jews in Cochin as the Christian Englishman is from the Moor or the Hindoo. The President of the Local Government Board [Herbert Samuel] visiting Morocco could not, I am sure, say for certain by appearance, whether an individual was a Moor or a Jew. How would the Jews occupy themselves? Agriculture is never attractive to ambitious people and the Jews in the main have long emerged into quicker less pastoral pursuits. I cannot see any Jews I know tending olive trees or herding sheep. Literature! Are there any great or even remarkable Jewish literary men of today? It is hardly worth transplanting one third of the Jewish peoples of the world for the sake of Zangwill!

Montagu was also scathing about the Hebrew language, writing:

The Jewish community, which it is hoped to restore to Palestine, would have no common tongue. Hebrew to the vast majority of Jews is a language in which to pray but not a language in which to speak or write. Those who are most familiar with it are the least well educated and the least likely to found a state. Few people who advocate a Jewish nation in Palestine could conduct two minutes conversation in Hebrew.

Montagu's memorandum ended with a direct attack on all Zionist Jews, when he wrote:

If only our peoples would cease to ask for special favours and cease to cry out together at the special disadvantages which result from asking special favours, if only they would take their place as non-conformists, Zionism would obviously die and Jews might find their way to esteem.

The Prime Minister, H. H. Asquith, had remained somewhat sceptical towards the idea of a Jewish home in Palestine, and did not need Montagu's arguments to influence him. In a letter to a friend on 19 March 1915 Asquith went so far as to describe the Jews as 'a scattered & unattractive tribe'. But the excitement created by the thought of a possible defeat of Turkey had survived even the initial setback at the Dardanelles on 18 March, and nine days later, on 27 March, when it had become clear that the Royal Navy would not be able to reach Constantinople, the Colonial Secretary, Lewis Harcourt, in a Cabinet memorandum entitled, tersely, 'The Spoils', still looked at the Ottoman Empire as a fertile field for territorial change, writing that 'it would be unfortunate if France became the guardian of the Christian Holy Places in Palestine'. Harcourt suggested that the Holy Places should be either 'in British hands', or even, if that was impossible, 'under the protection of the United States'.

Between the naval setback at the Dardanelles in March 1915 and the triumphant entry of British troops into Jerusalem in November 1917, many different schemes and proposals were put forward concerning the future of Palestine, most of them within the context of the changing fortunes of the war, and according to the shifting state of inter-allied relations. While Russia remained an active ally, Tsarist interests were also taken into consideration; so much so that on 17 April 1915 a Conservative Member of Parliament, Sir Mark Sykes, explained to a secret meeting at the Foreign Office, called to discuss the future of the Ottoman Empire, one possible plan for 'the establishment of a special Russian administration in the region of Jerusalem, Bethlehem and Jaffa'. Another possibility, Sykes told the meeting, was that 'Palestine would be erected into an Egyptian province' under British administration.

The British naval setback at the Dardanelles in March 1915 had barred any rapid conquest of Constantinople, and the severe difficulties encountered by the ensuing military landings on 25 April 1915 postponed still further the day on which a defeated Turkey would lie prostrate before the Allied armies. For their part, the Zionists were determined to show that they too could play their part in the war against Turkey, and had pressed for some specifically Jewish military force since the idea was first put forward by Pinhas Rutenberg and Vladimir Jabotinsky in September 1914.

Many Palestinian Jews had been forced to flee to Egypt on the outbreak of war, and were eager to fight against the Turks. Jabotinsky, who had gone to Egypt, urged the establishment there of a Jewish unit, and on 19 March 1915, the day after the first naval bombardment at the Dardanelles, a British officer, Lieutenant-Colonel J. H. Patterson, had been appointed to command an entirely new military force, the Zion Mule Corps. On March 23 the first group of volunteers had paraded in Alexandria, and were sworn in. Five British, and eight Jewish officers commanded more than 500 men; the senior Jewish officer was Captain Joseph Trumpeldor, who in 1904 had fought in the Russian army at the siege of Port Arthur, where he had lost his left arm, been taken prisoner by the Japanese and received a high Tsarist order for gallantry and zeal. Trumpeldor had settled in Palestine in 1912, inspired by the thought that the Jewish people could be liberated from national oppression through an independent existence in Palestine. He had worked for a time at the Deganiya collective farm, and had been active in the defence of Jewish settlements against Arab attack.

On 17 April 1915 the Zion Mule Corps had sailed from Egypt for Gallipoli; on April 25 they took part in the military landing at Cape Helles and by the end of July more than half of them had been killed or wounded. Trumpeldor himself was shot through the shoulder, but had refused to leave the battlefield for hospital. A year later, Colonel Patterson wrote, in his book *With the Zionists in Gallipoli*: 'Many of the Zionists whom I had thought somewhat lacking in courage showed themselves fearless to a degree when under heavy fire, while

85

Captain Trumpeldor actually revelled in it, and the hotter it became the more he liked it, and would remark: "Ah, it is now *plus gai!*" '

While 500 Jewish soldiers fought in the trenches of Gallipoli, the Arabs were likewise becoming involved with the British. On 14 July 1915 the Sherif of Mecca, Sherif Hussein, wrote to the British authorities in Cairo for British acknowledgement of 'the independence of the Arab countries'. An answer must be sent, the Sherif wrote, within thirty days, 'and if this period should elapse before they receive an answer, they reserve to themselves complete freedom of action'.

On 6 August 1915, before Hussein's ultimatum had reached Cairo, a second allied military landing at Gallipoli opened up, albeit briefly, a renewed hope for victory. Hussein's message reached Cairo on August 18, and instructions were at once sought from London. On August 30 Sir Reginald Wingate, the Governor-General of the Sudan, suggested in a telegram to Cairo, that 'I should personally recommend the insertion of a pious aspiration on the subject of the Sherif's ideal of an Arab union'. In other words, Wingate explained, 'something might be added to ensure his remaining definitely on our side until our success at the Dardanelles enables us to give more authoritative expression to our views'.

Replying to Sherif Hussein's ultimatum, Sir Henry McMahon declined to discuss the question of frontiers, as it would, he wrote in his letter of August 30, 'appear to be premature to consume our time in discussing such details in the heat of war', especially as the British had learnt 'with surprise and regret' that some Arabs, 'far from assisting us, are neglecting this, their supreme opportunity, and are lending their arms to the German and the Turk, to the new despoiler and the old oppressor'.

The hope of victory at the Dardanelles did not long survive the August landings. But within two months it was no longer victory, or even stalemate, that threatened, but defeat. On 11 October 1915, to the deepest alarm of Britain and France, the Bulgarians entered the war on the Turkish side, at once strengthening Turkey's power to resist at Gallipoli, and endangering still further the lives of the Allied troops seeking at least to hold on to their precarious positions on the peninsula. That same day Lloyd George told his Cabinet colleagues that 'it would be a great disaster to withdraw from Gallipoli, but at the same time, if we made another effort there which failed, it would double the number of men we might lose'.

It was the British intelligence officers in Cairo who then proposed a solution to the Gallipoli danger. It was a solution which was, over the next twelve months, to create an area of dispute of serious consequence to Zionist hopes. The solution concerned the possibility of some more specific territorial pledge by Britain in return for an Arab revolt behind the Turkish lines. For in the middle of October 1915 it suddenly seemed possible to reverse the worsening military situation at Gallipoli by making some definite territorial pledge to the Arabs within the Ottoman Empire. This opportunity arose, not from a spontaneous Arab offer of help, but from a threat of active Arab support for the Turks.

On 12 October 1915 a British intelligence officer in Cairo, Colonel Gilbert Clayton, informed his commanding officer, General Maxwell, that 'the Young Arab party' in the Ottoman Empire were about to be thrown 'definitely into the arms of the enemy', with the result that the whole 'machinery' of the Arabs would 'at once be employed against us throughout the Arab countries'. That same day General Maxwell telegraphed from Cairo to Lord Kitchener that urgent action was needed as the Young Arab Committee was already in direct negotiation, not only with the Turks, but also with the Germans, both of whom are 'spending money to win their support'. If the British were to reject the Arab overtures, or to delay their reply to Hussein, 'the Arab party will go over to the enemy and work with them'. On the other hand, Maxwell added, active Arab assistance 'in return for our support, would be of the greatest value in Arabia, Mesopotamia, Syria and Palestine'.

The Arab threats reported in Maxwell's telegram had an immediate effect, and on October 24 Sir Henry McMahon sent his second letter to Sherif Hussein. Britain now agreed 'to recognise and support the independence of the Arabs within the territories included in the limits and boundaries proposed by the Sherifs of Mecca'. But there were still two qualifications, for even this pledge depended not only upon active Arab military support in helping to ensure 'the expulsion of the Turks from the Arab countries', but also on certain territorial 'modifications' which McMahon listed. It was the exact nature of these modifications that Hussein subsequently declined to accept, and that McMahon himself defined only vaguely. According to McMahon's letter of October 24, those 'portions of Syria lying to the west of the districts of Damascus, Hama, Homs, and Aleppo cannot be said to be purely Arab, and should be excluded from the proposed limits and boundaries'.

Did this exclusion refer, *inter alia*, to Palestine? Seven years later, McMahon himself wrote to the Colonial Office: 'It was as fully my intention to exclude Palestine as it was to exclude the more northern coastal tracts of Syria.' And at the time, in the letters themselves, no mention whatsoever was made, by name, of 'Palestine', or 'Jerusalem', or the 'Sanjak of Jerusalem', within whose borders lay not only the Arab towns of Jaffa, Ramla, and Beersheba, but also Jerusalem itself, with its Jewish majority, and many of the Jewish villages, including Tel Aviv, Rishon le-Zion, Gederah and Petah Tikvah.

Despite McMahon's second letter to Hussein, no immediate Arab uprising of the sort envisaged by Clayton or Maxwell took place, and the Allied troops at Gallipoli continued to die without any pressure being applied to the Turks from behind their lines. There seemed no way, now, that the British position at Gallipoli could be maintained. On November 24 a British force which had landed at Basra and advanced towards Baghdad was itself defeated by the Turks

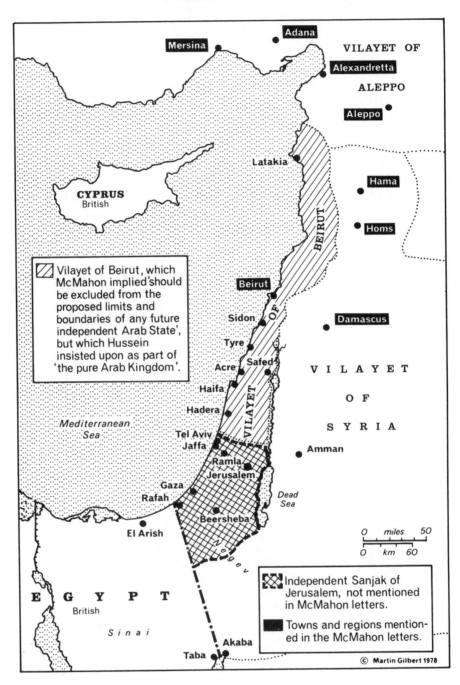

VILAYET OF

Adana

Mersina

Alexandretta

ALEPPO

Aleppo

Latakia

CYPRUS
British

Hama

Homs

BEIRUT

Vilayet of Beirut, which
McMahon implied 'should
be excluded from the
proposed limits and
boundaries of any future
independent Arab State',
but which Hussein
insisted upon as part of
'the pure Arab Kingdom'.

Beirut

Sidon

Tyre

Acre Safed

Haifa

Hadera

Mediterranean
Sea

Tel Aviv
Jaffa

Ramla
Jerusalem

Gaza

Rafah

Beersheba

El Arish

Damascus

V I L A Y E T

O F

S Y R I A

Amman

VILAYET OF

Dead
Sea

0   miles   50

0   km   60

E G Y P T
British

S i n a i

Negev

Akaba

Taba

Independent Sanjak of
Jerusalem, not mentioned
in McMahon letters.

Towns and regions mentioned in the McMahon letters.

© Martin Gilbert 1978

and forced to retreat, and on December 7 the British Cabinet decided to evacuate the Gallipoli peninsula. A week later, on December 14, McMahon wrote again to Hussein. This time the sense of urgency had waned. Taking note of Hussein's desire not to exclude 'the vilayets of Aleppo and Beyrout' from the area of Arab independence. McMahon added that 'as the interests of our ally France are involved, the question will require careful consideration'. McMahon also declared, in this, his third letter to the Sherif, that:

... in the meantime it is most essential that you spare no effort to attach all the Arab people to our united cause and urge them to afford no assistance to our enemies.

It is on the success of these efforts and on the more active measures which the Arabs may hereafter take in support of our cause, when the time for action comes, that the permanence and strength of our agreement must depend.

During 1916 the focus of British policy towards Palestine changed. Under the Sykes-Picot agreement of May 1916, the Vilayet of Beirut would fall within the proposed French sphere of influence, while Jerusalem and the area around it would become an international 'enclave', excluded from the area of Arab independence east of the river Jordan. This decision was made partly with reference to the Zionist hopes concerning Palestine, for, as the Sykes-Picot agreement noted, 'the members of the Jewish community, throughout the world, have a conscientious and sentimental interest in the future of the country'. Haifa, Acre, and the bay between them, however, were to be left open as a possible British outlet on the sea for the British sphere of influence in Mesopotamia, and for the terminus of a British controlled Baghdad-Haifa railroad.

The Sykes-Picot agreement was a close secret. But during April 1916 Sykes himself had communicated the Zionist aspects of it, through an intermediary, to Weizmann, Sokolow, and Rabbi Moses Gaster. On April 16 Gaster wrote in his diary: 'We are offered French-English condominium in Palest. Arab Prince to conciliate Arab sentiment, and as part of the Constitution, a Charter to Zionists for which England would stand guarantee and which would stand by us in every case of friction.' Gaster added: 'It practically comes as a complete realisation of our Zionist programme.'

Gaster's enthusiasm was premature, but the Zionist cause was soon to be powerfully argued on a more receptive stage. Meanwhile, in Palestine itself, the condition of the Jews had worsened considerably, and, in the hope of an eventual Allied victory, a group of Palestinian Jews had begun to work behind the Turkish lines, collecting military information which might be of help to the British in their eastward advance from Egypt. The group called itself NILI, this being the initial letters of the Hebrew biblical verse, from the book of Samuel, 'The Strength of Israel will not lie.' A prime mover in the NILI espionage work was Avshalom Feinberg, the son of a Jewish immigrant from the Crimea, but

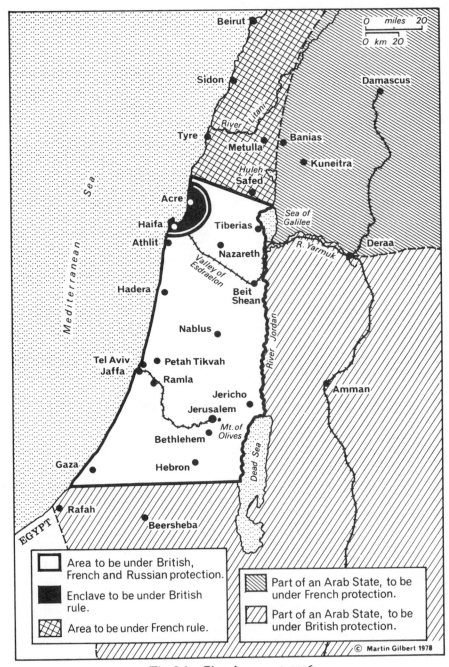

The Sykes-Picot Agreement, 1916

himself born in Palestine in the Jewish farm village of Gederah. Feinberg had worked at the agricultural experimental station established by Aaron Aaronsohn, whose whole family were drawn into the espionage ring. Aaron Aaronsohn himself set off in the summer of 1916 on a fictional 'Turkish official mission' to Germany, crossed the German border into neutral Denmark, made contact with British agents there, and on 24 October 1916 reached London, where he offered the British army important intelligence information about the location, strength and tactics of the Turkish forces. Meanwhile, on 5 June 1916, the Emir Hussein had launched the Arab revolt in the Hedjaz by declaring war on the Turks. On 10 June the Turks surrendered the Red Sea port of Jedda to Hussein's son Feisal, and a month later Mecca, the holiest city of Islam, had been captured by the Arab forces.

In September 1916, while Aaronsohn was on his way to London, Arthur Ruppin completed, in Jerusalem, his book, *Syria, an Economic Survey*, in which he examined the enormous economic potential of Palestine. For his pains, Ruppin was summoned to the Turkish Commander-in-Chief, Jemal Pasha, and ordered to leave within eight days. 'When I asked why I was being ordered to leave,' Ruppin recorded in his memoirs, 'he answered that he would not enter into a discussion with me. He was the representative of the Sultan and his will was law. I ought to know that I would *never* return to Palestine.' Yet Ruppin, in exile in Constantinople, still persevered with his plans and dreams, writing in his diary on 31 December 1916: 'I have drawn up a settlement programme for the next thirty years, regardless of whether future conditions will allow us to continue our work or not.' And his aim: 'I want to settle about one million Jews in Palestine within thirty years.'

9

The Evolution of
the Balfour Declaration
1917

THE anguish of the Jews when confronted by Christian or Muslim persecution; their own efforts to rebuild and revitalize Jewish life in Palestine;
and their realization that a British victory over the Turks could lead to a
British sponsored Jewish commonwealth in Palestine, produced, during 1917,
the conditions needed to advance the Zionist cause. For Jews all over the world,
the prospect of British troops entering Jerusalem brought with it the chance of
the first Jewish self-government since before Roman times.

On 24 October 1916 Aaron Aaronsohn reached London, and proceeded to give
the War Office invaluable material on the Turkish military situation. In particular,
he showed that one possible line of advance for the British forces was not through
Gaza, which was strongly defended, but through Beersheba; he was able to
point out to the War Office the location of those fresh-water wells without which
no such diversionary attack would be possible. While he was in London,
Aaronsohn also spoke of the future of Palestine to Sir Mark Sykes, who was
much impressed by all that Aaronsohn was able to tell him about the pre-war
achievements of the Jewish settlements. On 15 January 1917, largely as a result of
Aaronsohn's discussions, a note was prepared for the British Government by
Lord Drogheda to the effect that the Italian Government, with whom the
British were negotiating, must not only be made to recognize British railway
rights in the proposed Baghdad-Haifa railway, but must also 'generally respect
the civic and colonising rights of the Jews in Palestine'.

The Zionists were now aware of the extent to which their aspirations in Palestine
were becoming recognized as a legitimate object of British support. Nine days
after Lord Drogheda's note, Jabotinsky and Trumpeldor sent a joint memorandum to the new Prime Minister, David Lloyd George, urging the establishment of a Jewish Legion. Trumpeldor was already a veteran of the Allied forces,
and that same week Jabotinsky enlisted as a private in the Jewish unit which was
attached to the 20th Battalion of the London Regiment, then in training in
England. The first issue of a new weekly magazine, *Palestine*, appeared on January
26. Its editor was Harry Sacher, a young Zionist whom Weizmann had befriended,
and who shared Weizmann's determination, as *Palestine* declared in its first

issue, 'to reset the ancient glories of the Jewish nation in the freedom of a new British dominion in Palestine'.

Two days after the first issue of *Palestine* had appeared, Weizmann had his first meeting with Sir Mark Sykes, whom Lloyd George had appointed to the War Cabinet secretariat, as an Assistant Secretary with special responsibility for British policy towards Palestine. Weizmann sought to persuade Sykes that Britain alone, and not some international body, or an Anglo-French condominium, should determine the future of Palestine; on February 7 Sykes discussed the problem privately with the Zionist leaders. Among the Zionists themselves there were different views as to what was needed: Nahum Sokolow told Sykes that he wished to see 'a Jewish society' in Palestine; Moses Gaster wanted the Jews in Palestine to be recognized 'as a nation'; Harry Sacher favoured a 'Jewish State in Palestine under the British Crown'. All were agreed, however, that the Jewish future in Palestine must be guarded under British, not French, patronage.

Sykes listened sympathetically to the Zionists; Aaronsohn had already convinced him of the reality of Jewish enterprise in Palestine. He was aware, also, of the Arab presence, telling his listeners that in his view 'the Arabs could be managed, particularly if they received Jewish support in other matters'.

The importance of Sykes's attitude was at once understood by the Zionists. 'It's the first time in the history of our movement that we have come so close to the heart of the matter,' Weizmann wrote to Jabotinsky on the following day. There was a further advance on February 14, when Sykes wrote direct to Jabotinsky, who was still in training with the London Regiment, proposing that the idea of a Jewish Legion should be kept alive so that, if circumstances were to prove propitious, it could be proceeded with. On February 28 Sykes wrote to his French opposite number, Georges Picot: 'If the great force of Judaism feels that its aspirations are not only considered but in a fair way to realisation, then there is hope of an organised and developed Arabia and Middle East.'

On March 21 the War Cabinet discussed the coming British military advance into Palestine. Both Lloyd George and Balfour raised, sympathetically, the question of Zionist aims. When Balfour saw Weizmann on March 22, he spoke of the possibility of 'an Anglo-American Protectorate over Palestine', but, as Weizmann wrote to the editor of the *Manchester Guardian*, C. P. Scott, on the following day: 'Attractive as such a project may appear it is always fraught with the danger that there are two masters and we do not know yet how far the Americans would agree with the British on general principles of administration.'

On March 26 the British forces advanced towards the Turkish-held town of Gaza, the gateway to Palestine from the south. It was now widely known that one result of a British victory would be the furthering of Zionist policies. On March 30 the *Daily Chronicle* told its readers: 'The project for constituting a Zionist State under British Protection had much to commend it,' while *The Times*

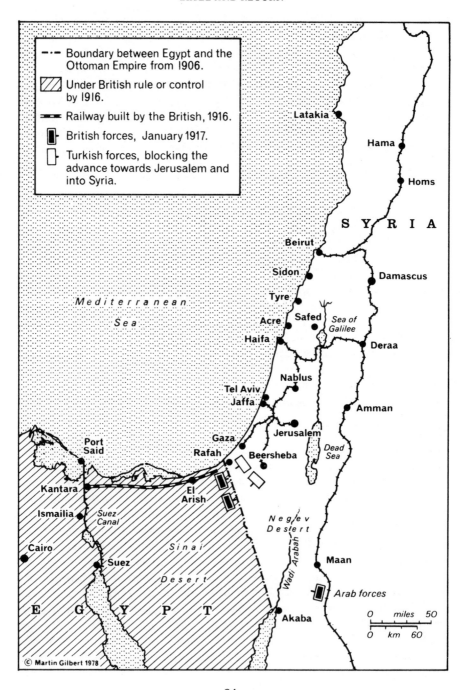

Boundary between Egypt and the Ottoman Empire from 1906.

Under British rule or control by 1916.

Railway built by the British, 1916.

British forces, January 1917.

Turkish forces, blocking the advance towards Jerusalem and into Syria.

Latakia

Hama

Homs

S Y R I A

Beirut

Sidon

Damascus

Tyre

Mediterranean
Sea

Acre   Safed   Sea of
Galilee

Haifa

Deraa

Nablus

Tel Aviv

Jaffa

Amman

Port
Said

Gaza

Jerusalem

Rafah

Dead
Sea

Beersheba

Kantara

El
Arish

Ismailia   Suez
Canal

Negev
Desert

Cairo

Sinai

Maan

Suez

Desert

Arab forces

E G Y P T

Akaba

0   miles   50

0   km   60

© Martin Gilbert 1978

94

commented: 'For the Jews and the Arabs, who form the majority, the Allies are carrying on a real war of liberation.'

On March 25 Jabotinsky had again urged the Foreign Office to support the immediate creation of a Jewish Legion, explaining that his Jewish unit was about to be sent to France, and that it 'begged to be sent to Palestine'. The recruiting campaign in the East End, Jabotinsky informed the Foreign Office, was going well, as a result of the hopes created by events in Russia. Within the Foreign Office, Sir George Clerk noted that: 'A solution of the East End Jew problem would be very welcome, especially to the Home Office.' But Clerk went on to warn that if Jabotinsky's idea of a Jewish Legion were accepted, the British Government 'may be laying stores of trouble, if they encourage a scheme which commits them to Zionism'.

Clerk's views were not those of the Prime Minister, for when Lloyd George saw Weizmann on April 3, Lloyd George 'was very emphatic on the point of British Palestine' – as Weizmann reported to Sokolow on the following day – and indeed, a few hours after seeing Weizmann, Lloyd George had sent for Sir Mark Sykes, who was about to proceed to Cairo, and instructed Sykes on 'the importance of not prejudicing the Zionist movement and the possibility of its development under British auspices'. The Jews, Lloyd George told Sykes, might render the British 'more assistance than the Arabs'. In reply, Sykes told Lloyd George that 'the Arabs probably realised that there was no prospect of their being allowed any control over Palestine'.

The British Press continued to support the new policy. According to the *Sunday Chronicle* of April 15, the Zionist movement would turn the British presence in Palestine into 'a source of pride and a pillar of strength', while the *New Europe* declared, four days later, that 'a British Palestine must be a Jewish Palestine'. During April the military situation worsened and, by mid-April, with the failure of the Battle of Gaza, the British conquest of Palestine seemed once more remote. This setback, however, did not deter the Zionist leaders from continuing their efforts, not only for private statements of support, but also for some official and public declaration that their aims were to be accepted as a part of the British war effort. Nor did it lessen the determination of the NILI group in Palestine to do their utmost to help the British in their military advance.

While the eastward march of the British army was still blocked by the Turks at Gaza, two members of the NILI group, Avshalom Feinberg and Yosef Lishansky, set off on foot across the Sinai desert, hoping to reach the British front line. They were spotted, however, by Bedouin, and their route barred. Lishansky managed to escape, but Feinberg was shot dead: fifty years later, in 1967, his remains were discovered near the coastal village of Rafah, lying under a palm tree which had grown from some dates he had been carrying with him on his journey.

Lishansky managed to reach the British lines, and conveyed his intelligences.

So too, in April 1917, did Aaron Aaronsohn's sister, Sarah. Having done so, both Lishansky and Sarah Aaronsohn insisted on returning to Palestine to continue their clandestine, and dangerous work, made more difficult for them on account of the hostility of many Palestinian Jews, who feared severe Turkish reprisals if the NILI group were caught. The Turkish butchery of hundreds of thousands of Armenians was a grim and recent precedent, striking fear into many Jewish families. So too were the public hangings in Jerusalem of several leading Arabs, including the Mufti of Gaza and his son. Against this background, the bravery of the NILI group was a remarkable example of heroism and tenacity.

One Englishman whom the work of NILI, and the character of Aaron Aaronsohn, had greatly influenced, was a former member of the Arab Bureau in Cairo, Captain William Ormsby Gore. On April 14 Ormsby Gore commented, in an official Foreign Office memorandum, that the Zionists wanted a British victory, not to have 'political control' of Palestine, but to further their cultural and ideological aims. 'All that Zionism seeks now', he wrote, 'is to give the Jewish people freedom to settle, acquire land and build up industries and schools.'

Throughout April, May and June, the Zionists pressed the British Government for a public declaration of support for 'a Jewish Palestine under British Protectorate', as Weizmann put it to Sokolow on April 27. The British Government were receptive for, as 1917 progressed, the course of the war seemed to be turning against the Allies. The Russian revolution on March 1917, in which the Tsar had been overthrown, failed to bring back the Russian fighting spirit. The United States, having entered the war in April, expected that it would take as much as a year before her troops were ready for action in Europe in any appreciable numbers. For Britain, it was becoming a matter of urgency to stimulate both Russian and American patriotism. On May 5, Lloyd George's private secretary, Philip Kerr, wrote to Ronald Graham, a senior Foreign Office official, urging the Foreign Office to support Jabotinsky's scheme. As Kerr explained:

> . . . the raising of a Jewish unit for use in Palestine, if coupled with assurances from the British Government of their sympathy with the desire of many Jews to settle in Palestine and build up a community within it, might produce a very beneficial effect in making the Jews in America and Russia much keener on helping to see the war through.

Kerr added a note of caution. 'I think', he told Graham, 'that the British Government can affirm their sympathy for Zionist ideals without committing themselves to a full Zionist programme.'

On April 20 Jabotinsky had again urged on the Foreign Office the creation of a Jewish force, in order to revive Jewish war morale. The Jews, he wrote, must have a goal, and 'such a goal can only be Palestine'; and on May 6 Jabotinsky wrote direct to Ronald Graham, explaining why a Jewish Legion was important to the Jews:

Without exaggerating my modest forces, and provided no miracles are expected, I simply think that there is in Russia plenty of inflammable material for a great pro-war movement and that setting it ablaze is only a question of a strong concentrated will and of a good battle cry. The battle-cry, so far as Jews are concerned, is Palestine – a goal which implies victory – and a legion as a live link connecting every Jew with the fortunes of the war.

While Jews and Zionists in both Russia and Britain were helping the Allied cause, in Palestine, itself, the Jewish population was increasingly the victim of Turkish persecution. On May 11 Ronald Graham received a telegram, sent through Sir Reginald Wingate in Cairo, reporting on the most recent atrocities. The telegram, from several leading Palestinian Jews, read as follows:

During Passover the entire Jewish population of Jaffa expelled towards North. Homes, property sacked, population in flight, robbed in connivance with Turkish authorities. Jews, resisting, pillaged, hanged. Thousands wandering helplessly on roads, starving. Overcrowding of Colony increasing misery, disease. Masses of young Jerusalem Jews deported, northward, destination unknown.

As the interests of the British Government and the Zionists were drawing closer, an attempt was made by a number of anti-Zionist Jews to oppose the Zionist efforts. On May 24 *The Times* published a letter from two leading British Jews, D. L. Alexander and C. G. Montefiore, rejecting what they called the Zionist belief that 'all the Jewish communities of the world' constituted 'one homeless nationality, incapable of complete social and political identification with the nations among whom they dwell'. Weizmann answered this claim that the Jews were not a nationality. His letter was published in *The Times* on May 28. 'The fact that the Jews are a nationality', he wrote, 'is attested by the conviction of the overwhelming majority of Jews throughout all ages right to the present time, a conviction which had always been shared by non-Jews in all countries.' Weizmann added his regret 'that there should be even two Jews who think it their duty to exert such influence as they may command against the realization of a hope which has sustained the Jewish nation through 2,000 years of exile, persecution, and temptation.'

On June 13 Weizmann sent Ronald Graham a letter, asking that the British Government 'should give expression of its sympathy and support to Zionist aims and should recognize the justice of the Jewish claims to Palestine'. Weizmann pointed out that an all-Jewish Congress of eight of the provinces of southern Russia had voted by 333 votes to 26 in favour of Zionism. 'These eight provinces', he pointed out, 'represent a population of two million Jews.' Jews in Italy, South Africa and Canada had all, Weizmann wrote, 'expressed their approval of the Zionist policy'.

Six days after this letter, A. J. Balfour, the Foreign Secretary, saw both Weizmann and Lord Rothschild, and asked them, as Weizmann reported to

Harry Sacher on June 20, 'to submit to him a declaration which would be satisfactory to us which he would try and put before the War Cabinet for sanction'. Weizmann asked Sacher to draw up a document on the lines, as Weizmann wrote, 'That the British Government declares its conviction, its desire or its intention to support Zionist aims for the creation of a Jewish national home in Palestine.'

The initiative now lay with the Zionists, in whose hands the draft declaration underwent many changes. On July 2 Harry Sacher proposed a bolder version, that 'The British Government declares that one of its essential war aims is the reconstitution of Palestine as a Jewish State,' but Sokolow warned Sacher on July 10: 'If we want too much we shall get nothing.' The idea of asking for full statehood was, however, supported by Herbert Sidebotham, who wrote, in a memorandum on July 11: 'by a Jewish State is meant a State composed not only of Jews, but one whose dominant national character . . . shall be as Jewish as the dominant national character of England is English.' That same day Sacher explained to Sokolow: 'We must control the *State* machinery in Palestine; if we don't the Arabs will. Give the Arabs all the guarantees they like for cultural autonomy; but the State must be Jewish.'

Sacher's arguments were in vain, and when Lord Rothschild gave Balfour the Zionist draft on July 18, Sacher described it as 'inadequate', and 'defective in form'. The draft referred to British acceptance of the principle that Palestine should be reconstituted as 'the national home of the Jewish people'. As the pressure from anti-Zionist Jews mounted, several amendments were made. But the phrase 'national home', enshrined in the Zionist draft of July 18, survived intact. The British Government realized from the outset that a pro-Zionist policy could have serious repercussions. 'The great thing to guard against', William Ormsby Gore minuted on August 18, 'is the appearance of a Christian power "forcing" the realisation of Zionist aims. Such forcing would arouse a conflict with the Arab population of Palestine at once, and would upset a certain powerful section of non-Zionist Jews.'

Interest in the future of Zionism was growing in British political circles. On the same day that Ormsby Gore issued this private caution, the weekly magazine *Palestine* published the official proposal of the British Labour Party for the establishment in Palestine of 'a free State under international guarantee, to which such of the Jewish people as desire to do so may return, and may work out their own salvation, free from interference by those of alien race and religion'. The magazine *Palestine* pointed out that, as opponents of imperialism, the Labour Party sought, by reference to an 'international guarantee', to free the future Jewish Palestine from the stigma of imperialism, and to ensure its place 'in the peace draft of international democracy'.

On August 23 the Zionist cause was again strongly challenged by Edwin Montagu, the most senior Jew in Lloyd George's Government. In a memorandum circulated to his Ministerial colleagues, Montagu, nervous that Zionism posed a threat to the position of Jews like himself who had been accepted in British public life, declared that 'Zionism' had always seemed to him 'to be a mischievous political creed, untenable by any patriotic citizen of the United Kingdom'. His memorandum continued:

If a Jewish Englishman sets his eyes on the Mount of Olives and longs for the day when he will shake British soil from his shoes and go back to agricultural pursuits in Palestine, he always seemed to me to have acknowledged aims inconsistent with British citizenship, and to have admitted that he was unfit for a share in public life in Great Britain, or to be treated as an Englishman.

Later in his memorandum, Montagu declared:

I assert that there is not a Jewish nation. The members of my family, for instance, who have been in this country for generations, have not the sort or kind of community of view or of desire with any Jewish family in any other country beyond the fact that they possess to a greater or to a lesser degree the same religion. . . .

Montagu expressed in his memorandum the fear that any declaration such as that proposed could only increase anti-semitism, create injustice to the Arabs, and result in chaos even for the Jews. According to his interpretation:

When Jews are told that Palestine is a national home, every country will immediately desire to get rid of its Jewish citizens, and you will find a population in Palestine driving out its present inhabitants, taking all the best in the country, drawn from all quarters of the globe, speaking every language on the face of the earth, and incapable of communicating with one another except by means of an interpreter.

Above all, it was the danger of anti-semitism in Britain itself that had made Montagu so hostile to any British support for Zionism. Even at present, he wrote, 'many a non-Jew in England wants to get rid of us'. And he went on to explain:

More and more we are educated in public schools and at the Universities, and take our part in politics, in the Army, in the Civil Service, of our country. And I am glad to think that the prejudices against intermarriage are breaking down. But when the Jews have a national home, surely it follows that the impetus to deprive us of rights of British citizenship must be enormously increased.

Once Palestine was admitted to be the Jewish national home, Montagu warned, all Jews living outside Palestine 'will be foreign Jews'. As for the Zionist Organization, he added, it was 'largely run, as my information goes, at any rate in the past, by men of enemy descent or birth, who by this means have dealt a severe blow to the liberties, position and opportunities of service of their Jewish fellow countrymen'.

The War Cabinet discussed Montagu's memorandum on September 3. Neither Lloyd George nor Balfour were present. After Montagu had elaborated on his arguments, 'it was urged', as the official minutes of the meeting recorded, 'that the existence of a Jewish State or autonomous community in Palestine would strengthen rather than weaken the situation of Jews in countries where they were not yet in possession of equal rights'. As for countries like Britain, where the Jews 'were identified with the nation of which they were citizens', it was argued, against Montagu's main contention, that 'their position would be unaffected by the existence of a Jewish national community elsewhere'.

At the War Cabinet of September 3, the Zionists had a powerful ally in Lord Robert Cecil, the Minister of Blockade, who had tried, but in vain, to persuade his colleagues not to postpone the issue of a declaration, as 'there was a very strong and enthusiastic organisation, more particularly in the United States, who were zealous in the matter', and who was convinced that 'it would be of most substantial assistance', both to Britain and the Allies, 'to have the earnestness and enthusiasm of these people on our side'. Cecil's arguments failed to convince the War Cabinet to issue the declaration; instead, it was decided to postpone any decision to a future date.

Throughout September, Weizmann sought to combat Montagu's influence. On September 18 he saw Leopold Amery, a member of the War Cabinet secretariat, and was, as Amery recorded in his diary, 'very interesting in his scorn for Montagu and all that class of "tame Jew" who doesn't want to be bothered with Zionism or national aspirations, and only regards the nuisance it may be to himself'.

While Weizmann and Lord Rothschild were together preparing a letter to Balfour, in answer to Montagu, the course of the war both on the eastern and on the western fronts had begun to worsen considerably for Britain and its Allies. For three months, from June to August, the Russians had launched a successful military offensive on the eastern front; but, with the spread of Bolshevik anti-war propaganda behind the lines, a mood of despondency had begun to influence the advancing armies and from September 1 the Germans had begun to reverse the tide, capturing Riga on September 3, and driving the Russians back towards Petrograd.

The German success provoked yet another outburst of Russian anti-semitism, for the wretched Jews of the Pale welcomed the German occupation, hoping there would be an improvement on the rigours of Russian rule. On September 2, three days after the fall of Riga, a Kiev newspaper *Razsvet* declared:

Russian people, awake from your sleep! A short time ago the sun shone and the Russian tsar used to visit Kiev. Now you find Jews everywhere!

Let us throw off that yoke, we can no longer bear it! They will destroy the Fatherland. Down with the Jews!

Russian people, unite! Bring the tsar back to us.

Fear for the outcome of the war was not confined to the eastern front; on September 20 the British forces on the western front launched their own massive offensive in the Ypres salient, towards the Passchendaele ridge. Within four days more than 10,000 British soldiers had been killed. Although the attack was to be renewed, and the Commander-in-Chief, Sir Douglas Haig, was confident of success, in England the prospect of further trench warfare with such high casualties cast a pall of apprehension.

The Foreign Office was particularly anxious to enlist the support of Russian Jewry in reviving the eastern war effort, now severely hampered by the continuing German advance, and by the increasingly widespread demoralization throughout the Russian armies. On September 22 the Germans captured the Baltic fortress town of Jacobstadt; two days later, on September 24, Ronald Graham pressed his superiors not to delay the pro-Zionist declaration. 'The Zionist leaders are rendered uncertain, if not dissatisfied', he minuted, and their propaganda on behalf of the Allies 'has practically ceased'. Graham continued:

It cannot be doubted that Zionist propaganda among the Russian Jews was extremely useful to us. Goldenburg, the Agent sent by Dr Weizmann, did very useful work at the Zionist Congress in Petrograd in the summer.

We are anxious to induce Monsieur Sokolow to proceed to Russia as soon as possible with a view to impressing the British case upon the Jews and to arousing Jewish enthusiasm for the expulsion of the Turks from Palestine. But he will not go until this question of an assurance is settled, not will Dr Weizmann take any more active steps.

Apart from Russia, Zionist propaganda in favour of the Allies is also desirable.

Graham went on to comment on the divisions within England between the Zionists and anti-Zionists. The opposition to the Zionist movement came, he wrote, 'from a small group of eminent and influential Jews', and was based upon what Graham believed to be 'unfounded apprehensions with regard to the effect of the movement on Jews who desire to remain entirely British'.

Graham's conclusion was: 'Apart from the merits of the question itself, our political interests seem to lie in encouraging the Zionists.' Commenting on this, Balfour minuted: 'Yes, but as this question was (in my absence) decided by the Cabinet against the Zionists I cannot do anything until the decision is reversed.'

On October 3 Weizmann answered the assimilationist, anti-Zionist view in a forceful memorandum, prepared for the War Cabinet meeting at which the long-delayed declaration would again be discussed. The memorandum was signed jointly by himself and Lord Rothschild. The 'anti-nationalists', Weizmann wrote, were represented 'by a small minority of so-called assimilated cosmopolitan Jews, most belonging to haute finance, who have lost contact with the development of Jewish life and ideas'. It was 'presumptious' of these Jews, for whom Judaism had become 'a mere religious formula', to take it upon themselves to represent the Jewish people 'at this critical time of their history'. Weizmann went on to tell Balfour that the Jewish masses all over the world now looked to Britain for the realization of their hopes. His letter continued:

Whether these masses are 'scientifically' justified in thinking of themselves as a nation is a mere academic question. The very existence of these masses and of their hopes throughout the ages, in spite of all destructive forces within and without, which have been making for their disappearance, is the most powerful testimony to the existence of the Jewish nation and to the tenacious will to persist, whatever some few Jewish assimilationists may decree to the contrary.

When the War Cabinet met on October 4, Balfour warned his colleagues that the German Government were making 'great efforts to capture the Zionist movement', and that although that movement was opposed in Britain by 'a number of wealthy Jews', it had behind it 'the support of a majority of Jews, at all events in Russia and America, and probably in other countries'. Balfour went on to tell his colleagues, as the official minutes recorded:

He saw nothing inconsistent between the establishment of a Jewish national focus in Palestine and the complete assimilation and absorption of Jews into the nationality of other countries. Just as English emigrants to the United States became, either in the first or subsequent generations, American nationals, so, in future, should a Jewish citizenship be established in Palestine, would Jews become either Englishmen, Americans, Germans or Palestinians.

What was at the back of the Zionist Movement was the intense national consciousness held by certain members of the Jewish race. They regarded themselves as one of the great historic races of the world, whose original home was Palestine, and these Jews had a passionate longing to regain once more this ancient national home. Other Jews had become absorbed into the nations among whom they and their forefathers had dwelt for many generations.

Balfour ended by reading to his colleagues what the minutes described as 'a very sympathetic declaration' which had been conveyed to the Zionists by the French Government, and he added 'that he knew that President Wilson was extremely favourable to the Movement'.

On October 5, the day after Balfour's encouraging report, events in Palestine took a tragic turn; for on that day the NILI spy, Sarah Aaronsohn, after four days of torture at the hands of the Turks, committed suicide. She had earlier insisted on returning from the security of Egypt to Palestine, knowing well the dangers but determined to continue her work, and that of her group, in advancing the day when Turkish rule over Palestine would come to an end. Sarah Aaronsohn's death was a blow to the work of NILI; but her work had not been in vain, and for those British who knew of it, the Allied cause had been thereby much enhanced.

Five months later Captain William Ormsby Gore sent a letter to the Foreign Office with details of the work of the Aaronsohn family. 'They were admittedly the most valuable nucleus of our intelligence in Palestine during the war,' he explained, and he added: 'In my opinion nothing we can do for the Aaronsohn family will repay the work they have done and what they have suffered for us.'

On the western front, the course of the battle for Passchendaele had worsened considerably, and, in the week ending on October 5, a further 5,000 British troops had been killed. In London, the fear of a German declaration in favour of Zionism, which would demoralize the efforts of both Russian and American Jewry, added to the problems of the proposed pro-Zionist declaration. Indeed, on October 8 the Foreign Office received a report from Heron Goodhart, the British Chargé d'Affaires in Berne, in neutral Switzerland, reporting that a meeting had taken place in Berlin between the Germans, Turks 'and a leading Zionist', at which 'certain promises had been made with regards to Palestine, with the intention of raising a new war loan in Germany'. At the same time, Goodhart reported, a senior German diplomat had held discussions 'with Zionist Jews' in Constantinople, while in Switzerland itself the German Minister 'had interviewed a prominent Swiss Jew on the same topic'.

These intelligence gleanings were vague, but they evoked the threat of a German counter-declaration. On October 6 Balfour had already telegraphed to Colonel House, in Washington, about the danger of German efforts 'to capture the Zionist movement'; Goodhart's details seemed confirmation of this concern. On October 16 Balfour learnt from Sir William Wiseman, a senior British negotiator in Washington, that the formula of the proposed British declaration had been put before President Wilson, 'who approves of it'.

Only one final obstacle now lay in the path of the British declaration: the continuing opposition of the anti-Zionist British Jews. Edwin Montagu, in another attempt to block the declaration, had urged his colleagues to consult ten 'representative Jewish leaders'. Four of those consulted opposed the declaration, including Montagu himself, and Claude Montefiore, and on October 17 the collective answers were circulated to the War Cabinet. Sir Herbert Samuel stressed that a Jewish Palestine under Turkish control would fall under German influence, while a Jewish Palestine under British control would not. Lord Rothschild supported the declaration as offering an opportunity 'for permanent and cordial relations between Jews, Armenians, Arabs and the other inhabitants of the country'. Weizmann focussed on the arguments of the anti-Zionists, of whom he wrote:

Although it is unfortunately true that a certain numbers of Jews, chiefly in western countries, are opposed to the idea of a Jewish national home in Palestine, it is no less true that these opponents, who are comparatively few in number, are almost exclusively to be found amongst those Jews who by education and social connections have lost touch of the real spirit animating the Jewish people as a whole.

103

Our opponents, therefore, are entitled to speak in their own name only, but have no right to speak for the Jewish masses whose hopes, aspirations, ideals and sufferings they do not share.

The real motive underlying their opposition is of an eminently individual nature. Our opponents are overcome by fear lest the existence of a Jewish national home compromises to a certain extent their own position in the eyes of the peoples in whose midst they are living and with whom they desire to be totally identified. This motive, which they do not conceal, is in itself an indication that they are conscious of being an isolated minority in Jewry and of having the bulk of the Jewish people not with them but against them.

It was not only Weizmann and his fellow Zionists who put forward Zionist arguments in the War Cabinet paper of October 17. A memorandum prepared within the Foreign Office also dealt with the positive reasons, historical as well as political, for a Jewish National Home in Palestine. The terrible suffering of six million Russian Jews both before and during the war had, the Foreign Office memorandum noted, 'brought home to many of them the consciousness of their unity and the necessity of a refuge of their own'. The Russian revolution of March 1917, with its call for liberty, 'far from weakening Jewish nationalism, did but deepen and intensify the national aspirations'. Of the Jews of war-time Vilna, subjected to all the rigours of German occupation and a war situation, the memorandum commented:

It is remarkable that in the darkest hour of their trial and struggle for existence, when they had to collect every penny to satisfy the vital needs of thousands of their starving brethren, they devoted part of the funds which were sent to them for the relief of the Jewish colonists in Palestine, and to the continuation of the educational work to prepare new settlers for the Palestinian colonies.

As well as the Foreign Office memorandum circulated to the War Cabinet on October 17, was one most persuasive note prepared by a Conservative Member of Parliament, Ronald McNeill. Palestine, he wrote, was capable 'under improved conditions of supporting a population of some 5 or 6 millions. For Jews wishing to escape poverty and persecution in various parts of Europe', Palestine would not only provide 'an asylum' but would also satisfy the 'secular national sentiment of the Jewish race'. McNeill went on to stress the importance of Zionism in the context of national movements:

The spirit of Nationality amongst the Jews was an active force for centuries before it became an influence among European nations, and it has shown an unconquerable persistence without parallel in the history of any other people. . . .

It would be a strange and glaring anomaly if, while professing to observe that principle, we were to deny or ignore the claims of nationality in the case of the people who have throughout history clung to them more tenaciously than any other.

The War Cabinet were to discuss the declaration on October 24, but the defeat of the Italian forces at Caporetto was so severe a blow to the Allies that it took complete precedence over all other matters. But within the Foreign Office this delay was most unwelcome. The situation on the eastern front had taken a decided turn against the Allies. The wave of defeatism in the Russian army had turned to mass desertion, and the collapse of all government authority, so much so that Russia's ability to remain at war was suddenly in doubt. Skilfully supported and encouraged by German money, the anti-war movement in Russia had brought almost all military activity to a halt. At the same time, German efforts to pose as sponsors of the Zionist movement continued unabated. It was therefore not surprising that a sense of urgency permeated the Foreign Office. 'I understand,' Ronald Graham minuted on October 24, 'that consideration by the War Cabinet of the assurance to be given by His Majesty's Government to the Zionists is again being postponed. I beg respectfully to submit that this further delay will have a deplorable result and may jeopardise the whole Jewish situation.' Graham added:

At the present moment uncertainty as regards to the attitude of His Majesty's government is growing into suspicion, and not only are we losing the very valuable cooperation of the Zionist forces in Russia and America, but we may bring them into antagonism with us and throw the Zionists into the arms of Germany. . . . We might at any moment be confronted by a German move on the Zionist question and it must be remembered that Zionism was originally if not a German at any rate an Austrian idea.

Graham's minute went on:

Information from every quarter shows the very important role the Jews are now playing in the Russian political situation . . . almost every Jew in Russia is a Zionist, and if they can be made to realise that the success of Zionist aspirations depends on the support of the Allies and the explusion of the Turks from Palestine, we shall enlist a most powerful element in our favour. . . . The moment this assurance is granted the Zionist Jews are prepared to start an active pro-ally propaganda throughout the world. Dr Weizmann, who is a most able and energetic propagandist, is prepared to proceed himself to Russia and to take charge of the campaign.

The Times shared this sense of urgency, and on October 26 stressed, in an editorial, the need to rally Jewish influence in order to combat 'the insidious German propaganda in Russia'. But that same day, a member of the War Cabinet itself, Lord Curzon, presented himself as an opponent of the declaration. His argument was not political, but demographic, and he spoke with the presumed authority of someone who was known to have travelled widely in the Near East. The problem in Palestine, Curzon insisted, was not a question of how many people it could support, 'but whether the land could support any populaiton'.

Curzon's argument could not be brushed aside: his position as a member of the small War Cabinet which had to make the decision was a strong one. Even Edwin Montagu was not a member of this inner body. But the answer to Curzon came, not from any of his Cabinet colleagues, but from Lloyd George's expert on the Near East, Sir Mark Sykes, the War Cabinet's Assistant Secretary who for nearly two years had been particularly responsible for Near Eastern affairs. On 30 October, the day before the War Cabinet was to meet again, Sykes replied specifically to Curzon's argument, stressing the contrast between the natural resources of Palestine and the apparent barrenness of the land. The barrenness was of human making, Sykes wrote, the result of Arab and Turkish neglect; the Arabs were a 'naturally idle and indolent race'. Given proper cultivation, the Jordan valley, for example, was 'a gigantic natural hothouse', capable of producing rice, tobacco and opium. Yet because it was part of the Turkish imperial domains, it had been left fallow.

In his memorandum of October 30, Sykes wrote with an authority that even Curzon could not match, or challenge. With roads, railways and cultivation, he declared, the existing population of 700,000 could be doubled in seven years. Even under the 'bad circumstances' of Turkish rule, the Zionists had shown what could be done. 'Since I first knew Palestine,' Sykes wrote, 'the area of sporadic cultivation had practically quadrupled in spite of every discouragement,' and he added: 'If Zionists do not go there I am confident someone will. Nature abhors a vacuum. It took the Turks and all their men to keep the country a desert before the war, and if it remains in their hands after the war they will be too exhausted to resist the spirit of the age.'

As these discussions continued in London, events in Palestine itself ensured that Britain would indeed soon be the arbiter of Palestine's destiny. At daybreak on October 31, helped by the intelligence which Aaron Aaronsohn had provided, the British army advanced against the Turkish defences around Beersheba. As they drove the Turks before them, the capture of Gaza itself became a certainty, while at the same time a way was opened to advance on Jerusalem from the south.

On the morning of October 31, while the battle for Beersheba was at its height, the War Cabinet met in London. All the arguments for and against a pro-Zionist declaration were now in front of them, and item twelve on the agenda was the question of the Zionist movement. As Foreign Secretary, Balfour presented the case in favour of the declaration, basing himself largely upon the views, and actual words, of Ronald Graham's minute of October 24 and drawing upon some of the details in Mark Sykes' memorandum of the previous day. The official War Cabinet minutes recorded Balfour's words as follows:

The Secretary of State for Foreign Affairs stated that he gathered that everyone was now agreed that, from a purely diplomatic and political point of view, it was desirable that some declaration favourable to the aspirations of the Jewish nationalists should now be made. The vast majority of Jews in Russia and America, as, indeed, all over the world, now appeared to be favourable to Zionism. If we could make a declaration favourable to such an ideal, we should be able to carry on extremely useful propaganda both in Russia and America.

He gathered that the main arguments still put forward against Zionism were twofold:

(a) That Palestine was inadequate to form a home for either the Jewish or any other people.

(b) The difficulty felt with regard to the future position of Jews in Western countries.

Balfour's exposition continued:

With regard to the first, he understood that there were considerable differences of opinion among experts regarding the possibility of the settlement of any large population in Palestine, but he was informed that, if Palestine were scientifically developed, a very much larger population could be sustained than had existed during the period of Turkish misrule.

As to the meaning of the words 'national home', to which the Zionists attach so much importance, he understood it to mean some form of British, American, or other protectorate, under which full facilities would be given to the Jews to work out their own salvation and to build up, by means of education, agriculture, and industry, a real centre of national culture and focus of national life. It did not necessarily involve the early establishment of an independent Jewish State, which was a matter for gradual development in accordance with the ordinary laws of political evolution.

Balfour went on to tell his colleagues that:

With regard to the second point, he felt that, so far from Zionism hindering the process of assimilation in Western countries, the truer parallel was to be found in the position of an Englishman who leaves his country to establish a permanent home in the United States. In the latter case there was no difficulty in the English-man or his children becoming full nationals of the United States, whereas, in the present position of Jewry, the assimilation was often felt to be incomplete, and any danger of a double allegiance or non-national outlook would be eliminated.

The War Cabinet's acceptance of what was to become known as the 'Balfour Declaration', made it clear that two pressing and potentially conflicting interests were now in harmony: the long-term needs and aspirations of Zionism, and the immediate, harsh dictates of war.

That same afternoon, one of the members of the War Cabinet Secretariat, Leopold Amery, who had helped to draft the declaration in its latter stages, wrote in his diary: 'After lunch Weizmann and Aaronsohn came in, the Cabinet having at last agreed to issue the declaration on Zionism, and fell on my neck with gratitude for my efforts on their behalf.' Amery added.

It certainly is pleasant to see the joy of a real enthusiast when after many years, he gets a step forward.

Aaronsohn is a real Palestinian, having lived there since childhood and been a farmer and cultivator. If all the Jews in their own country turn out as sturdy, frank-looking fellows as he, Zionism will certainly be justified.

On November 1 Ronald Graham urged the immediate publication of Balfour's declaration. 'The Zionist leaders', he minuted, 'are prepared to proceed themselves to send agents to Russia, America, Egypt etc'. These agents, Graham added, would help 'to work up a pro-ally and especially pro-British campaign of propaganda among the Jews'. Graham advised: 'The sooner this starts the better,' and thus it was that, on the following day, November 2, A. J. Balfour's letter was actually sent to Lord Rothschild. The declaration read:

His Majesty's Government view with favour the establishment in Palestine of a national home for the Jewish people, and will use their best endeavours to facilitate the achievement of this object, it being clearly understood that nothing shall be done which may prejudice the civil and religious rights of non-Jewish communities in Palestine or the rights and political status enjoyed by Jews in any other country.

Two days later, on November 4, Lord Rothschild replied, thanking Balfour for the interest he had shown 'in the wishes of the large mass of the Jewish people'. Rothschild's reply continued, 'I can assure you that the gratitude of ten millions of people will be yours, for the British Government has opened up, by their message, a prospect of safety and comfort to large masses of people who are much in need of it. I dare say,' Rothschild added, 'that you have been informed that already in many parts of Russia renewed persecution has broken out.'

IO
Hopes and Promises
1917-1919

THE Balfour Declaration achieved one of the main aims of the Zionists: the return of the Jews to Palestine had been recognized as a legitimate aspiration for world Jewry. But one imponderable condition remained: the Balfour Declaration, although approved by the United States, France and Italy, had been granted by Britain alone, and it would depend on Britain as to how it would be implemented. The Jews did not become masters of their own destiny in Palestine on 2 November 1917; that destiny still depended upon British rules and interpretations. It needed, also, further immigration, land purchase, investment, agricultural and industrial development, dedication, fair-dealing and the continual thrust of faith in the Jewish future, and idealism.

Britain's military conquest of Palestine was no longer in doubt. Following the conquest of Beersheba on the evening of October 31, the Turks sought in vain to hold Gaza, or to protect the approaches to Jerusalem. Gaza fell to the British on November 6, and the British troops, pressing forwards towards Jerusalem, liberated both Arab and Jewish villages in their daily advances. Reading of these military successes, Jews throughout the world felt that a new age was about to dawn, in which, in their own land, they would become, at least in part, their own masters.

For the British Government, the issue of the Balfour Declaration had been part of a two-way arrangement. Indeed, within twenty-four hours of the despatch of the Balfour Declaration from Balfour to Rothschild, and six days before it was made public, the British Foreign Office began to seek to exploit the Declaration in Britain's interest. On 3 November 1917 Ronald Graham met Weizmann, Sokolow and Aaronsohn in order to work out, as Graham recorded, the best way 'of obtaining full political advantage' of the Declaration. Various decisions were reached: Sokolow, Jabotinsky and the Russian Zionist leader, Yehiel Tchlenow would go at once to Russia; Aaronsohn would go to the United States; Aaronsohn's brother Samuel would go to Egypt; and Weizmann would go first to Paris, then to the United States, and finally to Russia. 'There is no question,' Graham noted, 'of the intense gratitude of the Zionists for the Declaration now made to them. . . . I believe that their wholehearted cooperation with us may achieve valuable results.'

The Permanent Under-Secretary of State for Foreign Affairs, Lord Hardinge, was likewise eager to see positive gains to the Allied cause as a result of the Jewish response. 'It is a pity', he noted on November 3, 'so much valuable time has been lost. With skilful management of the Jews in Russia the situation may still be restored by the spring.'

Yet on November 6, the day of the fall of Gaza, and while arrangements were still being made for Sokolow, Jabotinsky and Tchlenow to leave for Russia, all Lord Hardinge's hopes for the 'skilful management' of the Jews of Russia were dashed by events in Russia itself: that evening the Bolshevik leader, Vladimir Ilich Lenin, entered the capital, and within forty-eight hours the Provisional Government had been overthrown. By nightfall on November 8 the new Bolshevik regime had destroyed the Russian war-effort by declaring an immediate end to the war. At the same time, by handing over the estates to the peasants, they ensured that hundreds of thousands of peasants would at once leave the army units for their promised farms, thus effectively demobilizing what was left of the Russian fighting forces.

Lenin's anti-war declaration destroyed the immediate aim of the Balfour Declaration; no amount of Russian Jewish support for the war could reverse the no-war decree. But in the immediate aftermath of the Bolshevik success, it still seemed as if Russian Jewry might be of service to the Allied cause. In the confusion of war, news of the Balfour Declaration did not reach Petrograd until November 29. Three days earlier, on November 26, the British military representative in Petrograd, General Barker, alarmed at the rapid spread of anti-war feeling throughout Russia, telegraphed to the War Office in London: 'Would it be possible for Allies to make some sort of conditional promise that in the event of a successful termination of the war, Palestine would be given to the Jews.' Barker added: 'Such an announcement would immediately have a powerful effect in this country where Jewish influence is great and where craving for promised land and distinct nationality is greater even than in England.'

General Barker's telegram had already been made otiose by Lenin's first decree, nor could the publication of the Balfour Declaration in Russia on November 29 reverse the impetus of anti-war feeling. 'It is a misfortune that our declaration was so long delayed,' Graham noted despondently on Barker's telegram.

In London, Allenby's continuing advance against the Turks in Palestine excited those Englishmen who had been attracted by the Zionist cause – from its Middle Eastern aspect. 'It might be the destiny of the Jewish race', Sir Mark Sykes declared in a public speech in London on December 2, 'to be the bridge between Asia and Europe, to bring the spirituality of Asia to Europe, and the vitality of Europe to Asia.' Five days later, Sykes told a Zionist gathering in Manchester: 'No British Jew will be less British because he can look at the cradle of his race with pride. You know the Semite sleeps, but never dies.' But he went on to reflect also on the Arab future, telling his listeners:

Today the Arabs are seven or eight millions. There is a combination of man-power, virgin soil, petroleum and brains. What is this going to produce in 1950?

The Mesopotamia canal system will be reconstructed. Syria will become the granary of Europe. Baghdad, Damascus and Aleppo will each be as big as Manchester.

Therefore, I warn the Jews to look through Arab glasses.

British support for 'a national home for the Jewish people' in Palestine depended, in the first instance, upon driving the Turks out of Palestine. A further, major step forward towards this took place on December 9, when General Allenby's forces received the surrender of Jerusalem; in the battles for the city, nearly 20,000 Turkish soldiers, and 3,600 British and Allied troops had been killed. Allenby himself entered the Jaffa Gate on December 11. It was the thirty-fourth time in its history that Jerusalem had been conquered. For the Jews of Palestine it was a moment of relief and exhaltation. The British forces who had captured the city realized this, for, as Major Pirie-Gordon, the official British historian, recorded, with a direct reference to the Maccabees:

. . . from 0200 till 0700 that morning the Turks streamed through and out of the city, which echoed for the last time their shuffling tramp.

On this same day 2,082 years before, another race of conquerors, equally detested, were looking their last on the city which they could not hold, and inasmuch as the liberation of Jerusalem in 1917 will probably ameliorate the lot of the Jews more than any other community in Palestine, it was fitting that the flight of the Turks should have coincided with the national festival of the Hanukah, which com-memorates the recapture of the Temple from the heathen Seleucids by Judas Maccabaeus in 165 BC.

For the Jews, however, the joy of the conquest of Jerusalem was followed by a moment of sadness. On December 16, two members of the NILI spy group who had been captured by the Turks, Yosef Lishansky and Naaman Belkind, were executed in Damascus, and their bodies exposed in public.

Scarcely two months after the Balfour Declaration was issued, the question began to be discussed in London as to how the existing Arab majority in Palestine could be reconciled to any special privileges that might be given to the Jews. While the Balfour Declaration envisaged at least the possibility of an eventual Jewish majority, it was clear that it would be many years before such a majority would exist. Yet the British intention was equally clearly to make such a majority – even 'an independent Jewish State' – possible 'in accordance', as Balfour had told the War Cabinet on 30 October 1917, 'with the ordinary laws of political evolution'. How these laws were to be regarded was explained by Arnold Toynbee and Lewis Namier – the latter a Galician-born Jew – in a Foreign Office memorandum of 19 December 1917. As Toynbee and Namier saw it:

The objection raised against the Jews being given exclusive political rights in Palestine on a basis that would be undemocratic with regard to the local Christian and Mohammedan population is certainly the most important which the anti-Zionists have hitherto raised, but the difficulty is imaginery. Palestine might be held in trust by Great Britain or America until there was a sufficient population in the country fit to govern it on European lines. Then no undemocratic restrictions of the kind indicated in the memorandum would be required any longer.

For the Allies, the first six months of 1918 were dominated by the need to avert defeat on the western front; then, from July 1918, on how to defeat the German army, still entrenched on French and Belgian soil. Zionism, and even the defeat of Turkey, took second place, and, with both Jerusalem and Baghdad under British military rule, the 'eastern' question seemed less urgent. The ever-present dangers on the western front were themselves made even more urgent when, in March 1918, the new Bolshevik Government in Russia concluded a peace Treaty with the Germans at Brest-Litovsk, freeing hundreds of thousands of German soldiers for service on the western front, at least two months before United States troops could arrive in sufficient numbers to make up the balance again.

But the War Cabinet did receive evidence of the problem of Palestine during 1918: 'local Arabs', General Clayton reported on January 14, 'still evince some uneasiness at Zionist activity and fear a Jewish Government of Palestine as a result.' But at a meeting of the War Cabinet's Middle East Committee five days later, at which Curzon, Balfour and Lord Hardinge were among those present, Sir Mark Sykes pointed out that Arab unease arose largely due to a misunderstanding of Zionist aims and intentions. Sykes gave as an example the Arab belief that Zionism 'involved the expropriation of Arab proprietors and the handing over to future Jewish tutelage of Christian and Moslem sites'. Both these objections, Sykes pointed out, 'had been clearly and emphatically disavowed by the responsible leaders of Zionism'.

At its meeting on January 19, the Middle East Committee decided to send out to Palestine a Zionist Commission, led by Weizmann, to help 'in establishing friendly relations between the Jews on the one hand, and the Arabs and other non-Jewish communities on the other'. Among the Commission's other objects were to assist 'in restoring and developing the Jewish colonies', and to report 'on the possibilities of future Jewish developments in Palestine in the light of the declaration of His Majesty's Government'.

With Allenby's forces in full control of Jerusalem, and southern Palestine, it was possible for the Zionist Commission to make important progress. For the Arabs, however, with Damascus still under Turkish rule, there could be no progress towards their independence. On February 21 Leopold Amery noted in his diary that he was keen 'not to make too much of a splash locally with Zionism until the Arabs have got a slice of the cake themselves, i.e. Damascus'. But on March 2 Balfour wrote direct to Allenby, asking him to allow the Zionist Commission 'considerable latitude and authority to investigate questions relating to the whole future economic possibilities of Palestine as a whole'. Balfour specifically mentioned, as areas relevant to the Commission's activities, 'Crown, waste and unoccupied lands, as well as the existing Jewish colonies'.

Not only did the Zionist Commission carry out its work in respect of future Jewish developments in Palestine; Weizmann also made a strenuous effort to reach agreement with Emir Feisal, a son of King Hussein, and commander of the Arab forces which were about to declare themselves at war with the Turks.

The British supported Weizmann's efforts, so much so that on March 3 Sir Mark Sykes wrote direct to Feisal from the Foreign Office, urging him to give his support to a Jewish national home in Palestine. 'I know', Sykes told Feisal, 'that the Arabs despise, condemn and hate the Jews, but passion is the ruin of princes and peoples.' The fate of the Empire of Spain in the seventeenth century, and of the Empire of Russia 'in our time', both showed 'the road of ruin that Jewish persecution leads to'. The Jewish race, 'despised and weak', were nevertheless universal, all powerful, 'and cannot be put down'. If you challenge them, 'you are like the prince who broke the Roc's egg in the fable and who ruined himself and his nation'. But remember, Sykes told Feisal:

. . . these people do not seek to conquer you, do not seek to drive out the Arabs of Palestine, all they ask for is to be able to do what they have not done elsewhere, to return to the land of their forefathers, to cultivate it, to work with their hands to become peasants once more.

This is a noble thought in the soul of the Jews, they do not seek wealth, or power, that is in London and New York, in Rome and Paris truly and in Vienna and Berlin. Here are these people after 2000 years of wandering looking for something that wealth and power cannot bring, that is the soil of the earth which bore them.

O Faisal, I stood by your side when we came into Jeddah, and I heard your cry when you saw Jeddah your home rising out of the water. It is that same feeling that moves the Jews to seek for Palestine, they do not desire to go there in millions, what they desire is to be able to feel that in Palestine a Jew may live his life and speak his tongue as he did in ancient times.

Zionism, Sykes continued, was a 'noble and true impulse'. If Feisal were to welcome it, there would be 'happiness and prosperity'. If he could welcome Zionism, it would bring 'hope for your cause'; if he spurned it, he would have against him 'a force which cannot be seen, but which is felt everywhere'; and Sykes added:

It is no use to acquiesce in the Jewish movement; to say – I hate it, but I will bear it, I will tolerate this so long but presently we will deal with the Jews.

O Faisal, as I hope for my children's prosperity, I entreat you – banish such ideas, look on the Jewish movement as the great key to Arab success, as the one guarantee of strength when the nations come together in council.

Stand up for Arab rights; uphold the rights of the Palestinian peoples; make good arrangements, but always as between friend and friend, equal and equal, and above all recognise that the Jews desire to live their national life in Palestine: recognise them as a powerful ally.

On May 30 Weizmann explained to Balfour what he had in mind as the basis of an agreement between the Zionists and Feisal. If Feisal wanted 'to build up a strong and prosperous Arab Kingdom', Weizmann wrote, 'it is we Jews who will be able to help him, and we only. We can give him the necessary assistance in money and organising power. We shall be his neighbours and we do not represent any danger to him, as we are not and never shall be a great power.'

On June 4 – two years after the outbreak of the Arab revolt – Weizmann met Feisal near Akaba, on the Red Sea. 'We are lucky in having Weizmann as head of the Zionist Commission,' General Clayton wrote to Sir Mark Sykes on June 18. 'He has done very well with Feisal and at least has established excellent personal relations. He has also had long discussions with Lawrence and they quite agree on the main principles.' Clayton added, of Lawrence and Weizmann: 'Both are looking far ahead and both see the lines of Arab & Zionist policy converging in the not distant future.'

A renewed Arab offensive was soon successful, and on June 10 the Turks were surrounded in Maan. At the same time, three Hebrew battalions, numbering in all 5,000 men, were serving in Allenby's army. Among the very first recruits in Palestine itself was the son of Mendel Beilis.

Five weeks later, on July 18, Feisal replied to Sykes's pro-Zionist appeal. He despised no one, he wrote, on account of his religion, and he added:

... far away as I am from the world's centre, I have a perfect notion of the importance of the Jews' position, and admiration for their vigour and tenacity and moral ascendancy, often in the midst of hostile surroundings.

Therefore on general grounds I would welcome any good understanding with the Jews. . . .

I admit that some ignorant Arabs despise the Jews, but ignorants everywhere are the same, and on the whole such incidents compare favourably with what the Jews suffer in more advanced lands.

During the summer and autumn of 1918 there seemed good propsects both for Arab acceptance of the Jewish National Home, and for the success of what that Home could accomplish. In the first week of August Ronald Storrs went with Dr Weizmann to Mikveh Israel, one of the Jewish settlements liberated by Allenby's army less than a year before. On August 9 Storrs wrote to Sykes: 'I confess that until that moment I had not been aware of what could be done in this country under skilful management and treatment.' Mikveh Israel, Sykes wrote, was 'amazing', and he had been 'filled with hew hope for the future'.

During September and October 1918 the Germans were driven back behind the western front, while in Palestine Allenby's army, advancing northwards from

Jerusalem, defeated the Turks at Megiddo – ancient Armageddon – on September 25, and occupied Damascus five days later. Among the first troops to enter Damascus were the Arab forces, with T. E. Lawrence as one of their principal advisers. Allenby and Feisal both reached the city on October 3.

In all the theatres of the war, the Allies were turning four desperate years of war into victory. In the Balkans, Skopje was taken by the combined British and French armies on September 30. On the western front, the German fortifications of the Hindenburg Line were broken on October 9. On October 24 the Italians began their successful attack on the Austrians at Vittorio Veneto, north of Venice.

The Eastern Committee of the War Cabinet met in London on October 29. Like several other similar committees that week, it had to make important decisions in an atmosphere of impending peace. T. E. Lawrence, who had just returned to England from Damascus, told the Committee that Feisal wished to be free to choose whatever advisers he wished. His preference was for British and American Zionist Jews. The Zionists, Lawrence added, would be acceptable to the Arabs on certain conditions: Feisal would rule Syria, based on Damascus, while Palestine remained in British hands.

On October 30, less than twenty-four hours after this meeting of the Eastern Committee, the Turks surrendered to the Allies. Palestine was firmly under British military control, less than a year after the issue of the Balfour Declaration. On November 28, in honour of that anniversary, T. E. Lawrence told the *Jewish Guardian*: 'Speaking entirely as a non-Jew, I am decidedly in favour of Zionism; indeed, I look on the Jews as the natural importers of western leaven so necessary for countries of the Near East.'

On December 2, four days after Lawrence's pronouncement, Arnold Toynbee expressed his view, in a Foreign Office minute, of one of the territorial aspects of the new Jewish National Home. According to Toynbee, 'it might be equitable', as he put it, to include in Palestine:

... that part of the Arabah or Jordan trough – between the lower end of the Sea of Galilee and the upper end of the Dead Sea – which lies east of the Jordan stream. The Arabah is a sub-tropical district, at present desolate, but capable of supporting a large population if irrigated and cultivated scientifically.

'The Zionists', Toynbee concluded, 'have as much right to this no-man's land as the Arabs, or more.'

On December 12, a petition from several leading Arabs of Palestine was sent to the Foreign Office. Signed by individual Arabs from Haifa, Safed, Gaza, Acre and Hebron, its tone was uncompromising. 'Should the Jews immigrate in great numbers into Palestine,' the petition declared, 'they will doubtless defraud the natives of their rights.' It was, according to the petitioners, the 'fanaticism, egotism and vicious ambitions' of Zionism that had already 'dragged humanity into the abyss of this terrible war'. Three weeks later a young Foreign Office official, Archibald Clark Kerr, minuted: 'The appointed Governments are all so wedded to Zionism that this approach is foredoomed to failure.'

Meeting in London in December 1918, Weizmann and Feisal continued to try to find some common ground between the Zionist and Arab positions. On December 17 Weizmann telegraphed to his Commission colleagues that Feisal 'was sure that he would be able to explain to Arabs the advantages to country and thus to themselves of Jewish Palestine'. Feisal had gone on to promise that at the forthcoming Paris Peace Conference 'he would declare that Zionism and Arab movements were fellow movements and complete harmony prevailed between them'.

At the beginning of January, as a result of further discussion between Weizmann and Feisal, and with the approval of T. E. Lawrence, an agreement was reached between the Arab leader and the head of the Zionist Commission. This 'Weizmann-Feisal Agreement', as it came to be known, was completed on 3 January 1919; Article Four declared that all 'necessary measures' should be taken 'to encourage and stimulate immigration of Jews into Palestine on a large scale, and as quickly as possible to settle Jewish immigrants upon the land through closer settlement and intensive cultivation of the soil'. In taking such measures, the agreement went on, 'the Arab peasant and tenant farmers shall be protected in their rights, and shall be assisted in forwarding their economic development.'

Weizmann and Feisal agreed that the boundary between 'the Arab State and Palestine' would be determined by a commission agreed upon by them both; in Palestine, the Muslim Holy Places would be under Muslim control; no law would be made to interfere 'in any way with the free exercise of religion.' In addition, the Zionist Organization would use 'its best efforts' to assist the Arab State 'in providing the means for developing the natural resources and economic possibilities thereof'.

The Weizmann-Feisal agreement of 3 January 1919 marked a high point in Zionist hopes. Nor did it come one moment too soon; for, throughout the two previous years, while Europe's attention was focussed on the final battles of the war, Jews had been suffering yet again from terrible persecutions. In the Ukraine, in Galicia, and throughout the eastern zones of war, Russian troops had, during 1917, attacked, plundered, raped and murdered Jews throughout the war zones. So cruelly had the Russians assaulted the Jews of Galicia that, in the summer of 1917, 400,000 of them had fled westwards, and as the Bolshevik, Ukrainian, Polish and German forces contended with each other during 1918, the Jews were once again the victims of looting and destruction. In Tsarist Russia their plight had been that of aliens; nor did the successors of the Tsar see them in a more favourable light. Neither the Bolshevik revolution in Russia, nor the Nationalist movements in Poland and the Ukraine, offered any real hope of true equality to the Jews of the former Russian or Austro-Hungarian Empires.

The continuing persecutions in eastern Europe – including more than thirty pogroms in the Ukraine in 1918 – made international support for Jewish immigration to the newly liberated Palestine a matter of the utmost urgency in the minds of the Zionist leaders; for tens of thousands of Jews, all in desperate search of an immediate haven, the Balfour Declaration represented a new and real hope of salvation.

Within two months of the Weizmann-Feisal agreement of 3 January 1919, a Zionist mission was received in Paris by the Supreme Council, the central Allied negotiating body in Paris, on which Lloyd George represented Britain, Lansing the United States, and Clemenceau France. On that day, February 27, Nahum Sokolow read out to the Supreme Council the Zionist proposals: their long term aim, he explained, was 'the creation of an autonomous Jewish Commonwealth, it being understood' – and here the phraseology was precisely that of the Balfour Declaration – 'that nothing shall be done which may prejudice the civil and religious rights of existing non-Jewish communities in Palestine'.

The principal Zionist speaker was Dr Weizmann, who told the Supreme Council:

The Zionist Association demanded, in the name of the people who had suffered martyrdom for eighteen centuries, that they should be able, immediately peace was signed, to tell their co-religionists in the Ukraine, in Poland, and in other parts of Eastern Europe, that some of them would be taken to Palestine to be established on the land, and that there was therefore a hopeful prospect for Jewry. That was the essence of what the Zionists required. . . .

To this end, Weizmann told the Allied leaders, the nation which was to be given Palestine as a League of Nations mandate must first of all 'Promote Jewish immigration and close settlement on the land', while at the same time ensuring that 'the established rights' of the non-Jewish population be 'equitably safeguarded'.

Later in the discussion, the following altercation took place between the American Secretary of State and the Zionist leader:

Mr Lansing asked Dr Weizmann to clear up some confusion which existed in his mind as to the meaning of the words 'Jewish National Home'. Did that mean an autonomous Jewish Government?

Dr Weizmann replied in the negative. The Zionist Organisation did not want an autonomous Jewish Government, but merely to establish in Palestine, under a Mandatory Power, an administration, not necessarily Jewish, which would render it possible to send into Palestine 70,000 to 80,000 Jews annually. The Organisation would require to have permission at the same time to build Jewish schools, where Hebrew would be taught, and to develop institutions of every kind. Thus it would build up gradually a nationality, and so make Palestine as Jewish as America is American or England English.

Weizmann then told the Supreme Council that, 'Later on, when the Jews formed the large majority, they would be ripe to establish such a Government as would answer to the state of the development of the country and to their ideals.'

How did the Arab delegation at Paris react to these submissions? Three weeks earlier, on February 6, the head of the Arab delegation, the Emir Feisal himself, had already told the Supreme Council that because of Palestine's 'universal character', he accepted that it should be 'left on one side for the consideration of all countries interested'. On March 1 he expressed himself clearly and firmly in favour of the Zionist position, in a long letter to one of the American Zionist leaders, Felix Frankfurter. 'We Arabs,' Feisal wrote, 'especially the educated among us, look with deepest sympathy on the Zionist movement.' Feisal's letter continued:

Our deputation here in Paris is fully acquainted with the proposals submitted yesterday by the Zionist Organization to the Peace Conference, and we regard them as moderate and proper. We will do our best, in so far as we are concerned, to help them through: we will wish the Jews a most hearty welcome home.

With the chiefs of your movement, especially with Dr Weizmann, we have had and continue to have the closest relations. He has been a great helper of our cause, and I hope the Arabs may soon be in a position to make the Jews some return for their kindness. We are working together for a reformed and revived Near East, and our two movements complete one another. The Jewish movement is national and not imperialist. Our movement is national and not imperialist, and there is room in Syria for us both. Indeed I think that neither can be a real success without the other.

Feisal went on to warn, sympathetically:

People less informed and less responsible than our leaders and yours, ignoring the need for cooperation of the Arabs and Zionists, have been trying to exploit the local difficulties that must necessarily arise in Palestine in the early stages of our movements. Some of them have, I am afraid, misrepresented your aims to the Arab peasantry, and our aims to the Jewish peasantry, with the result that interested parties have been able to make capital out of what they call our differences.

'I look forward,' Feisal ended, 'and my people with me look forward, to a future in which we will help you and you will help us, so that the countries in which we are mutually interested may once again take their places in the community of civilised peoples of the world.'

Neither Feisal's letter to Frankfurter, nor the earlier agreement between Weizmann and Feisal, could provide a guarantee of future Jewish-Arab amity: indeed, in a handwritten note which he added to the agreement itself, Feisal had stressed that he would only 'carry out what is written in this agreement' on condition that 'the Arabs obtain their independence' in Syria. By July 1920 the French had deposed Feisal from the throne of Syria; two years later, however, with British support, Feisal did become king of an Arab state, Iraq, which gained complete independence in 1932.

II

'A National Idea of a Commanding Character'
1919-1921

FOR the thirty years beginning in 1918, the status of the Jews already in Palestine, and the future of those who wished to go there, was dependent upon British policy. Although a Jewish 'National Home' had come into existence in 1918, or was at least promised, the Jews themselves had to rely upon British goodwill, and British-controlled legislation, to secure or strengthen their legal and physical position there.

There was certainly no unanimity of pro-Zionist feeling among the British policy-makers during 1919 and 1920; sometimes the attitude was much more that of actual hostility. This hostile attitude was stimulated by those Englishmen who now found themselves the 'rulers' of Palestine. Thus, on the afternoon of 16 January 1919, Sir Alfred Money, the Chief Administrator of Palestine, while on a visit to London, called on Lord Curzon at the Foreign Office. Reporting on Money's views of Palestine later that same day, Curzon wrote to A. J. Balfour:

He had much to say about that country. But his main point, and that of Allenby, is that we should go slow about the Zionist aspirations and the Zionist State. Otherwise we might jeopardise all that we have won. A Jewish Government in any form would mean an Arab rising, and the nine-tenths of the population who are not Jews would make short shrift with the Hebrews.

Curzon went on to remind Balfour: 'As you may know, I share these views, and have for long felt that the pretensions of Weizmann & Company are extravagant and ought to be checked.'

Balfour himself, the author of the Balfour Declaration, shared at least some of Curzon's hesitations. 'As far as I know,' he replied three days later, 'Weizmann has never put forward a claim for the Jewish *Government* of Palestine. Such a claim is, in my opinion, certainly inadmissable and personally I do not think we should go further than the original declaration which I made to Lord Rothschild.'

Not only political considerations, but individual prejudice, played its part in some British attitudes to Zionism. In January 1919 the British Civic Adviser in Jerusalem, C. R. Ashbee, a man who was totally devoted to the reconstruction and rebuilding of Jerusalem as a modern city with parks and gardens and sanitation and water, and a devotee of the newly designed Zionist garden cities as far as planning and construction were concerned, wrote in his diary:

I have not met one Zionist yet whom I would really trust for a wise and sane constructive policy. I have met many cranks, and odds and ends of people. The wise Jews are lukewarm or hostile. There is something factitious, journalistic, about the whole movement that puts it on a level with other 'isms' where some kernel of a good idea is exploited for the benefit of unbalanced mediocrity. Walking down the streets of Jerusalem, an American friend pointed to the anaemic idle slum population drifting past her, and said to me: 'These people have not got the proper material for the making of a State.'

Ashbee added: 'Further the Jew is unthinkable without the bargain, he bears the brand of that mean fellow Jacob upon his brow, and with all the nobility of his convictions, and the grandeur of his Messianic idea one would not trust him, *qua* Zionist, not to exploit the Holy Land commercially in his own and his tribe's interest.'

Throughout 1919 and 1920 it was the part played by the Jews in the Bolshevik movement in Russia that gave opponents of Zionism their main focus for hostility. By contrast, the continuing persecution and murder of Jews in southern Russia made little impact. On January 21 the Chief of the Imperial General Staff, Sir Henry Wilson, noted in his diary that Weizmann, 'the Jew who is running the Zionist movement', had been to see him, and 'admitted Bolshevism was being run by Jews'. Wilson added, laconically: 'A clever rogue but a bad face.' Commenting on information just received about the anti-Jewish violence in the Ukraine, a Foreign Office senior official, J. D. Gregory, minuted on February 3:

The Jews deserve all they get. Their whole influence in Eastern Europe during the war was against us and our allies: nearly all the German and Austrian spies were Jews: and now they are busily engaged in undermining the foundations of European civilisation. It is little wonder that the two races which have suffered most, first from Jewish espionage and then from Jewish Bolshevism, should take a truculent revenge on them.

When, on February 4, Weizmann went once more to see Sir Henry Wilson at the War Office, Weizmann protested that the British officers in Palestine were both pro-Arab and anti-Zionist, a fact, Wilson noted in his diary, 'which is very likely, & quite right!' Two months later, on March 25, Lord Curzon expressed his own continuing opposition to Zionism in a letter to Balfour, in which he wrote:

I told you some time ago that Dr Weizmann had departed altogether from the modest programme upon which he agreed with you a year or more ago, and that the ambitions of the Zionists were exceeding all bounds. I do not know if there has been brought to your notice the report of a Conference of the Zionist leaders, which has just been held in this country, attended by Dr Weizmann himself, and devised for the purpose of constructing a programme for the Zionists in Palestine.

The results have been published. That part of the proceedings which was devoted to a political discussion was designedly kept secret; but the published record of the proceedings shows that the Zionists committed themselves to the following propositions as an essential part of their scheme:
  (1) Absolute control of immigration;
  (2) All Jewish holidays to be observed officially;
  (3) Immediate control of water-rights, carrying with it control of the land;
  (4) Jewish nationalisation of all public land and of the surplus land of all private estates exceeding a certain size;
  (5) Complete control of all public works;
  (6) Jewish supervision of all Educational Institutions;
  (7) Use.of Hebrew as main language in all schools.

'I confess', Curzon added, 'that I shudder at the prospect of our country having to adjust ambitions of this description with the interests of the native population' – a reiteration of his remarks to the War Cabinet in October 1917. 'I look back', Curzon went on, 'with a sort of gloomy satisfaction upon the warnings that I ventured to utter a year and a half ago in Cabinet as to the consequences of inviting the Hebrews to return to Palestine.'

Since the beginning of the year a British Jew, Israel Cohen, had travelled through Poland and the Ukraine, in the wake of the pogroms. Typical of his experiences, on January 5 he noted in his diary, while at Chrzanow:

Visited restaurant where everything looted: big supplies of meat, bread, cake, wines, spirits, etc. (bought in Vienna for expected celebration of Polish independence); everything destroyed, curtains, mirror, tables, safe. . . . Also saw former confectionery shop plundered, everything smashed, floors covered with debris; general shop of widow also demolished and ransacked. Went to other small shops, owner of one, brawny, broad-shouldered man told me he had been $4\frac{1}{2}$ years in army, $1\frac{1}{2}$ years on Russian front: this was his reward.

In March 1919, 300 Jews were murdered in the town of Zhitomir, a death toll far exceeding that of the usual pre-war pogrom; deaths on this scale were repeated week by week, as the local Ukrainians vented their hatred of Moscow-based Bolshevism on the local Jews. During the summer of 1919, the Ukrainian death toll rose above 60,000, the largest number of Jews murdered in a single year since the Chmielnicki massacres more than 270 years before. But for some influential British officials, Palestine was not so much a haven for the persecuted as a meeting point for undesirables; thus, on June 1, the British Ambassador in Paris, Lord Bertie of Thame, having talked to Edmond de Rothschild, wrote in his diary: 'He does not realise that a Jew State in Palestine would be the gathering together there of all the scum of the Jewish populations of Russia, Poland, Germany, Hungary and what has been the Austrian Empire.'

On 2 July 1919 the Syrian General Congress, meeting in Damascus, challenged the Emir Feisal's acceptance of Zionism, and, in a strongly worded memorandum, demanded the union of Palestine with Syria, and an immediate end to all Jewish immigration: 'We oppose', the Congress declared, 'the pretensions of the Zionists to create a Jewish commonwealth in the southern part of Syria, known as Palestine, and oppose Zionist migration to any part of our country.' The Congress memorandum went on to protest 'against any private engagement aiming at the establishment of Zionism in the southern part of Syria'.

The British Government, however, felt itself firmly committed to a pro-Zionist policy. On June 19 General Clayton had telegraphed to the Foreign Office from Cairo for approval of a Palestine ordinance to re-open land purchase 'under official control'. Zionist interests, he stated, 'will be fully safeguarded'. Clayton's telegram was forwarded to Balfour, who was then with the British delegation at the Paris Peace Conference, and who replied by telegram on July 5 that land purchase could indeed be continued 'provided that, as far as possible, preferential treatment is given to Zionist interests'.

In London, Weizmann continued to press for the fullest possible Jewish rights of immigration, settlement and self-defence. At the same time, he sought to protect the Jews already in Palestine from the often openly expressed hostility of the British military authorities there. On August 9 Lord Curzon wrote to Balfour:

> This is merely a line to say how much startled I am at a letter from Dr Weizmann to you, dated July 23, in which that astute but aspiring person claims to advise us as to the principle politico-military appointments to be made in Palestine, to criticise sharply the conduct of any such officers who do not fall on the neck of the Zionists (a most unattractive resting place), and to acquaint us with the 'type of man' whom we ought or ought not to send.

'It seems to me', Curzon added, 'that Dr Weizmann will be a scourge on the back of the unlucky mandatory, and I often wish you would drop a few globules of cold water on his heated and extravagant pretensions.'

The British Cabinet in 1919 was predominantly Conservative. But the anti-Zionist group spanned both political parties. Edwin Montagu, a Liberal, and Lord Curzon, a Conservative, were equally opposed to Britain accepting the Mandate for Palestine, and with it the responsibility of furthering the Jewish National Home. The influence of the Prime Minister, Lloyd George, was, however, paramount, and at a special Cabinet meeting on the morning of August 20, he asserted his support for a British Palestine. One of the Ministers present, H. A. L. Fisher, made a note of the discussion in his diary. Curzon, he wrote, 'dilates on difficulties of our accepting responsibilities for Palestine'. One of the difficulties which Curzon stressed was, as Fisher recorded, 'Quarrels beween Arabs and Jews.'

The Cabinet met again later that afternoon, at 10 Downing Street. The possibility was raised of offering all the conquered provinces to America as

Mandates. 'Assuming America won't play,' Fisher noted, 'shall we offer France Syria, America, Cilicia and Palestine.' In that case, Britain would restrict her territorial gains to Constantinople and the Straits. Another suggestion was to make Constantinople an 'international state' and for Palestine to 'go to France'. Edwin Montagu was, as Fisher recorded, 'very strong on the Turks being kept at Constantinople & our not attempting Palestine'. But the decision that was finally reached reflected, not Curzon's doubts or Montagu's opposition, but Lloyd George's views. As Fisher wrote: 'The PM very vehement about our keeping Palestine. The Biblical associations. Immense prestige attaching to Jerusalem. We have conquered it. The French did practically nothing. Even in San Francisco they appreciated the capture of Jerusalem.'

Lloyd George's views prevailed, and by the third week of September he had persuaded both his colleagues, and the French Government, to accept the principle of a British Mandate for Palestine, as well as British Mandates for Transjordan and Iraq, while France was to receive full control over the Lebanon, and eventual control over Syria.

What was to be the future of the Arabs in such an arrangement? T. E. Lawrence believed that the Emir Feisal would be satisfied by what would emerge, even if his position in Syria were to be under overall French influence. By the time that the Mandates were formally allocated, Lawrence wrote to Curzon on September 27, 'the Zionists will have a centre in Jerusalem, and for concessions they will finance him'. Lawrence added:

Zionists are not a Government, and not British, and their action does not infringe the Sykes-Picot agreement. They are also Semites and Palestinian, and the Arab Govt. is not afraid of them (can cut all their throats, or better pull all their teeth out, when it wishes). They will finance the whole East, I hope, Syria and Mesopotamia alike. High Jews are unwilling to put much cash into Palestine only, since that country offers nothing but a sentimental return. They want 6%.

Another Foreign Office expert on the Middle East, Major Young, who, like Lawrence, had taken a leading part in the Arab revolt, agreed that it might be possible for both the British and French to 'step out of Arab Syria altogether', and to leave the Emir Feisal 'to be financed as he pleases, preferably by the Zionists'. But Lord Curzon was strongly opposed to any plan for Zionist economic influence in the Arab world or for a Zionist-Arab union of the sort which Lawrence had long envisaged, as in his message to the *Jewish Guardian* a year before when he had written of the Jews as the 'necessary leaven' in Arab lands. On September 28 Curzon minuted on Lawrence's suggestion:

I strongly deprecate the idea of Feisal being run by the Zionists which I consider would be fatal. What would be the result? With Zionists already in the ascendancy in Palestine and financing, administering, arming and controlling Syria, they would become one of the most formidable factors in the East. This would be the 'New Jerusalem' with a vengeance.

Curzon went on to note that Weizmann himself had, as Curzon phrased it, 'let the cat out of the bag to me in conversation', but that, despite Weizmann's enthusiasm for Zionist-Arab co-operation, 'I offered him no sort of sympathy or encouragement'.

For Weizmann and the Zionists, a dilemma of enormous proportions had now emerged. The future of the Jews in Palestine had become the object of inter-allied, and international controversy; of political rivalries, and of the dictates of personal prejudice. In Palestine itself the Jews continued to build up their settlements, to plough their fields, to plant their vineyards, to educate their children, to welcome their fellow-Jews from outside and to seek autonomy in their community life. But as they did all this, they faced a daily pressure of both British and Arab hostility.

The pressures on the Jews were enormous: on 28 August 1919 an American Commission of Enquiry, known as the King-Crane Commission, had published a report in which it criticized Zionist ambitions, and recommended what it called 'serious modification of the extremist Zionist programme for Palestine of un-limited immigration of Jews, looking finally to making Palestine distinctly a Jewish State'. The King-Crane Commission went on to state that the Zionists with whom it had spoken looked forward 'to a practically complete dispossession of the present non-Jewish inhabitants of Palestine, by various forms of purchase'. In addition, the Arabs, forming nine-tenths of the population of Palestine, were 'emphatically against the entire Zionist programme', a view 'shared very generally by people throughout Syria'. In their conclusion, the Commissioners felt 'bound to recommend that only a greatly reduced Zionist programme be attempted'; a reduction that would 'have to mean that Jewish immigration should be definitely limited, and that the project for making Palestine a distinctly Jewish common-wealth should be given up'.

Undeterred, the Zionists continued to facilitate the development of the Jewish National Home. On September 19 they received unexpected support from *The Times*, which protested against any transfer to France of land east of the river Jordan: 'The Jordan river will not do as the eastern frontier of Palestine, and in Galilee Palestine should also include a good part of the Litani River in the narrows between Lebanon and the Hermon range. To realize the Biblical ideal of a united people from Dan to Beersheba not only must Palestine have a good military frontier east of Jordan, but access to the waters of the Litani is needed for the economic development of Northern Galilee.' The leading article con-tinued: 'Our duty as the Mandatory power will be to make Jewish Palestine not a struggling State, but one that is capable of vigorous and independent national life.' That same day, Weizmann himself wrote at length to Winston Churchill, then Secretary of State for War, to protest against the 'most trying and unpleasant series of experiences' which the Zionists had encountered hitherto at the hands of the British Military Administration. For the first year and a half of British rule, Weizmann wrote, the official British conduct had been 'cold and unsympathetic'. Now, he hoped, it would become 'appreciative of the Jewish destiny of the country'. Weizmann explained to Churchill that the Zionist Organization was 'very anxious to have freedom to send to Palestine a variety of experts to make a general investigation of the country and to prepare plans, so that when the political adjustments in Paris have been made, the Jewish people can proceed, without loss of time, with the task of reconstituting Palestine as their National Home'.

Three days later Weizmann wrote to Churchill again, sending him documents which showed, for example, 'the readiness with which Arabs are learning Hebrew in Palestine', and which were evidence, as Weizmann put it, 'of the rapprochment which is in progress between Jews and Arabs in Palestine'. But Churchill does not appear to have been particularly impressed, for in a memorandum which he wrote for his Cabinet colleagues a month later, on October 25, arguing that the Ottoman Empire ought, perhaps, not to be broken up, he wrote, echoing the argument of the King-Crane Commission: 'Lastly there are the Jews, whom we are pledged to introduce into Palestine and who take it for granted that the local population will be cleared out to suit their convenience.'

During 1919, anti-semitism became more widespread, and was not confined to Russians or eastern Europeans. An example can be seen in a telegram sent to the Foreign Office on 12 October 1919 by the British Government's representative in Georgia, John Wardrop, who informed Lord Curzon that if the 'Bolshevism of German-Jewish intrigues' could be 'crushed' in the Caucasus, the beneficial result would at once be apparent 'as far as frontiers of India and China'. Wardrop continued:

I cannot too strongly insist as I have been doing for last two years that nearly all the present misery of world is due to Jewish intrigues.
Your Lordship will understand what I mean on reference to Zachariah Ch. XII: (Jerusalem) is become a burdensome stone for all people, a cup of reeling, a pan of fire amongst wood, a torch of fire among sheaves.
In England and America as well as in this part of world a diabolical plot is being carried out for (? ruin) and enslavement of Christendom.

On October 16, only two days after Wardrop's secret telegram reached the Foreign Office in London, a public event took place in a Munich beer cellar which foreshadowed the fate of the Jews of Europe: a speech by Adolf Hitler, then aged thirty, who had entered post-war German politics as a rabble-rouser and overt anti-semite. Advertised by a local anti-semitic newspaper, the

Münchener Beobachter, the meeting drew seventy people. Hitler was not the main speaker but, when he spoke, his denunciations of the Jews held his audience spellbound for half an hour.

In the autumn and winter of 1919, Hitler's anti-semitism was confined to the beer halls of Munich, and the war-weary of Bavaria. But it reflected a far wider evil. That same autumn a British edition of the *Protocols of the Elders of Zion* was published in London, and circulated by, among others, H. A. Gwynne, the editor of a national newspaper, the *Morning Post*, whose readers were frequently regaled with stories of the activities of Jewish Commissars in Bolshevik Russia. In sending a copy of the *Protocols* to Churchill on November 27, Gwynne wrote: 'I think they will pay perusal.'

Evidence of the Jewish role in Bolshevik Russia created, throughout 1919 and 1920, a hostile attitude towards the Jews which made a strong impact; thus on 18 December 1919 a Foreign Office representative in eastern Poland, P. Wright, sent a full report, not only on Jewish Bolshevism, but on the eastern Jews in general. The 'village Jew', Wright asserted, 'lives in barbarous filth.' The Jews of Poland had a 'sensitive nerve, their love of money aggravated by centuries of exclusive enjoyment'. Jews and Poles could not be reconciled. 'The Jew,' Wright declared, 'claims a right to all the profits, and the Pole to kick the Jew whenever he feels the inclination.' For Wright, some of the Jews were hardly human; in his report he gave, for example, an account of the murder of a Polish soldier by a Jew who had practised, he wrote, one of 'those horrible mutilations practised by Jewish Chassidim murderers and which is one of the many ways in which they do not seem to be European.' Yet Wright's report also made it clear why there was no future for Jewish life in eastern Europe. Describing how the Poles in a certain area had shot a number of Jews suspected of Bolshevik sympathies, he continued:

> The Jewish ladies arrested, but exempted from the execution, were kept in prison without trial and enquiry. They were stripped naked and flogged. After the flogging they were made to pass naked down a passage full of Polish soldiers. The Jews arrested, but excepted from the execution, were next day led to the cemetery where those executed were buried, and made to dig their own graves, then, at the last moment, they were told they were reprieved; in fact, the gendarmerie regularly tormented the survivors.

'The victims', Wright added, 'were respectable lower middle-class people, school teachers and such like.'

By the end of 1919, more than 100,000 Jews had been murdered in the Ukraine and Poland, some in savage anti-Bolshevik-inspired attacks on Jews who had supported the Bolshevik forces, but most of them in equally violent attacks on innocent Jewish men, women and children. There were British officials who understood the plight of these eastern European Jews. On the last day of 1919 a member of the Eastern and Egyptian Departments of the British Foreign Office, Eric Forbes Adam, had expressed what the National Home could mean to the Jews when he wrote: 'it is thought that eventually some three (3) million instead of the present 60,000 Jews may be able to settle, and that hope and self-respect may be given to a large part of Eastern Jewry who can never actually go to live in Palestine.'

Another non-Jew who understood Zionism was the South African Prime Minister, Jan Christian Smuts. In 1917 Smuts had been a member of the Imperial War Cabinet, and had watched at close hand the evolution of the Balfour Declaration. In a speech at Johannesburg on November 3, marking the second anniversary of the Declaration, Smuts declared, in words which were both fateful, and prophetic:

From those parts of the world where the Jews are oppressed and unhappy, where they are not welcomed by the rest of the Christian population, from those parts of the world you will yet see an ever increasing stream of emigration towards Palestine; and in generations to come you will see a great Jewish State rising there once more.

Writing in the *Illustrated Sunday Herald* on 8 February 1920, another non-Jew, the British Secretary of State for War, Winston Churchill, encapsulated the main contemporary attitudes towards both Zionism and the Jews. 'Some people like Jews and some do not.' he wrote, 'but no thoughtful man can doubt the fact that they are beyond all doubt the most formidable and the most remarkable race which has ever appeared in the world.'

The conflict between good and evil, Churchill wrote, reached its greatest intensity 'in the Jewish race'. The Jews had evolved a system of ethics 'incomparably the most precious possession of mankind, worth in fact the fruit of all other wisdom and learning put together'. They had also produced Bolshevism, a system of morals and philosophy 'as malevolent as Christianity was benevolent'. Indeed, he continued, 'it would almost seem as if the gospel of Christ and the gospel of Antichrist were destined to originate among the same people: and that this mystic and mysterious race had been chosen for the supreme manifestations, both of the divine and the diabolical'.

Later in his article, Churchill wrote at length about 'the schemes of the International Jews', declaring:

The adherents of this sinister confederacy are mostly men reared up among the unhappy populations of countries where Jews are persecuted on account of their race. Most, if not all, of them have forsaken the faith of their forefathers, and divorced from their minds all spiritual hopes of the next world.

This movement among the Jews is not new. From the days of Spartacus-Weishaupt to those of Karl Marx, and down to Trotsky (Russia), Bela Kun (Hungary), Rosa Luxembourg (Germany), and Emma Goldman (United States), this world-wide conspiracy for the overthrow of civilisation and for the reconstitution of society on the basis of arrested development, of envious malevolence, and impossible equality, has been steadily growing. . . .

This Jewish conspiracy, Churchill went on, using language reminiscent of the *Protocols of the Elders of Zion* which had been sent to him scarcely two months earlier, had provided 'the mainspring of every subversive movement during the Nineteenth Century'; now, this 'band of extraordinary personalities from the underworld of the great cities of Europe and America' had gripped the people of Russia 'by the hair of their heads and have become practically the undisputed masters of that enormous empire'. Jews, he added, had even achieved an 'evil prominence' not only in Bolshevik terror in Russia, but also in Bela Kun's regime in Hungary.

Among the main sufferers of Jewish Bolshevism, Churchill continued, were millions of 'innocent' Jews, 'helpless people' on whom the brigands of Russia did not hesitate 'to gratify their lust for blood and for revenge'. As a result, one now saw in Russia 'the most brutal massacres' against Jews, and 'an eager response to antisemitism in its worst and foulest forms'.

Churchill then appealed to world Jewry to abandon Bolshevism, and to turn instead to Zionism: 'The struggle which is now beginning between the Zionist and Bolshevik Jews,' he wrote, 'is little less than a struggle for the soul of the Jewish people.' And he continued:

It is particularly important in these circumstances that the national Jews in every country who are loyal to the land of their adoption should come forward on every occasion, as many of them in England have already done, and take a prominent part in every measure for combating the Bolshevik conspiracy. In this way they will be able to vindicate the honour of the Jewish name and make it clear to all the world that the Bolshevik movement is not a Jewish movement, but is repudiated vehemently by the great mass of the Jewish race.

Zionism, Churchill believed, offered to the Jews 'a national idea of a commanding character'. Palestine would provide 'the Jewish race all over the world' with, as he put it, 'a home and a centre of national life'. Dr Weizmann's 'fiery energies', the support of British Jews, and the 'full authority' of Lord Allenby were all, Churchill wrote, 'directed to achieving the success of this inspiring movement'. Palestine itself could only accommodate 'a fraction of the Jewish race', but, Churchill continued,

. . . if, as may well happen, there should be created in our own lifetime by the banks of the Jordan a Jewish State under the protection of the British Crown which might comprise three or four millions of Jews, an event will have occurred in the history of the world which would from every point of view be beneficial, and would be especially in harmony with the truest interests of the British Empire.

Churchill's article ended with an appeal for the building up 'with the utmost rapidity' of a 'Jewish national centre' in Palestine; a centre, he asserted, which might become 'not only a refuge to the oppressed from the unhappy lands of Central Europe', but also 'a symbol of Jewish unity and the temple of Jewish glory'. On such a task, he added, 'many blessings rest'.

The anti-Jewish killings continued in Russia during 1920. Westwards, in Germany, the year 1920 also saw a growth in anti-semitism. At a meeting in Munich on February 24 a new party formulated its policy. Inspired by Adolf Hitler, the party's 25-point programme contained eight points specifically directed against the Jews of Germany. Under Hitler's plan, the Jews, after 2000 years of continuous settlement, were to be excluded altogether from all the rights and privileges of citizenship. 'Only those who are members of the nation can be citizens,' point 4 declared. 'Only those who are of German blood, without regard to religion, can be members of the German nation. No Jew can, therefore, be a member of the nation.' All Jews who had reached Germany since 1914 were to be expelled. If food shortages were to become severe, all Jews were to be forced to leave. No Jew could be either a newspaper editor, or contribute to the Press.

On April 4 an Arab-led anti-Jewish riot broke out in Jerusalem. 'I regret to say,' Churchill reported to the House of Commons at the end of the month, 'that about 250 casualties occurred, of which nine-tenths were Jewish.' The Jewish leader, Vladimir Jabotinsky, who had tried to arm the Jews in self-defence, was sentenced to fifteen years penal servitude. Two Arabs were also sentenced to fifteen years in prison, for raping two Jewish women. Following protests in the House of Commons by Lord Robert Cecil and others, Jabotinsky's sentence was reduced to a single year.

Where could the Jews find safety? On 19 April 1920, in a 'secret and personal' letter to Lord Allenby, a British General, William Congreve, who was command-ing the British troops in Palestine at the time of the Jerusalem riots, wrote bluntly of how 'the majority of Englishmen have an inherited feeling against the Jew'. Congreve pointed out to Allenby the effect of this feeling on the British officers in Palestine, who had also 'a sympathy with the possessor of the soil', and had thus given vent on a few occasions to making 'inadvisable remarks'. These remarks had led to protests, not only from Weizmann and the Zionists, but also from a senior British officer in Palestine, Colonel Meinertzhagen – who was not a Jew. But Allenby himself defended the growing anti-Zionist feeling, writing to Lord Curzon on April 19:

A large section of Moslem and Christian opinion in Palestine, coherent and powerful, views Zionist aspirations with deep suspicion. It is useless for Meinertz-hagen or Weizmann to avoid the issue by throwing blame on the military administration. Moslem and Christian feeling is deeply stirred. Jewish propaganda has increased in strength and confidence.

Allenby, having been given evidence of Meinertzhagen's pro-Zionist sympathies, asked for the Colonel's recall, and Meinertzhagen returned to London, to a desk job at the War Office. But the doubts of men like Allenby as to the effect of a pro-Zionist policy on the Arabs of Palestine did not prevail, and on 24 April 1920, at the San Remo Conference, Lloyd George accepted a British Mandate for Palestine. Sir Henry Wilson, who accompanied Lloyd George to the Conference, recorded the day's events in his diary:

Then we dropped down to Monte Carlo, spent half-an-hour on the terrace. The day was absolutely perfect and everything looking its best except the horrible crowds of Jews, Dagos of all sorts, painted women, most of them as ugly and dirty as sin. . . .

This afternoon there was a two-hour battle by the Frocks (the politicians) about acknowledging and establishing Zionism as a separate state in Palestine under British protection.

During the 'battle' at San Remo, the French representative, Philippé Berthelot, expressed hostility towards the Jewish National Home, and urged the British not to proceed with the implementation of the Balfour Declaration. But Curzon pointed out that 'the Jews themselves attached a passionate importance to the terms of this declaration and that they would not only be disappointed but deeply incensed' if the pledge were not renewed. When Berthelot continued to argue against the Jewish National Home, Curzon told him that he thought 'that the Jews themselves were really the best judges of what they wanted'.

At one point in the discussion Lloyd George told the Conference that Britain's task of governing Palestine 'would not be rendered less difficult by the fact that it was to be the national home of the Jews, who were an intelligent race but not easy to govern'.

Writing from San Remo two days later, Sir Henry Wilson reported succinctly to General Congreve how the politicians had 'finally decided the fate of Palestine under the Zionists, Syria under the French, Arabia under the Arabs, and Palestine under a British Mandate'. The dual nature of Palestine's future could not have been more clearly noted. Wilson added: 'I quite agree with you that the whole lot, Arabs, Jews, Christians, Syrians, Leventines, Greeks etc are beastly people and not worth one Englishman.'

In Britain a further step forward towards the establishment of a Jewish National Home was taken in the summer of 1920, with the appointment of a former Cabinet Minister, Herbert Samuel, as Britain's first civil High Commissioner in Palestine. Samuel was not only a Jew, but an early advocate of some form of substantial Jewish presence in Palestine. On July 10 Arthur Ruppin recorded in his diary the ceremony on the Mount of Olives on Samuel's arrival:

The scene, which lasted from four until about five o'clock, made a deep impression on all the Jews, including even myself, though generally I am not as impressionable as other Jews. Until now, pronouncements about a Jewish National Home and the decisions at San Remo had only been words on paper; but now they rose before us embodied in the person of a Jewish High Commissioner. The king's message that the Jewish National Home was to be established by stages in Palestine, delivered by Samuel in this banquet hall in the presence of the highest officials and dignitaries from all ranks of the population, sounded like a fanfare to wake the dead. Many of the Jews present had tears in their eyes.

For Lord Curzon, and other opponents of Zionism, Samuel's appointment was very much a step in the wrong direction. 'I should never, myself, have made the Balfour Declaration,' Curzon wrote to Allenby on July 16, and he went on to explain his personal intention 'to give it the narrower and more prudent rather than the wider interpretation'. Curzon added:

Neither should I have appointed a Jew as the first High Commissioner. But Samuel is a sensible man. He has been better received than seemed likely, and I have earnestly pressed upon him the necessity of going slow. He has, I think, a good staff, and if only we can curb the immoderate aspirations of the Extreme Zionists – who would exasperate a Job – we may get through the critical times.

Despite such opposition, the Prime Minister remained a staunch supporter of the Jewish people, and often expressed his admiration for them even in the privacy of the Cabinet room. On August 2 the Minister of Education, Herbert Fisher, after having lunched with Lloyd George, recorded in his diary: 'He talked about the Jews, whom he put first, and of the Scots, whom he put second among the nations.'

Curzon also commented on Lloyd George's attitude. Indeed, in a letter to Balfour on August 20, he expressed powerful misgivings. 'The task of reconciling Zionist aspirations with Arab deserts in Palestine,' Curzon wrote, 'is one that the experience of the last six months has made all our administrators unwilling to undertake,' and he added: 'The Prime Minister clings to Palestine for its sentimental and traditional value, and talks about Jerusalem with almost the same enthusiasm as about his native hills.'

The year 1920 was a fateful one for the Jews, for it saw not only Lloyd George's determination to accept the Palestine Mandate for Britain, but also, in Germany, the evolution of Adolf Hitler's crude anti-semitic views from the obscurity of individual prejudice to the publicity of the popular mob. Indeed, the anti-semitic views enunciated by Hitler with the launching of his 25-points in Munich that February were reiterated by him in speech after speech throughout 1920, culminating in a speech in another Munich beer house on 13 August 1920, in which he spoke for two hours on the theme of 'Why We Are Against the Jews', and promised his listeners that his party alone 'will free you from the power of the Jew!' There must, he said, be a new slogan: 'Anti-Semites of the World, Unite! People of Europe, Free Yourselves!' and he demanded what he called a 'thorough' solution, in brief, 'the removal of the Jews from the midst of our people'.

In Palestine, one of the Arabs who had been charged with incitement to violence during the riots of April 1920 was the twenty seven year old Haj Amin el-Husseini, a member of one of the leading Palestinian Arab families. An outspoken opponent of the Jewish National Home, he had broken his bail and fled across the Jordan, but had been sentenced in his absence to ten years imprisonment. On 7 July 1920, when Sir Herbert Samuel had proclaimed an amnesty for all those who had been sentenced by the military courts, Haj Amin had been specifically excluded. But, seven weeks later, when Samuel himself had been in Amman, he announced a special pardon for Haj Amin, and the fugitive returned to Jerusalem. Only six months later, on 8 May 1921, with Samuel's support, Haj Amin was appointed Mufti of Jerusalem, and later, again with Samuel's approval, he became President of the newly created Supreme Moslem Council. This latter post gave Haj Amin full authority over considerable religious funds, and made him effective head of the Muslim community in Palestine. As an inducement to loyalty, half of his salary was paid by the Government of Palestine. Yet, henceforth, he was to be a leading instigator of a sequence of protests, of riots, and, after 1936, of murder – against Jews, against British soldiers and civilians, and against several hundred moderate Arabs who opposed his extreme activities.

In pursuance of his aim to see a Jewish National Home established in Palestine, Lloyd George entrusted Winston Churchill, who became Colonial Secretary in January 1920, to supervise the details of the emergence of the formal League of Nations Mandate.

Almost the first letter which Churchill received in his new Cabinet post was one from T. E. Lawrence, who, on 17 January 1921, reported on his discussions with the Emir Feisal, who had, Lawrence wrote, 'agreed to abandon all claims of his father to Palestine'. In return, Feisal wanted both Mesopotamia and Transjordan to become Arab States. This was accomplished within two years, when Feisal himself became ruler of Mesopotamia, and his brother, Abdullah, ruler of Transjordan. Mesopotamia, as Iraq, became independent in 1932, Transjordan in 1946. As part of Britain's policy towards Transjordan, all the Jewish National Home provisions of the Palestine Mandate were specifically excluded from the whole of Transjordan, some of whose western areas had originally been seen, both by the British and the Zionists, as a potential area of Jewish settlement.

Churchill visited Palestine in March 1921, where he was greeted by a petition from the Haifa Congress of Palestinian Arabs, dated 14 March 1921. It read: '1. We refuse the Jewish Immigration to Palestine. 2. We energetically protest against the Balfour Declaration to the effect that our Country should be made the Jewish National Home.'

In his reply, Churchill stated the case for the Zionists in a powerful manner. 'It is manifestly right', he told the Palestinian Arab leaders on March 28,

> ... that the Jews, who are scattered all over the world, should have a national centre and a National Home where some of them may be reunited. And where else could that be but in the land of Palestine, with which for more than 3,000 years they have been intimately and profoundly associated? We think it would be good for the world, good for the Jews, and good for the British Empire.

The Arab protest continued, and the violence that followed Churchill's visit was severe. Arab violence in Jaffa on May 1 led to the British High Commissioner in Palestine, Sir Herbert Samuel, ordering an immediate temporary suspension of Jewish immigration. Ten days later the Senior Naval Officer in the Eastern Mediterranean, Captain Seymour, sent to the Admiralty his report on the riots, in which he wrote: 'Further immigration of foreign Jews into Palestine has been prohibited as a temporary measure and this has given satisfaction to the Arabs.'

The suspension of immigration, made on the authority of Sir Herbert Samuel, did not entirely impress the Colonial Office, and a telegram was drafted for Churchill by one of his senior advisers, Major Young, which was despatched to Samuel on 14 May 1921. 'The present agitation', the telegram read, 'is doubtless engineered in the hope of frightening us out of our Zionist policy. ... We must firmly maintain law and order and make concessions on their merits and not under duress.'

Although the total prohibition of Jewish immigration, which the Arabs continued to demand, was never acceptable to Churchill, the idea of some limit to Jewish immigration was discussed between Samuel and the Colonial Office, and it was decided to set up a limit based on what was described by Samuel as 'the economic absorbtive capacity of Palestine'. This idea of some limit took rapid shape, and within two years it had become government policy, to the dismay of the Zionist leaders, who saw it as an erosion of what they believed was the principle of freedom of immigration implied in the 'National Home' phraseology of the Balfour Declaration.

For good or ill, the future of Zionism was now linked to British policy and British prejudice. But it was still up to the Zionists to take the initiative, if their numbers were to grow and their efforts to flourish. On June 4 Arthur Ruppin wrote in his diary: 'It is absolutely clear to me that Zionism will perish altogether if we do not soon make a start developing Palestine agriculturally.' He had decided to go to Prague, for the next meeting of the Zionist General Council, because, as he wrote in his diary: 'I shall want to shout this for all the world to hear, because our people, continuing to rely on the Balfour Declaration, apparently do not understand the gravity of the situation.' Ruppin added: 'The declaration will not be worth the paper it is written on if we do not infuse it with life and strength by practical accomplishments in Palestine.'

12

The Palestine
Mandate Secured
1921-1922

ON June 22 Churchill explained the British position on Zionism to the Dominion Prime Ministers, at a meeting of the Imperial Cabinet. Among those present were the New Zealand Prime Minister, William Massey, and the Canadian Prime Minister, Arthur Meighen. 'The Zionist ideal', Churchill told them, 'is a very great ideal, and I confess, for myself, it is one that claims my keen personal sympathy.' But the Balfour Declaration, he added, was more than an ideal. It was also an obligation, made in wartime, 'to enlist the aid of Jews all over the world', and Britain must be 'very careful and punctilious', he explained, 'to discharge our obligations . . .'.

Arthur Meighen questioned Churchill about the meaning of a Jewish 'National Home'. Did it mean, he asked, giving the Jews 'control of the Government'? To this Churchill replied: 'If, in the course of many years, they become a majority in the country, they naturally would take it over.'

On July 5 Dr Weizmann, who had just returned from the United States, told Colonel Meinertzhagen that he feared for the future of Zionism. 'He says the British Government is whittling down the Balfour Declaration,' Meinertzhagen recorded in his diary, 'that immigration has practically stopped, that the bulk of the British Officers in Palestine are not in sympathy with the movement and that the Zionists are not getting those concessions which are necessary for the establishment of the Home of the Jews in Palestine'.

Meinertzhagen shared Weizmann's worries, writing in his diary on July 5:

Sir Herbert Samuel has been weak. The moment the Jaffa rioting broke out, he and his staff seem to have been hypnotized by the danger and everything was done to placate the Arab. Immigration was stopped, elective assemblies were discussed, whereas what the Arab wanted was a good sound punishment for breaking the peace and killing Jews.

The Arab is fast learning that he can intimidate a British Administration. Samuel has not been able to stand up to the solid block of anti-Zionist feeling among his military advisers and civil subordinates. . . .

On July 22 Churchill, Lloyd George, and A. J. Balfour met Weizmann, at Balfour's house in London, to try to reassure Weizmann that British policy had not changed. At this meeting, Weizmann protested that the Balfour Declaration was being whittled away, and that Sir Herbert Samuel himself was undermining it. Weizmann pointed out that, on June 3, Samuel had declared, in an official speech, that 'the conditions of Palestine are such as not to permit anything in the nature of mass immigration'. Such a statement, Weizmann pointed out, was 'a negation of the Balfour Declaration'. Churchill asked Weizmann to explain why this was so. Weizmann explained that the Balfour Declaration 'meant an ultimate Jewish majority' whereas Samuel's speech 'would never permit such a majority to eventuate'.

According to the minutes of the meeting, Churchill 'demurred at this interpretation' of Samuel's speech, while Lloyd George and Balfour both agreed 'that by the Declaration they had always meant an eventual Jewish State'.

On August 5 one of the principal Middle East advisers at the Colonial Office, Major Young, sent Churchill a forceful minute, in which he stressed that both he and the head of the Middle East Department, John Shuckburgh, felt that Herbert Samuel had been pressed 'not only by Arabs, but also by British officials who are not in sympathy with Zionist policy', into taking action 'which was not altogether justified' in restricting Jewish immigration. The Cabinet, Young believed, should give Samuel clearer guidelines as to the policy to be pursued, particularly as a delegation of Palestinian Arabs was on its way to London, intent on protesting, at the highest level, against the Balfour Declaration.

Young himself favoured a policy which, he had written to Churchill on August 1, involved 'the gradual immigration of Jews into Palestine until that country becomes a predominantly Jewish state', and he went on to argue that the phrase 'National Home' as used in the Balfour Declaration implied no less than full statehood for the Jews of Palestine. There could be 'no half-way house', he wrote, between a Jewish State and 'total abandonment of the Zionist programme'. It was, he continued, 'insufficient for us merely to tell the Arab Delegation that we do not intend to waver in our policy – the fact of the matter is that we *have* wavered, and we must be prepared to take a stronger line'.

On August 2 Young discussed the future of Palestine with Dr Weizmann. But his sympathetic attitude did not set Weizmann's mind at rest. On August 10 the Zionist leader wrote to an American friend: 'Whenever you think you have won a real support out of this "other world" it proves at the end to be a mirage and one has to pay bitterly with one's nerves (and) self respect for the few minutes of fictitious joy and satisfaction. And so we stand again before the sphinx.'

On August 12 the Palestinian Arab Deputation, having reached London, sent the Colonial Office a memorandum setting out their demands. Their first was for a National Government, responsible to a Parliament 'elected by those natives of Palestine who lived in the country before the war'. Their second was for 'the abolition of the principle of the creation of a National Home for the Jews in Palestine'. The Zionist aim, they continued, was the establishment of a Jewish State in Palestine; such an aim 'threatens our very existence as a nation'. The third Arab demand was for a total ban on all Jewish immigration until a National Government had been set up. The fourth demand was for the cancellation of all laws made since the British occupation; the fifth demand was for Palestine to be allowed to join 'her Arab neighbouring sister-states . . . under one confederated government, with one language, one Customs regulation etc. etc.'

On August 15, three days after receiving these demands, Churchill himself received the members of the Deputation. The Secretary to the Deputation, Shibly al-Jamal, protested bitterly against the Balfour Declaration, against the employment of Jews in the administration, and against the use of Hebrew – together with English and Arabic – as one of the three official languages of the Mandate. But Churchill answered firmly. The Jews, he said, 'are to be encouraged to go to Palestine and found there a home for themselves'. A few moments later Churchill reiterated: 'It undoubtedly is intended the Jews shall be allowed to come freely into Palestine in proportion as there is room, and there is a good livelihood, provided of course they develop the resources of the country.'

On August 17, two days after Churchill had received the Arab Deputation, the Cabinet met to discuss the future of the Palestine Mandate. H. A. L. Fisher recorded the discussion in his diary: 'I propose offering it to America which is welcomed'. Fisher added:

'The PM indulges in a fancy sketch of the huge population of Palestine in ancient times. The Arabs must not be too much pampered. The Jews are the people for cultivating the soil.'

According to the official minutes of the meeting, it was agreed, at one point during the discussion, 'that the Arabs had no prescriptive right to a country which they had failed to develop to the best advantage'.

The Cabinet decided to retain the Mandate, for, as the official minutes recorded, 'stress was laid on the following consideration, the honour of the government was involved in the Declaration made by Mr Balfour, and to go back on our pledge would seriously reduce the prestige of this country in the eyes of the Jews throughout the world'. Nevertheless, also contained in the Cabinet's conclusion was the warning that, 'It was not expected that the problem could be easily or quickly solved, especially in view of the growing power of the Arabs in the territories bordering on Palestine.' Here once more was the warning, first raised by Herbert Samuel in 1915, that the Arab forces outside Palestine would eventually play an important, if not a predominant part in determining the future of the British promise to the Jews.

On August 22 the Arab Deputation called on Churchill again at the Colonial Office. He at once rebuked their leader, Musa Kazim Pasha, for refusing to see either Dr Weizmann or Nahum Sokolow, and for being unwilling 'to get to a practical friendly agreement with them'. Churchill then asked if he could speak 'as man to man in a friendly way', and when they agreed, he spoke to them without prevarication:

The British Government mean to carry out the Balfour Declaration. I have told you so again and again. I told you so at Jerusalem. I told you so at the House of Commons the other day. I tell you so now. They mean to carry out the Balfour Declaration. They do. What is the use of looking at anything else? The Government is not a thing of straw, to be blown by the wind this way and that way. It is bound to carry out the Declaration. It contains safeguards for the Moslems, just as it contains clauses satisfactory for the Jew.

Churchill told the Arabs: 'You are not addressing your minds to the real facts of the case,' and he went on to say that he had no power, or desire, to repudiate the Balfour Declaration. Nor did he believe that the Jews were in any way a threat to the Arabs:

I have told you again and again that the Jews will not be allowed to come into the country except in so far as they build up the means for their livelihood according to the law. They cannot take any man's lands. They cannot dispossess any man of his rights or his property or interfere with him in any way.

If they like to buy people's land, and people like to sell it to them, and if they like to develop and cultivate regions now barren and make them fertile, then they have the right, and we are obliged to secure their right to come into the country and to settle.

Later in the discussion, Churchill stated unequivocally that Britain could not grant representative government to Palestine, because, as he said, 'we are trustees, not only for the interests of the Arabs but also for the interests of the Jews. We have a double duty to discharge.' The Arabs could not have representative Government, he said, because that would give them the power to halt Jewish immigration. The British Government, he added, 'wants to see Jews developing and fertilising the country and increasing the population of Palestine'. It was 'a great pity', he continued, that there were so few people in Palestine, which had once been 'three or four times' more populous. He wanted to see more wealth in Palestine, 'instead of it being occupied by a few people who were not making any great use of it'. It was Britain's intention, Churchill declared, 'to bring more Jews in. We do not intend you to be allowed to stop more from coming in. You must look at the facts.'

The Arab Deputation had been at the Colonial Office for nearly an hour. But, before the meeting ended, Churchill spoke to them at length about the need to accept Jewish immigration as a permanent and irrevocable feature of Palestinian life. During his final speech, he declared:

... the Jews are a very numerous people, and they are scattered all over the world. This is a country where they have great historic traditions, and you cannot brush that aside as though it were absolutely nothing. They were there many hundreds of years ago. They have always tried to be there. They have done a great deal for the country. They have started many thriving colonies, and many of them wish to go and live there. It is to them a sacred place. Many of them go there to be buried in the city which they regard as sacred, – as you regard it as sacred.

Why cannot you live together in amity and develop the country peacefully? There is room for all as long as they are not brought in in great numbers before there are means of livelihood for them; before the electrical and other means of power are created which will make waste places fertile; before the hills have had terraces made upon them; before irrigation and proper agricultural development. Of course, if they were brought in before these things were done, you would have reason to complain. . . .

Churchill's speech continued:

Many of the British Officials in Palestine are very, very friendly to the Arabs, more so than to the Jews. The Jews make continued outcry on that subject, that the British officials and the British military authorities are unduly partial towards the Arabs. No one has harmed you, and no one is harming you. More than one and a half millions of money was invested in Palestine last year by the Jews, and many years must pass before there can be any question of Jews having the majority, or having any control or predominant influence in the Country. . . .

'Give the Jews their chance,' Churchill urged the Palestinian Arab leaders, and he ended his speech:

The Jews have a far more difficult task than you. You only have to enjoy your own possession; but they have to try to create out of the wilderness, out of the barren places, a livelihood for the people they bring in. They have to bring them in under conditions which make for the general good of the population, and which supplant no one, and deprive no one of their rights and liberties.

On August 23 Hubert Young reported on Churchill's discussions with the Arab Delegation to one of Weizmann's closest advisers, Harry Sacher. Young told Sacher 'that Mr Churchill had not received a very favourable impression' of the Arab Delegation. During the discussion, Sacher reiterated the Zionist position that in any future Palestinian constitution, the Zionists 'would desire adequate safeguards for the Jewish National Home'. His fear was that the Arabs might eventually be granted veto powers on Jewish immigration. These worries were shared by Dr Weizmann, who, despite Churchill's remarks to the Arab Delegation, doubted that British policy would ultimately uphold the promises of the Balfour Declaration.

On August 31, in a long letter to the Chief Secretary to the Palestine Administration, Sir Wyndham Deedes, Weizmann set out his fears in detail. He had not been impressed, he wrote, by Churchill's contribution to the discussion at Balfour's house on July 22. On that occasion, he said, Churchill had tried to defend Herbert Samuel's arguments in favour of restricting Jewish immigration, and had reacted 'sulkily' to Weizmann's questionings. As a result of the meeting of July 22, Weizmann had drawn the conclusion that the British leaders saw no common ground in British and Jewish interests. If this were in fact so, Weizmann told Deedes, 'then this should be told to us honestly and straightforwardly. We are an old people, full of sores. We bleed out of every pore and it is a great sin, which will bitterly revenge itself, if we are simply put off by pious promises.'

Weizmann had been particularly depressed by a remark which Churchill had made to him at the meeting of July 22, when he had stated quite bluntly, as Weizmann told Deedes, that nine tenths of the British in Palestine were 'opposed to the policy' of a Jewish National Home. In his letter to Deedes, Weizmann commented bitterly that in future the Jews would have to be taught 'to rely only on themselves'. His letter continued:

Unless there will be a definite change of the course I don't see how we can demand millions from the Jews for an Arab Palestine, how we can continue to pour in about half a million pounds a year into the country. Our lives, our honour are not safe there, our prestige is being ruined. British public opinion which three years ago was distinctly in our favour is being systematically formed against us and I fear chiefly by those '9/10'.

Of the Balfour Declaration nothing is left but mere lip service. The rock on which the policy has been built up is shattered! I know that all that will have far reaching consequences. But out of this present – terrible crisis, the Zionist idea will emerge triumphantly after much tribulation, because we are indestructible. The God of Israel in His wisdom is trying His people. Ukraine, Poland, Bolshevism – all that is not enough. We must be pogromed in Palestine, submitted there to restrictions and difficulties.

'Such', Weizmann added, 'are the ways of Providence, and I believe faithfully that it is all for the good in the end'.

On the fourth anniversary of the Balfour Declaration, violence broke out again in Palestine. 'A disturbance took place in Jerusalem this morning,' Samuel telegraphed to the Colonial Office on November 2, 'when a small crowd of Arab roughs appeared in the Jaffa Road. They were dispersed by the police but soon after gathered for an attack on the Jewish quarter. This was averted by the police. Some shots were exchanged between this crowd and the crowd in the Jewish quarter. . . . Four Jews and one Arab were killed.'

The Middle East Department was angered by the Arab attack, and by the somewhat feeble action taken to halt it. It was, wrote one young official, Gerard Clauson, on November 3, 'a pity that when the first mob gathered the Police only dispersed it, instead of rounding it up. They knew trouble was in the wind.' And he added: 'It was quite certain that this demonstration was deliberately organized.' The Arab aim, Colonel Meinertzhagen noted, was to make it impossible for the Government to carry out the terms of the Balfour Declaration;

it was essential, he believed, to 'remove all doubts about our intentions', otherwise the Arabs would continue to seek to alter the policy by violence.

Despite the urgings of Churchill and his Colonial Office advisers, the Palestinian Arab delegation adamantly refused to enter into negotiations with the Zionists. For his part, Dr Weizmann was increasingly depressed that the British Government had not made greater efforts to convince the Arabs of the permanence of the Jewish National Home; indeed, on December 13 he wrote to Wyndham Deedes of his fears that the British aim was not to build a Jewish National Home in Palestine, but rather, as he expressed it, 'an Arab National Home in which a few Jews will be inserted'.

The Colonial Office knew of Weizmann's discontent. But they took no action to counter the strong anti-Zionist feelings of the British officials in Palestine, nor did they intervene when General Congreve issued an army order which referred at one point to 'the grasping policy of the Zionist extremists', and described the sympathies of the British army as 'rather obviously with the Arabs, who have hitherto appeared to the disinterested observer to have been the victims of an unjust policy, forced upon them by the British Government'. Congreve's order had been issued on October 29. Throughout November and December Churchill himself had been urged to denounce it, particularly by Colonel Meinertzhagen. But, in a departmental minute on December 1, John Shuckburgh advised Churchill against any action. Shuckburgh wrote, 'It is unfortunately the case that the Army in Palestine is largely anti-Zionist and will probably remain so whatever may be said to it.'

Before the Mandate was itself finalized, the British Government made a major contribution to the development of the Jewish National Home. This took the form of granting the Zionists a monopoly control over the development of the electrical resources of Palestine, according to a scheme which had been drawn up by the Russian-born Jewish engineer, Pinhas Rutenberg, to harness the waters of Palestine.

The Rutenberg scheme was accepted by the British Government as an integral part of its Mandate commitment to the Jews. In a formal communication from the Foreign Office to the United States Government, dated 29 December 1921, it was officially stated that 'so far as Palestine is concerned, Article II of the mandate expressly provides that the administration may arrange with the Jewish Agency to develop any of the natural resources of the country, in so far as these matters are not directly undertaken by the Administration'. The reason for this, the Foreign Office letter explained, 'is that in order that the policy of establishing in Palestine a national home for the Jewish people could be successfully carried out, it is impractical to guarantee that equal facilities for developing the natural resources of the country should be granted to persons or bodies who may be motivated by other motives'. It was on this basis that the Rutenberg electrical concession was granted, as a monopoly, to the Zionists.

One of those in the Colonial Office whose task it was to give effect to this policy was Churchill's principal adviser on Middle East affairs, John Shuckburgh, who minuted on 17 January 1922:

I admit that the electrification of any portion of the railways in Palestine may at first sight appear premature. It may be well asked why the needs of Jaffa and Jerusalem cannot be served by a form of traction which is deemed sufficient for the infinitely heavier traffic between, let us say, London and Liverpool, or Paris and Marseilles. The answer is that in this, as in all matters relating to Palestine, we stand under the shadow of the Balfour Declaration. The Rutenberg concession has always been regarded as the more practical example of the policy of setting up a National Home for the Jews. It is so regarded by the Zionists themselves.

And Shuckburgh went on to point out:

We are always trying to divert the attention of the Zionists from political to industrial activities, and preaching to them from the text that their best chance of reconciling the Arabs to Zionist policy is to show them the practical advantages accruing from Zionist enterprise. For these reasons we support and encourage Mr Rutenberg's projects.

The Colonial Office was, at the same time, aware of Palestinian Arab hostility. On March 3, at a meeting of Arab supporters held at the Hyde Park Hotel in London, the principal Palestinian Arab speaker, Shibly Jamal, was reported by Shuckburgh to have used language 'about the necessity of killing Jews if the Arabs did not get their way'. Such a threat could only underline the dangers that still beset the Zionist movement.

Evidence of the extent to which the Zionists could not necessarily depend even upon British support was soon forthcoming. On May 24 John Shuckburgh sent Churchill the final draft of Sir Herbert Samuel's memorandum on the future of Palestine. In it, Samuel described as 'impracticable' Weizmann's much quoted remark of 1919 that Palestine would become 'as Jewish as England is English'. The British Government, Samuel insisted, 'have no such aim in view'. Nor did they wish to see 'the disappearance or the subordination of the Arab population, language or culture in Palestine'. Samuel also stressed that the Balfour Declaration did not contemplate 'that Palestine as a whole should be converted into a Jewish National Home, but that such a Home should be founded *in Palestine*'.

Samuel's memorandum went on to state once again that further Jewish immigration could not be permitted to exceed 'whatever may be the economic capacity of the country at any given time to absorb new arrivals'.

Samuel's statement was accepted by the Colonial Office as a guideline for future British policy, and was published as part of the Palestine White Paper of 30 June 1922. The Zionists themselves formally accepted the White Paper. But they were unhappy about fixing so specific an economic condition on future immigration, fearing that unsympathetic, and even anti-Zionist High Commissioners in the future, would abuse the concept of an economic absorptive capacity, in order to halt future immigration. Samuel was convinced, however, that his formula was the right one for the peaceful development of Palestine. On June 12 one of the Middle East Department's advisers, Eric Mills, noted, in a departmental minute: 'Sir H. Samuel told me that he thought the country could not support economically more than 6,000 immigrants per annum. If that be so then there is no conceivable chance that the Jews will ever be a majority in Palestine.'

It was for reasons such as those given by Mills that, during the spring and summer of 1922, the evolution of the Jewish National Home created unhappiness among many Zionists. In a letter to *The Times* published on May 13, Israel Zangwill went so far as to state that 'the utmost that now seems predictable is a rise of a Semitic Switzerland, in which the Jews would have an equal national status with Arabs'. Such a development, he believed, would certainly be a British asset, but, 'as a Jewish political asset, or as the solution of the Jewish problem, it will be comparatively worthless'. According to Zangwill:

What the Jews need as a people is not a centre, but a circumscribing circumference, such as every other people enjoys; not an 'airy nothing', but 'a local habitation'; not a spiritual sophistication, but a solid surveyable territory.

It was this that was supposed to have come to my sorely-tried race as the outcome of the Great War; partly as the expression of the nationalist ideals of the war programme.

Read a recent book on my shelves, of four hundred pages, devoted to the 'extra-special' slaughter of Jews in all the shambles of Europe, and you will admit that in these days of universally renascent anti-Semitism, a spiritual Zion is no more a solution of the Jewish problem than Mr Belloc's fantastic scheme of re-established Ghettoes.

During the summer of 1922, influential anti-Zionist forces were mustered to speak in Parliament on behalf of the Arab majority and to demand representative institutions which would enable the Arabs to halt Jewish immigration. There was particularly strong criticism of the Rutenberg concession, which was seen as the beginning of Jewish domination.

On June 21 a Liberal Peer, Lord Islington, introduced a motion in the House of Lords, declaring that the Palestine Mandate was 'inacceptable to this House', because it was 'opposed to the sentiments and wishes of the great majority of the people of Palestine'. The Rutenberg scheme, Islington alleged, would invest the Jewish minority with wide powers over the Arab majority. 'Zionism', he declared, 'runs counter to the whole human psychology of the age.' It involved bringing into Palestine 'extraneous and alien Jews from other parts of the world', in order to ensure a Jewish predominance. Jewish immigration, he added, would be a burden on the British taxpayer, and a grave threat to Arab rights and development. 'The Zionist Home', he asserted, 'must, and does mean the predominance of political power on the part of the Jewish community in a country where the population is predominantly non-Jewish.'

Lord Islington's arguments were challenged by Balfour himself, who, in his maiden speech in the House of Lords, spoke emphatically in favour of Jewish immigration and investment, and denied that the Arabs would suffer in any way as a result. But, as the debate continued, it was clear that a majority of the Peers present were bitterly opposed to Zionism. Lord Sydenham matched Lord Islington in the strength of his anti-Zionism. 'Palestine is not the original home of the Jews,' he said, referring to biblical times. 'It was acquired by them after a ruthless conquest, and they never occupied the whole of it, which they now demand.' The Jews, Lord Sydenham continued, 'have no more valid claim to Palestine than the descendants of the ancient Romans have to this country.' The Romans, he added, had occupied Britain 'nearly as long as the Israelites occupied Palestine, and they left behind them in this country far more valuable and useful work'. The 'only real claim' to Palestine, he believed, 'is that of its present inhabitants'. Sydenham then spoke of the effect of Jewish immigration since 1919:

Palestinians would never have objected to the establishment of more colonies of well-selected Jews; but, instead of that, we have dumped down 25,000 promiscuous people on the shores of Palestine, many of them quite unsuited for colonising purposes, and some of them Bolsheviks, who have already shown the most sinister activity.
The Arabs would have kept the Holy Land clear from Bolshevism.

A few moments later Lord Sydenham declared:

What we have done is, by concessions, not to the Jewish people but to the Zionist extreme section, to start a running sore in the East, and no one can tell how far that sore will extend.
Zionism will fail . . . but the harm done by dumping down an alien population upon an Arab country – Arab all round in the hinterland – may never be remedied. . . .
The Mandate as it stands will undoubtedly, in time, transfer the control of the Holy Land to New York, Berlin, London, Frankfurt and other places. The strings will not be pulled from Palestine; they will be pulled from foreign capitals; and for everything that happens during this transference of power, we shall be responsible.

The views of the anti-Zionist Lords prevailed. In the division, sixty Peers voted against the Balfour Declaration, and only twenty-nine for it.

On the day after the Lords debate, Hubert Young warned Churchill, in a departmental minute, that the anti-Zionist vote 'will have encouraged the Arab Delegation to persist in their obstinate attitude'. Unless the Lords' vote could be 'signally overruled' by the House of Commons, he wrote, 'we must be prepared for trouble when the Delegation gets back to Palestine'. Young feared an Arab policy of 'non-cooperation' with the British, if the Balfour Declaration were not specifically upheld in the Commons.

Churchill spoke in defence of the Zionists on July 4, telling the House of Commons:

... anyone who has visited Palestine recently must have seen how parts of the desert have been converted into gardens, and how material improvement has been effected in every respect by the Arab population dwelling around. On the sides of the hills there are enormous systems of terraces, and they are now the abode of an active cultivating population; whereas before, under centuries of Turkish and Arab rule, they had relapsed into a wilderness.

There is no doubt whatever that in that country there is room for still further energy and development if capital and other forces be allowed to play their part.

There is no doubt that there is room for a far larger number of people, and this far larger number of people will be able to lead far more decent and prosperous lives.

Apart from this agricultural work – this reclamation work – there are services which science, assisted by outside capital, can render, and of all the enterprises of importance which would have the effect of greatly enriching the land none was greater than the scientific storage and regulation of the waters of the Jordan for the provision of cheap power and light needed for the industry of Palestine, as well as water for the irrigation of new lands now desolate.

The granting of the Rutenberg concession did not involve, Churchill said, 'injustice to a single individual'; it did not take away 'one scrap of what was there before', and it offered to all the inhabitants of Palestine 'the assurance of a greater prosperity and the means of a higher economic and social life'. Churchill then asked the House of Commons:

Was not this a good gift which the Zionists could bring with them, the consequences of which spreading as years went by in general easement and amelioration – was not this a good gift which would impress more than anything else on the Arab population that the Zionists were their friends and helpers, not their expellers and expropriators, and that the earth was a generous mother, that Palestine had before it a bright future, and that there was enough for all?

Were we wrong in carrying out the policy of the nation and of Parliament in fixing upon this development of the waterways and the water power of Palestine as the main and principal means by which we could fulfil our undertaking?

Critics of the Rutenberg concession had insisted that it was for the Arab majority to develop the economic wealth of Palestine. Churchill sought to rebut this argument:

I am told that the Arabs would have done it themselves. Who is going to believe that? Left to themselves, the Arabs of Palestine would not in a thousand years have taken effective steps towards the irrigation and electrification of Palestine.

They would have been quite content to dwell – a handful of philosophic people – in the wasted sun-scorched plains, letting the waters of the Jordan continue to flow unbridled and unharnessed into the Dead Sea.

It was the non-commercial aspect of the Rutenberg concession which Churchill wished to stress, for it revealed an aspect of Zionism which had made a profound impression on him. The offer of a major concession in Palestine, he pointed out, had 'fallen extremely flat outside the circles of the Zionist followers'. He continued:

Nearly all the money got up to the present time has come from associations of a Jewish character, which are almost entirely on a non profit-making basis.

I have no doubt whatever – and, after all, do not let us be too ready to doubt people's ideals – that profit-making, in the ordinary sense, has played no part at all in the driving force on which we must rely to carry through this irrigation scheme in Palestine. I do not believe it has been so with Mr Rutenberg, nor do I believe that this concession would secure the necessary funds were it not supported by sentimental and quasi-religious emotions.

Churchill continued his speech with a defence of Rutenberg himself: 'He is a Jew. I cannot deny that. I do not see why that should be a cause of reproach. . . .' And he then declared: 'It is hard enough, in all conscience, to make a New Zion, but if, over the portals of the new Jerusalem, you are going to inscribe the legend, "No Israelite need apply", then I hope the House will permit me to confine my attention exclusively to Irish matters.'

Churchill then appealed to the House of Commons to allow the Government 'to use Jews, and use Jews freely, within limits that are proper, to develop new sources of wealth in Palestine'. It was also imperative, if the Balfour Declaration's 'pledges to the Zionists' were to be carried out, for the House of Commons to reverse the vote of the House of Lords.

The House divided at the end of Churchill's speech. His appeal was successful. Only thirty-five votes were cast against the Government's Palestine policy, and 292 in favour.

The success of the Rutenberg Debate effectively freed the Colonial Office from the pressure of the anti-Zionists, and left the way clear for presenting the final terms of the Mandate to the League of Nations. On July 5 Churchill telegraphed Sir Wyndham Deedes – who was administering the Government of Palestine in Samuel's absence – that the House of Commons vote 'has directly reversed House of Lords resolution'. As a result, 'every effort will be made to get terms of mandate approved by Council of League of Nations at forthcoming session and policy will be vigorously pursued'.

On July 22 the League of Nations approved the Palestine Mandate. Henceforth, the anti-Zionists, however strongly they expressed their criticisms, could not uproot the Jewish National Home. 'I am more pleased than I can say at the

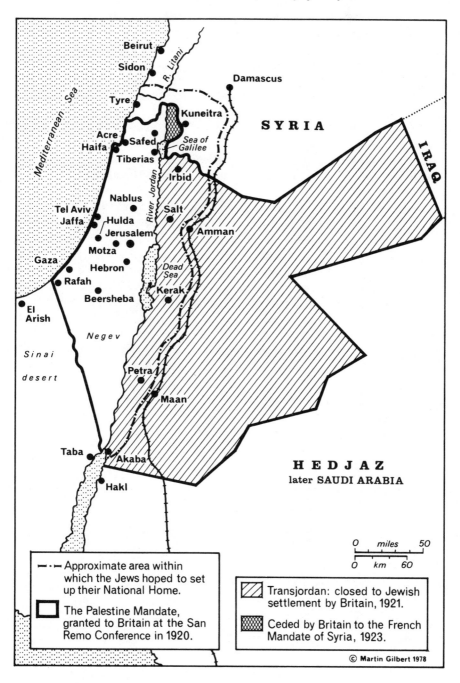

Beirut

Sidon

R. Litani

Damascus

Tyre

Kuneitra

SYRIA

Acre

Sea of Galilee

Safed

Haifa

Tiberias

River Jordan

IRAQ

Irbid

Nablus

Tel Aviv

Salt

Jaffa

Hulda

Jerusalem

Amman

Motza

Gaza

Dead Sea

Hebron

Rafah

Kerak

Beersheba

El Arish

Negev

Sinai

desert

Petra

Maan

Taba

Akaba

HEDJAZ

later **SAUDI ARABIA**

Hakl

Mediterranean Sea

O   miles   50

O   km   60

— · — Approximate area within which the Jews hoped to set up their National Home.

The Palestine Mandate, granted to Britain at the San Remo Conference in 1920.

Transjordan: closed to Jewish settlement by Britain, 1921.

Ceded by Britain to the French Mandate of Syria, 1923.

© Martin Gilbert 1978

passing of the Mandate,' Colonel Meinertzhagen wrote in his diary that night. 'It will once and for all convince the Arabs and their anti-Zionist friends that the Zionist policy has come to stay and that all their obstruction has been of no avail.'

The terms of the Mandate were powerful aids to the fulfilment of Zionism. Under Article 4 the Zionist Organization was recognized as the 'appropriate Jewish agency', to work with the British Government 'to secure the co-operation of all Jews who are willing to assist in the establishment of a Jewish national home'. Article 6 instructed the Palestine Administration both to 'facilitate' Jewish immigration, and to 'encourage' close settlement by Jews on the land, 'including State lands and waste lands not required for public purposes'. Under Article 22, Hebrew, as well as English and Arabic, was to be an 'official language' of Palestine.

On the evening of 22 July Arthur Ruppin was sitting in his study in Jerusalem when Eliezer Ben Yehuda, the pioneer of modern spoken Hebrew, came to see him in a state of great excitement. It was more than forty years since Ben Yehuda had come to live in Palestine; now he had just seen a telegram which had arrived from London, announcing that the League of Nations had just confirmed Britain's Palestine Mandate. 'The Ben Yehudas were elated,' Ruppin recorded in his diary, telling him, in Hebrew: *now we are in our own country.*' But Ruppin himself was hesitant. 'I could not share their enthusiasm,' he wrote. 'One is not allocated a fatherland by means of diplomatic resolutions.' And he added: 'If we do not acquire Palestine economically by means of work and if we do not win the friendship of the Arabs, our position under the Mandate will be no better than it was before.'

13

Persecutions,
Riots and Refugees
1923-1933

T HE granting of the Palestine Mandate to Britain provided a major stimulus
to Zionist enterprise and development. But it neither lessened Arab
opposition to Zionism, nor improved the lot of Jews elsewhere. Throughout 1923
the Jews of the Soviet Union found their independent activities curtailed: the
Jewish Social-Democratic Party was declared illegal, and all Jewish self-defence
groups disbanded. In Germany, a new wave of anti-semitism was witnessed by
Arthur Ruppin, who wrote in his diary on 30 October 1923, while in Munich, of
how the 'anti-Semitic administration in Bavaria expelled about seventy of the
350 East European Jews from Bavaria during the past two weeks, and it is said
that the rest will also be expelled before too long'.

Throughout the world, the Jewish fate was still surrounded by uncertainty; in
1924 even the United States Government gave persecuted Jewry cause for
concern, with the introduction of a new Quota Act, which severely restricted
immigration into the United States. By its reliance upon national quotas, this
Act fell particularly harshly on potential Jewish immigrants, the majority of
whom were from a very small number of countries, and in particular from Poland,
whose quota was quickly filled. So effective was this new legislation that, in 1925,
more Jews were able to enter Palestine than the United States, and did so.

But even Jewish settlement in Palestine was subject to increasing difficulties,
both economic and political. 'What continually worries me,' Arthur Ruppin
wrote in his diary on the last day of 1924, 'is the relationship between the Jews
and Arabs in Palestine. Superficially, it has improved, inasmuch as there is no
danger of pogroms, but the two peoples have become more estranged in their
thinking. Neither has any understanding of the other. . . .' The Palestinian Arab
Congress had, indeed, already specifically rejected any such understanding: on
6 October 1924, in a report to the Permanent Mandates Commission of the
League of Nations, the Congress had gone so far as to declare:

The daily slight frictions between Arab and Jew, whose ideas, principles,
customs and modes of life take diametrically divergent lines cultivate and solidify
hatred between both communities, and there must come a time when it will
accumulate to such a degree as to defy all moral or political restraints.

It is a gross error to believe that Arab and Jew may come to an understanding if only each of them exchanges his coat of extremism for another of moderation. When the principles underlying two movements do clash, it is futile to expect their meeting halfway.

On 1 April 1925 the Hebrew University of Jerusalem was finally inaugurated: the culmination of more than three decades of Zionist hopes and preparation. Yet even this event could not escape the growing Arab discontent, and Balfour, who had come specially to Jerusalem for the ceremony, was allowed neither to listen to the Christian Arab choirboys at St George's Cathedral, nor to enter the Moslem Arab sanctuary on the Temple Mount.

In the autumn of 1925 Arthur Ruppin took the initiative in trying to bring Jews and Arabs together by means of a new organization, Brit Shalom. 'We want to prepare the ground', he wrote in his diary on November 18, 'for an understanding between Jews and Arabs,' under the watchword: 'Palestine, a Bi-national State'. But, from the outset, the Arab leaders rejected even this attempt at conciliation.

During 1926 the economic situation in Palestine worsened; unemployment rose, and many Jews returned to Europe. 'With the means at our disposal,' Ruppin noted in his diary on 1 January 1927, 'it may be possible to provide a livelihood for 2-3,000 immigrants a year, but we want to bring in 25-30,000! I cannot see how Zionism can make any progress with no more than its present financial resources.'

In Europe, anti-semitism continued to provoke violent attacks against Jews and their property: in 1926 it erupted again in Rumania. In Palestine, the Jewish sense of unity was strengthened by the apparent undiminished hostility of the local British officials. On 10 January 1927 a British supporter of Zionism, Josiah Wedgwood, wrote to the Viceroy of India, Lord Irwin:

We have a very second rate lot of officials in Palestine, lazy, blind and sulky. We foolishly recruited them from Egypt and they talk and think Levantine French. . . .

I am shortly off to Bucharest to tell them what I think about Dagos who persecute Jews. I have become a sort of patron saint among the Jews, who will I believe soon bracket me with Cyrus and Lord Balfour!

'If you get a chance on your way back,' Wedgwood added, 'stop off at Palestine and go to see the new Jewish colonies. They are really remarkable – an agricultural population with their heads up.'

In 1928 the British Cabinet considered a request by the Zionist Organization for a British Government loan. The money would be used, Dr Weizmann explained in a note of January 21, 'for the sole purpose of promoting and expediting close settlement by Jews on the land, as contemplated by the Mandate'. This request was supported by Lord Balfour, who informed his Cabinet colleagues on March 5 that he was 'not so sure' that since 1920 Britain had in fact carried out its obligations to the Jews 'in a very generous spirit'. It was not Britain, he wrote, which had as yet provided either money or immigrants: 'The supply of money is due to Jewish idealism; the supply of immigrants is due to Jewish idealism combined with Jewish misery.'

Balfour pointed out that the Jews had already put money into Palestine to benefit all its inhabitants. He gave, as an example, the £100,000 a year spent on sanitation by the Jewish National Fund, 'though the whole community (and not the Jews only) benefit by it'. In other colonial and dependent territories such work was either not done, or was paid for out of taxes levied on all the inhabitants. Both Leopold Amery – then Colonial Secretary – and Winston Churchill – then Chancellor of the Exchequer – supported the proposed Zionist loan. But the Cabinet rejected it; and, in doing so, marked a step away from what had earlier been regarded as one of Britain's obligations under the National Home provisions of the Mandate.

In Palestine itself there was a serious increase in Arab hostility against the Jews during 1928. Even the Muslim Holy Places were said to be threatened, and on September 8 the Mufti submitted a memorandum to the Palestine Government warning of 'the unlimited greedy aspirations of the Jews', whose aim, he declared was, 'to take possession of the Mosque Al-Aqsa'. On September 23, when the Jews put up a screen at the wailing wall to divide the men from the women, the Mufti again declared that 'the Jews' aim is to take possession of the Mosque of Al-Aqsa gradually'.

Three days later on November 1, the Mufti presided over a Moslem Conference which urged restrictions on Jewish worship at the wailing wall, including preventing the Jews 'from raising their voices or making speeches'.

Disturbances at the wall itself continued, and on 11 June 1929 the High Commissioner wrote to the Mufti, defending the right of the Jews 'to conduct their worship' as in the past. But growing tension between the two communities led, on August 23, to an attack by crowds of Arabs on individual unarmed Jews in the Old City of Jerusalem. According to the Official Report of the Shaw Commission of Enquiry, 'large sections of these crowds were bent on mischief if not on murder'.

Arab attacks on Jews spread throughout Palestine. When news of the violence in Jerusalem reached Hebron, the Jewish school there was attacked, and a Jew killed. On August 25 a large Arab mob made what the Shaw Report described as 'a most ferocious attack' on the Jewish quarter. 'This savage attack,' the Report continued, 'of which no condemnation can be too severe, was accompanied by wanton destruction and looting.' Within five hours, more than sixty Jews had been killed, including many women and children. In the village of Motza, just inside Jerusalem, 'the horrors of Hebron were repeated on a smaller scale', leaving six Jewish men, women and children dead, their bodies mutilated in their homes. On August 26, 'Arab mobs', as the Shaw Report described them, killed and wounded forty-five Jews in Safed. In the suburbs of Jerusalem more than 4,000 Jews were forced to leave their homes, many of which were looted.

When the attacks ended at nightfall on August 29, 133 Jews had been killed. Eighty-seven Arabs had also died, mostly shot by British troops and police seeking to halt the violence. 'In a few instances', the Shaw Report noted, 'Jews attacked Arabs and destroyed Arab property. These attacks, though inexcusable, were in most cases in retaliation for wrongs already committed by Arabs.' As for Press incitements before the riots, the Report concluded that the 'worst offenders' were 'a number of newspapers published in Arabic', which were not only provocative, but even 'reproduced extracts from that discredited work, the *Protocols of the Learned Elders of Zion*'. Above all: 'among the members of the various Moslem associations in Palestine were many whose desire to see the adoption of more violent methods than the Executive officially countenanced led them as individuals to prosecute among the more ignorant Arab people a campaign of propaganda calculated to excite them'.

The Arabs had also been alarmed, the Shaw Report noted, by the Zionist decision to enlarge the Jewish Agency by what was considered to be 'a strong body of wealthy non-Zionists who were expected to provide funds for the futher Zionist activities in Palestine'. News that the Jewish Agency had in fact been enlarged had 'spread quickly and was, in our opinion, a cause of increased apprehension and alarm among all classes of Arabs'.

How far the Mufti himself was involved in the disturbances was a matter of dispute. The Commission of Enquiry devoted eight pages to showing that he had 'cooperated with the Government in their efforts both to restore peace and to prevent the extension of disorder'. But one member of the Commission, Henry Snell, dissented, and, in a 'note of reservation' published with the Report, he wrote, of the Mufti:

I have not the least doubt that he was aware of the nature of the anti-Zionist campaign which was conducted by some of his followers and that he realised the danger of disturbance which is never absent when religious propaganda of an exciting character is spread among a Moslem people.

I therefore attribute to the Mufti a greater share in the responsibility for the disturbance than is attributed to him in the report.

I am of the opinion that the Mufti must bear the blame for his failure to make any effort to control the character of an agitation conducted in the name of a religion of which in Palestine he was the head.

Despite the end of the killing, the propaganda continued. 'O Arab!', declared a Jerusalem Arab students' leaflet widely circulated on 11 September 1929, 'Remember that the Jew is your strongest enemy and the enemy of your ancestors since olden times. Do not be misled by his tricks, for it is he who tortured Christ (peace be upon him), and poisoned Mohammed (peace and worship be with him).' The leaflet urged an Arab boycott of all Jewish trade, in order 'to save yourself and your Fatherland from the grasp of the foreign intruder and greedy Jew'.

The British were well aware of the nature of Arab propaganda. As early as September 5 the Officer Commanding the Troops in Palestine had telegraphed to the War Office in London with details of a manifesto 'full of falsehoods and inflammatory material which has been issued to Moslems in other countries'. Two weeks later, on September 29, the new High Commissioner, Sir John Chancellor, telegraphed to the Colonial Office:

... the latent deep-seated hatred of the Arabs for the Jews has now come to the surface in all parts of the country. Threats of renewed attacks upon the Jews are being freely made and are only being prevented by visible presence of considerable military force.

Chancellor went on to point out:

Propaganda against immigration of Jews with Palestine has recently been conducted amongst Arabs in neighbouring countries on an extensive scale, and if there is any recrudescence of the disturbances in Palestine it is doubtful if incursions into Palestine by Arabs from beyond the frontier could again be prevented.

That same day, September 29, the President of the Arab Executive in Palestine, Musa Kazim Pasha, warned a senior British official in Palestine that unless the Jewish National Home policy was changed, 'there would be an armed uprising'. Musa Kazim Pasha added that such an uprising would involve, not only the Arabs of Palestine but 'participation of Moslems from Syria, Transjordan and perhaps Iraq'.

In a further telegram to the Colonial Office on October 12, Sir John Chancellor pointed out that the Arabs of Palestine had recently obtained 'a considerable number of arms' from both Transjordan and the Hedjaz. Further arms were known to have come from Syria. A week later Chancellor noted that opinion of the 'ignorant Arab masses' was being deliberately inflamed by those who were 'ill-disposed' towards the Mandate, while on October 26 a Police Report warned that 'gangs of criminals to attack Jews and British officials have been formed and will first function in areas at Haifa and Nablus'.

The Jews were shaken by the intensity of the Arab violence, but determined not to surrender all that they had created in the past fifty years. On October 25, after a visit to one of the Jewish villages destroyed, Arthur Ruppin wrote in his diary:

On Tuesday, I went from Tel Aviv to visit Huldah, most of which was destroyed and burnt to ashes during the disturbances. Many of the trees have also been burnt. There is nobody there. The place makes a terrible impression.

I remembered what hopes we had when we built the first house there twenty years ago. But I was not depressed: we shall rebuild what has been destroyed. On the whole, it is strange that I am one of the few optimists. I have a profound mystical belief that our work in Palestine cannot be destroyed.

In Ruppin's view, a Jewish community in Palestine would not only continue to exist, but would also 'animate Jewry in the Diaspora'.

As a result of the 1929 violence the British Government set up a Commission of Enquiry, headed by Sir Walter Shaw, to examine the causes of Arab unrest. On 18 December 1929 the Commission examined a senior member of the Zionist Executive, Harry Sacher, who told them, emphatically, that the 'Jews have no intention of dominating or being dominated in respect of any other people in this country. They look upon their own right to create their own civilization as being neither greater nor less than the right of the Arabs to create their civilizatio.'

Among the other Zionists who gave evidence was Arthur Ruppin, who told the Commissioners – as he noted in his diary on December 31 – 'that enough land would become available for Jewish settlement' as the Arab farmers 'changed over to intensive farming', a change-over which they would be able to afford 'with the money they would acquire through selling part of their land to the Jews'.

Published in March 1930, the Shaw Report made it clear that British opinion was swinging slowly but definitely against the Zionists. According to its conclusion: 'the claims and demands which from the Zionist side have been advanced in regard to the future of Jewish immigration into Palestine have been such as to arouse among Arabs the apprehension that they will in time be deprived of their livelihood and pass under the political domination of the Jews.' The Report continued: 'There is incontestable evidence that in the matter of immigration there has been a serious departure by the Jewish authorities from the doctrine accepted by the Zionist Organization in 1922 that immigration should be regulated by the economic capacity of Palestine to absorb new arrivals.'

The Shaw Report recommended an early declaration of the British Government as to the policy which was to be pursued 'in regard to the regulation and control of future Jewish immigration into Palestine'. But was even this what the Arabs required? On 1 May 1930 the Colonial Secretary in the Labour Government, Lord Passfield, after a meeting with an Arab delegation headed by Musa Kazim Pasha and the Grand Mufti, Haj Amin, told the Cabinet's Palestine Committee that 'briefly, the Arabs did not accept the Mandate, wished for the abandonment of the Balfour Declaration, demanded the establishment of democratic institutions and the prohibition of the sale of land to the Jews'. Passfield also told his colleagues, as the minutes recorded:

The Jews had in the past purchased and drained small uninhabited tracts of swamp where they had formed colonies, which, although not yet self-supporting, were still being maintained. The acquisition and draining of such land was beyond the present means of the Arabs, and might be permitted in future.

Another point to be noted was that the Arab population was increasing more rapidly than the Jews.

At present it appeared that all we could tell the Arabs was that their representations were viewed with sympathy, that the question of land was being carefully enquired into, and that there was no intention of allowing them to be dispossessed ... one of the great difficulties was the nomad Arab population, numbering some 100,000. These Arabs wandered over the country, and their goats committed serious depredations.

A second official report, written by Sir John Hope-Simpson, was issued in October 1930. Instructed to examine Shaw's conclusions in detail, it concluded that, given existing Arab farming methods, there was insufficient land in Palestine to meet the needs of Jewish immigrants. Based on this second report, the Government issued a White Paper intimating that future Jewish immigration might have to be curtailed even more rigorously than in the past. The Zionists were dismayed, and Weizmann himself resigned as President of the Zionist Organization and the Jewish Agency. At a meeting with the Colonial Secretary, Lord Passfield, and the Foreign Secretary, Arthur Henderson, on November 17, Weizmann declared: 'We feel our work in Palestine has been during the last few years constantly subjected to scrutiny and enquiry. It is like a plant which is being constantly taken out of the soil to look at its roots; it is not very good for the plant.'

At a second meeting between Passfield, Henderson and the Zionist leaders on November 18, Weizmann warned that two-thirds of the Jewish people 'live under conditions which, without any attempt on my part to harass your feelings, are such as to destroy slowly but surely the vital elements of a great race'. The mass of Jews in those lands were eager to emigrate. Both Poland and Rumania had instituted anti-semitic policies, and declared that they had 'too many' Jews. In Turkey, and in Arab countries, the Jews were likewise 'seeking an outlet', and yet, Weizmann continued: 'While they are seeking an outlet every door of those countries into which the Jews emigrated in the past is gradually being closed before them: America, South Africa, Canada, Mexico, each used to be a country of immigration; they are closed now. . . .'

A few moments later, Arthur Henderson asked Weizmann whether it was 'anti-racial', or economic, causes that barred the Jews' way. It was both, Weizmann replied, and he went on:

We have, throughout our history, not disappeared among the nations with whom we have lived. We have remained different; different in religion, different in outlook, and we have therefore been placed as a minority among the people with whom we have lived; they belong in the majority, we were placed in a position which rendered us economically inferior to that majority, so a complex situation has been produced which, as I said, in its external effects moves the Jews to go from one country to another, and today the world is closed to our emigration;

155

with the possible exception of Brazil and Argentina, and with the possible exception of a small infiltration into any other country, there is no room in the world for the mass of Jews who can find no room in their respective countries.

The moral effect of this situation has combined with an age-long tradition of attachment to Palestine, a tradition which forms an integral part of our religion, a tradition which, I think, has made us what we are; a stubborn, stiffnecked attachment to a country which many of us have not seen, but which has been the central part of our history, which has made us look upon Palestine as the country where we wanted to find the realisation of an age long dream.

Following Weizmann's protests, Ramsay MacDonald agreed to abandon the immigration clauses of the 1930 White Paper. Even so, in the letter which he wrote to Weizmann and which he read out in the House of Commons on 13 February 1931, MacDonald warned that if, in consequence of the existing Zionist policy of only using Jewish labour, Arab labour were to be replaced 'that is a factor in the situation which the Mandatory is bound to have regard'.

In spite of MacDonald's 'retraction', the situation inside Palestine was worrying the Zionists. On 3 December 1931 Arthur Ruppin wrote to a friend: 'Undoubtedly the Arabs have greatly strengthened their political position during the past few years and are much less ready to make concessions to the Jews than they were ten years ago,' Ruppin no longer saw any hope in reliance upon Arab goodwill. His letter continued:

At most, the Arabs would agree to grant national rights to the Jews in an Arab state, on the pattern of the national rights in Eastern Europe. But we know only too well from conditions in Eastern Europe how little a majority with executive power can be moved to grant real and complete national equality to a minority. The fate of the Jewish minority in Palestine would always be dependent upon the goodwill of the Arab majority, which would steer the state.

To the Jews of Eastern Europe, who form the overwhelming majority of all the Zionists, such a settlement would be completely unsatisfactory, and it would kill their enthusiasm for the Zionist cause and for Palestine. A movement which would agree to such a compromise with the Arabs would not be supported by the East European Jews and would very soon become a *Zionism without Zionists.* . . .

On the last day of 1931 Ruppin wrote, pessimistically, that it was in his view 'doubtful whether a Jewish minority will be able to preserve its national individuality and independence against an arab majority if the latter controls the machinery of state'. His pessimism was fully justified, for three months later, on 9 April 1932, the new British High Commissioner in Palestine, Sir Arthur Wauchope, telegraphed to the Colonial Office: 'I have learnt from my private conversations that the Jews' objection to any Legislative Council is due to belief that the Arab leaders chiefly desire a Legislative Council in order to check the advancement of a National Home for the Jews. They are not altogether incorrect in this belief.'

The reiterated Arab demand for a Legislative Assembly, coupled with Arab hostility to Jewish immigration, led the British to adopt a policy of cautious verbal restraint. On April 12, at a meeting of the Cabinet's Committee on Palestine, the official minutes recorded general agreement with the view 'that considerable embarrassment had been caused by past pronouncements of a too specific and definite nature, and that it would be desirable to publish as little as possible with regard to the Government's intentions'.

On 30 January 1933 Adolf Hitler became German Chancellor, and anti-semitism took on an open, official, and hysterical tone. 'From a moral point of view,' Arthur Ruppin noted in his diary on February 14, 'the situation of the Jews in Germany is frightful. A catastrophic collapse of all the hopes of the liberal Jews to assimilate among the German people.' On March 21 the British Ambassador in Berlin, Sir Horace Rumbold, informed the Foreign Secretary, Sir John Simon, of how the Jews had been singled out for ill-treatment and abuse. Bruno Walter, the conductor, had been prevented from conducting a concert at Leipzig, while all over Germany Jewish musicians were dismissed from orchestras, Jewish actors driven off the stage, and Jewish judges refused entry into court. 'Dreadful things happen all the time,' Rumbold's wife wrote to her mother on March 22, 'and as the press is muzzled are never heard by the public. All sorts of terrorising of Jews and Socialists, and 40,000 are supposed to be in prison ... endless writers and professors, etc., are persecuted, whilst old government officials are ruthlessly turned out, often without pensions. It is hateful and uncivilized!'

On March 28 Rumbold sent Simon a further report of the 'gross injustice' to which the Jews were being subjected. 'Throughout the public services,' he wrote, 'they are being systematically removed from their posts.' Two days later he wrote again, giving Simon details of a Manifesto which had just been issued by the Nazis, in which local organizations throughout Germany were instructed 'to carry on anti-Jewish propaganda among the people'. Typical of the daily anti-semitic actions, Rumbold reported, Lion Feuchtwanger, the distinguished Jewish writer, had had all his literary manuscripts seized.

For the Jews of Germany, the advent of Hitler was the beginning of a new and terrible era, accentuated at the end of March by the announcement of a total boycott of all Jewish shops to be held on April 1. In vain did the Italian Ambassador in Berlin urge Hitler to desist from this measure. But Hitler told the Ambassador that, unlike Mussolini, he had studied the Jewish question 'for long years, from every angle, like no one else'. In five or six hundred years, Hitler predicted with what he called 'absolute certainty', his name would be honoured in all lands 'as the man who once and for all exterminated the Jewish pest from the world'.

The anti-Jewish boycott took place on 1 April 1933, a black day for Germany's half million Jews. Not only Jewish-owned shops, but Jewish doctors and lawyers, and Jewish-owned cafes, were to be shunned and abused. On the following day Lady Rumbold wrote to her mother:

I *fully* intended to go into a shop to buy something even if it was picketed by Nazis. We tried Wertheimer, a dense crowd was standing at each entrance and in front of the doors 2 or 3 Nazis aggressively blocking the way. We saw that it was impossible without making a scene to push past. We then went down the Kurfurstendam. Nearly every other shop is Jew there. We walked along with the crowds. The shops were mostly open, but in front of each Jew shop were 2 or 3 stalwart Nazis standing blocking the door. . . .
Obviously no one felt inclined to make a scene or provoke an incident. So the crowds just processed along, and the Nazis just terrorized and dominated!
On every Jew shop was plastered a large notice warning the public not to buy in Jewish shops. In many cases special notices were put up saying that sweated labour was employed in that particular shop, and often you saw caricatures of Jewish noses. It was utterly cruel and Hunnish the whole thing, just doing down a heap of defenceless people. Also any number of cafes were placarded, and of course quite empty. Then on the address plates at the entrances of blocks of flats of Jewish doctors, lawyers, or businessmen were plastered with these placards.

Three days later Lady Rumbold added: 'To see people pilloried in this fashion, a very large number of them quite harmless, hardworking people, was altogether revolting, and it left a very nasty taste in the mouth. I shall never forget it.'

On an almost daily basis, Sir Horace Rumbold continued to inform the British Foreign Office of further terror measures against the Jews. 'Large concentration camps,' he wrote on April 5, 'are being established in various parts of the country, one camp near Munich being sufficiently large to hold 5,000 prisoners.' This was Dachau, in which thousands of Jews were to be tortured, and several hundred murdered, even before the outbreak of war; and in which tens of thousands were to be murdered, and starved to death, during the war years.

The terror was not confined to the new camps. On April 8 the *Manchester Guardian*, which had followed closely the advent of Nazi Germany, informed its readers of how, in many villages, atrocious scenes had taken place. The paper gave the following example, among several:

A few days ago a man was sentenced to a year's imprisonment for spreading the 'false rumour' that a Jew had been hanged by Brown shirts – the 'rumour', as a matter of fact, was true: the Jew, a certain Mr ——, was beaten by Brown Shirts and hanged by his feet, so that his head was suspended off the ground. When the Brown Shirts had finished with him he was dead.

The first British Cabinet Committee to discuss the question of a new rush of refugees from Germany had met on April 7. It concluded that, so far as Palestine was concerned, 'the number of Jewish refugees who could be allowed to enter the country is strictly conditioned by what the country can absorb. The matter is strictly one for the High Commissioner, but there is no reason to suppose that room could be found in Palestine in the near future for any appreciable number of German Jewish refugees.' In answer to another question that had been raised during the Cabinet Committee, it was decided, according to the official minutes of the meeting, that, 'The number of refugees who might be transmigrated to the Colonies generally, must be treated as negligible.'

On 18 August 1933 the Home Secretary, Sir Samuel Hoare, who was a member of the Cabinet Committee on refugees, sought the opinion of the new Viceroy of India, Lord Willingdon, as to the possibility of at least 'a few' German Jewish doctors being found employment in India. But Willingdon was sceptical, replying ten days later: 'I personally feel perfectly sure that it will be little use any of these gentlemen coming out to try and get useful employment in India.' Later, when Sir Samuel Hoare spoke to the President of the Royal College of Physicians, Lord Dawson of Penn, on November 23, about the possibility of German Jewish refugee doctors being allowed into Britain, Lord Dawson told him, according to Hoare's note of the conversation, that 'the number that could usefully be absorbed or teach us anything could be counted on the fingers of one hand'.

The new German persecutions, combined with the continuing anti-Jewish feelings in Poland and Rumania, did lead, however, to a great influx of Jews into Palestine. By the end of 1933, the number of Jews reaching Palestine exceeded 30,000 for that year alone, the highest annual figure of the Mandate years. Of these 13,000 were from Poland, over 5,000 from Germany. The Jewish population now stood at more than 230,000, nearly 20 per cent of the total. For the Zionists, the arrival of large numbers of refugees seemed to be a hopeful sign, for the future of Palestinian Jewry as well as for the immediate needs of those who were in search of a home free from persecution. 'If we could work at this pace for another five years,' Ruppin noted in his diary on December 31, 'we would reach the figure of almost 500,000 and then we would no longer have to live in fear, as we do today, that a serious Arab revolt would ruin all our work.'

14

'Formidable in Action. . .
Strong in Restraint'
1933-1937

IMMEDIATELY following the Nazi victory in Germany, Arab protests against Jewish immigration to Palestine were renewed. In March 1933, in a manifesto issued in Jerusalem by the Arab Executive Committee, it was announced that 'the general tendency of Jews to take possession of the lands of this holy country and their streaming into it by hundreds and thousands through legal and illegal means has terrified the country'. The manifesto called on all Arabs 'to get ready for the serious acts which will be imposed' at the forthcoming Assembly to be held in Jaffa; on March 26 this Assembly, at which Haj Amin, the Mufti of Jerusalem, was predominant, ordered 'the immediate execution' of a boycott of all 'Zionist goods, products and commercial premises'.

The Jews did not allow themselves to be intimidated or deterred, but began to augment the arms supplies which, since the riots of 1929, they had been building up for their own defence. In August 1933 the Zionist Congress in Prague demanded that the Jewish National Home should be built up 'as speedily as possible and on the largest scale'. Within a month, Musa Kazim Pasha, the President of the Arab Executive, demanded an immediate halt to all Jewish immigration, and, in the last week of October, Arabs attacked public buildings and the police in Nablus, Jaffa and Jerusalem. In the resulting violence, one policeman and twenty-six rioters were killed; the Arabs had decided to challenge both the British and the Jews.

In 1934 a further 42,000 Jews entered Palestine, in 1935 more than 61,000. Both figures were 'records': that of 1935 was more than double that of 1933. Two years later the Palestine Royal Commission headed by Lord Peel commented:

So far from reducing economic absorptive capacity, immigration increased it. The more immigrants came in, the more work they created for local industries to meet their needs, especially in building: and more work meant more room for immigrants under the 'labour schedule'. Unless, therefore, the Government adopted a more restrictive policy, or unless there were some economic or financial set-back, there seemed no reason why the rate of immigration should not go on climbing up and up.

Parallel with the activities of the Zionists, a new organization led by Vladimir Jabotinsky, the Revisionist Movement, began to press for even more rapid Jewish immigration, and for immediate Jewish settlement, not only in Palestine, but also in Transjordan. In 1934 the Revisionists brought to Palestine a ship with 117 'illegal' Jewish immigrants: their first venture in a move which was to see fifteen more ships set off that same year from the ports of the Black Sea towards Palestine. Other 'illegals' were also brought by private organizations, and by the Mosad Aliyah, a Zionist-sponsored organization. In the six years between 1934 and 1939, nearly fifty ships in all made the hazardous journey, many of them intercepted by the British Navy, and their human cargo either interned or deported.

The aims and methods both of the Zionists and of the Revisionists continued to rouse hostility and criticism in British circles: in a 'very secret' memorandum dated 28 March 1934, the then Colonial Secretary, Sir Philip Cunliffe-Lister, set out for his Cabinet colleagues, at their request, his view of the Palestine situation. Among the Jews, he wrote, 'illicit immigration' had assumed 'alarming proportions', and would be strictly combatted. His memorandum continued:

> But there is no use blinking the fact that to-day Arabs and Jews are diametrically opposed on the whole subject of immigration. The Arabs claim that nothing will satisfy them except a complete embargo on all further immigration; and Jewish extremists do not make matters easier by their claims to unlimited immigration, and by their avowed determination to make Palestine not merely a National Home, but a Jewish State. As I have warned my colleagues before, Arab hostility is to-day not merely hostility to the Jews, but hostility to the British Government as the authors of immigration.

Cunliffe-Lister went on to criticize the continuing Jewish Agency policy of employing only Jewish labour. Such a policy, he wrote, 'must tend to reduce Arab employment', even if the general influx of Jewish capital and trade led to greater import and export activity, with the creation of 'more employment for the Arabs' in the ports of Jaffa and Haifa. So important was this question, Cunliffe-Lister believed, that the only way to resolve 'the enmity between Arab and Jew' lay in the Jews 'abandoning the principle of the exclusive employment of Jews', and he added:

> Such a change of policy will be anathema to the Jewish extremists. It will be difficult for Jewish leaders who see its wisdom and necessity. The theme of the prospectus on which they raise money is 'Jewish money for Jewish settlers', and when even the moderate Jewish leader is appealing to his constituents, I have no doubt that the picture of the Jewish National Home often expands into one of the Jewish State.

Cunliffe-Lister regretted that whereas, in his private conversations with Weizmann, Sokolow, and Rutenberg in the summer of 1933, the Jewish leaders had seemed willing 'to modify their policy', Weizmann himself had recently, in public speeches, 'reaffirmed the principle of exclusive Jewish employment'. Cunliffe-Lister commented:

If the Arabs were cleverer propagandists, they could put their case against exclusive Jewish employment in a very telling way. They could say that the charge against Hitler is that he had refused Jews employment in Germany: is it reasonable that Jewish immigrants to Palestine, entering in increasing numbers, should refuse employment to the Arab population?

The Jews were caught in a dilemma. On the one hand, fearing a repetition of the Hebron, Safed and Motza massacres, they armed themselves, and, anxious to build a Jewish entity, and to increase the possibilities for Jewish immigration, they employed only Jews in the major Zionist enterprises. On the other hand, desirous of improving relations with the Arabs, in the autumn of 1935 they added 50 per cent to the land reserved for Arabs in the Huleh basin: land allocated to a Jewish group by the Administration. It was, above all, events in Germany which dominated Jewish thinking, making Palestine seem more than ever an essential focus of Jewish hopes. On 15 September 1935 a Nazi Convention, being held in Nuremberg, accepted two special statutes, known subsequently as the Nuremberg Laws, whereby no Jew could be a German citizen.

The Nuremberg Laws created, in Germany, a barrier between Jews and non-Jews that existed nowhere else in the modern world. Marriages between Jews and non-Jews were forbidden; extramarital relations between Jews and non-Jews were forbidden; nor could Jews employ any non-Jewish German women under the age of forty-five. In a series of thirteen specific regulations following on the Nuremberg Laws, Jews were barred from all official and professional life in Germany. On October 30 Winston Churchill wrote, in an article for the *Strand* magazine of how the Jews 'were to be stripped of all power, driven from every position in public and social life, expelled from the professions, silenced in the Press, and declared a foul and odious race'. Churchill continued, in a denunciation which provoked an immediate protest from Berlin:

The twentieth century has witnessed with surprise, not merely the promulgation of these ferocious doctrines, but their enforcement with brutal vigour by the Government and by the populace. No past services, no proved patriotism, even wounds sustained in war, could procure immunity for persons whose only crime was that their parents had brought them into the world. Every kind of persecution, grave or petty, upon the world-famous scientists, writers, and composers at the top down to the wretched little Jewish children in the national schools, was practised, was glorified, and is still being practised and glorified.

Churchill was not exaggerating; on November 12, a senior member of the British Mandate Administration in Palestine, Eric Mills, having completed a tour of Central Europe and Germany, wrote to the Chief Secretary in Jerusalem:

'While before I went to Germany I knew that the Jewish situation was bad, I had not realised as I now do, that the fate of German Jews is a tragedy, for which cold, intelligent planning by those in authority takes rank with that of those who are out of sympathy with the Bolshevik regime, in Russia; or with the elimination of Armenians from the Turkish empire.' Mills added: 'The Jew is to be eliminated and the state has no regard for the manner of his elimination.'

Since the achievement of German unity in 1870, the Jews of Germany had been loyal and valuable citizens, numbering more than half a million by 1914. In the days of the Kaiser they had contributed substantially to the prosperity, the culture and the welfare of the Empire. During the First World War 100,000 of them had served in the German army, and, among these, many had won the highest awards for courage. Twelve thousand had died on the field of battle. After the war the Jews had suffered, with their fellow non-Jews, all the rigours of inflation and economic chaos. In the fourteen years of the Weimar Republic, assimilation was widespread: by 1927 more than 44 per cent of all Jewish marriages were with non-Jews, and at least 1,000 Jews a year either converted to Christianity, or dissociated themselves from the community. The urge to be exemplary citizens was strong in them. But none of this counted against the vitriolic hatred which Nazism now aroused.

No Jew could escape the Nazi determination to drive the Jews from German life, and to make them suffer in the process. Neither assimilation nor conversion could act as a shield. The story of one Jewess is typical of many; Bertha Pappenheim was seventy-five years old when Hitler came to power. Her life had been devoted to the cause of German orphans and delinquent women. Since 1895 she had been a pioneer of women's social welfare. A prominent Jewess, she was strongly and openly opposed to Zionism. After 1933 she spoke out against the emigration of Jews from Germany, fearing its disruption on Jewish family life. But in 1936, aged seventy-eight, she was taken by the Gestapo 'for questioning', and died as a result of her interrogation.

Neither quality of past service, nor respected position in society; neither ability nor age, could protect a Jew in Nazi Germany. Everywhere, schoolchildren were taught that the Jewish people in their midst were the enemies of Germany. Villages competed with each other to declare themselves 'Jew-free'. And young men in uniform sang the new 'patriotic' songs, in which race hatred predominated. One of the most popular of these songs proclaimed:

> When Jewish blood spurts from the knife,
> Then all goes twice as well!

The Zionists were determined to establish the link between the anti-Jewish persecutions in Germany and the need to keep Palestine open for Jewish refugees. Among those who accepted this link was Churchill, who told the House of Commons on 24 March 1936:

... there is in our minds an added emphasis upon this question of Jewish migration which comes from other quarters, at a time when the Jewish race in a great country is being subjected to most horrible, cold, scientific persecution, brutal persecution, a cold 'pogrom' as it has been called – people reduced from affluence to ruin, and then, even in that position, denied the opportunity of earning their daily bread, and cut out even from relief by grants to tide the destitute through the winter; their little children pilloried in the schools to which they have to go; their blood and race declared defiling and accursed; every form of concentrated human wickedness cast upon these people by overwhelming power, by vile tyranny.

I say that, when that is the case, surely the House of Commons will not allow the one door which is open, the one door which allows some relief, some escape from these conditions, to be summarily closed, nor even allow it to be suggested that it may be obstructed by the course which we take now.

The British government still maintained its attitude that Palestine was not a suitable place for any substantial additional number of Jewish refugees. But the Palestinian Arabs made it clear that they were bitterly opposed to the idea of Palestine being made a haven for any more European refugees whatsoever: they regarded even the existing number as too large, pointing out that since 1933 the Jewish population of Palestine had increased from 230,000 to 400,000, reaching by 1936 one third of the total population of Palestine. In protest against any further Jewish immigration, the Arabs began a general strike on 15 April 1936, and on May 7 the Arab leaders, meeting in Jerusalem, demanded an immediate end to all Jewish immigration, a ban on any further Jewish land purchase, and an Arab majority Government. Jewish farms were attacked all over Palestine: Jewish houses were burnt, shops looted, and whole orchards destroyed. Attacks on individual Jews led, within a month, to the deaths of twenty-one Jews, several of them women and children.

The British responded to this Arab violence by announcing, on May 11, that they intended 'to suppress all outbreaks of lawlessness'; six Arab rioters had been killed by the police by the middle of May. The Jewish Agency urged the Jews to exercise restraint, and while Jews continued to be killed throughout Palestine – leading to a total death toll of eighty by October – no Jewish reprisals took place. British troops, however, killed more than 140 Arabs, and thirty-three British soldiers were killed, in a series of armed clashes with Arab bands.

For the Jews, it was galling to see what little effect the British protection could have. During the summer of 1936 thousands of Jewish acres were destroyed, Jews were killed while travelling in buses, or even sitting in their houses. On May 18 it was announced in the House of Commons that a Royal Commission would be set up to investigate the cause of unrest in Palestine, and on July 29 Lord Peel was chosen as Chairman, with Sir Horace Rumbold, the former British Ambassador to Berlin, as his deputy. On August 30 the Arab leaders announced that they would continue both with their strike, and with their campaign of violence, but the Commission decided nevertheless to go ahead with its deliberations. On September 4 the High Commissioner, Sir Arthur Wauchope, wrote to the new Colonial Secretary, William Ormsby Gore: 'From start to finish the Arab leaders have refused to face realities and made no effort to end methods of violence.'

On November 12 Sir Arthur Wauchope welcomed the Commissioners officially at Government House, in Jerusalem, pointing out in his speech that a Royal Commission was 'the highest form of inquiry known in the British Empire . . . impartial, independent and uncontrolled by the Government of the day'. Peel, in his reply, spoke of the Arab decision to boycott the inquiry. 'It would be most unfortunate,' he said, 'if without their advice and assistance we were compelled to arrive at conclusions and to make decisions.' But the Arabs insisted on staying away, refusing to participate in any discussions that might consolidate the Jewish National Home.

For two days the Commissioners made an extended tour of Palestine, visiting the main Arab centres, and several Jewish settlements, as well as Tel Aviv. John Martin, the Commission's Secretary, later recalled an incident which had, he believed, made a considerable emotional impact on Lord Peel and his colleagues. While visiting a Jewish agricultural settlement, the Commissioners had seen a man living in a rough hut, but with a piano, and musical scores. Sir Horace Rumbold was certain that he had met the man before. On asking his name, it appeared that he was a well-known German musician, from Leipzig, who had once played at the British Embassy in Berlin. 'We all felt uncomfortable about his plight,' Martin later recalled. Rumbold began to commiserate with the man. 'This is a terrible change for you,' he said, condoling. But the musician replied, to Rumbold's surprise: 'It *is* a change, from Hell to Heaven'.

On November 18, at the Commission's first public session, Eric Mills was examined about Jewish immigration. He informed the Commissioners that on his estimate there were, in mid-1936, 940,000 Arab and 370,000 Jews living in Palestine, and that 134,000 of the Jews had arrived since Hitler had come to power in Germany three and a half years before. Pressed to say how effective was the work of the British Passport Control Officers, who scrutinized potential Jewish immigrants in Warsaw and Berlin, Mills answered that it was as effective as need be.

On November 24, Lewis Andrews, the acting Director of the Department of Development for the Galilee District, told the Commissioners that although he and his officials had made every effort to collect evidence of the Arab charge that Arab farmers had been displaced by Jews, little evidence had been forthcoming. The Arabs had been invited, and encouraged to complain, but few had done so. 'The only answer I can give', Andrews told Lord Peel, 'is that there were not so many people displaced as we imagined.' He put the total figure at no more than two thousand, many of whom had found employment 'in other agricultural industries or in orange groves . . .'.

November 25 was given over to the evidence and cross-examination of Dr Weizmann. In a moving speech, Weizmann outlined the history and aims of Zionism. The Jewish problem, he said, was 'a problem of the homelessness of a people . . . almost everything to the east of the Rhine is today in a position politically and economically, which is, if I may say so – and I am not given to exaggeration – something which is neither life nor death. . .' . It was not only a German problem, he insisted. 'The German tragedy . . .', he continued, 'is in size much smaller than the Polish; it is of manageable proportions and, moreover, the German Jews are stronger, economically stronger; they can resist the on-slaught much better than the Polish Jews, who have been ground down now for almost a century. . . .'

Continuing his evidence, Weizmann spoke of the six million Jews of eastern and central Europe for whom, he said, 'the World is closed', and he drew the Commissioners' attention to the Polish assertion that there were 'a million Jews too many' in Poland alone. Why the one million figure had been chosen, out of Poland's three million Jews, he did not wish to discuss. But these millions, he said:

. . . are citizens of Poland; they have been connected with the fate and destinies of Poland for well nigh a thousand years. They went through all the vicissitudes through which the Polish nation went. They are out to make their contribution to Poland, good, bad or indifferent as everybody else. Why should they be singled out as being a million too many? . . .

What does it mean? Where can they go? Is there any place in the world which can rapidly absorb a million people whoever they may be, Jew or non-Jew? The poor Polish peasant, perhaps ignorant and not very subtle, when he hears his own Government making a pronouncement like that, may possibly interpret it as meaning 'Here is a superfluous people standing in my way, which must be got rid of somehow'.

Beyond Poland, Weizmann continued, were the Jews of Rumania, Latvia, Lithuania and Austria, where one found 'practically the same picture', an un-wanted people, and he went on:

. . . it is no exaggeration on my part to say that to-day almost six million Jews – I am not speaking of the Jews in Persia and Morocco and such like places, who are very inarticulate, one hears very little of them – there are in this part of the world six million people doomed to be pent up in places where they are not wanted, and for whom the world is divided into places where they cannot live, and places into which they cannot enter.

Weizmann went on to explain to the Commissioners the appeal of Palestine. 'We are a stiff-necked people and a people of long memory,' he said. 'We never forget.' And he went on:

Whether it is our misfortune or whether it is our good fortune, we have never forgotten Palestine, and this steadfastness, which has preserved the Jew through the ages and through a career which is almost one long chain of inhuman suffering, is primarily due to some physiological or pathological attachment to Palestine.

We have never forgotten it; we have never given it up. We have survived the Babylonian destruction. We have survived the Roman destruction. The Jews put up a fairly severe fight and the Roman invasion, which destroyed half of the civilised world, did not destroy small Judea; and whenever they once got a chance, the slightest chance, there they returned, there they created their literature, their colonies, towns and communities, and if the Commission would take the trouble to study the post-Roman period of the Jews, and the life of the Jews in Palestine, they would find that there was not a single century in the nineteen centuries which have passed since the destruction of Palestine as a Jewish political entity, not one single century in which the Jews did not attempt to come back.

It is a fallacy, if I may submit if, to think that those 1900 years were, so to say, a desert of time; they were not. When the material props of the Jewish commonwealth were destroyed, the Jews carried Palestine in their hearts and in their heads wherever they went.

Weizmann went on to tell the Commissioners something of what the Jews had already achieved in Palestine, and how Palestine could prosper. In 1920, he said, there had been 'no Treasury, no funds, no experience, a broken up people, no training, a people which for centuries had been divorced from agricultural pursuits . . .' . After only sixteen years 'we stand before an achievement on which I think we can look with a certain amount of respect and on which, I will not hide from you, we look with a certain amount of pride'. The Jewish-owned land in Palestine amounted to only 400,000 acres, but into that land had been sunk 'the sweat and blood of our pioneers'.

On November 26 Weizmann again appeared before the Commissioners, to give evidence about the April disturbances; the session was not open to the public, and is not referred to in the evidence of the Palestine Royal Commission. But Weizmann's wife, Vera, in a diary which she kept throughout the sittings of the Peel Commission, wrote of how her husband:

. . . gave his evidence in camera for $2\frac{3}{4}$ hours. What a difference to his feelings on his return. He looked pale, sad & worn out. His first words were: I feel the c's mind is made up; we shall have to make concessions.

They are convinced that our case is a good one, but the Imperial interests are of the first consideration; they can't afford to quarrel with the Arabs. We have come to an impass. The British can't afford to enforce peace by force; the public opinion would not tolerate it. If they were sure of European peace for the next three years, they might [have] acted differently. Therefore for the next few years they will have to go slowly & see to the future more remote.

Ch. is afraid least should they crystallise the N.H. [National Home] and enforce the immigration not exceeding the Arab natural increase, which will mean a permanent jewish minority. Such were Ch's general impressions.

Lord Peel asked: 'can you & we take upon us the responsibility of bringing thousands of jews in without giving them a proper protection?' Ch. – 'we think in different categories, my lord. The Jews protected in Poland would prefer to live unprotected in Palestine'.

They all were most kind and understanding with the exception of Rumbold. He asked 'When will the J.N.F. be finished?' 'Never' said Chaim, 'England is never finished. . . .'

On November 30 the Commission examined Moshe Shertok, head of the Political Department of the Jewish Agency. Rumbold asked Shertok if the town of Tel Aviv was being built up deliberately as 'a sort of artificial creation with a view to getting more and more immigrants in and creating a sort of snowball process'. Shertok replied: 'you might call the whole process of settlement of Palestine a snowball process. Naturally every wave of immigrants creates possibilities of salvation not only for themselves but for those coming after them. There is a succession of immigration waves into this country.' Rumbold questioned Shertok about how far the Jewish Agency policy of granting labour certificates to European Jews took into account 'the economic absorptive capacity' of Palestine. Shertok claimed that it did. When Rumbold pointed out that the granting of certificates to German Jews since 1933 'really had nothing to do with the absorptive capacity of the country', Shertok replied tersely: 'We are never oblivious of the conditions under which our people live in the Diaspora.'

In his statement five days before, Chaim Weizmann had dealt with this same question. 'Belgium may be overpopulated', he had told the Commissioners, 'but when a Belgian comes from exile back home he is not asked at the frontier whether he falls within the absorptive capacity of Belgium.'

Moshe Shertok's evidence continued for two more days. Palestine, he told the Commissioners on December 2, offered 'a promise of a future for large numbers of young people from abroad'; the Jewish Agency had 365 training centres in twenty-four countries, whose aim was 'to prepare those people for the career of a manual labourer in Palestine' and to see them, once they had emigrated, 'in all occupations from the very roughest'. They were being taught Hebrew, agriculture and hard labour. In all, there were 6,500 'pioneers' in training. Shertok was confident that all who wished to go to Palestine would find work.

On December 3 Shertok was joined by another senior member of the Jewish Agency, Eliahu Epstein, who told the Commissioners about Arab immigration, and the danger of a 'deterioration of the standards of life in Palestine' if Syrian Arabs from the Hauran continued to cross the border, as they had done in large numbers, since the establishment of the Mandate, particularly in time of drought. As many as 8,000, Epstein calculated, had entered illegally, and remained in Palestine, in the previous five years.

On December 8 Epstein and Shertok elaborated these complaints. Arab immigration from neighbouring countries, Epstein asserted, 'is causing a number of social and economic evils'. Shertok added that there were cases 'where an Arab peasant takes on a Haurani as a farm hand, leaving him in charge of the farm, while he himself goes to a Jewish colony to be employed by a Jewish orange grower, in view of the difference between the wage he gets from the Jewish orange grower and the wage paid to the Haurani'. Shertok added that even the Government, through contractors, made use of this cheap, illegal labour. The Hauranis, Epstein declared, were a simple-minded people, who 'lay themselves open to incitement by agitators'; nor did any Arab equivalent of the Jewish Agency exist to help them. They lived, Epstein asserted, 'in very unhygienic and insanitary conditions, often on the beach'.

In his evidence, Epstein pointed out that as many as 10,000 illegal Arab immigrants, some from the Hauran, some from Transjordan, were being employed by the Government in the port of Haifa. Rumbold was eager to examine the conclusions of this argument. 'If you debar various people from Transjordan and Hauranis from coming in to work in the port,' he asked, 'your contention is that the Government would then be able to employ Jews, it would give more opportunity to Jewish labour? Is that your contention?' Epstein was equally blunt in his reply. 'Yes,' he said, '. . . our main contention is that, so far as there is an absorptive capacity in Palestine for immigrants from outside, that should be primarily used to allow Jews to come in and get that employment.'

The Jewish Agency had already taken over many of the functions of government in relation to the Jewish immigrants. The Commissioners soon found that in its assertiveness, its competence, and its ambition, it was quite prepared to take over the full responsibilities of government. On December 8 Arthur Ruppin, who was then head of the Institute of Economic Research at the Jewish Agency, explained some of the work which it had done. Cows had been imported from Holland, poultry from the United States, banana trees from Africa. Co-operative settlements had been established 'in which the people did not feel that they were administrated to by the administrator, but in which they had a feeling that they were creating something by their own force'. Swamps had been drained, deserts irrigated, citrus groves established. Schools and farms had been established, financed largely by the Women's International Zionist Organization WIZO, to train girls in agriculture, so that the wife of the farmer could be a farmer herself. In the towns, the Jewish Agency had opened infant welfare centres, and, by its own exertions and funds, had reduced the level of infant mortality, both Jewish and Arab.

In the countryside as well, Ruppin asserted on December 9, his second day of giving evidence, Arabs gained by Jewish enterprise. They had found in the Jews an expanding and profitable market for their produce, they had learnt from the Jews innumerable techniques of building and irrigation. Ruppin urged the Mandatory authorities to act with greater vigour, to spend more on education, to assist farmers by cheap loans, to develop their own irrigation schemes, and to realize that even the water supply could be greatly increased if the Government were prepared to make the effort. 'The mountains of Palestine must not remain barren,' he urged. 'They can be made green and fertile.'

Rumbold was angered by Ruppin's attack. In demanding a dynamic policy, he declared, Ruppin and his colleagues in the Jewish Agency were 'inferring that the Government had been behindhand in developing the natural resources of the country. . . . Have you ever reflected that the Government have been administering this country under the Mandate only for 14 years.' To which Ruppin replied: 'Yes.' Rumbold persisted in his questioning. 'You seem to think', he went on, 'the Government has got an inexhaustible purse which is to be put at your disposal, but that is not so.' Ruppin replied that Jewish immigration had brought much wealth to Palestine; the Government had a budget surplus of six million pounds, and if it undertook large-scale drainage and irrigation works the cost would be spread 'over a long series of years'. He continued:

It may be that we are impatient, but we are being pressed very much by Jews who would like to settle here and who cannot settle here if the development activities are not carried out in rather quick tempo. I understand all the difficulties, and I am far from accusing the Government. I am concerned here not so much with the past; I am concerned with the future, and I believe quite a lot of things could and should be done now.

On December 14 Rumbold clashed again with another member of the Jewish Agency, Dr Maurice Hexter, whom he pressed about the limit of Jewish settlement. If the Jews were given all the land which Ruppin had estimated as irrigable – $1\frac{1}{2}$ million dunams – 'would you admit', Rumbold asked, 'that that was the last possibility of settlement for Jews and that there was nothing more. . .'. 'Would you admit,' he repeated, 'that that finished the possibilities of the settlement of Jews on the land.' Hexter replied that it would depend on 'what possibilities existed and would turn out to be available later'. To this Rumbold replied: 'I see. It is an unending process, an unending vista of possibilities.' To predict 'the end of the race', Hexter retorted, 'is a very hazardous thing'.

As the Peel Commissioners proceeded with their interviews and questionings, the Zionist leaders feared that Britain might, in the face of Arab pressure, give up all idea of an eventual Jewish majority in Palestine. On 13 December 1936 Dr Weizmann had spent the night at Government House in Jerusalem, and two days later, the High Commissioner, Sir Arthur Wauchope, sent the Colonial Secretary, William Ormsby Gore, an account of Weizmann's conversation with him:

He had heard that it was generally held that there was a solid block of Arab people who could make the position for the British in Palestine so difficult and so constantly threatened that the English were tempted to say that they had done their duty, a National Home is now established, formed and existing, and it is neither their duty nor their interest to go on allowing immigration when that course will only mean war or constant strife against Arabs in Palestine actively supported by so formidable a combination.

Dr Weizmann considered this terribly false reasoning. . . . Consider Iraq – a country quite unfit for self-government, hostile Kurds, hostile tribes on the Euphrates – Dr Weizmann did not mention Saudi Arabia, but asked is it a Federation of this sort that is to compel England to break her promises and throw over the Jews?

Were England to decide to 'throw over the Jews', Weizmann told the High Commissioner, 'the 400,000 Jews in Palestine would never submit. They would show themselves to be as formidable in action as they had hitherto shown themselves strong in restraint.' England would then be faced, Weizmann warned, 'with 400,000 Jews all in revolt in Palestine backed by millions of Jews in America and elsewhere determined to gain their just rights and the fulfilment of the promises made to them.'

Towards the end of their discussion – which had been continued on the morning of December 14, Wauchope asked Weizmann to what he attributed the growing Arab extremism. He replied at once, 'Abyssinia. Mussolini had made the Arabs believe that England would always give way to force.'

Weizmann posed two alternative courses for Britain. One was to accept that the Arabs would always oppose all Jewish immigration, and 'meet this attitude' by admitting 300,000 Jews in the next two or three years. 'When the Jews were $\frac{3}{4}$ million,' Weizmann told Wauchope, 'they could hold their own in Palestine.' The second alternative, Weizmann continued: 'is for the British Government to play false by the Jews, discard the principle of absorptive capacity, and condemn the Jews to be a permanent minority'.

The head of the Eastern Department of the Foreign Office, George Rendel, on reading the text of Weizmann's interview with Wauchope, resented the implication that Palestine must provide a solution for a problem which was not, in his view, a Palestinian problem at all. While sympathetic to the Jewish plight in Europe, he explained, in a departmental minute on January 9, his reasons for opposing the continued Jewish immigration into Palestine which Weizmann's plea envisaged:

The position of the Jews is indeed a tragic one, and commands the utmost sympathy. They are suffering an intense persecution in Germany, and the problem of the disposal of the surplus Jewish population of Poland is clearly becoming one of the major difficulties of central European politics. It would be idle to belittle or ignore the gravity of the problem created by the troubles and misfortunes of European Jewry.

But this is a world problem of the same type as that of the pressure of the surplus populations of Japan and Italy, or of the redistribution of raw materials and the opening up of markets. It is a major world problem which may easily bring about disaster if no solution can be found.

It is submitted that, even if Palestine were, as the Jews like to represent it, a practically empty place capable of absorbing a very much larger number even than at present of Jewish refugees, it is neither practical nor just to regard the Palestine problem simply as an escape from a major world problem of these proportions.

On December 26 Professor Coupland, one of the members of the Peel Commission, went to Rehovot to see Dr Weizmann. Coupland had begun to see a means of reconciling Arab and Jewish aspirations. He believed that part of Palestine could be given to the Jews, and part to the Arabs; a partition not only of land, but of sovereignty. The Jews would have their State, albeit in a much truncated form; the Arabs would be free, in the areas allotted to them, from any Jewish settlement or expansion, just as Transjordan had been entirely closed to Jewish settlers since its establishment, by Britain, in 1922. Coupland's historical research had convinced him that two peoples, each with a separate sense of national identity, could not live together as equal partners in a single state. In this way, a Jewish 'mini-State' would come into being, and the Balfour Declaration be superseded and annulled.

On December 28 the Commissioners continued with their enquiries, examining the Russian-born Dr Avraham Katznelson, Director of the Health Department of the Zionist Executive, and the American-born Henrietta Szold, a pioneer in the field of social services since her arrival in Palestine sixteen years before. When the Commissioners pointed out that the increased Jewish immigration had brought much greater demands for health services among the Jews, Henrietta Szold replied that the Jews had 'also brought a great deal of capital into the country'. For his part, Dr Katznelson pointed out that, from the moment the immigrant landed at Haifa and paid two shillings for his first two inoculations, 'he is paying more than the Government actually spends ... it perhaps cost Government not 2 shillings but a few pennies and the immigrant pays for all the services provided for his needs'. In addition, the Jewish Agency paid the full cost of school hygiene, infant welfare, adult hospitalization and all dispensary services.

All the Jews were asking for, Katznelson went on, was for Government support 'to a very modest extent'. The Jewish Agency had already paid £290,000 towards their medical services, while the Government grant was only £60,000. 'We are not requesting a complete system of health services on a European standard,' Katznelson insisted. 'We are requesting the minimum which in our opinion is quite practicable within the limits of the Government resources.' When Rumbold tried to claim that the Government could not be expected to give special benefit to the richer – that was, Jewish – section of the population, Katznelson pointed out that the Jewish community was composed of the poor as well as the rich, and the poorer Jews had themselves organized a medical service costing nearly £200,000 'by means of health insurance and the membership dues of the workers'.

On December 30 the Commissioners examined several representatives of the General Federation of Jewish Labour, or Histadrut. Golda Meyerson – later Golda Meir – pointed out that as the Government itself had no Unemployment Insurance Scheme, the Histadrut had set up its own scheme; yet it had been unable to secure Government assistance. For education, she added, the Government paid only £7,000 towards the total cost of £53,000; this created a serious burden because 'our people are such that they consider education a primary need for the family. . . .'.

To another Labour representative, Dov Hos, who appeared before the Commissioners on December 30, Rumbold put the question: 'Would it be correct to say all these numerous institutions you have founded here and which are, many of them, very admirable, would it be correct to say you expect the Government to supplement with funds various organisations which you have founded here and that if they do not do so that constitutes a grievance?' To which Hos replied that the Jewish institutions to which Rumbold had referred 'as a rule, perform duties which in other countries the Government is performing, and in our opinion the Government should perform here'. Where the Jews established hospitals or schools, he added, 'that is relieving Government from the responsibility and expense connected with them'.

Rumbold's patience was at an end. 'Now let me tell you this,' he expostulated:

Lord Cromer was in Egypt for twenty-five years and he took over a country which was in a very bad way indeed. It took him nearly twenty-five years to restore that country to prosperity. . . . My impression is that the task here is more difficult than that Lord Cromer had, because not only was this country completely derelict when the Mandatory Power took over, but the Mandatory has had to develop the country having regard to the unique experiment, the injection of an alien race into the body politic of this native race. . . .

The Jews were outraged to be called an 'alien race'. Dov Hos replied that the Jews would not describe themselves as an alien race, but as 'children returning to their country, to the country where they lived or to a country where they are going to have their home'. Jewish immigration, he added, carried with it not only 'enthusiasm and devotion to the work, but the actual possibilities of development which were not inherent in this country, which did not exist here before the arrival of the Jews'.

The Commissioners had been surprised by the extent of Jewish criticism, and by the obvious determination of the Jewish community to expand and flourish. The rapid growth of Tel Aviv seemed to them a deliberate attempt to encourage continual Jewish immigration. On 5 January 1937 they closely cross-examined the Mayor of Tel Aviv, Israel Rokach, about plans for the growth of his city. Once more, it became clear that the Jews had no intention of curbing their expansion. At the same time, they resented the attitude of the Mandatory Power in not contributing more than 6 per cent towards the city's annual budget. With more 'goodwill and understanding' Rokach asserted, the Government could do much to help improve the town's facilities. When Rumbold asked why the municipality paid a higher wage to its police force than was paid by the Government to its police, Rokach declared that 'there is a standard of living in Tel Aviv which lays it down that a minimum amount must be paid to a man, especially a family man'.

When Lord Peel commented that Tel Aviv's growth reminded him of a large American town, Rokach mentioned that he hoped Tel Aviv would grow as large as Los Angeles. Rumbold commented sarcastically: 'With the cinema business and all?'; to which Rokach replied: 'No, without the cinema business. We want culture, but not the cinema.' Lady Rumbold was less scathing of the influx of Jews to Tel Aviv, writing to her mother on 6 January 1937: 'Ugly as it really is, that mushroom town, we were impressed by the happy, cheerful, & *very* busy people running about in it. They feel it is their *own*, & that they are free, not looked down on & despised & constantly being harried (& worse). So tho' they are a strangely unpleasing race, one admires this effort of theirs. . . .'

On January 7 the Commission held its last public session with a Jewish witness, David Ben Gurion, who declared that the aim of the Jewish Agency, of whose Executive he was the Chairman, was 'to make the Jewish people master of its own destiny not subject to the will and mercy of others – to make it like any other free people'. But, he insisted, it was no part of the Jewish aim 'to dominate anybody else'. The Arabs, he added, 'have a right not to be at the mercy of the Jews'.

Ben Gurion ended his evidence by a discussion of Arab-Jewish relations. He applauded the fact that the people of Egypt, Iraq, and Syria had achieved independence, and declared that there was:

. . . no conflict of interest between the Jewish people as a whole and the Arab people as a whole. . . . We need each other. We can benefit each other. . . . It is our belief that a great Jewish community, a free Jewish nation, in Palestine, with a large scope for its activities, will be of great benefit to our Arab neighbours, and from the recognition of this fact will come a lasting peace and lasting co-operation between the two peoples.

Five days later, when the Commission began to examine the Arabs, who had belatedly agreed to attend, it became apparent that the possibility of such co-operation was remote. Reginald Coupland had already come to such a conclusion, and at a secret session on January 8 asked Dr Weizmann direct whether he would agree to the partition of Palestine into two separate political units, one Jewish, the other Arab. Recalling the incident twelve years later, Coupland told John Martin that Weizmann had said 'he would think it over'. A week later, on January 16, Coupland went privately to see Weizmann near Haifa, at the Jewish village of Nahalal. Coupland recalled that although they only spoke together for 'less than an hour', Weizmann had told him 'that personally and provisionally, and provided the frontiers were drawn to his satisfaction, he favoured the idea of Partition'.

The first Arab witness was the Mufti of Jerusalem, Haj Amin, who came before the Commission with nine other members of the Arab Higher Committee. The Balfour Declaration, he declared, was 'extremely prejudicial to the interests of the Arabs. . . . The Jews were enabled to acquire large areas in the most fertile of Arab lands. . . . Every hope which the Arabs had of attaining independence was frustrated.' The Jews, Haj Amin alleged, had as their 'ultimate aim' the recon- struction of the Temple of Solomon on the ruins of the Moslem Holy Places in Jerusalem.

The Mufti wanted the Balfour Declaration annulled, and Palestine made over to a sovereign Arab body. When Rumbold asked him whether Palestine could 'assimilate and digest' the 400,000 Jews already there, the Mufti replied in a single word: 'No.' Later, in answer to a question from the Commissioners on January 13, another Arab leader, Awni Bey, who had been one of the Hedjaz delegates at the Paris Peace Conference in 1919, declared: 'Every Arab in Palestine will do everything possible in his power to crush down that Zionism, because Zionism and Arabism can never be united together.' Awni Bey rejected the idea of Arab-Jewish co-operation within a single state, telling the Commissioners: 'What we say is that we want a National Palestine Government . . . we object to the existence of 400,000 Jews in this country.'

The Arabs and Jews had revealed apparently irreconcilable positions. The Jews were devoting much energy and money to building up their own admini- strative activities, and to creating, through the Jewish Agency, a virtual state within a state. The Arabs saw this activity as a threat to their existence, and as proof of a wider Zionist 'conspiracy' to drive them out of Palestine altogether. The Government of Palestine believed that it could hold the ring, by firm rule, by constant scrutiny of all land sales and urban expansion, and above all by restricting Jewish immigration. The Arabs rejected the idea of such a 'balance'; the Jews rejected any limit on immigration. Reflecting on these differences, Professor Coupland became convinced that Arab-Jewish co-operation was impossible, and argued in favour of two separate national states, one Arab and one Jewish, with Britain retaining control only over Jerusalem and the Holy Places.

When the Commissioners reached London their work continued. On January 19 they received a long letter from Dr Weizmann, who had also returned to London, setting out his answers to the various questions which he had been asked at secret sessions held on November 26, December 16 and December 23. In answer to Rumbold's question about when the Jewish National Home would be completed, Weizmann declared:

The Jewish National Home is no home unless its doors remain open to as many Jews desirous of entering Palestine as the country can economically absorb . . . the Mandate cannot be terminated until after the League of Nations had satisfied itself that the Jewish National Home has developed to such a stage that its further free growth is assured by its own strength, or that such constitutional and other safeguards have been provided in the place of the Mandate as would effectively guarantee a continued growth of the National Home unhampered by any political limitations.

In answer to the suggestion that there should be a halt to Jewish immigration, Weizmann replied that such a move 'would be encouraging in the Arabs the belief that disturbances bring their rewards . . .'.

During March Lloyd George was questioned by the Commissioners, and gave them an account of what had been in his mind at the time of the Balfour Declaration in 1917. 'The idea was . . .', he told them:

. . . that a Jewish State was not to be set up immediately by the Peace Treaty without reference to the wishes of the majority of the inhabitants. On the other hand, it was contemplated that when the time arrived for according representative institutions to Palestine, if the Jews had meanwhile responded to the opportunity afforded them by the idea of a national home and had become a definite majority of the inhabitants, then Palestine would become a Jewish Commonwealth.

On March 12 Winston Churchill was called before the Commissioners. In answer to a question from Lord Peel, he declared that the Jewish right to immigration ought not to be curtailed by the 'economic absorptive capacity' of Palestine, and he spoke of 'the good faith of England to the Jews'. The British Government had certainly committed itself, he said:

to the idea that some day, somehow, far off in the future, subject to justice and economic convenience, there might well be a great Jewish State there, numbered by millions, far exceeding the present inhabitants of the country. . . . We never committed ourselves to making Palestine a Jewish State . . . but if more and more Jews gather to that Home and all is worked from age to age, from generation to generation, with justice and fair consideration to those displaced and so forth, certainly it was contemplated and intended that they might in the course of time become an overwhelmingly Jewish State.

Rumbold took up the questioning. Was there not, he asked, 'harsh injustice' to the Arabs if Palestine attracted too many Jews from outside? Churchill replied that even when the Jewish Home 'will become all Palestine', and it eventually would, there was no injustice. 'Why', he asked, 'is there harsh injustice done if people come in and make a livelihood for more, and make the desert into palm groves and orange groves? Why is it injustice because there is more work and wealth for everybody? There is no injustice. The injustice is when those who live in the country leave it to be desert for thousands of years'.

1. Theodor Herzl with his fellow Zionist leaders, Jerusalem, 2 November 1898, waiting to greet the Kaiser.

2. Chaim Weizmann and the Emir Feisal, near Akaba, 4 June 1918.

3. Churchill on Mount Scopus, 29 March 1921.

4. General Allenby, Lord Balfour and Sir Herbert Samuel at the opening of the Hebrew University, Jerusalem, 1 April 1925.

5. Sir Mark Sykes, a supporter of both Zionist and Arab aspirations.

6. Arthur Ruppin, pioneer of the Kibbutz movement.

7. 'Jews are not wanted here': a sign photographed in Germany in 1935.

8. A synagogue in the Sudetenland destroyed during the Kristallnacht, 18 November 1938.

9. A protest by Jerusalem Jews against the 1939 White Paper.

). Watched by the Nazis, Jewish refugees leave Memel, 25 March 1939.

t. A ship with 'illegal' Jewish immigrants approaches the shores of alestine after a perilous journey from the Black Sea.

12. The Zionist Congress, at Geneva, hears the news of the Nazi-Soviet Pact, 24 August 1939. David Ben-Gurion is seated between Moshe Sharett (far left) and Chaim Weizmann.

13. The Mufti of Jerusalem greeted by a senior Nazi official in Berlin, 1941.

4. Jewish refugees from Transnistria
each Palestine by rail from Turkey,
uly 1944.

. Golda Meir on hunger strike, in
otest against the British refusal to
ow Jewish refugees to travel to
lestine through Italian ports in
oril 1946.

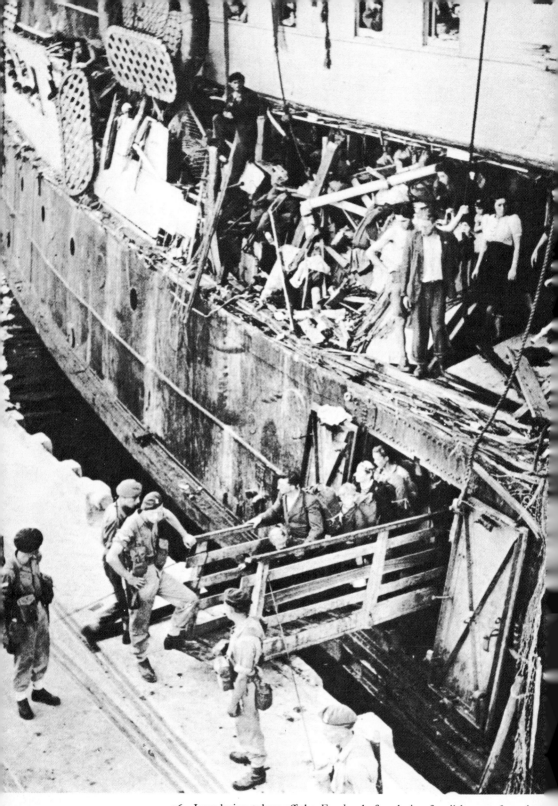

16. Jews being taken off the *Exodus*, before being forcibly transferred to another ship and returned to Europe, July 1947.

When Rumbold spoke up for the Arabs who were, he said, 'the indigenous population', subjected in 1918 'to the invasion of a foreign race', Churchill objected to the phrase 'foreign race'. The Arabs, he said, had come in after the Jews. It was the 'great hordes of Islam' who 'smashed' Palestine up. 'You have seen the terraces on the hills which used to be cultivated,' he told the Commissioners, 'which under Arab rule have remained a desert.' Rumbold insisted that the backwardness had come under Turkish rule, but Churchill insisted that 'where the Arab goes it is often desert'. When Rumbold spoke of the Arab civilization in Spain, Churchill retorted: 'I am glad they were thrown out.' It was 'for the good of the world', he told Lord Peel a few moments later, 'that the place should be cultivated, and it never will be cultivated by the Arabs'.

Towards the end of the session, Rumbold asked Churchill when he would consider the Jewish Home to be established, and Britain's undertaking fulfilled. 'At what point?' Rumbold asked; to which Churchill replied: 'when it was quite clear the Jewish preponderance in Palestine was very marked, decisive, and when we were satisfied that we had no further duties to discharge to the Arab population, the Arab minority.'

15

Jewish Hopes
and Arab Pressures
1937

EVEN before the Peel Commissioners had reached any final conclusion, the pressures from Arab Governments, and Muslim leaders outside Palestine became acute, as Weizmann himself had feared. On 4 January 1937 the British Ambassador in Baghdad, Sir Archibald Clark Kerr, reported to the Foreign Office that, according to the Prime Minister of Iraq, the 'solution of the problem of Arabs in Palestine' was more important 'than any other question of the day'. Two days later George Rendel, the head of the Eastern Department of the Foreign Office, noted on Clark Kerr's telegram: 'It will be remembered that it was extremely difficult to restrain the Iraqis from attacking Iraqi Jews during the recent disturbances in Palestine.'

The potential pressure of Arab States opposed to what Britain might decide for Palestine was detailed on February 13 by another member of the Eastern Department of the Foreign Office, Lacy Baggallay, who gave it as his opinion that even King Ibn Saud of Saudi Arabia 'would probably cease to exert any moderating influence', if a solution emerged which did not satisfy Arab opinion outside Palestine. 'Diplomatic remonstrances,' alone, Baggallay warned, even over countries like Iraq and Egypt, where Britain had considerable influence, 'may not suffice of themselves to prevent the despatch of active assistance'. On a suggestion by Wauchope for allowing the Jews to form armed units for their own defence against the repeated attacks of Arab bands on Jewish settlements, Baggallay minuted: 'I can conceive nothing more likely to convince Arab opinion that his Majesty's Government was definitely and finally committed on the side of the Jews . . . there is no advantage in furnishing a little additional security in Palestine at the cost of creating a situation which might lead to the use of our forces in Iraq, Egypt and possibly (if our difficulties led some power like Italy to stir up trouble elsewhere) in Arabia too.'

Within the Foreign Office, opinion had hardened against the Jews. On February 18 the Permanent Under-Secretary of State, Sir Robert Vansittart, noted: 'We shd set our faces most resolutely against the recruitment of Jews for use against Arabs. This wd be a vast mistake.'

During April, the Government prepared to announce the decision of the Peel Commission for the establishment of two separate States in Palestine, one Jewish, the other Arab, and with Jerusalem and a corridor to the coast excluded from both. Inside the Foreign Office this decision was looked at primarily, as Baggallay noted on April 22, 'from the point of view of our relations with the surrounding Arab countries'. Eight days later, on April 30, the Foreign Secretary, Anthony Eden, received a message about Palestine from the Secretary of State in Washington, Cordell Hull. The message read, as the Foreign Office reported, that:

> . . . in Mr Hull's view the Jews were for the greater part democratically-minded and opposed to the dictatorship outlook; to that extent perhaps they were deserving of special sympathy. At the same time Mr Hull and the United States Government fully understood our great responsibilities in view of the number of Moslems within the British Empire.

The Arabs outside Palestine quickly made their opposition felt towards any form of partition, or 'mini-State' for the Jews. On May 31 the Saudi Arabian representative in London, Sheikh Yusuf, had gone to the Foreign Office to stress, as Rendel noted, 'that what was really worrying the Arabs was the proposal that Palestine should be divided'. To the Colonial Office, potential Jewish criticism of partition seemed most dangerous, not for its effects on the plight of world Jewry, but for its effects on American Presidential policy. As the Colonial Secretary, William Ormsby Gore, wrote to Anthony Eden on June 5: '. . . the abolition of the mandate and the end of the Balfour declaration, and the division of Palestine into two self-governing states, is strong meat for an uninstructed America with $3\frac{1}{2}$ million Jews, some of them "near" the President'.

Among those who protested direct to Ormsby Gore was Dr Weizmann, who wrote to him on June 15, stressing the Zionist insistence on 'the whole of the Galilee', 'a strategically defensible frontier' east of the coastal plain, the inclusion of the Negev in the Jewish State, room 'to absorb a substantial immigration', and permanent Jewish control over 'the new Jewish quarters of Jerusalem'.

In Palestine itself the possible geographic aspects of the Peel proposals caused considerable alarm in Jewish circles. There were rumours that the Peel Commission would, among its other decisions, limit the Jewish area around the Sea of Galilee to the western shore. But to place the eastern shore within the Arab State would effectively cut off the Jewish State from the main water resources of the area, and from control of the Sea itself. The Zionists decided to act at once, and to set up a settlement on the eastern shore, at Ein Gev. One young Jew, Teddy Kollek, an immigrant from Austria, has described in his memoirs how:

> . . . we summoned up our energies and carried out a lightning-quick settlement of the 'tower and stockade' type on the eastern side of the lake. It was completed within one day in June 1937.
>
> Hundreds of people came in dozens of trucks and, within a few hours, put up a stockade around the area, a few huts, and a watchtower with a searchlight.
>
> By evening we were settled, and a few hours later, when we heard the Peel

179

Commission Report broadcast over the radio, one of our members started chanting, 'Now we belong to Emir Abdullah' (the emir of Transjordan).

We all laughed and danced. Spirits were high. We had succeeded. We were right on to the water and ready to fight for it. . . .

In presenting the Peel Commission Report to the Cabinet on June 25, Ormsby Gore had strongly advised his colleagues to accept the partition of Palestine into a Jewish and an Arab state, calling the report 'a lucid and penetrating analysis' which had led him to accept 'without hesitation the Commission's diagnosis of the root of the trouble as a conflict of irreconcilable national aspirations'. He also accepted that partition, although a 'drastic and difficult operation', has 'the best hope of a permanent solution, just to both parties and consonant with our obligations both to Jews and to Arabs'.

Another assessment of the effect of Partition reached the Cabinet from the Commander of the British Forces in Palestine, Lieutenant-General Dill, who telegraphed to the Chief of the Imperial General Staff on June 29:

Report so cuts across Zionists' aspirations that Jewish resistance to it will be strenuous. Long-sighted Doctor Weizmann may be willing to accept and bide his time, but if he does he is unlikely to carry world Jewry with him. Although Jewish opposition to report may be frantic, consider it unlikely to take form of armed resistance. Nevertheless Jewish restraint on reprisals is likely to weaken.

General Dill also gave his view of the Arab reaction:

Report likely to split Arabs, larger proportion being in favour of acceptance while Mufti and dangerous elements being against. Report likely also to split Jewry, larger proportion being against and very few in favour. Period of discussion among Arabs likely before any armed outbreak, though political assassinations may take place immediately. In event of armed rebellion removal of Mufti likely to cause early collapse.

The Jews, Dill concluded, were likely 'to turn every political stone to undermine Report but unlikely to use force'.

All of Dr Weizmann's geographical worries were confirmed when the Royal Commission published its Report on July 7. The Jewish State was to be a small one. Not only the Negev, and the eastern half of the Sea of Galilee, but even the Rutenberg concession works on the Jordan river were to be excluded from it.

According to the Report, the Arabs were afraid that they would be 'overwhelmed and therefore dominated by Jewish immigrants'. The Report went on to point out that even if Jewish immigration were restricted to 30,000 a year – the number for 1936 – Jews would outnumber the Arabs by 1960, while if immigration remained at the 1935 figure of 60,000, then the Jews would outnumber the Arabs by 1947. To avoid an immediate exacerbation of Arab fears, the Commissioners recommended an annual limit to Jewish immigration of

The Peel Commission Proposals, 1937

12,000, for a period of five years. But they warned that this would be only a palliative, not a solution. The Arabs would continue to want the Jews out of Palestine, in order to have for themselves 'the same national status as that attained, or soon to be attained, by all the other Arabs of Asia'.

As it was impossible to devise any form of government for Palestine which would satisfy both Arabs and Jews, the Report concluded that partition into two separate States, with Jerusalem remaining under British control, 'seems to offer at least a chance of ultimate peace'. Partition would mean 'that the Arabs must acquiesce in the exclusion from their sovereignty of a piece of territory, long occupied and once ruled by them'. For their part, the Commissioners concluded, 'the Jews must be content with less than the Land of Israel they once ruled and have hoped to rule again'.

On July 16 Jabotinsky wrote privately to Churchill to protest about the Peel partition plan. Although, he wrote, the Jews themselves had not 'fully realized' the full implications of the report, 'they surely want, above all, room for colonisation and a Holyland that is a Holyland'; partition, he was convinced, 'kills all their hopes'.

The Peel Commission report was debated in the British Parliament on July 21, when Sir Archibald Sinclair, the leader of the Liberal Party in the House of Commons, attacked the partition scheme with vigour, insisting that the Jews would never be content with so small a State as the Report proposed. According to Sinclair, the Jews, 'established along an indefensible coastal strip, congested, opulent, behind them the pressure of impoverished and persecuted World Jewry' would 'be fired by the urge to reach by force or by contrivance the goal of Mount Zion and the Jordan Valley'.

In August 1937, at the Twentieth Zionist Congress, held in Zurich, partition itself was accepted, but the geographical area of partition suggested in the report was voted to be 'unacceptable'.

In contrast to the Zionist reaction, the Arabs rejected the Peel Report with its Jewish State, however small that State might be. On July 26 Sir Miles Lampson telegraphed from Cairo to report his conversation with the Egyptian Prime Minister, Nahas Pasha. 'To start with,' Nahas told him, 'Egypt could not regard with equanimity prospect of an independent Jewish State as her neighbour. Apart from questions of defence etc, who could say the voracious Jew would not claim Sinai next? Or provoke trouble with Jewish community in Egypt itself?' Nahas wanted an independent Arab State in Palestine, with strictly limited Jewish immigration. 'Arabs', he said, 'should not be plucked up by the roots to make way for strangers in their native land.' That same day George Rendel noted that if partition went ahead, the Palestinian Arabs 'will be more and more resentful of the Jewish State, which cuts them off from the sea, and it is difficult to see how we shall be able to prevent them from embarking on a series of raids and incursions'. Rendel's comment arose from a letter from

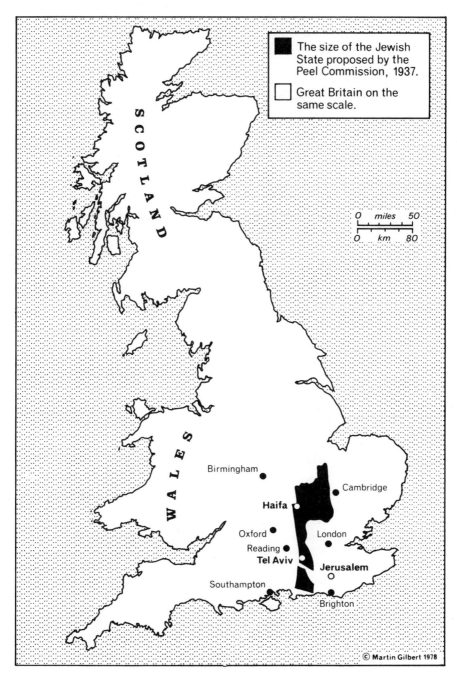

The size of the Jewish State proposed by the Peel Commission, 1937.

Great Britain on the same scale.

SCOTLAND

WALES

0 miles 50
0 km 80

Birmingham

Cambridge

Haifa

Oxford

London

Reading

Tel Aviv

Jerusalem

Southampton

Brighton

© Martin Gilbert 1978

Jabotinsky which had been published in the *Daily Telegraph* on July 23, in which the Revisionist leader had warned of the danger of 'Arab irridentism coveting the capture of the Jewish State'. As Jabotinsky wrote:

A dwarfish State whose defenders can never grow to more than a handful, but full of riches and culture, will be surrounded not by the Arab Palestine only but by an Arab Federation from Aleppo to Basra and Sanaa (for the report openly invites the proposed 'Arab State' to join such a Federation). It will inevitably be coveted and inevitably attacked at the first opportunity; and the meaning of 'opportunity' is any moment when the British Empire will find itself in trouble elsewhere.

Could the 'mini' State proposed by the Peel Commissioners either defend itself against a possible future Arab attack, or absorb the hundreds of thousands of Jews who would surely seek refuge – and a new life – in it? Such was the question that tormented the Zionists. 'There is a general mood of uneasiness', Arthur Ruppin wrote in his diary on August 15. 'Neither those who are for nor those who are against are satisfied.'

On July 30, nine days after the Peel Commission Report was debated in Parliament, William Ormsby Gore explained the change in British policy to the Permanent Mandates Commission of the League of Nations, at Geneva. During his explanation, Ormsby Gore stressed the extent to which the Jewish fate in Palestine was now bound up – in Britain's view – with the attitude, not of the Arabs of Palestine alone, but of the whole Arab world, and indeed of the Muslim world as well:

Now, the next point I wish to get into your mind is how greatly the situation in the neighbouring countries round Palestine has changed since the mandate was originally drafted and since we undertook the obligations of that mandate. In those days we were in mandatory control of Iraq, France was in mandatory control of Syria, we had a Protectorate in Egypt. That has all been changed, and the significant fact noted by the Royal Commission is the enormous interest which the neighbouring Arabic-speaking countries take in the affairs of Palestine. The situation has changed. Iraq is now a sovereign, independent State, a Member of the League. The French mandate over Syria is being transformed, and partition is to take place there into two sovereign States and the special area in the north round Alexandretta. British power in Egypt has gone, and Egypt is now completely self-governing, and a termination to our occupation is agreed.

In those circumstances, how long can we go on adhering strictly to the mandate in Palestine of seventeen years ago? And more than that: we have ample evidence that it does not stop at the Arab world. We have had an Imperial Conference this year and the principal Indian delegate was a Punjab Mohammedan, an elected member of the Council of State in India. He, as is recorded, made at our Imperial Conference a strong plea on the Arab side and for the Arab case.

Ormsby Gore went on to warn that even the Jews in Arab lands were now 'in danger because of Palestine', and he added: 'the whole relation between the Jew all over the world and the Moslem all over the world is likely to become a serious one, and is likely to deteriorate, unless we can find a solution to the Palestine problem'.

It was the very vulnerability of any 'mini-State' to outside Arab and Muslim pressures that had most alarmed Jewish and Zionist opinion from the moment that the partition plan was announced. In a 'Note on the Palestine Partition Scheme' which he wrote specially for Winston Churchill, the Revisionist leader Vladimir Jabotinsky pointed out that 'such a Jewish State would be destined to be eventually captured by the neighbouring Arab States, the conquest being probably accompanied by destruction and massacre'.

The British Colonial Secretary, William Ormsby Gore, was still hopeful that the partition of Palestine would work, despite Arab hostility. On 13 August 1937 he first explained this hostility to the Permanent Mandates Commission of the League of Nations, telling the Commission, as its official minutes recorded:

Undoubtedly, Jews had poured millions of money into Palestine. They had benefitted not only themselves but the Arabs economically; and yet, in spite of the Arabs having better economic conditions than they had ever had before, their intensity of hostile feeling had increased rather than diminished.

As he had said before, the Arabs would rather be poor without the Jews than rich with them. He had always taken the view that men sacrificed their lives and rose in rebellion and engaged in war, not for economic reasons but for reasons of race, of sentiment, of religion, and that those passions in the human heart were far more powerful than economic interests. They always had been, and always would be. Men aspired to political liberty, to freedom, to the development of their own civilisation, to the conservation of their position in the world; and they fought for those things, and not for a better material life.

That was the fundamental fact in Palestine to-day.

Nevertheless, Ormsby Gore argued, the Arabs in Palestine 'had not hitherto regarded themselves as "Palestinians", but as part of Syria as a whole, as part of the Arab world'. They could, therefore, be transferred out of many areas allocated to a Jewish sovereign state. 'They would', Ormsby Gore declared, 'be going only a comparatively few miles away to a people with the same languages the same civilisation, the same religion. . . .' Ormsby Gore continued:

He was quite satisfied that not all the Arabs would wish to leave the Jewish State: some would realise that they would have opportunities in the Jewish State. But that some would want to leave on grounds of sentiment, he equally had no doubt; and, if homesteads were provided, and land was prepared for their reception not too far from their existing homes, he was confident that many would make use of that opportunity.

It would be one of the first duties of the mandatory Power, if the League approved of its proceeding with that plan, to make an intensive survey of Trans-Jordan with a view to ascertaining how much it would cost, and where such homesteads could be provided.

This concept of a transfer of Arabs eastwards, across the Jordan, was Britain's last attempt to find some way in which the Jews might become a majority in at least a part of the lands west of the Jordan. Henceforth, there was growing up in official British circles a stereotype of the Palestinian Jew as altogether alien to Palestine. On August 14, the day after Ormsby Gore's proposal to transfer the Arabs eastwards, a distinguished British colonial civil servant, Lord Hailey, who had in the past been Governor of two vast Indian provinces, told the same Permanent Mandates Commission at Geneva, 'that the British public would never with any conviction support a scheme which involved the subordination of an indigenous Arab population to a new population largely consisting of Polish and German colonists'.

In September, in Damascus, four hundred Arabs, representing all the Arab States as well as Palestine itself, resolved that Palestine was 'an integral part of the Arabian homeland', and insisted that Britain had to chose 'between our friendship and the Jews'. By the end of the year violence had broken out again: on September 26 Arab terrorists murdered Lewis Andrews, the District Commissioner for Galilee, who had been responsible for arranging the Peel Commissioners' travels through Palestine.

At a Cabinet meeting three days after Andrews's murder, Ormsby Gore told his colleagues that it was 'essential to take action in regard to the recent murders', and he went on:

Mr Andrews was perhaps the most promising member of the Palestine Civil Service and had been attached to the Royal Commission during their visit. It was at his house that the Royal Commission had met the Arab leaders and it was known that his name had been placed first on the Mufti's black list. The circumstances of the murder were most despicable, as Mr Andrews, who had attended service in the Church of England where he had read the Lessons, had been shot as he left the building

This murder had been accompanied by many other murders of moderate Arabs, and a reign of terror seemed to have been inaugurated.

As a result of Ormsby Gore's representations, British troops began an intensive military campaign against Arab terrorists, and on October 6 he was able to report to the Cabinet that, among other measures, a strict local Press censorship had been imposed, 'prohibiting any reference to the Grand Mufti', while, of the ten members of the Arab Higher Committee, three were abroad, including the Mufti himself, and one had evaded arrest, but five had been arrested and deported to the Seychelles. These stern measures, Ormsby Gore told the Cabinet on October 8, had already had 'a salutory effect'. The source of the terrorism was referred to by the Acting High Commissioner, W. D. Battershill, in a letter which he sent on October 12 to Sir John Shuckburgh at the Colonial Office. The 'actual gunmen', he wrote, 'live in Palestine scattered amongst the villages near and around Haifa and in the North generally. They are directed by some Palestinians who live in Damascus.' Battershill continued: 'There is no doubt that there are some hundreds of Palestinians there preaching openly in the streets of Damascus sedition of the worst kind against H.M.G.'

On October 15 Ormsby Gore sent Battershill's report to Anthony Eden at the Foreign Office. 'I am afraid,' he wrote, 'it is clear that Damascus is now the centre of the organization behind the gunmen.' At the end of the month further evidence reached the Foreign Office direct from the British Consul in Damascus, Gilbert Mackereth, who sent Eden details of the activities of Palestinian 'bandits' in Syria on October 25, and again five days later, after his own life had been threatened for the third time 'by Palestinian terrorists'. On November 15 Mackereth wrote directly to Rendel. One could sympathize, he wrote, with the pan-Arab and anti-Zionist activities of the Arab world, but there was in his view another aspect to the present anti-British and anti-Jewish campaign. 'It should not be thought', Mackereth wrote, 'that the Arab nationalists, either in Palestine or Syria, offer themselves as heroes in a noble cause,' and he went on to explain:

During the past two months they have been scouring the slums of Syrian towns for known criminals (many of whom have already served long terms as punishment for savage assaults). I have myself compiled in the course of my efforts to prevent them from going to Palestine a list of about one hundred and fifty Syrians and Palestinians resident in Syria who have in this way been canvassed; many have been hired and have gone to Palestine with a sordid and purely mercenary mission to create what havoc they can.

So far, though I write subject to correction, not a single honourably known Syrian or Palestinian from Syria has crossed the frontier to join any of the groups of bandits who in Palestine pass their time blowing up passenger trains, menacing and murdering officials, defenceless soldiers, policemen and civilians, extorting money at the point of the revolver from Arab, Christian and Jew alike, cutting telephone wires, destroying the oil pipeline, and performing a hundred other anti-social acts.

I do not refer to Arabs generally as bandits, bad hats and thugs, but I believe I can fully justify the use of these epithets in the cases where I have used them. I chose the terms deliberately in the hope of thus distinguishing their activities from a legitimate manifestation of proper Arab feeling.

It was not only in the Arab world that Zionism was under attack. In October pressure had mounted among the Muslim members of the official Legislative Councils in British India, to oppose any form of Jewish statehood in Palestine, in however small or circumscribed an area. These were the very same senior Indian politicians upon whom Britain was devolving an ever larger measure of responsible government. On October 10 the Viceroy received a protest signed by all the Muslim members of the Central Legislatures, declaring that Britain had 'surrendered itself to the world Jewry intrigue and is involved in financial transaction with them'. The feeling was 'growing in India', according to the Muslim protest, that 'if things do not improve it would be very difficult to control it'. The protest continued: 'We beg His Excellency to inform the responsible Ministers in England of our feelings and sentiments, who should not lose us for the sake of foreign Jews, who at a crisis would not be able to give any help.'

The Foreign Office took this protest seriously. Despite its 'ill considered terms', a member of the Eastern Department, Terence Brenan, noted, 'we cannot afford to ignore the warning', and George Rendel wrote, of the Indian Muslim reaction to Britain's Palestine policy, that it was 'a reaction which, I think, is likely to grow stronger and more dangerous the longer the policy is continued'.

Egyptian hostility to any future Jewish State was also discussed in the British Foreign Office. On October 15, Ronald Campbell, of the Egyptian Department, warned of the dangers, as he saw it, of adopting a policy 'which would be hateful to the Arabs'. George Rendel had devised a more unusual argument against a Jewish State, minuting that same day:

> . . . the culture of the leading Jews in Palestine, as I know by personal experience, is predominantly German. The Jewish immigrants of the better class are mostly of German origin or tradition, and have not only kept a culture of a strongly Germanic character, but have even retained a curious loyalty to Germany and to German ideals. A Jewish state is therefore likely to acquire a very Teutonic complexion, and it is by no means inconceivable that if there was some turn of the wheel in Europe, a no longer actively Jew-baiting Germany might find a ready-made spiritual colony awaiting her in a key position in the Middle East.

It may even be, Rendel added, that if trouble broke out in Europe, 'we shall not be able, after all, to count so completely on the friendship of the Jews of Galilee as we are at present inclined to assume'.

Rendel's fear of Jewish disloyalty in favour of Germany went against his own views expressed only four months earlier. On June 8, when a senior German Embassy official, von Selzam, had called on Rendel at the Foreign Office to protest about the possibility of a Jewish State in Palestine as likely to constitute 'a focus of anti-German feeling', Rendel himself had told von Selzam that 'the harm had already been done, since the expulsion of the Jews from Germany had in effect created an anti-German organisation wherever Jews were to be found, and it seemed to me that it would make very little difference whether these Jews were in England or in Palestine'.

Simultaneously with Rendel's new view of potential Jewish disloyalty, evidence continued to reach the Foreign Office, on an almost daily basis, of widespread Muslim hostility to the proposed Jewish 'mini' State. On October 19 the Foreign Office received a telegram from Tripoli about local Arab protests there against the proposed partition; protests which, while being centred in the mosques, were known to be encouraged by the Italian authorities, apparently with Mussolini's approval. Nevertheless, the protests were judged to be of importance, and on October 20 Rendel minuted: 'Our policy of creating a Jewish State in Palestine for the sake of Jewish immigrants from Poland and Central Europe has provoked the uncompromising hostility of practically all the Arabs of Palestine, and of the neighbouring Arab territories.'

One of the territories concerned was Egypt: on October 20, at a Muslim Brotherhood demonstration at Port Said, there were cries of 'down with the Jews', and seven days later David Kelly, of the British Embassy in Cairo, warned the Foreign Office of the danger of Palestine becoming a political issue in Egypt, which was, the report noted, 'predominantly a Moslem nation . . . instinctively sympathetic to the tribulations, supposed or otherwise, of her co-religionists'. Yet Kelly went on to note that the Muslim sense of outrage was not necessarily spontaneous, but that internal Egyptian political rivalry 'may', as he wrote, 'provoke an artificial and inconvenient interest in the Arab cause in Palestine'.

Despite Kelly's caution, the stage was clearly set for a radical change in British policy, and for the beginning of the end of the plan of partition. Neither the continuing flow of refugees from the persecutions in Germany, nor the reviving anti-semitism in Poland, affecting as it did more than three million Jews, could weigh against the threats and pressures of the Arab world. On October 27, in a Foreign Office memorandum entitled 'Palestine. Immediate Problem', Rendel gave the reasons for a new policy. Firstly, he wrote, 'bands of Arabs from neighbouring countries are waiting to take the first opportunity to cross into Palestine to assist in the guerilla warfare which is being proposed against the Mandatory Powers'; they were doing so because they regarded the partition policy 'as involving their ultimate extinction'; inevitably, the Arab rulers themselves would give the Palestinian Arabs 'an increasing degree of sympathy and support'. Nor was the strength of the Arabs confined to their influence within the Arab world, for, as Rendel wrote:

. . . we have many enemies in Europe, and there are clear signs that the Arabs are already turning to them for help against us. Our Palestine policy will thus not only earn us the hostility of all the Arabs, both inside and outside Palestine, but is calculated to bring about an increasingly close association between those Arabs and our European rivals, the consequence of which may be far-reaching and extremely serious to ourselves.

'It would be natural,' Rendel noted, for the Jews to welcome the current British efforts to suppress Arab terrorism in Palestine, 'so much so', he wrote, that Britain should be committed to the 'suppression or extermination' of the Arabs, 'and, as a natural corollary, to unqualified and un-hesitating support of the non-Palestinian Jews in their dreams of Palestinian colonisation', but this, he warned, would create 'so dangerous a situation in an area of such vital strategic importance to us, that no local Zionist success in Palestine could be worth the sacrifice involved'.

In seeking to prepare the groundwork for a new solution, there remained the dilemma of Arab terrorism. Not only had a British District Commissioner, Lewis Andrews, been murdered at the end of September, but each week moderate Arabs were being killed by Arab extremists. Rendel criticised Mackereth's description of those extermists as terrorists: 'The trouble in Palestine is political and not criminal, though naturally our political opponents are using criminal measures, since no others are at present open to them,' and on November 5 he wrote that many of those whom Mackereth described as 'thugs' were, in fact, 'sincere Arab patriots'.

The Foreign Office were not alone in this sympathetic attitude towards the Arab killings in Palestine. On October 9 a British academic, Thomas Hodgkin, had written to the *New Statesman and Nation*, defending even the murder of Lewis Andrews. His letter read:

Of the accounts which I have read of the death of Mr L. Y. Andrews, District Commissioner of Galilee, almost all seem to have been discoloured by a certain amount of jingo resentment at the murder of a British official by members of a subject race; none have attempted to give an objective explanation of this and other recent acts of terrorism in Palestine.

The Palestine Arabs are not by temperament inclined to violence. They have turned to terrorism as a political weapon, as the Indians of Bengal, the Egyptians, the Irish, and other subject peoples of the British Empire have turned to it in the past, because no other effective political instrument was available. Terrorist movements under British imperialism, like the Nihilist movement in Tsarist Russia, can be understood only as the expression of strongly held political beliefs which are denied an adequate constitutional outlet.

However much one may disparage killing for political ends, it is surely misleading to describe an action like the assassination of Mr. Andrews as a 'dastardly murder'. (*The Times*, in a leading article of October 2nd, describes it so). Would any liberal-minded person speak in such terms of the killing of some prominent Gestapo official by an opponent of the Nazi regime? Yet that is exactly the light in which the assassination of Mr. Andrews would appear to most Palestine Arabs.

Hodgkin's letter was commented on within the Foreign Office. 'I think this letter has a great deal of good sense in it,' Rendel minuted on October 28, 'though it is of course written from a very "left" and "anti-Imperialist" point of view.' On that same day, Terence Brenan noted that there was 'unfortunately a lot of truth in this letter'. In his own view: 'The whole history of the last 20 years in Palestine have made it abundantly clear that by no other means than terrorism could the Arabs hope to get what they consider to be a square deal.'

On October 29 four British Government departments sent representatives to discuss the Palestine question: the War Office, the Colonial Office, the Foreign Office and the Air Ministry. Rendel represented the Foreign Office. 'I suggested', he wrote in his report, 'that the hostility of the Palestine Arabs to the transfer of territory which they regarded as their own to Jewish immigrants from Central Europe, whom they regarded as aliens, was a deep-seated and natural sentiment which was likely to grow stronger as our policy developed.'

At the beginning of November further evidence of outside Arab hostility reached the Foreign Office from Saudi Arabia. 'I have no doubt', minuted another Middle East expert, Sir Reader Bullard, on November 2, 'that the Arab Higher Committee, although they probably despise the Saudi royal family as camel drivers, will try to bribe Ibn Saud to intervene actively on their behalf, if they have not already done so.' It would be 'asking a great deal', Bullard added, to ask Ibn Saud 'to stop "volunteers" from crossing over into Trans-Jordan & Palestine to help the insurgents'. On November 3 Rendel urged the Foreign Office to remember, as he put it, that Ibn Saud 'is genuinely in something approaching despair about our Palestine policy', and he went on to explain that:

... he has now realized that the formation of a compact homogeneous and independent Jewish state on the Mediterranean coast of the Arab countries, with some six million Jews from Central Europe desperately trying to get into it, will mean so serious a threat to any hopes of the creation of an independent and prosperous Arabia that it is his duty, as the leading independent Arab sovereign, to make almost any sacrifice to try to prevent it.

Rendel was now ready to put forward his solution: the scrapping of partition, and the imposition on the Jews of Palestine of permanent minority status. The Government had already announced, in the House of Commons on November 3, that only 8,000 new Jewish immigrants would be allowed into Palestine in the eight months between August 1937 and March 1938, under a newly redefined 'economic absorptive capacity', while a former Military Governor of Jerusalem, the much-respected Sir Ronald Storrs, had told a meeting in London on October 19, as reported in *The Times* on the following day, that 'no Zionist was going to force us to pump in immigrants at a rate which was going to continue the present state of battle, murder and sudden death'.

Since the publication of the Peel Report in July, Ormsby Gore had continued to support partition, and on November 9, in a secret Cabinet memorandum, while recognizing the danger that the Jewish 'mini' State 'may temporarily accentuate Arab hostility in the countries surrounding Palestine', he nevertheless argued against any 'compromise with the demands of the Arab world within and without Palestine which involve at the best the toleration of the Jews in Palestine as a permanent minority'. It was a continuance of the 'present uncertainty', Ormsby Gore added, that would tend in his opinion 'to increase Arab intransigence'.

It was George Rendel who, on November 11, set out the Foreign Office answer to Ormsby Gore, in a thirteen-page memorandum. Palestine must remain a single country, he wrote, and reassurance must be given to the Arabs 'that they will no longer be in danger of becoming a minority in their own country, or of finding practically its only fertile portions taken from them and handed over in full sovereignty to alien immigrants'. The Jews, Rendel argued, should never be allowed to reach 'more than 40 per cent of the total population of the country'.

On November 13 Rendel's views were endorsed by Sir Robert Vansittart, who noted that he hoped that Anthony Eden himself 'will adopt the line of this memorandum'. On November 15 Rendel noted that 'Mr Eden had been so swamped with vitally urgent work connected with China, Germany, Spain etc that it had really been physically impossible for him up till now to go into the question of Palestine'. Yet Eden did try to find the time to read the various documents which the Foreign Office had prepared for him, and was impressed by a memorandum, which had been written by the Foreign Office's Assistant Adviser for League of Nations Affairs, Roger Makins, on November 12. What worried Makins was the possible hostility of the 'Middle East States' at the League of Nations in Geneva. 'I would view with dismay', Makins wrote, 'the possibility that Egypt, Iraq, Turkey and Persia would work against us at Geneva.' Such opposition, Makins warned:

... would, in my opinion, be far more serious than the possible opposition which would be confined to this issue, of the States with large Jewish populations, such as Poland and Roumania.

Such opposition would be unlikely to affect the general policy of Poland and Roumania, or their relative positions on the balance of power. The alienation of the Moslem countries might be total.

On reading this argument on November 15, Eden himself noted: 'This is important. I have great confidence in Mr Makins' judgement, & little doubt that he is right.' Makins's argument, Eden added, 'should find its place in our memorandum for the Cabinet'.

On reading Rendel's detailed draft of November 11, Eden made certain small amendments. He also intimated, through Vansittart, that he did not want any specific mention of the figure '40 per cent'. But Eden had already promised Ormsby Gore to send him the Foreign Office views. 'I have therefore redrafted the present paper', Rendel minuted, 'in the form of a Cabinet paper, in the first person, which could be circulated over the Secretary of State's initials.' This was indeed done, and it was therefore as a Cabinet paper signed by Eden himself, that the Foreign Office memorandum was circulated to the Cabinet on the evening of November 19. The memorandum declared:

The Arabs are not a mere handful of aborigines, who can be disregarded by the 'white coloniser'. They have a latent force and vitality which is stirring into new activity. If any stimulus were required to their growing nationalism, it is hard to imagine any more effective method than the creation of a small dynamic State of hated foreign immigrants on the seaboard of the Arab countries with a perpetual urge to extend its influence inland.

For the Arabs, the Foreign Office memorandum continued, Palestine was 'an Arab country, the best area of which is being handed over to an alien and particularly dangerous invader . . .'. The Middle East was, in his words, 'an organic whole', so much so that 'Arab opposition in neighbouring countries is even more serious'; the countries specifically listed were Syria, Egypt, Iraq, Saudi Arabia and the Yemen.

The Foreign Office memorandum continued, written, as Rendel had arranged, in the first person, as if by Eden himself:

It has been suggested to me that there is only one way in which we can now make our peace with the Arabs, and avoid the dangers I have indicated above, that is, by giving the Arabs some assurance that the Jews will neither become a majority in Palestine, nor be given any Palestinian territory in full sovereignty. . . .

If this could be agreed upon, the memorandum commented, 'we should, I think, go a long way towards recovering the confidence and friendship of the Middle Eastern States, and greatly strengthen our moral and political position in that vital area'. One way of doing this, and to enable Britain both 'to re-establish peace with the Arab and Moslem world', and to fulfil 'our obligation to the Jews', was 'the establishment of a fixed numerical proportion between the two races'.

What effect would a permanent Jewish minority have on wider Arab opinion? Such a solution, the memorandum asserted 'would be welcomed by King Ibn Saud, who would probably agree, if it were adopted, to abandon his old claims to Akaba and Ma'an, and his new claim to a corridor to Syria'. Not to adopt such a policy, however, was likely not only to involve the British Government 'in continuing military commitments of a far-reaching character in Palestine itself, but also to bring on them the permanent hostility of all the Arab and Moslem Powers in the Middle East'.

What possible chance had the hopes of Palestinian Jewry, or the needs of European Jewry, against such arguments, in which the possibility of the Jews being masters of their own destiny was pitted against Britain's strategic aims from the Suez Canal to the Straits of Bab el Mandeb; and against Britain's future relations with four separate existing Arab sovereign States, including two, Iraq and Saudi Arabia, whose oil was already referred to in the documents as a vital British need.

The Foreign Office Cabinet paper of 19 November 1937 marked the beginning of Britain's new policy. Its aim, as Eden himself explained in a personal message to the British Ambassador in Washington on November 26, was to seek some alternative to the Peel Commission, an alternative 'which would not give Jews any territory exclusively for their own use'.

Dr Weizmann, who had returned to his home at Rehovot, in Palestine, understood exactly what was happening in London. On the last day of 1937 he wrote to Sir John Shuckburgh of how he had been told 'that under the pressure of Indian Moslems, Arab Kings, Italian intrigue and, last not least, anti-Zionist Jews', the notion was gaining ground 'in high quarters' that there should be, in Palestine, a single Arab State, and 'the reduction of the Jews to permanent minority status'. Weizmann went on to tell Shuckburgh:

Jews are not going to Palestine to become in their ancient home 'Arabs of the Mosaic Faith', or to exchange their German or Polish ghetti for an Arab one.

Whoever knows what Arab government looks like, what 'minority status' signifies nowadays, and what a Jewish ghetto in an Arab State means – there are quite a number of precedents – will be able to form his own conclusions as to what would be in store for us if we accepted the position allotted to us in these 'solutions'.

Weizmann's letter continued, angrily, but also anxiously:

It is not for the purpose of subjecting the Jewish people, which still stands in the front rank of civilisation, to the rule of a set of unscrupulous Levantine politicians that this supreme effort is being made in Palestine.

All the labours and sacrifices here owe their inspiration to one thing alone: to the belief that this at last is going to mean freedom and the end of the ghetto.

Could there be a more appalling fraud of the hopes of a martyred people than to reduce it to ghetto status in the very land where it was promised national freedom?

16
Jewish Hopes and
British Appeasement
1938

FROM the beginning of 1938, British policy focussed increasingly on the very solution which the Jews feared most: the fixing of permanent minority status on Palestinian Jewry, by means of a severe cut-back, and eventual ban, on Jewish immigration. But the British policymakers were not unaware of the Jewish viewpoint, and of the support which it had received at the League of Nations. Indeed, on 9 January 1938, Ormsby Gore informed the Prime Minister, Neville Chamberlain, that the Permanent Mandates Commission of the League of Nations 'still looks to Palestine as the chief place where persecuted Jews from Germany, Roumania and Poland can find a place of refuge'.

The Arab terror campaign continued: Jewish civilians, British officials, and Arab moderates all being its victims. On January 11 Leopold Amery wrote to Winston Churchill:

I see a poor devil of an archaeologist has now been murdered simply because he is British. If Billy Gore had any real courage he would let it be known that every additional murder would mean an enlargement of the Jewish State. As it is it looks unpleasantly like the old Irish business, a gradual acceptance of murder as the natural expression of political opposition, in fact as an argument whose reasonableness we end by acknowledging.

On February 1 the Revisionists, led by Jabotinsky, held a World Congress in Prague. Six days later they passed a series of resolutions, the principal one of which was their opposition 'to any plan whatsoever which would deprive the Jewish people of their right to establish a Jewish majority on both sides of the Jordan'. The Jewish Agency, and the 'Old Zionist Organisation', were described as 'traitors', who had abandoned 'the ideals of Zionism as propagated by Herzl'. In Palestine, the Revisionists decided to strike back at the repeated Arab attacks on Jewish settlements and travellers, attacks which the Jewish Agency had insisted must be met by restraint. Henceforth, most acts of Arab terror were met, often within a few hours, by equally savage acts of reprisal.

As the new policy emerged, only a few voices were raised against it. One of those who still hoped to see a Jewish National Home in Palestine was Cólonel Meinertzhagen, who wrote, on 7 February 1938, in a letter to *The Times*:

Much has been written about injustice to the Arabs. There is nothing in a Jewish State which conflicts with Arab rights. And, moreover, be it remembered that the Arabs are the only nation in the world with at least three kings and several sovereign States. The Jews are a nation without a home.

The Arabs of Palestine, Meinertzhagen added, 'far from contributing anything towards ultimate victory' in the First World War, 'actively opposed us and deserve no better treatment than others. The so-called promises made to the Arabs have received sufficient exposure in your columns . . . my advice to the Jews is never to lose sight of the fact that Palestine includes the area from Dan to Beersheba.'

The pressures which had come from the Indian Muslims in 1937 continued into 1938. One Liberal politician, Lord Lothian, returning from a visit to India, reported to the Colonial Office on March 9, as Ormsby Gore noted, that: 'On partition, the Moslems argued against the separation of any part of what had been Moslem territory from its neighbours, and the creation of any Jewish state. In general, the Indian attitude is that no Moslem could submit to Palestine, and especially Jerusalem, being handed over to Jewish rule.' Lothian went on to report that the Indian Muslims 'failed to see why the Jews were unwilling to be in the same position in Palestine as they were in London or under the Turkish Empire which had always befriended them in times of Christian persecution in the past'.

On his return from India, Lord Lothian had also gone to see Dr Weizmann, to whom he mentioned the idea of separate Jewish and Arab self-governing areas in Palestine, with 'several British Enclaves' to ensure an effective working society 'if only for railway administration and the like'. Weizmann had replied by stressing the need for 'real' self-government, not an imposed solution that fell short of it. As he told Lothian:

The one thing the Jews would and could never accept was the prospect of being in a permanent minority status in Palestine. The one thing the Jews now understood by the word *National* Home as distinct from a Home was some area where they had responsible self-Government and where they were in a majority, and no longer in a ghetto status. They did not want 'battle-ships and big guns', but they did want to be responsible for law and order in some place on the earth they could call their own.

On March 10 the Colonial Office informed the new High Commissioner in Palestine, Sir Harold MacMichael, that no more than 2,000 immigrants of independent means – with a personal capital of £1,000 – and not more than 1,000 Jewish workers, should be allowed to enter Palestine in the six months from April to September 1938. At the same time, Ormsby Gore was still fighting to preserve the 'mini' Jewish State proposed by the Peel Commission, and in a letter to Lord Halifax on March 15 he stressed that he was 'absolutely committed to partition'

He had committed himself, he explained, not only in the House of Commons and at the League of Nations, but to Weizmann 'personally'; and he had gone so far as to tell Eden that he would resign if partition was abandoned. Ormsby Gore continued: 'I am, of course absolutely convinced that the Peel Commission were right, and that the only solution of the Palestine problem compatible with the Balfour Declaration and with Article 22 of the Covenant is self-government for Jews and Arabs in separate areas within Palestine.'

In Palestine, the Jews had been confronted since the beginning of 1938 with an increase in Arab violence, including the murder of Jewish farmers, and sniping at Jewish buses and trucks. One route by which Arab bands infiltrated into Palestine was from the north, across the Lebanese border. Land was therefore bought by the Jews at Hanita, on the border itself, and in March 1938 the Jewish Agency's defence force, the Haganah, decided to fortify the site, clear the fields, and open an access road. Four hundred men were chosen to take part in the operation, which was to be completed in a single day, under the command of the leader of the Haganah field companies, Yitzhak Sadeh, with two deputies, Yigal Allon and Moshe Dayan. Dayan, born in Deganiah in 1915, had been named after the Russian-born pioneer, Moshe Barsky, whose death at Arab hands in 1913 had so upset Arthur Ruppin. In his memoirs Dayan recalled the pre-dawn operation:

. . . we moved out of our assembly point before dawn and headed northward for Hanita. We had to leave the vehicles on the road and laboriously climb the rocky slopes. While one group started hacking out a smooth track, the rest of us carried heavy loads of fortification equipment and materials by hand.

On the hilltop site we began erecting a wooden watchtower and the standard perimeter fence, a double wall of wood filled with earth and boulders. We hoped to do all this during the day so that the tented compound within would be defended by nightfall, when we expected the first attack. But night came and we had not completed the fortifications. There had been too much to do, and we were also hampered by a strong wind. We could not even put up the tents.

At midnight we were attacked. . . .

The founders of Hanita were successful: it survived, to become yet another outpost where Jewish farmers tilled the rocky soil, and Jewish soldiers sought to defend the remote perimeters of the Jewish National Home. A few weeks after Hanita had been established, a Captain in the British army, Orde Wingate, was to join these Jewish soldiers and help them to protect their fields and settlements from Arab attack by a method already pioneered by Yitzhak Sadeh – the night ambush of the would-be attacking forces. Dayan wrote, of Wingate:

There were times when he would march on, driven by an iron will. He had an unshakeable belief in the Bible. Before going on an action, he would read the passage in the Bible relating to the places where we would be operating and find testimony to our victory – the victory of God and the Jews.

The pressures against the Jews of Europe, and not only in Germany, had continued throughout 1935, 1936 and 1937. In Poland, anti-Jewish riots had broken out in Lodz in August 1935, and in Przytyk in January 1936. These riots spread throughout Poland in 1937: Jews were attacked in Brest in May, and in Czestochowa in June, while in August alone 350 attacks on individual Jews were recorded. In the first three months of 1938 more than eighty Polish Jews were killed and 500 wounded in attacks all over Poland. Similar violence had taken place in Rumania, beginning with an anti-Jewish riot in Czernowitz in October 1935, and spreading in June 1936 to Bucharest, Kishinev and Belz. Nor had these attacks abated in 1937, when further anti-Jewish attacks took place in Bucharest in February, and in several other towns during the summer, culminating on 18 December 1937 in legislation which specifically discriminated against Jews. It was against this background of murders, attacks on property, and 'legal' discrimination that tens of thousands of Jews thought of immigration, and looked towards Palestine.

For the Jews of Europe, already the victims of hatreds beyond their control, March 1938 saw a further deterioration in their hopes of a normal life, for on March 15 Hitler entered Vienna, and direct Nazi rule was at once extended to Austria. Within only a few days, the whole apparatus of anti-Jewish persecution—from the imposition of the Nuremberg Laws to the foul beatings, the torture, and deportation to Dachau concentration camp – was instituted in its most vicious form. Overnight more than 180,000 Jews were added to the German Reich, while an extra 40,000 people of Jewish descent – many of them baptized Christians – were declared to be, racially, Jews.

By the end of April more than 500 Austrian Jews had committed suicide. Others sought to flee across the borders into Czechoslovakia, Hungary and Switzerland; they were not always made welcome. In Vienna, itself, the humiliations continued, a terrible example of the collapse of civilized standards in the face of modern anti-semitic fervour, bolstered up by crude tyranny. One Jewish eye-witness of the Nazi 'rape of Austria', the twenty-one-year-old Ehud Ueberall – later Ehud Avriel – recalled in 1975 in his book *Open The Gates!*:

Jewish men, and especially women, were arrested in the streets and, under the scornful laughter of the Viennese, were forced to wash away the slogans painted during the desperate few weeks while Austria's fate lay in the balance. Jewish shops were broken into and plundered by the mob while Jews specially apprehended for the purpose stood in front (guarded by SA men, armed to the teeth) holding signs saying 'Aryans, don't buy at the Jews'.'

When dusk fell the emptied shops were abandoned by the looters. The SA then would collect the Jews who had been posted before the shops in one street, force them into a procession surrounded by Viennese of all ages, and, while their Austrian neighbours shrieked and spat into the Jews' faces, led them down the road into some dark alleyway where the Austrians were allowed to beat them viciously.

Jews were evicted from their flats by their own landlords or by jealous neighbours. Jewish students were turned out of their schools. The prisons became full of innocent people simply because they were Jews.

Throughout the spring and summer of 1938 the Jews sought to leave Austria. But it was not easy to do so. 'On the day Hitler took over Austria,' Ueberall recalled, 'there was a total of sixteen immigration certificates at the disposal of the entire Austrian Jewish community.' A few hundred visas were obtained during the summer for agricultural workers, who were able to proceed to England, Holland and Denmark. Those who left had, of course, to leave behind all their property, all their savings, and almost all their belongings. For those who remained, as Uerberall wrote, 'turned down by one foreign consulate after the other, they realized that no country would take them in'.

Ueberall's recollections are fully borne out by contemporary records. On May 31, D. St Clair Garner, the British Consul-General in Vienna, informed the British Ambassador in Berlin that 'the distress and despair amongst the Jews are appalling. This consulate-general is literally besieged every day by hundreds of Jews who have been told to leave the country and who come vainly searching for a visa to go anywhere.'

The fears of Austrian Jewry were not exaggerated. On the night of Sunday, April 17, the inhabitants of a Czech village on the Danube heard cries of distress from a breakwater in the middle of the river. Going out in boats, they found fifty-one Austrian Jews, including an eighty-two-year-old Rabbi, and many women and children. The Jews had been driven from Austria by storm troopers and dumped on the breakwater without either food or warm clothing. Several had been ill-treated and injured.

The expelled Jews were at once given shelter in Czechoslovakia; but within twenty-four hours of their arrival the Czech authorities refused to allow them to stay, and on the night of April 18 they were sent across the Hungarian frontier. The Hungarians, however, likewise refused to give the refugees a haven; indeed, on the night of April 19 they were driven back across the Austrian frontier, to the land from which they had been expelled less than forty-eight hours before. On reaching Austrian soil, they were at once arrested by storm troopers, and imprisoned in the local army barracks.

This incident, and others equally cruel, was widely reported in the world's Press. On April 24, in Chicago, a Conference of the United Palestine Appeal urged the settlement in Palestine of 100,000 Jews a year, for five years. In Britain, also, voices were raised in favour of opening Palestine to the growing number of refugees. But within government and official circles it is hard to find, in the mass of documents and minutes, many notes of compassion.

It was those who had consistently shown sympathy for the Jewish plight who understood what was happening to the Jews of Germany, and now of Austria, and it was one of these, Leopold Amery, who wrote to Malcolm MacDonald, the new Colonial Secretary, on 30 May 1938: 'There is no real comparison between the quite natural resentment of the Arabs at seeing the character of their country changed, though with material advantage to themselves, and the agony of the Jews of Central Europe, for whom there is really no other serious alternative city of refuge.'

Amery was a personal friend of the Zionist leaders and of many individual Jews, Zionist and non-Zionist. He knew well that the question of refugees was central both to Zionist and to Jewish concern. Yet the government was reluctant to recognize how desperate the needs were, and rejected the idea that, despite their Palestinian responsibilities, and despite their Imperial responsibilities, they were in any way involved in the unfolding tragedy of European Jewry. Thus the Governor of Kenya, Air Chief Marshal Sir Henry Brooke-Popham, wrote to the Colonial Office on June 18 to say that while in favour of the settlement of perhaps a few Jewish families in Kenya, he 'would not object to the carefully regulated influx of Jews of the right type, i.e. Nordic, from Germany or Austria for agricultural settlement in reasonably small number . . . in small groups of a size not too large to become part of the general economic and social life of our community'. Any Jewish 'enclave' as such, Brooke-Popham stressed, 'would be an undesirable feature in a colony which . . . should be developed on lines predominantly British'.

Hostility towards Jewish refugees was to be found elsewhere. On June 19 – the day after Brooke-Popham had sent his cautious answer to London, the *Sunday Express*, one of Britain's largest circulation newspapers, told its readers: 'There is a big influx of foreign Jews into Britain. They are over-running the country. They are trying to enter the medical profession in great numbers. . . . Worst of all, many of them are holding themselves out to the public as psychoanalysts'. The psychoanalyst, the newspaper alleged, 'often obtains an ascendancy over the patient of which he makés base use if he is a bad man'.

In Palestine, the situation had again worsened; it was made particularly bitter for the Jews by the death sentence passed on two young Revisionists, Slomo Ben Josef and Abraham Sein, for firing on an Arab bus. No one had been killed in the incident, and in England, the *Manchester Guardian* had appealed, on June 6, for clemency. But the Palestine Government decided that an example should be set, and Ben Josef was executed. On June 29 the British Consul General in Riga, Charles Orde, telegraphed the Foreign Office: 'Last night a stone was thrown through my study window wrapped in a paper bearing the message "The Jewish people will never forget the blood of their brother Ben Joseph." '

The situation of the Jews was becoming desperate. In Germany and Austria their thousand year old communities were rapidly being destroyed. In Poland and Rumania anti-semitism had again become open, vociferous and violent. Throughout Europe, the possibility of Nazi rule, or pro-Nazi regimes, encouraged and stimulated anti-Jewish feeling. In the Soviet Union, any attempt to express a specifically Jewish culture was suppressed, and all Zionist activity stamped out: indeed, several hundred thousand of the more active Jewish citizens, including all the Jewish Bolshevik leaders who had roused British hostility in the 1920s, had been wiped out in the Stalinist purges, then at their height. In Palestine, Arab attacks on Jews continued with terrible effect, despite the British decision to expel the Mufti and his senior advisers, and impose martial law. The execution of Ben Josef did not deter other young men in the Revisionist movement from seeking to revenge Arab killings by killings of their own, despite the repeated appeals by the Zionist leadership for restraint. Above all, the continuing restrictions on Jewish immigration from Europe were a constant source of distress for all Palestinian Jewry.

On the afternoon of July 4 Malcolm MacDonald discussed with Dr Weizmann the whole Palestine problem. If partition were rejected, Weizmann warned, and the Jewish State, however small, abandoned, 'the Revisionists would be greatly strengthened as against the moderates, and there would be serious trouble'. But, MacDonald replied, it was believed by 'many people who knew the Arab world' that Arab opposition to the Peel proposals 'was intense and permanent, and that the final adoption of the policy of partition would be followed at once by a considerable rebellion in Palestine which would receive material and moral support from Arabs and Moslems elsewhere'. In addition, MacDonald told Weizmann:

We should lose much of the friendship of the authorities and peoples of a number of important surrounding countries like Egypt, Saudi Arabia, Iraq and Syria. This would happen at a time when we were facing a very uncertain situation in Europe, in which both Germany and Italy were potential enemies; and serious trouble for us in Palestine would be an additional inducement to our enemies in Europe to start some active aggression, the outcome of which would be war.

MacDonald also warned of the danger of any policy that might 'arouse hostility amongst Moslems in India', at a time when Britain was trying to evolve a scheme of Federation in which Hindus and Muslims would both participate. Above all, MacDonald argued, the Arab rebellion in Palestine tied down 'considerable armed forces, thus immobilising them for action anywhere else'.

Replying to MacDonald, Weizmann declared that Britain:

... could make a very good case, for since the War we had given the Arabs generally 90 per cent. of what they wanted. They had a number of independent States, and under the Peel Commission's proposal a new area in the near East would come under complete Arab sovereignty. The Arabs were already greatly indebted to us, and they would not so lightly cast aside our friendship. Moreover, if we were now to abandon partition – having already in principle accepted it – the Arabs would not regard this as a concession from a generous British people. They would regard it as a concession wrung from a weak British people, as a result of the terrorist campaign.

The Germans and Italians would be quick to encourage this view throughout the Near East, where their propaganda was deliberately and continuously anti-British. They would rub in the lesson that Great Britain was effete, and the peoples of Egypt and Saudi Arabia and the other countries would regard the concession as fresh evidence of this fact.

During their discussion on July 4, Weizmann warned MacDonald that if Britain abandoned partition, she would lose the friendship of the Jews, 'which at present', he said, was something that Britain 'could really count on in peace or in war', and he went on:

The abandonment of partition now would leave the Jews completely disillusioned regarding the reliability of Britain. Even though he and individuals like him would understand our difficulties and the reasons for our policy, they could not convey that understanding to the great masses of their people. The moderates would be swept from office in the Zionist Organisation, and the extremists would come in. We should not even solve our problems in Palestine itself, for the 450,000 Jews now in Palestine would be in a trap. They would be a helpless and permanent minority; their position would get weaker and weaker, and their position would gradually become very distressing.

The official Colonial Office minute recorded the final, harsh exchange between the two men, after Weizmann had told MacDonald that:

... if a Jewish State were established in Palestine we could count absolutely on the support of that State. They would have a considerable Jewish army and they would be a source of various military supplies. They would be an extremely effective addition to our strength in that very important strategic quarter. He went so far as to say that, in his view, within a year of the establishment of a Jewish State we could withdraw our own military forces from Palestine.

I said that I thought this was very optimistic, though I appreciated the strength of the argument that we could count on the Jewish State being a friend and ally under all circumstances. But if it was also a source of trouble and friction in the Near East, to that extent it was an additional liability.

Dr Weizmann said that in establishing a Jewish State we would be creating the certainty of a new and powerful friend in the Near East, whereas we were only taking a risk of alienating the Arab peoples. He thought that we should at least be prepared to try the experiment.

I retorted that the experiment might prove fatal.

Where could the Jews turn? On July 6, following an initiative by President Roosevelt, an international conference opened in France, at the town of Evian, on Lake Geneva. The aim of the Evian Conference was to find some common policy towards the refugees: thirty-two countries were represented, with the United States in the chair. On British insistence, Dr Weizmann was not even allowed to address the delegates privately.

As the conference itself progressed, nation after nation declined to liberalize their immigration policies. The Australian delegate went so far as to announce that 'since we have no racial problem, we are not desirous of importing one'.

The British Government told the Evian Conference that nowhere in the British Colonial Empire was there any territory suitable for the large-scale settlement of Jewish refugees. No mention at all was made of Palestine until the closing session, when Lord Winterton, on behalf of Britain, explained that only very limited immigration could be considered. For its part, the United States adhered to its existing quotas: 27,370 refugees a year from Germany and Austria. Given such insistence on the letter of the law, it would have taken twenty years, until 1958, before all the Jews, even of the German Reich alone, could reach asylum in the United States.

The United States decision to maintain its strict quotas served as a guideline for other States; the delegate from Peru described the 'wisdom and caution' of the United States as being a 'shining example that guided the immigration policies' of Peru iteslf. Only the Dutch, the Danes, and the Republic of Santo Domingo agreed to let in refugees without restrictions.

On the last day of the Evian conference, July 15, a resolution was passed which stated that 'the countries of asylum' – such as they were – 'are not willing to undertake any obligation towards financing involuntary emigration'. Other resolutions expressed the Conference's 'sympathy' towards the plight of the refugees – Jewish and non-Jewish alike. On the following day a journalist from a Swiss newspaper asked one of the Jews present, Golda Meyerson, for her comments. 'There is one ideal I have in mind,' she replied, 'one thing I want to see before I die – that my people should not need expressions of sympathy any more.'

Since February 1938, with the resignation of Anthony Eden and his replacement by Lord Halifax as Secretary of State for Foreign Affairs, the policy of appeasement had been actively pursued. This affected not only Anglo-German relations generally, but also the refugee question. Returning from Evian, Lord Winterton informed his Cabinet colleagues, on July 20, that the American representative 'had wanted some clause of a denunciatory character towards the German Government, but the British delegation, under instruction from the Secretary of State for Foreign Affairs, have resisted this successfully'.

At the same meeting, of the Cabinet Committee on Refugees, there was a long discussion about the possibility of Jewish refugees finding a haven in some of the British colonies. But the Home Secretary, Sir Samuel Hoare, as the official minutes recorded, 'warned his colleagues that, while he was anxious to do his best, there was a good deal of feeling growing up in this country – a feeling which was reflected in Parliament – against the admission of Jews to British territory'.

During the summer of 1938, the British Government moved steadily away from Partition. The resignation of Ormsby Gore, who had become convinced that partition was the sole solution, had made this change of policy much easier, for it now had the support of the permanent officials in both the Foreign Office and the Colonial Office. But in Palestine itself, the violence continued. On June 19 seven Arabs were murdered by Arab terrorists for the so-called 'crime' of having worked for Jews. One of those murdered was a woman in her last month of pregnancy. Another woman had been tied to a tree before being shot dead. That same evening, a band of 300 Arabs crossed into northern Palestine from the Lebanon: their first victims were three Arab peasants.

At the beginning of July the Government of Palestine published its official Report for 1937, warning that public security in Palestine had been 'seriously disturbed by a campaign of murder, intimidation and sabotage conducted by Arab law-breakers'. On 'a few occasions', the Report noted, this campaign had 'provoked Jewish reprisals'.

The Report also noted that since 1922 the Arab population of Palestine had increased by 261,000, compared with a Jewish increase of 245,000, and that despite the heavy Jewish immigration of the early 1930s, the Arab population, by both its own immigration and a higher birthrate, had grown by a larger absolute number than the Jewish population. The Report also referred to those Arabs who were dispossessed of their land as a result of Jewish land purchase, noting that for the whole of 1937 only six Arab families had claimed to have been dispossessed: and that each had then been settled on Government land as compensation.

Arab attacks on Arabs continued throughout the summer. On June 24 two Arabs working in a Jewish-owned stone quarry near Haifa were wounded by Arab raiders. The wounded men were taken to hospital, but two of the raiders entered the hospital in search of them, killing by mistake another Arab, a patient from Nablus. On June 29 an Arab terrorist threw a bomb at a Jewish wedding party at Tiberias: seven Jews were wounded, including three children. Parallel with these events, a small band of Jewish terrorists struck back in violent acts of reprisal, after nine Jews had been killed during June in Arab attacks on individual Jews throughout Palestine. On July 6, a single Jewish terrorist bomb killed twenty-five Arabs in Haifa. On July 11 Arabs killed two Jews in Haifa, and on July 12 an elderly Jew was stoned to death in the city. The killings and counter-killings continued: on July 21 four Jewish workers were killed at the Dead Sea, and four days later, in Haifa, a Jewish terrorist bomb killed 39 Arabs in the melon market.

In Palestine, the Jewish newspaper *Davar* denounced the Jewish reprisals as both 'shameful and calamitous', while the newspaper *Haaretz* declared them to be 'a criminal gamble with the fate of the Jewish community'. The Zionist leaders were equally strong in their condemnation: the terrorists, declared David Ben Gurion, were 'miserable cowards', and Izhak Ben Zvi warned that they 'were stabbing the community in the back'. At the end of July the Jewish

Labour Organisation issued an official manifesto stating that the bloodshed of reprisals was 'a disgrace and a madness'.

Arab provocations showed no signs of abating, nor did the Arab leaders issue any appeal for moderation. On July 26 two Jews were killed in the Galilee, and two in Jerusalem, and in the last week of July, on the eve of a visit to Palestine by Malcolm MacDonald, there were twenty-seven separate Arab attacks on Jewish villages.

MacDonald was in Jerusalem on August 6 and 7, and in a Cabinet memorandum entitled 'Talks in Jerusalem', he gave his colleagues in London an account of his talks with the new High Commissioner, Sir Harold MacMichael, the Commander-in-Chief, General Haining, and the Inspector-General of Police, Major Saunders. MacDonald hoped also to talk to both Jewish and Arab leaders while he was in the city, but MacMichael told him, at the outset of their discussion, that 'he was afraid it would not be'. As the High Commissioner explained it, the power of Arab extremists was too strong, even for a High Commissioner:

He could easily get Jewish representatives up to Government House, but he would be at a loss to know which Arabs to invite. No Arab political leaders could safely come and discuss politics with him or me. It would put them in an exceedingly embarrassing position, and even in danger of foul play from terrorists afterwards. Even if they only came for a few minutes and a hand-shake they would be suspect.

The trouble arose, MacDonald was told by both MacMichael and Haining, 'from the comparatively small number of small bands, which consist for the most part of thorough-going brigands'. These were the permanent nucleus of much larger Arab terrorist forces, 'for they recruit to themselves by night various Arab peasants who are restless and anti-Jew, and who are not averse to joining in violent action for reasonable remuneration'. MacDonald then summarized his own conclusions, telling MacMichael and Haining:

. . . this picture seemed to indicate that the terrorist movement as such amongst the Arabs was not a spontaneous national movement of the Palestinian Arabs as a whole, but the result of strenuous agitation by political leaders and the activity, no doubt often accompanied by intimidation, of bands of banditti who had no genuine political significance, but were delighted at the chance to fish in troubled waters.

Was I correct in drawing this deduction, or did they think that the movement was really a sort of national movement?

They replied that they thought that terrorism was not a national movement. The moderate Arab leaders were opposed to it, and the great majority of Arabs in the country disliked it and began to feel that it was fruitless. But the power of intimidation of the terrorists was so great and Arab politicians generally were so lacking in courage that there was no lead against the terrorists amongst Arabs. If the Mufti were not sitting just across the border, other political leaders might arise; but whilst he is there the Arabs could not believe that he would not soon return to Palestine. . . .

MacDonald proposed a conference of both Jews and Arabs, to be held in London. He was worried, however, that the Palestinian Arabs 'might well be terrorised into saying that, if their representatives could not be the Mufti and his friends, they would send nobody'. The Egyptian Prime Minister, Mahmoud Pasha, whom he had seen in London on July 29, had urged him to 'recall these Arab leaders from their exile in order to negotiate with them', but MacDonald had rejected this advice, telling MacMichael and Haining: 'It seemed to me that to pursue such a course would be to abdicate a great deal of our activity in Palestine to men who were responsible for terrorism itself.'

On August 12, after his return to London, MacDonald spoke to Dr Izzet Tannous, an Arab Christian, who was in charge of the Arab Centre in London. Tannous urged MacDonald to allow the Mufti to return to Palestine, but MacDonald was firm in his refusal, telling Tannous:

. . . he and I took a different view as to the responsibility of the Mufti and his colleagues for the campaign of violence in Palestine. I did not say that they were responsible for every individual act which had been committed. But that they had encouraged and authorised the campaign in general I had no doubt.

We had plenty of information on that point. Indeed, it seemed obvious to me that the campaign was still at this moment being encouraged from a source outside Palestine. Terrorism could not continue without that encouragement. The bandits had to be organised and supported, they had to have the wherewithal to recruit villagers to join in their work. Money and arms were being collected from various sources, their distribution was organised mainly from one centre.

I had no doubt as to who had been and was still mainly responsible for the campaign of violence which was disgracing the Arab cause. It might be that people would come to me and say that if these leaders were allowed back to Palestine they would mend their ways, and really use their influence for peace. I would tell him frankly that I would not trust the word of the leaders who had been exiled, and I would not in any circumstances be responsible for their return now to Palestine.

On August 21, in a secret note to his Cabinet colleagues, enclosing transcripts of his London and Jerusalem conversations, MacDonald noted:

Great harm had already been done in Palestine by rumours that the wisdom of Partition had been questioned in the Cabinet, which have encouraged the Arab terrorists and those behind them to believe that if only they persist in their campaign they will force us to abandon this policy.

The extremists were so powerful, MacDonald added, 'that they virtually dictate Arab policy'.

As 1938 progressed, more and more boats, many of them organized by the Revisionists, brought Jews from Poland, Germany and central Europe across the Black Sea, through the Aegean Sea, and on to Palestine. These 'illegal' immigrants were determined not to remain in a Europe where their future was clearly bleak. The British Government responded to this traffic by putting pressure on all the Governments between Poland and Palestine, not to allow the refugees, or the ships, to pass.

On July 21 a success was scored in this anti-refugee campaign, for that evening the British Minister in Athens, Sir Sidney Waterlow, was able to telegraph to the Foreign Office in London that the Greek Government 'have now instructed their Missions abroad, including Vienna and Warsaw, not to issue transit visas through Greece to Jews whatever the destination stated'.

For many Jews, such British efforts to prevent refugees reaching Palestine were a matter of concern and distress. Yet unprovoked and savage Arab attacks on Jewish civilian settlements continued unabated. A telegram from the High Commissioner, Sir Harold MacMichael to Malcolm MacDonald's office, sent on July 24, gave a grim picture of the pattern of Arab violence. The village attacked was Kiryat Haroshet, 'a wooden straggling settlement', as MacMichael described it, 'over about three kilometres at the foot of Carmel Hills'. His report continued:

Within five kilometres there are some nine other Jewish settlements containing about 136 armed supernumeries but Haroshet lies at the extreme west. It held 4 Greener guns with 300 rounds and 10 rifles with 500 rounds. The gang engaged the attention of the Colony by firing from the rear and setting fire to two huts. Family of three was burnt in one and woman and child shot in the other. The attack began at 11.15 pm and the attackers had gone by midnight. When the police arrived supernumeries had used all their ammunition. It is believed that casualties were inflicted on attackers.

'Age of persons killed,' MacMichael added, 'are as follows:—two children 11 and 2, one man 33, two women 33 and 31.'

On 3 August 1938 David Ben Gurion gave his judgement on the British response to Arab terror. 'England', he said, 'has yielded to terror in matters of her nearest concern - in Ireland, in India, in Egypt. How much more likely, then, she is to yield when only Jews are concerned?'

Yet not all Britain's representatives had wanted to yield to the pressures of violence. Towards the end of July Sir Sidney Waterlow, from Athens, had sought to moderate the policy of halting without exception the attempt of 'illegals' to reach Palestine. On July 25, H. F. Downie, head of the Middle East Department of the Colonial Office, had written to the Foreign Office specifically to protest against 'Sir Sidney Waterlow's rather surprising suggestions that a number of Jewish illegal immigrants should be admitted to Palestine on humanitarian grounds'.

Ben Gurion and his fellow Zionists were becoming more and more embittered. In his speech of August 3 Ben Gurion declared:

Far too many of us think in our innocence that, because one fine or rainy day – for it usually rains in England in November – a British Cabinet Minister made a Declaration to the Jewish people, then Palestine is already in our pocket, the steady goodwill of the British people is guaranteed, and all we have to do is taste the fruits.

How very naive! The most formal promise in the world, no matter how many countries back it, will never fulfill itself. Since Balfour declared as he did, quite a few international treaties and pledges have been torn up or repudiated, promises and pronouncements forgotten. The Treaty of Versailles has been ripped to pieces. Where is the guarantee of Austria's independence? Where is the demilitarization of the Rhineland? Where are the restrictions upon the Reichswehr, and on traffic through the Dardanelles? Null and void – every single one. . . .

It may be that in Britain, too, a 'new king' will arise. Ministers come and Ministers go; a Pharaoh may come that knows not Joseph, that may want to forget the promises of his predecessors.

As the summer of 1938 drew to an end, the German Government began to abuse the Czechoslovak Government, whose State included three million German-speaking citizens, formerly part of the Austro-Hungarian Empire. On August 9 the British Foreign Office learnt, from its Consul-General in Munich, J. E. M. Carvell, that 'a new concentration camp' had been set up at Flossenburg, near the Czechoslovak frontier with Germany. Were Hitler to annex the Sudetenland, the predominantly German-speaking area of Czechoslovakia, as he threatened to do, it was clear that the tens of thousands of Jews of that area, as well as thousands more opponents of Nazism there, would have a ready place of incarceration nearby.

Should the Jews of the Sudetenland join the ever-growing trek of refugees? 'Dreadful, dreadful are the afflictions of the Jewish people,' a *Daily Express* editorial declared on August 23. 'Every warm heart must sympathise deeply with them in their plight.' But the editorial continued:

Certainly there is no room for the Jews in Britain, where we have 1,800,000 of our own people out of work and biting their nails. But places must be found for the Jews. There are plenty of uninhabited parts of the world where, given a touch of the Christian spirit, they may yet find happy homes.

Sometimes anti-Jewish sentiment was even more blunt. On September 17 the magazine *Everybody's*, in opposing the entry of refugee doctors and dentists to Britain, told its readers: 'Most of the alien doctors and dentists are Jews who are fleeing from Germany and Austria. And the methods these aliens are bringing into England are not always in accordance with the professional etiquette of this country.'

These prejudices did not bar out the refugees altogether. Between 1933 and 1939 more than 65,000 German and Austrian Jews, including many doctors, lawyers and other professional men, found asylum in Britain. But tens of thousands more were refused permission to enter, and those who were able to gain entry into Palestine were an even smaller portion of those who sought to enter.

At the end of September 1938 the British Government put pressure on Czechoslovakia to accede to Hitler's demands. The Czechs did so: at the Munich Conference, from which the Czechs themselves were excluded, the Czechoslovak State – after twenty years of independence – was made to cede the Sudetenland to Germany.

With the German annexation of the Sudetenland, yet more Jews – at least 20,000 – fell under Nazi rule; yet more innocent individuals became marked out for persecution and terror; and yet more refugees set out, with all their life's work and possessions behind them, along the ever-narrowing road towards the mirage, safety.

Britain's role in putting pressure on Czechoslovakia was seen by many observers as perfidy. The subject was discussed, in October 1938, between Dr Weizmann, and the Czechoslovak Minister in London, Jan Masaryk, who told him: 'But don't think, Dr. Weizmann, that we are the only victims. The British have built a house of three stories. On the first floor they put Haile Selassie. The second floor has now been allocated to us. But the third floor is reserved for you.'

Leopold Amery took a similar view, writing in his diary on October 11 that Britain's Palestine policy 'is a replica on a small scale of the European situation: absence of policy and fear of irritating those who mean mischief in any case'. Nor was Amery's instinct wrong, even though, on October 19 the advocates of partition received further support in the conclusions of yet another British Government Commission, headed by a senior Indian civil servant, Sir John Woodhead. The Woodhead report stated bluntly: '. . . no impartial person would think the Arabs justified in claiming sovereign rights over persons and property of Jews who have settled in other parts of Palestine on the faith of the Balfour Declaration and the Mandate'. On the question of Jewish land purchase, the Woodhead Commission stressed Arab fears that the Jews had taken the most fertile land, but this was not the view of Sir Alison Russell, a former Chief Justice in Tanganyika, who stated in his Note of Reservations:

It has been alleged that the Jews have acquired the best land in Palestine. It does not appear to me a fair statement. That much of the land now in possession of Jews has become the best land is a truer statement. . . . It was impossible not to be impressed when inspecting some of the bare rocky places where Jewish settlements have been or are in the course of being made. Such remarkable efforts may well disturb statistics.

In its actual boundary proposals, the Woodhead Report produced three separate schemes, each of which gave the Jews less land than the Peel Report had suggested. Even the scheme most favourable to the Jews excluded most of the Galilee from the proposed area of the Jewish State, while at the same time giving the Arab States substantial portions of Jewish-owned land south-west of Rehovot, and around Beisan. The only Jewish 'gain' between the two reports was that Woodhead included the Rutenberg concession area inside the proposed Jewish borders.

As Amery had forseen, however, fear of 'irritating' the Arabs led to even the Woodhead Plan being abandoned, despite the substantial area of Palestine which it would have allocated for an Arab State; for on October 24 Malcolm MacDonald told his colleagues on the Cabinet Committee on Palestine that if Britain were to insist upon the partition of Palestine into an Arab and a Jewish State, 'We should forfeit the friendship of the Arab world,' while Lord Zetland, the Secretary of State for India, said that whereas the opposition among Indian Muslims to giving the Jews 'control over any part of Palestine' was as yet 'not clearly defined', nevertheless, 'speaking generally, the feeling was against any Jewish sovereignty in the Holy Land'.

As the discussion proceeded, the Prime Minister, Neville Chamberlain, stated bluntly that as 'Palestine had become a Pan Arab question' any discussion of its future had to include not only the Arabs of Palestine but also those whom he called the 'Arab Princes' from the neighbouring Arab States, including Saudi Arabia, Transjordan and the Yemen. In its conclusion, the Cabinet's Palestine Committee of October 24 decided that the proposals of the Peel Commission should be abandoned, and that a public announcement should be made to the effect that 'the setting up of independent Arab and Jewish States, is impracticable'.

The Arab States whose involvement Chamberlain wished to see in any Palestine settlement had gained further British government approval at this time by showing sympathy to Chamberlain's policy of appeasement towards Germany. Thus Lord Halifax had told his Cabinet colleagues on October 19, à propos the Munich crisis: 'One of the most satisfactory features of the recent crisis had been the attitude of the Egyptian Government, which had responded admirably in every way.' Halifax had gone on to say that, in his view, 'the attitude adopted by the Egyptian Government was a complete justification (if justification was required) for the concessions we had made to the Egyptian Prime Minister when he visited this country in the summer'. Simultaneously with their much-appreciated support for Britain's appeasement policy, the Egyptians were also pressing Britain for a permanent restriction of Jewish immigration into Palestine: on October 19 the Egyptian Prime Minister, Mohammed Mahmoud Pasha, had written direct to Neville Chamberlain to urge him to adopt, in Palestine, a solution that would 'win for your country the good will and deep gratitude of Arabs and Moslems throughout the world'.

The extent to which Arab protests against Jewish immigration were being stimulated by religious as well as by political activists, was well known to the British government, as is made clear by a report from the Criminal Investigation Department, dated 1 November 1938. According to this report, the Mufti and his followers:

have steadily consolidated their position. .... A complete 'Jihad' (Holy War) has not yet been proclaimed, although Jihad has been preached in many village mosques in Palestine, Syria and Iraq. The more religious-minded seriously regard rebel activities in a religious light and the belief is growing in Arab circles in Palestine, that in the event of the British Government declaring a policy which is adverse to Arab interests, a complete Jihad will be declared by the more prominent religious leaders of Islam.

These Arab threats served, momentarily, to harden British policy. On November 9, in an interview with MacDonald, Izzet Tannous stated that Britain's offer to invite both Jews and Arabs to negotiate in London had been 'spoilt' by the exclusion of the Mufti from these negotiations. But MacDonald replied that the Mufti's conduct 'over many years' had shown that he was an influence 'always ready to stir up strife between the Arabs and the Jews'. If the Mufti went back to Palestine, MacDonald added, 'I had no confidence that he would not do this again.' Dr Tannous warned, however, that if the Mufti were not invited to London, 'he was afraid that no Palestinian Arabs would come'. Two days later, in an effort to placate the extremists, MacDonald telegraphed to the High Commissioner: 'I think that it is important that you should take any opportunity that offers of dispelling the impression that exclusion of Mufti necessarily means exclusion of all representatives of the Mufti's Party.'

On 28 October 1938 the German Government began the deportation of all Polish-born Jews, many of whom had been resident in Germany for ten and even twenty years. On November 7, Herschel Grynszpan, the seventeen year old son of Polish-born Jews, but himself born in Germany, driven to desperation by the news of the deportations, which included his parents, shot, and mortally wounded a young German diplomat in Paris. The diplomat's death on the afternoon of November 9 was at once used by the Nazis as an excuse for an orgy of destruction; that same night, more than two hundred synagogues throughout Germany, Austria and the Sudetenland were set on fire, and most of them totally destroyed; hundreds of Jewish-owned shops and warehouses were gutted; more than 30,000 Jews were seized and sent to concentration camps, and more than 1,200 Jews were murdered.

Following the *Kristallnacht*, or 'Night of Broken Glass', the German Government imposed an enormous fine on the Jews of Germany, confiscated all insurance claims, and made an extra effort to drive the remaining Jewish businessmen and traders out of German economic life, while holding most of the 30,000 arrested until early in 1939.

The British Government received full details of these events throughout November 11 and 12, when telegraphic reports reached the Foreign Office from the Embassy in Berlin and from the Consul-General in Frankfurt, R. T. Small-bones. 'I am informed that arrests of male Jews up to the age of 60 are being made on a large scale,' Sir George Ogilvie Forbes telegraphed from Berlin on November 11. All Jewish schools, newspapers and cultural organizations had been closed down. It was even rumoured that the Germans intended to confiscate all Jewish capital.

'Every synagogue in the district has been destroyed,' Smallbones reported on November 12, 'and all rabbis together with other religious leaders and teachers are under arrest.' On November 13 Ogilvie Forbes telegraphed again: the Germans had just announced that from the new year no Jew could be a retailer, an exporter, or a manager of a business. All damage done to Jewish property would have to be paid for by the Jews themselves, who would also have to pay a massive fine. Many Jews, Ogilvie Forbes reported, 'are wandering about in the streets and parks afraid to return to their homes', and he added: 'I can find no words strong enough in condemnation of the disgusting treatment of so many innocent people, and the civilised world is faced with appalling sight of 500,000 people about to rot away in starvation.'

The events of the *Kristallnacht* cast a fearful pall over the Jews of Germany, Austria and the Sudetenland. Once more, the pressure for emigration mounted, but on November 14, only four days after the night of terror, Lord Halifax told the Cabinet, as the official minutes recorded, that 'The government would shortly be confronted with a very difficult decision, namely, was it not to be regarded as fundamental to obtain a settlement with the Arabs?' Malcolm MacDonald, speaking immediately after Halifax, told his colleagues:

The government had to choose between its commitments to the world of Jewry and its commitments to the world of Islam. In spite of the adversities which it was now suffering, the world of Jewry remained extremely influential. For example, there were said to be 3 million Jews in the United States. On the other hand, the British Empire itself was to a very considerable extent a Moslem Empire, some 80 millions of our fellow subjects in India were Moslems. From the defence point of view it was literally out of the question that we should antagonise either the Moslems within the Empire or the Arab kingdoms of the near East.

MacDonald concluded: 'This might very well mean that we could not con-template even a distant future in which there could be a Jewish majority in Palestine.'

Here was the conclusion which the Jews feared most of all. An attempt to mitigate it was touched on at the end of the Cabinet of November 14, when, as

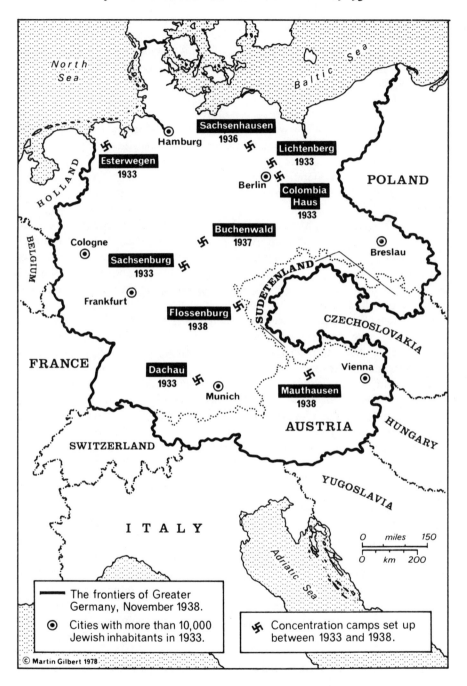

North
Sea

Baltic Sea

Sachsenhausen
1936

Hamburg

Lichtenberg
1933

Esterwegen
1933

Berlin

POLAND

Colombia
Haus
1933

HOLLAND

BELGIUM

Buchenwald
1937

Breslau

Cologne

Sachsenburg
1933

SUDETENLAND

Frankfurt

Flossenburg
1938

CZECHOSLOVAKIA

FRANCE

Dachau
1933

Munich

Vienna

Mauthausen
1938

AUSTRIA

HUNGARY

SWITZERLAND

YUGOSLAVIA

ITALY

Adriatic Sea

0   miles   150

0   km   200

The frontiers of Greater
Germany, November 1938.

Cities with more than 10,000
Jewish inhabitants in 1933.

Concentration camps set up
between 1933 and 1938.

© Martin Gilbert 1978

the minutes recorded, a 'brief discussion took place of the possibilities of Jewish settlement elsewhere than in Palestine'. The Cabinet agreed that the sending of Jewish refugees to places outside Europe 'would become an issue of first-class importance in the event of Jewish immigration into Palestine being restricted'. Mention was made 'of the possibilities of settlement' in Brazil, British Guiana and Western Australia.

How serious were these alternatives? On the day after the Cabinet meeting, Roger Makins, who was now working in the Central Department of the Foreign Office, noted that 'the pitiful condition to which German Jews will be reduced will not make them desirable immigrants', while that same day Neville Chamberlain told a deputation from the Council for German Jewry that the idea of a British Government loan was 'premature, and hardly worth discussing at this stage'.

Also on November 14, MacDonald reported to his Cabinet colleagues on a talk he had held with Weizmann two days before, when he had found Weizmann 'naturally very despairing about the situation of the Jews in Central Europe in general and Germany in particular'. So desperate was Weizmann that he asked MacDonald if the Government of Iraq might not agree 'to some development scheme along the Euphrates which would enable a considerably larger population to settle there'. For such a scheme, Weizmann believed, the Jews themselves 'would be ready to raise £20,000,000 or £30,000,000'. This could be used either to enable Iraq to take '300,000 Jews as direct settlers', or to take 100,000 Arabs from Palestine 'whose land would then pass to Jewish immigrants'.

Within the Foreign Office, those who had followed German affairs since the advent of Nazism understood what the new persecutions meant. On November 15 Michael Cresswell, who had only recently returned from several years in Berlin, noted on Ogilvie Forbes's most recent report: 'This far exceeds the other barbarities which the Nazis have been guilty of in the last 5 years. It is of a quite different order; with winter beginning in Berlin, the outlook for these miserable people is absolutely hopeless.' One could not be surprised, Cresswell added, 'if large numbers of them prefer suicide to death by starvation and exposure. At the same time, tens of thousands are being sent to concentration camps. . . .'

R. T. Smallbones, the Consul-General in Frankfurt, sent a further report to London on November 16, in which he told of 'scenes of indescribable, destructive sadism and brutality'; of householders locked into their lavatories while 'the mob entered and destroyed everything or threw everything on to the streets, where in some cases they were set on fire'. Smallbones reported that there had been 'innumerable cases of suicide' in Frankfurt and the near surroundings, and he added: 'I personally know of eleven acquaintances who have taken their lives to avoid being arrested.'

The *Kristallnacht* ended all hope of an improvement in the situation of the

214

half million Jews of Germany, Austria and the Sudetenland. But the situation of the Jews was ominous also in Poland, Germany's eastern neighbour, and a potential victim of German territorial aspirations. On November 20 the British Ambassador in Warsaw, Sir Howard Kennard, reported to Lord Halifax on Poland's hostile attitude towards the three million Jews who lived within the borders of the Polish State. Most Poles, he wrote, 'regard it as inevitable that in order to induce a state of mind favourable to emigration among the Jews, their position here must be made less comfortable'. Kennard added: 'Local excesses – not organised, as recently in Germany, but more or less spontaneous – are of not infrequent occurrence.'

Following the *Kristallnacht*, there was once again talk about alternate havens in remote colonial lands. But Weizmann knew that such talk would not provide any realistic alternative. On November 20 he wrote to the leader of the Liberal Party, Sir Archibald Sinclair:

All the fancy 'territorialist' projects are useless. It's merely dangling false hopes before the eyes of tortured people. It needs millions untold and years of labour before all these exotic countries could receive an appreciable number of refugees. One can absorb refugees quickly only in highly developed countries and there you meet with limiting factors inherent in the present social structure like unemployment and antisemitism!

Weizmann's letter continued:

We could *easily take now* into Palestine 50,000 people if they *would let us*. We could employ them and all the untold money which is being spent on giving these people temporary shelter could be used effectively for settling them permanently in Palestine. But they don't let us and here is the tragedy! Hence all the fanciful diversions.

17

'The Violation of the Pledge'
January-June 1939

O N November 21 the House of Commons discussed Jewish immigration
into Britain, in the wake of the *Kristallnacht*. During the debate several
Members of Parliament urged the Government to relax its immigration restrictions. More than 65,000 German and Austrian Jews had already found a haven
in Britain, but there was surely room for more. 'I speak', one Labour MP,
Alderman Logan, declared, 'as an orthodox Catholic, feeling to the depth of my
heart the cause of the Jew', and he continued:

I hear mention made of the question of money. If we cannot have civilisation
contented, if we cannot bring sunshine into the lives of people, without being
concerned with the question of money, civilisation is doomed. To-day an opportunity
is offered to the British nation to take its proper stand among the nations of the
world. . . .

The appeal of Logan and of those who felt as he did was answered by the
Home Secretary, Sir Samuel Hoare, who sought to remind the House of what he
called 'some of the difficulties' of a greater immigration. Hoare then explained
what he meant:

In this country we are a thickly populated industrial community with at the
present moment a very large number of unemployed. Competition is very keen
with foreign countries, and it is difficult for many of our fellow-countrymen to
make a livelihood at all and keep their industries and businesses going. It is quite
obvious that there is an underlying current of suspicion and anxiety, rightly or
wrongly, about alien immigration on any big scale. It is a fact, and we had better
face the fact quite frankly, that below the surface – I know it from my own daily
experience at the Home Office . . . there is the making of a definite anti-Jewish
movement.

I do my best as Home Secretary to stamp upon an evil of that kind. That is
the reason why I have prohibited demonstrations in certain parts of London where
inevitably they would stimulate this evil movement.

Faced with a fact of that kind, while I think very few hon. Members look upon
this problem with greater sympathy than I do, I have to be careful to avoid anything
in the nature of mass immigration which, in my view, would inevitably lead to the
growth of a movement which we all wish to see suppressed.

'That means', Hoare added, 'that we must keep a check upon individual cases of immigrants.'

The Jews could draw little comfort from such an answer. All over the world, individuals sought to help them, and humanitarian feelings were roused by their plight; but all over the world where regulations, visas and quotas held sway, Governments set up barriers which could not be crossed, and warned of anti-semitic reactions that could not easily be denied.

On November 28 Pinhas Rutenberg went to see MacDonald at the Colonial Office. Any restriction of Jewish immigration to 'a mere 15,000 or 20,000 or 30,000 Jews a year', Rutenberg told MacDonald, would be 'a capitulation to Arab pressure'. Hundreds of thousands of Jews 'were looking for a country to live in'. They could not be settled in British Guiana, and if too many went to Britain 'or other countries', there would be 'an anti-Semitic movement which would check the flow'. But they could go to Palestine, Rutenberg insisted, 'without any harm coming to the Arabs'. MacDonald replied, however, that there was a 'very strong anti-Semitic movement' which already existed in Palestine, 'and which was resulting in violence and bloodshed every day'.

As 1939 opened, the situation of the Jews of Europe reached a crisis. On 14 January 1939 the British Consul-General in Munich, John Carvell, sent Lord Halifax a harrowing account of the situation inside Dachau concentration camp, where, despite the daily release of two to three hundred Jews a day during December, 7,000 Jews still remained in the camp, including boys of seventeen from the Jewish Seminary at Würzburg, and 'professional men between the ages of 50 and 60'. According to Carvell: 'Apparently the first day of captivity was one of indescribable horror since no released prisoner has been able or willing to speak about it. It may be imagined that the prisoners herded together like cattle in a stockyard were tortured by the fear of the slaughter-house.'

Carvell went on to describe the harsh conditions in the camp, and noted:

Accounts of brutal treatment at the hands of the guards are too consistent to have been mere fabrications. Prisoners have been buffeted, kicked, and even beaten and bastinadoed with steel birches. Some guards never speak to prisoners without hitting them across the mouth with the back of the hand. The medical attendants are particularly callous in their disregard for prisoners requiring medical attention.

As a result of their ill-treatment, Carvell noted, many of those who were released 'are unable to walk and some have been carried to the station unconscious'.

Yet, despite such information, of which there was no shortage, few politicians saw any reason to support the Jews in their distress. One of those who did was the South African leader, Jan Smuts, who had, since 1917, consistently looked forward to the setting up of a Jewish State in Palestine. On January 16 Smuts wrote from Pretoria to Leopold Amery:

The Jewish persecutions are the most ghastly feature of the present international situation, and naturally one expects Palestine to take its fair share of the surplus Jewish population.

I fear it is not much use trying to conciliate the Arabs who are not satisfied with all the Independent Kingdoms – which *we* secured for them.

For the British Government, however, its new policy was about to be made public, as both Jewish and Arab leaders prepared to come to London for a Round Table Conference on the future of Palestine. The Colonial Secretary, Malcolm MacDonald, set out for his Cabinet colleagues the crux of the new policy in a secret Cabinet memorandum on January 18. As the MacDonald memorandum explained:

We cannot accept the contention that all Jews as such have a right to enter Palestine.

It would clearly be absurd to admit that all the millions of Jews in the world have a right, which they should be allowed to exert if they wished, to settle in Palestine.

We cannot avoid an eventual clash, if we continue to carry out the Balfour Declaration, between the forces of persecuted, desperate, brilliant, constructive Jewry in Palestine and the widespread pan-Arab movement which is rallying to the defence of its weakest brethren the Arabs of Palestine.

Arab detestation of the Jewish invasion into Palestine being what it is, it would be wholly wrong to suggest that this large Arab population should one day in their own native land and against their will come under the rule of the newly arrived Jews.

These paragraphs became the basis of the government's policy. At the same time, attempts were made to seek the opinions of various Colonial Governors as to the possibility of at least some small Jewish immigration elsewhere. There was even an attempt to see whether large-scale Jewish immigration to the Soviet Union might be possible. But, as Lord Halifax was informed by the British Consul in Moscow on January 21: 'Despite the absence of any anti-semitic policy on the part of the Soviet Government, an infinitely larger number of Jews have been executed in the Soviet Union in the last two years than in Germany under the Nationalist Socialist regime, while an equal if not larger number have been placed in the Concentration Camps.' This ruled out the Soviet Union.

Meanwhile, the pressures were growing against the mounting flood of illegal immigrants seeking to escape from eastern Europe. On January 24 the Foreign Office urged the British legation in Sofia to press the Bulgarian Government 'to take immediate steps to put an end' to the movement of illegal immigrants through Bulgaria.

The Foreign Office expert who drafted this telegram – C. W. Baxter of the Central Department – explained that same day to Malcolm MacDonald:

It seems to me that it is equally arguable that it is morally wrong for us to insist on sending more and more Jews into Palestine against the wishes of the Arab inhabitants of that country and the Middle East. After all, the moral satisfaction we may derive from sending more Jews to Palestine without Arab consent must be weighed against the moral right of the Arabs to have some say in the question of admission of aliens into their country.

Acutely aware of such attitudes, Dr Weizmann discussed Jewish immigration with Lord Halifax on January 24. Halifax noted, in his report of their conversation, that Weizmann was anxious that, 'while he was not particularly concerned with the numerical limit at which immigration might be fixed – a thousand more or less was, he said, a matter of no great importance on a long view – the thing that was fundamental was that His Majesty's Government should not undermine the whole basis of right by which Jews were in Palestine at all'. And Weizmann had gone on to explain to Halifax that 'it would be to place Jewry in an unbearable position were we to say that immigration was to be permitted only by agreement with the Arabs. This would have the effect of reducing the position of the Jews in Palestine to one of sufferance instead of one, as they claimed, of right.'

From this discussion, it was clear that the Zionists adhered to that very Jewish 'right' to enter Palestine which was established in the 'Churchill' White Paper of 1922, and which MacDonald had secretly rejected six days before Halifax's discussion with Weizmann. In order to overcome this problem, the Government now made an attempt to persuade Weizmann to abandon all Jewish rights in Palestine. This attempt was made at the specific suggestion of Lord Halifax, and with the support of the Minister for the Co-ordination of Defence, Sir Thomas Inskip. Would it not be possible, Halifax asked in a Foreign Office minute on January 26, to get 'the Jews themselves' to agree to give up their rights 'instead of having it forced on them'; and on the following day Malcolm MacDonald told the Cabinet that, 'If we could now persuade the Jews to make a unilateral declaration as had been suggested by Lord Halifax the whole atmosphere might be changed for the better.' MacDonald was afraid, however, that even if Dr Weizmann were prepared to entertain such a declaration 'his constituents would not for a moment allow him to make it'. Nevertheless, MacDonald agreed that a strenuous effort should be made to persuade Weizmann 'to give favourable consideration to this declaration'.

During the Cabinet of January 27, Lord Zetland, the Secretary of State for India, pressed for the immediate passing of the 33 per cent maximum Jewish population in Palestine. Zetland told the Cabinet that he was constantly being urged by the Indian Moslems to support the Arab claims in Palestine. The Minister of Health, Walter Elliot, declared that he attached 'greater weight to the United States than to Arabia at the present moment' but Zetland warned that 'this problem of Palestine was not merely an Arabian problem, it was fast becoming a pan-Islamic problem'. If the Conference failed to reach any agreement, he insisted, 'or ended in what was regarded as a substantial victory for the Jews, serious troubles in India must be apprehended'.

It was during the Cabinet meeting of January 27, that Malcolm MacDonald reinterpreted the Churchill White Paper statement of 1922, that the Jews were in Palestine 'as of right, and not on suffrance'. *As of right* MacDonald told his colleagues, referred only to those Jews who were already living in Palestine in 1922, and not to those who reached Palestine later, or might do so in the future.

The last week of January also saw serious obstacles raised against the possibility of some new Jewish haven being found outside Palestine; indeed, on January 30 the Chancellor of the Exchequer, Sir John Simon, wrote to MacDonald about Jewish settlement in British Guiana: 'It will indeed be a very serious business if the British tax payer, in addition to paying everything else which he is asked to pay for just now, has to pay for the settlement in various parts of the world of enormous numbers of refugees.'

On January 30 Hitler set out, in the Reichstag in Berlin, his designs towards what he called 'the Jewish world-enemy', telling his listeners, and the world:

One thing I should like to say on this day which may be memorable for others as well as for us Germans: In the course of my life I have very often been a prophet, and have usually been ridiculed for it.

During the time of my struggle for power it was in the first instance the Jewish race which only received my prophecies with laughter when I said that I would one day take over the leadership of the State, and with it that of the whole nation, and that I would then among many other things settle the Jewish problem. Their laughter was uproarious, but I think that for some time now they have been laughing on the other side of their face.

To-day I will once more be a prophet: if the international Jewish financiers in and outside Europe should succeed in plunging the nations once more into a world war, then the result will not be the bolshevization of the earth, and thus the victory of Jewry, but the annihilation of the Jewish race in Europe!

Even as Hitler spoke, more news was emerging from Germany about the conditions inside Hitler's camps. On February 2 the British Consul in Dresden, F. M. Shepherd, sent a full report to the British Embassy in Berlin, of the treatment of Jews at Buchenwald concentration camp. 'There was not even enough water to drink,' the Consul reported, 'and there were only 20 lavatories for 10,000 men.' One doctor, later released, had reported to the Consul that he 'had seen people beaten with barbed wire birches'. Of the 10,000 inmates, including 'professors and other leading Jewish men', as many as 350 had died since the previous November. Three weeks later, on February 25, the Foreign Office received a detailed and horrible account of the fate of individual German and Austrian Jews from the Tel Aviv based Association of Jewish Settlers from Germany and Austria; it had been sent from Tel Aviv on February 8, and listed

133 cases concerning the immediate families of German and Austrian Jews who had reached Palestine. The following seven cases were typical:

Father has been arrested and brought to a concentration-camp. Mother was burnt to death while worshipping in the synagogue which was set on fire. Her dead body was found among the debris.

Father died because of cruel treatment in concentration-camp. Mother has been left alone in Germany and is deprived of any means of livelihood.

Father-in-law was thrown out of the window by Nazis and died immediately. Mother-in-law remained in Nuremberg alone. Both children are in Palestine.

Father-in-law is a *shohet* (butcher according to Jewish rites.) He was filmed by the Gestapo and forced to dance while killing an animal. Now this film is shown in the exhibition 'Der ewige Jude' (The Wandering Jew) which is being held in Vienna. In view of the fact that thousands of people are visiting this exhibition, he is in acute danger of being assaulted and even killed by persons who have seen this film.

In September 1938, the mother (78 years old) fled to her son in Prerau (Czechoslovakia). Recently she was expelled from Czechoslovakia. She is almost blind and quite helpless.

Father was murdered in a concentration camp, mother, 57 years old, is left absolutely alone in Germany, is penniless, homeless and destitute. Is the only Jewess left in a small town, nobody dares to offer her refuge or help.

Aged father (71 years old) was imprisoned but subsequently released. His house was raided several times. He was robbed of his belongings and finally evicted from his flat. Now he is all alone and homeless. Palestine is his only hope.

During February and March 1939 new decisions were made by the Cabinet with regard to Palestine. Each of these decisions proved fatal to Palestine being kept open to refugees. The principle behind these arguments had been summed up clearly by Malcolm MacDonald at the Cabinet of January 27, when he had told his colleagues that 'He was satisfied that we could not afford to forfeit the confidence and friendship of a large part of the Moslem world. If we lost that now we would lose it for a long time, whereas if we reached a settlement in Palestine along the lines proposed, Jewish criticism in America would not have any permanent effect on Anglo-American relations.'

While Palestine was being closed, however, several territorial requests were being made, on behalf of Jewish refugees, not only of British Governors and High Commissioners, but also of foreign Governments. There was even a short time during which President Roosevelt put forward the thought that the Portuguese might be persuaded to open Angola to Jewish settlement, but it was the Permanent Under-Secretary of State at the Foreign Office, Sir Alexander Cadogan, who pointed out that in view of the lack of population in many of the

British Colonies it would not be very tactful for Britain to take part in pressing the Portuguese to open their Colonies instead. Cadogan believed in an alternative solution. On February 8 he wrote in a Foreign Office minute for Lord Halifax: 'Are we really trying to find a place for them in e.g. Northern Rhodesia? It would help enormously towards an "Arab" solution of Palestine if we could at the same time offer an alternative "home" elsewhere.'

But no such alternative home could be found. Nor could the pressure of American Jewry act as a counterweight, however that pressure was expressed. Indeed, American Jewish pressure had the exact reverse effect on the policy makers to pan-Islamic and Indian Moslem pressure. Thus Lacy Baggallay minuted on February 8: 'If Jewish immigration into Palestine is not stopped we shall be heading for trouble. We cannot hope to please both the Jews and Arabs. If our solution displeases the Jews, they will let off a lot of hot air – particularly those in the U.S.A. If our solution displeases the Arabs, they are likely to act.'

Six days later, on February 14, at one of the sessions of the London Round Table Conference on Palestine, Malcolm MacDonald openly told Chaim Weizmann the same story. 'If it came to a choice between Jewish or Arab support,' MacDonald asserted, 'he did not believe that, valuable as Jewish assistance would be, it would make up for what would have been lost by the lack of vital support of the Arab and Muslim world.'

Weizmann replied by expressing his scepticism of the enormous powers of the Arabs to destroy the British Empire. In his experience, Weizmann told MacDonald, 'those who knew the Arabs best knew them to be of mercurial temperament and did not paint so alarming a picture of Arab solidarity'. But Lord Halifax, at that same meeting, set out what he considered to be the wider, philosophical view to Weizmann. 'There was a contest', Halifax explained:

between the profoundest philosophies of human life. Their discussion must enable them to see lucidly how necessary it was for the Jews to reconcile administrative necessity and fundamental spiritual claims and rights. He would suggest that the Jews should of their own free will dispose of their rights by offering terms of conciliation and by the long view of their own problem be satisfied that all parties must give freely in order to reach a solution.

The Jews were being asked to 'dispose of their rights'; the Arabs were being offered an end to any possibility of a Jewish majority in Palestine. Yet Arab terrorism continued, and almost every week some Jewish woman or child died at the hands of Arab killers. But even this murder campaign did not deter the British in their policy. A reference to it was made by MacDonald at the Round Table Conference, when he told the Arab representatives, on February 18, that he knew there were men 'who were dying for the Arab cause who were noble men and he respected that sentiment', but, he stressed, his own view was that 'whilst he did not deny their patriotism, they were misguided'. Extremists did harm to their cause. 'He would refer to the massacre at Tiberias in which, for no reason, defenceless Jewish people were murdered, that was the worst case, but there were other similar cases not quite so bad.'

Even while the London Conference was sitting, the British Government were taking active steps to check, and if possible to halt, the continuing flow of 'illegal' Jewish immigrants fleeing from central Europe, and travelling down the Danube to the Black Sea, and on by ship to Palestine. This flow, which had begun in 1934, reached a peak of intensity early in 1939; indeed, during 1939 more than thirty ships, carrying in all nearly 17,000 refugees, sailed from the Rumanian Black Sea ports across the Black Sea, through the Bosphorous, on to the Greek ports, and thence to Palestine.

During February, all British Consuls had been instructed to warn shipping agencies not to take Jews on board for Palestine. But on February 24, in a telegram which was to set the pattern for future British policy, Sir Reginald Hoare, the Minister in Bucharest, informed MacDonald that, in spite of these instructions, 'I have little doubt that this exodus of Jews will continue.' Hoare added: 'We must ourselves take effective police and naval measures to prevent the smuggling of unauthorised refugees into Palestine either from the High Seas or over land.'

Measures were taken, and these measures were to a certain extent successful, so much so that Lord Halifax was informed by the King's Private Secretary, Sir Alexander Hardinge, on February 28, while the London Conference was still in session, that 'The King has heard from Lord Gort that a number of Jewish refugees from different countries were surreptitiously getting into Palestine, and he is glad to think that steps are being taken to prevent these people leaving their country of origin.' Two days later, on March 2, the Foreign Office telegraphed to Sir Nevile Henderson, the British Ambassador in Berlin:

There is a large irregular movement from Germany of Jewish refugees who as a rule, set out without visas or any arrangements for their reception, and their attempt to land in any territory that seems to them to present the slightest possibility of receiving them. This is a cause of great embarrassment to His Majesty's Government and also, it appears, to the American Government, and the latter have expressed a wish that you should join American Chargé d'Affaires in Berlin in bringing situation to the attention of appropriate German Authorities and requesting them to discourage such travel on German ships.

Henderson did as he was instructed, urging the German Government 'to check unauthorized emigration' of Jews from the German Reich.

These pressures were relentless; on March 8, when it was learnt in London that 850 Jews had embarked for Palestine at the Rumanian port of Galatz, aboard the *Astir*, a senior Foreign Office official, A. W. G. Randall, minuted: 'I think we should reprove the Rumanian Government at once.'

As for the colonial, or imperial alternative, this was typified on March 3 by an

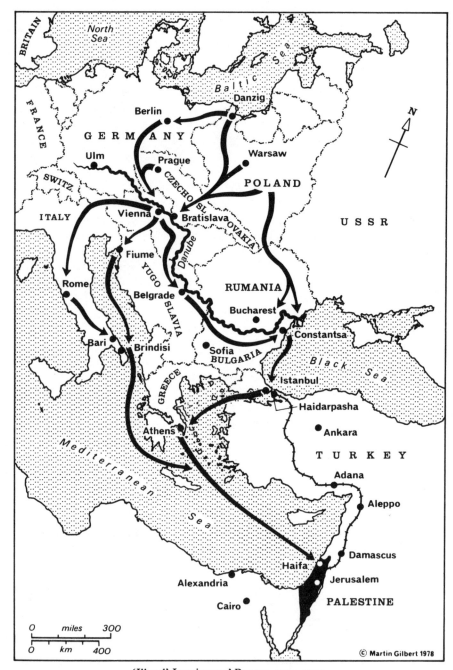

'Illegal' Immigrants' Routes, 1934–1939

India Office comment on a proposal to send Jewish refugees to Burma, 'there is no possibility of contemplating large scale settlement by European refugees in view of the strong objections which would be felt against such settlement to the prejudice of the indigenous races concerned.'

Similar replies were given by every colony approached. On March 13 the Governor of Southern Rhodesia gave his reasons for turning down a request from sixteen Jews for refuge, informing the British Consul-General in Alexandria: 'My Government regrets they are unable to accede to request of the sixteen German Jews mentioned in your telegram to migrate to this Colony. Capacity of Southern Rhodesia for absorbing aliens is definitely limited. Numerous applications are being received, and only those of a suitable type with connections here, as agriculturalists with sufficient capital, are being admitted.'

In London, the Round Table Conference was drawing to a close. Despite the absolute refusal of the Palestinian Arabs to accept any Jewish immigration, the other Arab States had acted as mediators, and a solution had been found. Yet it was a solution entirely against every Zionist request and hope; 'the Jews for their part' Neville Chamberlain told the Cabinet's Palestine Committee on March 6, 'must be made to face up to the fact that a veto on immigration was inevitable after the initial period'. Two days later Malcolm MacDonald reported to the Cabinet of March 8 that whereas the Palestinian Arabs 'had proved very difficult' in accepting any further Jewish immigration whatsoever, the representatives of the neighbouring Arab States, while supporting the Palestine Arabs in public, had, in private, 'indicated that they are prepared to contemplate the immigration of 50,000 Jews over a period of five years, provided that the Arabs were in a position to veto the continuance of Jewish immigration after that date'.

On March 15 German troops occupied Prague, and the Jews of Bohemia and Moravia were added to the ever growing number of second-class citizens, whose future in the Third Reich was a matter for the gravest concern. In all, 118,000 former Czech citizens were designated Jews, according to the Nuremberg Laws. With the imposition of Nazi rule, the pattern of Vienna was repeated: Jewish books were banned, Jewish property was confiscated, Jewish shops were looted, individual Jews were beaten up, and synagogues were burnt. Everywhere in the German Reich the Jews were the daily victims of abuse and persecution. 'Only when this Jewish bacillus infecting the life of people has been removed,' Hitler declared at Wilhelmshaven on April 1, 'can one hope to establish a cooperation among the nations which shall be built up on a lasting understanding.'

At the London Round Table Conference, the representatives of Iraq, the Yemen, Transjordan and Saudi Arabia now applied their maximum pressure. It took the form, as it had done earlier, of urging 'moderation' upon the Palestinian Arabs, who were demanding an immediate veto on Jewish immigration. The Arab States were soon able to persuade the Palestinian Arabs that as, under the new British policy, the total Jewish population would never exceed 33 per cent of the whole, a veto could easily be deferred for five years on all those Jews above an initial 75,000 who would be allowed in between 1939 and 1944.

Despite Jewish protest, the Cabinet now took the view that it was the Jews who should have made some compromise agreements with the Arabs in the past. The current impasse arose, Halifax told his Cabinet colleagues on March 22, 'through no fault of the Arabs but through failure of the Jews to co-operate with the Arabs', and on the following day, when the White Paper was finalized, Malcolm MacDonald informed his colleagues: 'We must not enable the Jews to hold up constitutional progress by refusal to co-operate with the Arabs.'

Dr Weizmann, leaving England on March 24, wrote to Neville Chamberlain: 'Never before have I left England with so heavy a heart. A cloud hangs over the relations between the Jewish Agency and British ministers. Through all the ups and downs of more than 20 years I have found support in the thought that, to quote Lord Balfour's words "We are partners in the great enterprise",' an enterprise, Weizmann added, 'which means life or death to my people'.

The new policy, with its harsh implications for almost all refugees, was put into effect with amazing rapidity, even before the proposed White Paper was published by the Government, or debated in Parliament. Indeed, during April, anti-refugee pressures were put in addition on the Governments of Hungary and Yugoslavia. Nor were these pressures always unwelcome to the Ambassadors who received them. On April 11, an Independent Member of Parliament, Miss Eleanor Rathbone, wrote to Winston Churchill: 'When I was in Prague on refugee business I heard from everyone – refugee workers, journalists, etc – that the British legation was completely aloof, uninterested and unhelpful over refugee questions.' And she added: 'In Bucharest, the British Minister (as admitted to me by a member of his family) was strongly anti-Semite, though the persecution of Rumanian Jews had already begun.'

On April 20 the Cabinet's Palestine Committee discussed possible United States' objections to the British policy of preventing Jewish refugees from going to Palestine. But Lord Halifax was able to report to his colleagues that he had discussed this very question with the American Ambassador, Joseph Kennedy, and that Kennedy had told him 'that we ought not to over-estimate Jewish influence in the United States'. Later in the same Cabinet meeting, Neville Chamberlain declared, with all the authority of his Premiership, that it was of 'immense importance' from the point of view of strategy, 'to have the Moslem world with us', and he added: 'If we must offend one side, let us offend the Jews rather than the Arabs.'

Continual efforts were made to put this policy into practical effect. On April 25 the British Minister to Greece, Sir Sydney Waterlow, was able to telegraph to the Foreign Office from Athens: 'As a result of my representations Greek

Government have now issued an order to Greek Port Authorities and Consular Officers abroad to the effect that it is from now on forbidden to transport Jews to Palestine in Greek ships if they are not in possession of passports or valid visas.' Waterlow added, as his personal opinion: 'I am satisfied that this order will go a long way to putting an end to this traffic.'

In Palestine itself, the search for 'illegal' immigrants continued even for those who managed to slip ashore. On April 22 the High Commissioner, Sir Harold MacMichael, was able to telegraph to Malcolm MacDonald: 'On information given by Arabs to the military and police, 218 illegal immigrants were captured yesterday in orange groves south of Rehovot.' For the policy-makers in London, these 'illegals' were not true refugees at all. On April 26 Patrick Reilly minuted that the Jews who were seeking to reach Palestine from Czechoslovakia were people who 'need not leave anyhow': some of them, he added, 'are definitely criminals or spies.'

The terrible conditions on board the refugee ships were made even worse by the long delays and even longer return voyages which British policy imposed upon them. On April 3 the British Vice-Consul in Constantsa, Anthony Kendall, reported to the Foreign Office on the progress of the ship *Sandu*, with 350 refugees from central Europe on board, which had been forced to return to Rumania from Palestine. Even though the Jewish Agency had been able to send food and water on board at Haifa, after twenty-five days at sea, the Consul reported, 'the filth and congestion had to be seen to be believed'. The conditions on the ship were 'absolutely shocking'.

On April 28 the Foreign Office received a press cutting from the *New York Times*, dated April 23, with an article by Joseph Levy, describing conditions on board another ship, the *Assimi*, which had likewise managed to reach Haifa. According to Levy: 'When a police officer announced the Government's order for the steamer to leave, the passengers tore off their clothing and screamed that they would rather be killed than sent back to sea. Some prayed and recited psalms.'

On May 8 the British Minister to Greece, Sir Sydney Waterlow, suggested that the 700 refugees on board a third ship, the *Astir*, should be allowed temporarily into Cyprus. But this prompted Patrick Reilly to ask, on May 9: 'Why should the British Empire take these refugees. We have nothing to show that they are in any way suitable settlers.' Reilly added: 'Their position is horrible, for they have been on this small ship since 7 March.' But the policymakers did not allow themselves to be influenced by the conditions on board the *Astir*, and that same day, May 9, Randall noted that the Colonial Office 'could hold out no hope that they would be allowed into Cyprus, which is too near Palestine anyhow'.

Meanwhile, as the *Astir* proceeded on its journey towards Palestine, the Foreign Office continued to put pressure on Rumania not to allow the boat to go on, and there was anger when that pressure failed. On May 9 the Foreign Office telegraphed to Sir Reginald Hoare, the British Minister in Bucharest, that the 'failure of Rumanian authorities to prevent their departure has caused serious embarrassment to His Majesty's Government, who are entitled to ask that Rumanian Government should assist in a difficult situation by taking the refugees back'.

On May 10 Sir Sydney Waterlow was able to report success for Britain in the wider, pan-Arab sphere. 'Egyptian Minister here,' he telegraphed to the Foreign Office from Athens that day, 'has informed me that Palestine Government's action in arresting and ordering away vessels having on board illegal Jewish immigrants has had profound effect in Egypt, as well as proof of good faith and intentions.' Waterlow's telegram continued: 'Such concrete action had far more value in the eyes of an Oriental than any number of promises and agreements,' and he went on to urge continued vigilance, and action. 'For this reason,' he added, 'it seems to me most desirable that every effort should be made to prevent steamship *Astir* landing her passengers in Palestine.' He intended his own part in this to be a positive one. 'I will endeavour', he promised, 'to furnish early information of her movements.'

By the end of April 1939, the Palestine White Paper was finalized, imposing upon Palestine severe restrictions which would fix an upper limit of 100,000 on the number of Jewish immigrants to be admitted over the following five years, after which the Arabs would have an effective veto on any further Jewish immigration. MacDonald himself was well aware of some unfairness in this decision. 'As regards the policy itself,' he told his Cabinet colleagues on May 1, 'he had admitted frankly that certain points had been inserted to meet Arab pressure and which, perhaps, would have been omitted if the matter were looked at on strict merits.'

On 9 May 1939 a special Cabinet Committee on Refugees discussed a proposal to settle 500 Jewish families in British Guiana. Sir John Simon's economic objection had been overcome by a pledge from British Jewry to finance the settlement. But nevertheless the proposal was opposed, for, as Malcolm MacDonald told the Committee, 'Lord Moyne and his colleagues on the Royal Commission on the West Indies were sceptical as to the possibilities of any extensive white settlement in British Guiana.' MacDonald himself had another reason for hesitation, telling his Committee that he was 'afraid that when the refugee settlers became British subjects (i.e. after five years) they would acquire the right to migrate into the United Kingdom if they wished'.

The Cabinet met on May 17 for a final discussion of the new White Paper. On the question of the legality of their measure, which Herbert Samuel had challenged, Lord Halifax told his colleagues that 'he would much prefer it if the League of Nations could be induced, either to approve our policy as being consistent with the Mandate, or to say that the Mandate should be modified so as to make it consistent with our policy'. MacDonald warned, however, that the Council of the League 'was much under the influence of Zionist opinion', and might want to take the matter to the International Court at the Hague.

There was also a discussion of the Mufti's rejection of the new plan. But MacDonald was not disposed to take this too seriously, and, as the official Cabinet minutes recorded, 'emphasised the importance of making it clear that the Mufti was not a national leader, but merely the head of a faction whose supporters had shot a very large number of their fellow Arabs'. In all, MacDonald told the Cabinet, 'some 370' moderate Arabs had been murdered by the Mufti's men 'in the last few months'.

MacDonald ended with the observation that the White Paper 'would be opposed by both sides'. That, he said, 'was perhaps some indication that it was a just settlement'.

The new Palestine White Paper was published by the Government on the evening of May 17. On the morning of May 22, *The Times* published a letter by Sir Horace Rumbold, Professor Coupland, and all the other surviving members of the Peel Commission (Lord Peel having died in September 1937) to say that the 'cessation of immigration' did not, as they put it, 'eliminate the fear of domination; it only transfers it from Arab minds to Jewish'.

That same day, the House of Commons debated the new White Paper, against which Leopold Amery spoke with much force, telling the House that the Government's watchword had now become 'appease the Arabs', and to do so 'by breaking faith with the Jews'. Amery went on:

The White Paper is a direct invitation to the Arabs to continue to make trouble. As for the Jews, they are now told that all the hopes that they have been encouraged to hold for 20 years are to be dashed to the ground, all their amazing effort wasted – in so far as it was an effort to create a National Home – all the pledges and promises that have been given to them, broken. That is to be their reward for loyalty, for patience, for almost unbelievable self-restraint.

After protesting that the Jews were now to be 'a permanent minority' in Palestine, Amery continued:

Let us not forget of whom we are asking this. These are not like the Jews in Germany, a helpless, hopeless minority. They are a formidable body of people. They are composed largely of younger men who have undergone military training and are quite capable of defending themselves, of holding their own, if only we allowed them. They are people who have felt the breath of freedom and who mean to remain free. They are people who believe the land in which they are living is their own, not merely by old sentimental association, or even international sanction, but because, such as it is to-day, they have created it.

Addressing himself directly to Malcolm MacDonald, Amery asked:

Does my right hon. Friend believe that these people will be content to be relegated to the position of a statutory minority, to be denied all hope of giving refuge and relief to their tortured kinsfolk in other countries; that they will wait passively until, in due course, they and the land they created are to be handed over to the Mufti?

Amery ended his speech by telling the House of Commons that he would feel 'ashamed' if he did not vote against the Government. On May 23, the second day of the debate, Winston Churchill spoke with force and bitterness against what he believed was both a betrayal of the Balfour Declaration, and a shameful act of appeasement. His speech began:

I say quite frankly that I find this a melancholy occasion. Like my right hon. Friend the Member for Sparkbrook (Mr Amery), I feel bound to vote against the proposals of His Majesty's Government. As one intimately and responsibly concerned in the earlier stages of our Palestine policy, I could not stand by and see solemn engagements into which Britain has entered before the world set aside for reasons of administrative convenience or – and it will be a vain hope – for the sake of a quiet life. Like my right hon. Friend, I should feel personally embarrassed in the most acute manner if I lent myself, by silence or inaction, to what I must regard as an act of repudiation.

During the course of his speech Churchill drew attention to a factor of the Palestine problem which had been much commented on in Britain during the previous two years: the large Arab as well as Jewish immigration into Palestine since the beginning of the Mandate. The extent of this Arab immigration had been commented on by several Jewish witnesses to the Peel Commission. Not only Jewish immigrants, but Arab immigrants had been drawn to Palestine by its new-found prosperity, and the Arabs like the Jews had been drawn from a wide geographic area. The Palestine census of 1931 had shown that many Arabs then resident in Palestine had been born in countries as far away as Morocco, Algeria, Tripoli and Yemen. This fact had so impressed itself on Churchill that he told the House of Commons during his speech:

So far from being persecuted, the Arabs have crowded into the country and multiplied till their population has increased more than even all world Jewry could lift up the Jewish population. Now we are asked to decree that all this is to stop and all this to come to an end. We are now asked to submit, and this is what rankles most with me, to an agitation which is fed with foreign money and ceaselessly inflamed by Nazi and by Fascist propaganda.

Of the proposed Arab veto on all Jewish immigration after 1944 Churchill declared emphatically: 'Now, there is the breach; there is the violation of the pledge; there is the abandonment of the Balfour Declaration; there is the end of the vision, of the hope, of the dream.'

After warning that the appeasement of the Arabs 'will cast our country, and all that it stands for, one more step downwards in its fortunes', Churchill ended

Countries from which both Arabs and Jews emigrated, 1922-1931, to settle in Palestine.

Countries from which Jews or Arabs alone emigrated, 1922-1931, to settle in Palestine.

IRELAND

Atlantic Ocean

GREAT BRITAIN

SPAIN

FRANCE

GERMANY

LATVIA

AUSTRIA

POLAND

LITHUANIA

MOROCCO

Mediterranean Sea

CZECHOSLOVAKIA

HUNGARY

SOVIET UNION

ALGERIA

ITALY

RUMANIA

TUNISIA

YUGOSLAVIA

BULGARIA

Black Sea

TRIPOLI

GREECE

TURKEY

Caspian Sea

CYRENAICA

SYRIA

PALESTINE

EGYPT

TRANSJORDAN

Persian Gulf

IRAQ

PERSIA

N

Red Sea

SUDAN

SAUDI ARABIA

ABYSSINIA

YEMEN

Indian Ocean

0   miles   400

0   km 400

© Martin Gilbert 1978

his speech 'upon the land of Palestine', directing his criticisms first against Malcolm MacDonald and then against Neville Chamberlain. 'It is strange indeed', he said, 'that we should turn away from our task in Palestine at the moment when, as the Secretary of State told us yesterday, the local disorders have been largely mastered.' And he went on:

It is stranger still that we should turn away when the great experiment and bright dream, the historic dream, has proved its power to succeed.

Yesterday the Minister responsible [Malcolm MacDonald] descanted eloquently in glowing passages upon the magnificent work which the Jewish colonists have done. They have made the desert bloom. They have started a score of thriving industries, he said. They have founded a great city on the barren shore. They have harnessed the Jordan and spread its electricity throughout the land. . . .

It is 20 years ago since my right hon. Friend [Neville Chamberlain] used these stirring words:

'A great responsibility will rest upon the Zionists, who, before long, will be proceeding, with joy in their hearts, to the ancient seat of their people. Theirs will be the task to build up a new prosperity and a new civilisation in old Palestine, so long neglected and misruled.'

Well, they have answered his call. They have fulfilled his hopes. How can he find it in his heart to strike them this mortal blow?

The final vote was 268 to 179 in favour of the Government's White Paper policy, one of its smallest majorities since the formation of the National Government in 1931: an eighty-nine vote majority, as opposed to their usual two hundred and fifty.

The MacDonald White Paper – known henceforth to the Jews as the 'Black Paper' – led not only to widespread distress among world Jewry, and strong protests throughout the Jewish community in Palestine, but also to a widespread feeling among the majority of Jews both in Palestine and beyond that henceforth the future, not only of Jewish immigration into Palestine, but of the whole nature of a future Jewish entity there, depended first and foremost, not upon the British with whom power lay, but upon the renewed efforts, struggles and perseverance of the Jews themselves. By making the possibility of Jewish statehood more remote, and even impossible, under the now amended Mandate system, the policies of the MacDonald White Paper, both in curbing immigration and in ending all hopes even of a Peel-type 'mini' State, had the reverse effect to their intentions, by stimulating and sharpening the Jewish goal of statehood and full independence. The obstacles seemed formidable: on May 22 Josiah Wedgwood drew the attention of the House of Commons to what he called the 'unjust law' whereby although the city of Jerusalem had a substantial Jewish majority, 77,000 Jews and 49,000 Arabs, 'the Government insists upon the mayoralty and the administration being in the hands of the Arabs'. That, Wedgwood said, 'is something nobody can justify'.

Since the German occupation of Prague on March 15 the lot of the 118,000 Jews of Bohemia and Moravia had worsened with every passing week. At the same time the British Government found itself with funds available for political refugees from Czechoslovakia left over from the time of the Munich Conference. Did these funds apply to Jewish refugees, 25,000 of whom managed to leave Bohemia and Moravia in the four months between the German occupation and the outbreak of war? On May 19, two days after the publication of the Palestine White Paper, a young Foreign Office official, G. M. Warr, had minuted: 'we can presumably agree that the political refugees should be treated as more urgent than the Jews.'

On May 26 an Inter-Departmental Conference, at which Foreign and Colonial Office representatives were present, discussed the question both of those 'illegal' immigrants already on their way to Palestine, and of those who might soon set off. The official minutes of the conference recorded:

. . . The subject could be conveniently divided into two parts. (1) How to prevent further Jewish refugees from Central and South Eastern European countries from embarking on ships en route for Palestine. (2) What, if any, steps should be taken with regard to the two Greek ships mentioned.

1. It was agreed, however . . . that strong pressure should be brought at once upon the Governments of the remaining countries [Greece, Hungary, Poland, Rumania and Yugoslavia] to take effective measures to put a stop to the traffic. . . .

2. The following alternative courses of action were considered:
   (a) to admit them to Palestine.
   (b) to decline all responsibility.
   (c) to obtain permission for them to disembark in the port of embarkation.
   (d) to secure permission for them to land temporarily in some British colony in the Eastern Mediterranean, with a view to their ultimate settlement in a proposed Jewish colony elsewhere.

It was agreed that while (a) must be avoided at almost any cost, (b) might occasion serious criticism in this country on the ground of callousness, and that therefore a fresh attempt should be made to secure (c).

One conclusion of the Conference of May 26 was that the Rumanian Government 'should be asked to take them back'; and in order to bring 'the utmost moral pressure to bear' on the Rumanians actually to accept the Jews back, and to set them *en route* to the eastern European towns from which they had fled, it was agreed that the British Government 'should offer as their own contribution to the solution of the problem, to supply free of charge, food, water and any necessary medical supplies at the Roumanian port of embarcation in each case sufficient for a short period, say 15 days, while the negotiations were proceeding with the Roumanian Government'.

Once more, the idea of 'a proposed Jewish colony elsewhere' had been raised. But on the following day a Government Minister, Lord Winterton, wrote as

233

follows to the Foreign Office about the possibility of Kenya – which had been raised at the Evian Conference in 1938. 'Nothing', he declared in a letter to A. W. G. Randall on May 27, 'could be more calculated to injure any organized Settlement Scheme in any territory, British or otherwise, than an unorganized flow of refugee immigrants pari passu with the formation of the settlement, and unconnected with it'. Writing of what he had said at Evian, Lord Winterton told Randall that: 'my recollection is that I spoke on more than one occasion of a "trial settlement" in Kenya. I think that I *safeguarded the position* further by indicating, without mentioning figures, that if the experiment succeeded it would only eventually provide for the settlement of a small number of families.' The figure mentioned, Winterton thought, had been 'at least' three hundred.

The focus of Foreign Office attention now turned to the Danube. On the same day that Lord Winterton was especially barring out Kenya to any substantial Jewish settlement, the British Ambassador in Belgrade, Sir Ronald Campbell, was pressing the Yugoslav Government 'to cooperate with His Majesty's Government ... in putting a stop to attempts at illegal immigration into Palestine'. Three days later, on May 30, Campbell handed the Yugoslav Foreign Minister an *aide memoire* in which he stated that the British Government were 'deeply concerned at the increase in attempts to land at ports in Palestine Jewish refugees embarked in ships flying the Greek or some other flag at ports in various European countries, including Yugoslav ports in the Adriatic'. The *aide memoire* continued:

A number of these embarkations have lately been taking place in Roumanian ports, and many of the Jewish refugees so embarked come from neighbouring countries. His Majesty's Minister at Bucharest has accordingly been instructed to suggest that the Roumanian Government take steps to make the entry into Roumania of persons in transit dependent in every case on proof of permission to enter a third country, or alternatively to take proper steps to prevent the embarkation at a Roumanian port of any person not possessing a visa for a third country.

His Majesty's Representatives at Warsaw, Budapest, and Athens have also been instructed to approach the governments to which they are accredited in the matter and to urge them to cooperate with His Majesty's Government and the other Governments concerned in putting a stop to these attempts at illegal immigration into Palestine. His Majesty's Government earnestly hope that the Yugoslav Government will use their best endeavour to the same end.

Within the Foreign Office in London, Randall had pondered the proposal of the Inter-Departmental Conference of May 26 for paying the Rumanians fifteen days' worth of food and water before sending the Jewish refugees back towards Poland, central Europe, and above all Germany. Randall was very much against this British contribution, for, as he explained in a departmental memorandum on June 1:

The payment could only be offered by us if it was strictly limited, on the other hand it could only be attractive to the Roumanians if there was no limit, since there is no prospect of the negotiation at the end of a fortnight resulting in disposing of the majority of the cases who are German.

The question has to be faced what should be done with the non-Roumanian Jews when the limited period for which we might be prepared to pay for them came to an end. I confess I see no satisfactory answer to this question.

We could not press the Roumanian Government to return the German and Czechoslovak Jews to their country of origin; the proposed temporary solution of Cyprus has, I understand, been firmly rejected by the Governor; it is unthinkable that a miscellaneous crowd of Jews could be admitted to any other part of the Empire.

We therefore seem driven back, pending an approach to the Treasury, to making one more attempt to place the responsibility where it really lies, namely on the Roumanian and Greek Governments. . . .

Four days after Randall wrote this memorandum, with its added information that even Cyprus had now been barred as an alternative to Palestine, the House of Commons debated the refugee question. During the course of the debate, Josiah Wedgwood spoke with much bitterness against the Colonial Office and Foreign Office policy in carrying out the White Paper with such vigour. 'Conduct worthy of Hitler,' he declared, 'conduct worthy of the Middle Ages, cannot be carried on by the British Government in 1939.' Wedgwood added, with a direct reference to Malcolm MacDonald: 'He may succeed in stopping this illegal immigration, but if he does the report of it will stink in the nostrils of posterity.'

18

Towards the Abyss
July-December 1939

DURING the summer of 1939 the number of Jewish 'illegal' immigrants seeking to reach Palestine grew considerably. In response, the British Government continued, with mounting vigour, to seek to stop the ships reaching Palestine. Every country that allowed Jews to pass through found itself faced with strong British displeasure. In June 1939 British anger was turned against the Rumanian Government; on 9 June Patrick Reilly, of the Foreign Office, protested against 'the Roumanian Govts complete failure to stop the scandalous traffic of illegal immigrants into Palestine'.

According to the Rumanians, however, passengers coming down the Danube in *one* ship, and then transferring to another, were never legally within Rumanian jurisdiction. Such was the law of the Danube – according to the Definitive Statute of 1921. Commenting on this on June 14, Randall minuted for his Foreign Office colleagues: 'The Roumanian argument about the international status of the Danube is plausible, but it also reveals an absence of any wish to collaborate with HMG to stop this traffic.'

The British enquiries into places of refuge other than Palestine continued throughout the summer of 1939. On June 3 the Foreign Office received information from the Indian Ocean island of Socotra. Officially, it was reported 'Jewish refugee settlement in Socotra is quite impractical'. But, as a further minute explained, the ruler of Socotra, a Muslim, had made it clear that 'if only they were Christians and not Jews there would be no trouble'.

Then, on June 15 the Foreign Office learned, from the British Legation in Bogota, that the Colombian Government had decided to suspend Jewish immigration, and had just refused to issue 1,500 immigration permits to Jewish applicants. Randall noted: 'This is disappointing, but the same thing is happening all over S. America.' That same day the Foreign Office received a report from Sir John Maybin, the Governor of Northern Rhodesia, on the possibility of Jewish settlement there. Large-scale Jewish settlement had been proposed, by one of Churchill's former advisers at the Colonial Office, Major, and now Sir Herbert Young. But, as the Governor wrote:

I am frankly alarmed at the thought of European children being born and brought up in such a regime where an insufficient and ill-balanced diet would be inevitable and no amenities of life possible. The result, as I foresee it, would be physical degeneration.

To these physical dangers would be added the even more serious danger of mental and moral degeneration. The educational facilities even for our present European population are far from satisfactory.

The Governor's objections continued:

I am sure that you will agree that it would be unfair to allow European children to grow up in this Territory ill-nourished and ill-educated, and that very grave problems for the future would be created thereby. It will strain our resources to provide education for the existing population. To increase that strain by intro-ducing a large number of settlers who would contribute little directly or indirectly to the revenue might well create a problem beyond our financial means.

Commenting on the Governor's arguments, a senior member of the Foreign Office, Sir Orme Sargent, an opponent of the appeasement of Nazi Germany, noted caustically on June 23: 'I can imagine a great many of these argument were being used with equal sincerity to prove that Jewish colonisation in Palestine was bound to fail on economic & climatic grounds.'

On July 6, in a debate in the House of Lords, several Peers urged a British Government loan towards the resettlement of Jewish refugees in British Guiana. But on July 7, at a meeting of the Cabinet Committee on Refugees, Sir Samuel Hoare, the Chairman of the Committee, confirmed Britain's support for the Evian Conference decision, 'that no participating Government would give direct financial assistance to refugees'. It was essential, Hoare explained, that Britain should 'put first the general financial stringency, which precludes consideration of any further burden on the British taxpayer except on urgent grounds'. On July 13 one of the United States representatives on the Intergovernmental Committee for Refugees, Robert Pell, reported to Washington that the British Representative on the Committee, Sir Herbert Emerson, had told him:

... that it was not the intention of the British Government to permit 'mass settlement' in Guiana or anything resembling the situation in Palestine. He said at most it would agree to the establishment of a group of 50 here and 50 there interspersed throughout the territory and not forming a homogeneous mass of Jews. He said that the idea which seemed to be held in American circles that something akin to a Jewish state could be set up anywhere in the world was Utopian in the extreme . . . .

During the autumn of 1939 the British Government made several attempts to influence United States opinion against the 'illegal' immigration. But there were counter-sympathies difficult to combat: in particular a further report sent by Joseph Levy to the *New York Times*, and published on June 2, which had roused sympathy throughout the United States for the plight of the refugees during their perilous journey towards Palestine. The ship concerned was a Greek cattle boat, the *Liesel*, with 906 Jews on board, which had reached Palestine on June 1. The passengers, who included 300 women and children, had come from Poland, Rumania, Germany and Czechoslovakia. Allowed by the authorities to enter, their number was to be deducted from the next immigration schedule. 'It goes without saying,' Levy noted, 'that the British soldiers and constables here are happy when the human contraband they have apprehended are finally released. They look sympathetically upon joyful reunions of long separated families.'

In his article, Levy also wrote of some less fortunate refugees, 424 in all, who had left Danzig nearly three months before, and were 'now stranded on the Island of Crete in utter destitution, starvation and sickness. These castaways lack elementary sanitary necessities.' Levy's article continued:

Under normal conditions illegal immigrants constitute the best constructive elements for the country, since those whose entry is effected with the approval of national Jewish organisations are previously trained for Palestine life and labor conditions.

But groups organised by the Revisionists are based on the wider assumption that any Jew willing to go to Palestine is acceptable.

It is no secret that the Jewish population of Palestine is sympathetic and helpful to all organisations now taking the latter wider view.

It is interesting to note that even the Palestine Arabs in general are not antagonistic toward these illegal immigrants. Many of the latter recount instances of Arab charity when they wandered unknowingly into Arab villages. While some of the Fellaheen ran to report them to the police, the refugees report, others sheltered the newcomers, sharing their bread and olives.

On July 22, in order to attempt to lessen the impact of Levy's article, the Colonial Office prepared a special note on the subject of 'illegal' immigration. This note was sent confidentially to all British Consuls in the United States, for use in trying to win American sympathy for the British point of view. 'Every country which operates a quota system,' the note read – a clear reference to the strict United States legislation, 'must protect its laws from infringement, and its citizens from mass-invasion.' The immigration traffic itself was 'a dirty, sordid, crooked business'. The Jews of Palestine, in helping the immigrants to get ashore, were 'palpably neglecting their duties as citizens', and, having been in favour of law and order during the earlier Arab riots, it 'ill becomes them of all people to play the other game now'. The Colonial Office note also sought to point out to the British Consuls, and through them to the American public, that:

The idea is fostered by Jewish circles that they are justified in trying to break the law by virtue of some super-legal higher morality, and in extenuation they cite the persecutions in Greater Germany, and the desperate plight in which many European

238

Jews now find themselves. But in this view they, like so many other lawbreakers, are thinking only of themselves, and fail to realise that what they are doing is fundamentally anti-social – as anti-social as the German persecution of which they complain.

A phrase had been used in this Colonial Office note to the effect that the Jews from Poland and Rumania were not *bona fide* refugees. This argument had first reached London from the Chargé d'Affaires in Warsaw, Clifford Norton, who had written on 6 July, about the Jews reaching Poland from Prague; 'It is true that many of those not more or less earmarked by the Refugee Organisation are non-political refugees, mostly Jews who left the Protectorate perhaps prematurely in panic'. Yet Norton had also given a graphic picture of what fate might be in store if these Jews returned to Prague: 'if I began to tell you', he wrote to Randall, 'the stories *we can vouch for* . . . nostrils or cheeks slit, swastikas branded etc, you would agree that one can feel little certainty as to what might happen to them'.

Reading Norton's report, and ignoring his account of the terrors which a return to Czechoslovakia might involve, on July 24 Patrick Reilly minuted:

The problem of the Czech refugees is an extremely difficult one, particularly as regards the refugees in Poland. A great many of these are not in any sense political refugees, but Jews who panicked unnecessarily & who need not have left: many of them are quite unsuitable as emigrants & would be a very difficult problem if brought here.

On July 30 Neville Chamberlain commented on the persecution of the Jews of Germany in a letter to one of his sisters. 'I believe the persecution arose out of two motives; A desire to rob the Jews of their money and a jealousy of their superior cleverness.' His letter continued: 'No doubt Jews aren't a loveable people; I don't care about them myself; – but that is not sufficient to explain the Pogrom.'

On July 30 the House of Commons again debated the refugee policy, and Britain's financial contribution. Several MPs, among them Josiah Wedgwood, Alfred Duff Cooper, and Leopold Amery, spoke bitterly against the Government's policy of not accepting that many of the Jews who fled were really refugees, in the technical sense.

During the debate, MacDonald revealed that, to show its displeasure at the continuation of 'illegal' immigration, the Government had decided 'a short while ago' to suspend all legal immigration. This suspension, he told the House, would remain in operation for a further six months. At the same time, 'illegal' immigrant ships would still be intercepted and turned back.

Duff Cooper, who had resigned from the Cabinet after Munich, was speaking for the first time on Palestine. 'It seems to me,' he said, 'that the latest announcement that because illegal immigration is succeeding, legal immigration has to be stopped, is another lamentable proof of failure. It is like a petulant schoolmaster who, because some boys play truant, keeps in those who come to school.' The Jews and Arabs, Duff Cooper went on, were both 'old friends' of Britain. If two old friends come to you for help, you help the one who has 'the greatest need', clearly, in this instance, the Jews; and he added: 'Before these islands began their history, a thousand years before the Prophet Mohammed was born, the Jew, already exiled, sitting by the waters of Babylon, was singing: "If I forget thee, O Jerusalem, may my right hand forget its cunning." '

During his speech Duff Cooper spoke of what a 'hateful experience' it was for the Arab to see his land 'passing out of his hands into those of another race', but he went on to ask: 'What hateful experiences are other races going through at the present time? Compare it, for a moment, with the long torture that is being inflicted on the Jews.' His speech ended with an appeal to the Government not to close Palestine to the Jews, and he declared:

In the course of their long persecution, they have begun once again to see a hope of return. It is us, it is the British people, British statesmen, the fore-runners of right hon. Gentlemen on the Front Bench, who have raised that hope in their hearts. It is the strong arm of the British Empire that has opened that door to them when all other doors are shut. Shall we now replace that hope that we have revived by despair, and shall we slam the door in the face of the long-wandering Jew?

On the day after this debate Lord Beaverbrook's mass-circulation *Daily Express* commented scathingly on the financial aspects: 'Jews all over the world should be willing to help the persecuted and homeless of their own race. Our own Exchequer cannot bear the burden.' The Jewish organizations had, however, almost exhausted their funds, which came entirely from private donations. On August 2 an all-Party deputation went to see the Chancellor of the Exchequer to urge him to make available to Jewish refugees a sum of £2 million, as a separate sum from the £4 million which had originally been proposed for Czechoslovak refugees in general. But this request was rejected, and on August 4 Lord Winterton told the House of Commons that extra funds were not available for 'these unfortunate refugees'.

At the very moment when British funds had been refused, Jewish refugees were being denied entry into more and more countries, among them Argentina, Brazil, Colombia and Nicaragua, while at the same time France, Belgium, Holland and even Switzerland were tightening their entry regulations and frontier controls. As far as entry into the United States was concerned, since April 1939 its refugee quotas had been completely filled, not only for the remaining eight months of 1939, but for the whole of 1940 and 1941 as well; nor could any number of appeals to President Roosevelt give the refugees any hope of a change in United States policy.

On 31 July 1939 a specific question was asked in the British Parliament about the plight of those Jewish refugees from Czechoslovakia who had crossed over the frontier in to Poland. The question was directed to Chamberlain, but a note in the Foreign Office files states: 'PM does *not* wish to see.' Nevertheless, some answer had to be given by someone. Despite Clifford Norton's letter of July 6, and a further detailed despatch from Katowice, in Poland, of July 7, both of which had been discussed at the Foreign Office for a week before the Parliament-ary question, the Under-Secretary for Foreign Affairs, R. A. Butler, told the House of Commons that the Prime Minister 'has received no very recent reports on the position of refugees from Czecho-Slovakia in Poland.'

For the Cabinet meeting of August 4, Malcolm MacDonald had asked that the question of illegal immigration be put specially on the agenda. At the meeting itself he gave his colleagues a report of what was being done. As a first step, the High Commissioner in Palestine had been authorized 'to make the recent drastic announcement that no immigration quota would be issued for the next six-monthly period October 1939–March 1940'. It was essential, MacDonald said, 'that we should adhere firmly to this decision', which was already making the Jewish leaders realize 'that they would have to use their influence to stop illegal immigration in order to secure the resumption of legal immigration'.

The second step in progress, MacDonald added, was the 'strong representa-tions' being made by the Foreign Office to certain Governments 'against their laxity in the matter of the discouragement of this traffic'. MacDonald continued:

Very strong representations had been made in particular to Roumania, Poland and Greece, and the first results of this action had been good. Roumania and Greece had taken action which should secure much stricter surveillance, and while the good effect of our representations might not last, since the power of Jewish money was great, for the present at any rate the results were good.

MacDonald's reference to what he called 'the power of Jewish money' was ill-chosen. In reality, the situation of European Jewry in 1939 was precarious and weak, and the funds of the Jewish charitable institutions nearly exhausted. In mid-August news of just how desperate the Jewish situation was in Europe reached the Foreign Office from Slovakia, when a full report of the fate of Slovak Jewry reached them on August 17, through the League of Nations High Com-missioner for Refugees.

The report was distressing. Non-Jews, private Slovak citizens, encouraged by the Germans, 'do all they can to rob and plunder Jewish property and persecute the Jewish people'. Other Slovaks, 'unable to show their hatred of the Germans, so vent their wrath instead upon the Jews'. More than 85,000 Jews were affected by the new mood. 'Jew-baiting' was a frequent occurrence. All but a tiny pro-portion of Jews had been excluded since the previous March from all the professions, and from the universities. Many Jewish shops and businesses had been forced to close. For this reason, many Slovak Jews were joining the 'illegal' movement to Palestine: 'Their nerves can stand no more', the Report explained. 'Fear of the unknown in other countries is more pleasant to them than present persecution and feeling that they are trapped.' Several thousand had already fled, and some had even succeeded in reaching Palestine. 'This made the others more reckless,' the report added, 'especially as conditions in Slovakia grew worse.'

What was the Foreign Office reaction to this report? On August 18 Patrick Reilly minuted:

I don't know whether our relations with the Slovak Govt through HBM Consul at Bratislava are such as to make it possible for him to take any useful action with the Slovak Govt. If so, he might use our willingness to apply some of the Govt fund to Slovakia as an inducement to get the Slovaks to reduce pressure on Jews to leave, or at least to discourage them from trying to go to Palestine.

On August 23 news of the Nazi-Soviet pact effectively sealed the fate of Poland, and with it the fate of Poland's three million Jews. The news of the pact was announced in the middle of one of the sessions of the twenty-first Zionist Congress, being held in Geneva. On the following day Arthur Ruppin, one of the Palestine delegates, noted in his diary: 'the news exploded like a bomb.'

In his final words to the Congress on the evening of August 24 Weizmann told the delegates: 'If, as I hope, we are spared in life and our work continues, who knows – perhaps a new light will shine upon us from the thick black gloom,' and he ended: 'The remnant shall work on, fight on, live on, until the dawn of better days. Towards that dawn I greet you. May we meet again in peace.' The official protocol of the Congress recorded how, at this point: 'Deep emotion grips the Congress. Dr Weizmann embraces his colleagues on the platform. There are tears in many eyes. Hundreds of hands are stretched out towards Dr Weizmann as he leaves the hall.'

On September 1 the Germans invaded Poland, and Warsaw was subjected to the most severe bombing raid hitherto known. But even the coming of war did not soften British policy towards the Jews. Further pressure was put on Turkey on September 1 'to do what they can to delay ships carrying illegal immigrants', as Halifax telegraphed to the British Ambassador in Ankara, while on September 8, five days after the British declaration of war on Germany, the American Ambassador in Berlin, who had been put in charge of all British interests, telegraphed to London with a request from the State Department. The request read: 'Please ascertain from British Government whether German nationals of the Jewish race who hold immigration permits issued by British authorities in Germany will be allowed to enter Great Britain and if so advise procedure to be followed in stamping or visaing their passports.' This was the British answer, dated September 18:

On the outbreak of war all visas previously authorised or granted became void, and it is left to the individual to make an entirely fresh application which will be dealt with in accordance with the war time regulations which do not contemplate the grant of visas to refugees of this nature.

It was on September 18, the same day as this decision, that Dr Weizmann went to see Malcolm MacDonald, as a matter of urgency, to plead with MacDonald for permission to allow 20,000 Polish Jewish children to enter Palestine. These 20,000 would still not complete the 25,000 special quota of immigrants envisaged in the White Paper four months before, and, in a letter to MacDonald, Weizmann had written, movingly, for 'immediate permission' to move the children from Poland to Palestine. 'The economic burden of supporting them,' Weizmann added, 'will naturally fall upon the Jewish people, inside and outside Palestine. We pledge ourselves to provide for them. It therefore depends on your decision alone whether the lives of Jewish children shall be saved or not.'

Weizmann's appeal was discussed in the Colonial Office that same afternoon, in MacDonald's room, and with MacDonald present. The official minutes of the meeting were taken by Lacy Baggallay. Its decision, its arguments, and its tone, constituted a terrible blow to Jewish hopes. As the minutes recorded:

Mr. MacDonald said that his own view had at first been that we should make some effort to meet this request, on humanitarian and other grounds. On reflection, however, he had felt that it must be turned down. Technically it might be possible for us to admit 20,000 Polish Jewish children to Palestine straight away without going back on our pledge to the Arabs not to exceed the immigration figures laid down in the White Paper and our decision to hold up the current immigration quota owing to illegal immigration.

The position about the 25,000 refugees is that it has always been intended that they should be introduced gradually over the five-year period, and in fact the first quota period made provision for a certain number of these refugees, although it subsequently had to be cancelled for the reason already mentioned. In any case, it has always been contemplated that these refugees should include persecuted Jews of all countries, and not only Poland.

It might be possible to get round the technical difficulty of our promise with regard to illegal immigration by keeping the children in Cyprus or some such British territory until the new quota period began, and then introducing them into Palestine. But he thought that, even though this might not actually be breaking our promise, it would certainly be so regarded by the Arabs.

Furthermore, there were technical difficulties about getting the children there and making arrangements for the reception of so large a body at once, whatever Dr. Weizmann might say about accepting responsibility for their maintenance. The position in all the Middle Eastern countries was delicate, and he thought that to accept Dr. Weizmann's proposal might have serious consequences.

There was, furthermore, the consideration that H.M.G. were at war and everything must be subordinated to the winning of the war. However brutal it might sound, to remove 20,000 children from Poland at this moment would *pro tanto* simplify the German economic problem.

As against this must be set the possibility of hostile comment in America and other countries should this chance of relieving distress in Poland be missed. But here against the distress weighed equally on Christians and Jews alike, and the Christians were far the more numerous. On the whole, therefore, he felt that, without saying anything about Arab sentiments, he should reply to Dr. Weizmann that the acceptance of his request might prejudice the successful prosecution of the war, and, for that reason, must be turned down.

Even American pressure for some relaxation of British Colonial restrictions met with a negative response. On September 25, a week after Weizmann's meeting with MacDonald, a special War Cabinet Committee on refugee problems decided, and so informed the United States Government, that Britain could not assist the emigration in war time of 'Reich nationals', and that large-scale settlement in British colonies was to be 'suspended' for the duration of the war.

In fact, less than a thousand refugees had been allowed to enter British Colonial Dependencies in the six months from March to September 1939, the very six months when the Colonial alternative had been so much discussed. The following figures for those six months up to September 30 are taken from the official Colonial Office statistics: Cyprus, 291 Jews; Kenya, 216; Northern Rhodesia, 186; Malaya, 88; Hong Kong, 43; British Honduras, 23; British Guiana, 19; Swaziland, 13; Ceylon and the Bahamas, 10 Jews each; the Gold Coast and Malta, 7 each; the Bechuanaland and Nyasaland Protectorates, 6 each; Jamaica, 5; Fiji, the Uganda Protectorate and Sarawak, 3 each; and the Leeward Islands and Gibraltar, one Jew each. Fourteen further colonies had refused to take any Jews at all: these included Barbados, the Gambia, Mauritius, Nigeria, the Seychelles, the Somaliland Protectorate and Tanganyika.

With the coming of war, the British Government had not only continued, but even intensified, its attempts to halt the flow of 'illegal' Jewish refugees; indeed, Royal Navy ships, ostensibly on contraband duty, were used during the winter of 1939 to intercept immigrant ships. The success of this policy, and of the pressures which continued to be applied on foreign Governments, was commented on by J. S. Bennett, the official in the Colonial Office responsible for Jewish immigration, when he noted on 15 September 1939:

Rumania has prohibited the departure of Jews to any destination. Turkey has been asked to obstruct (on sanitary and safety grounds) the passage of ships carrying Jewish immigrants through the Bosphorus. Greece has introduced legislation with heavy penalties for any of their nationals engaging in the trade.

Panama had promised to put a stop to the irregular use of her flag. All other countries concerned have been strongly pressured to cooperate and have undertaken to do so. We can only wait and see.

On September 20 the Permanent Under-Secretary of State at the Colonial Office, Sir John Shuckburgh, alarmed at the number of 'illegals' who had succeeded in leaving central Europe, expressed, in a departmental minute, his hope that, as a result of the outbreak of war, 'some of the sources of supply may dry up'. Five days later the Foreign Office rejected a suggestion by the Italian Ministry of Foreign Affairs to help facilitate the passage of German Jewish refugees seeking to reach Palestine through Italian ports: such help would, it was argued, be contrary to the decision of the Cabinet Committee on Refugees to 'suspend' the emigration of Reich nationals in war time. On September 26 a further Foreign Office minute by G. M. Warr of the Western Department explained that 'no refugees who were in Germany at the outbreak of war would be admitted to the UK'. A 'few', he wrote, might be allowed in from neutral countries, 'but these cases would have to be carefully considered'.

Since the outbreak of the war, all 'illegal' refugees who did manage to reach Palestine were being interned in a camp at Athlit, just south of Haifa. This decision alarmed the officials of the Colonial Office, one of whom, Harold Downie, the head of the Middle East Department, suggested to Malcolm MacDonald on October 10 that it should be publicly announced that when the war was over these internees would be 'transferred to the country from which they came'. MacDonald agreed, noting four days later that, in his view, the British Government should adopt the policy of 'sending them back to mainland Europe after the war'.

As 1939 came to an end, British pressure on foreign Governments continued; so much so that, on December 20, the Colonial Office wrote to the Foreign Office of Turkey's continuing laxity in allowing refugee boats to pass through the Bosphorous on their way from the Black Sea. 'We therefore suggest,' the Colonial Office letter read, 'that the Turkish Government might be invited to enact legislation prohibiting their merchant marine from engaging in this traffic, on the lines of the law enacted by the Greek Government at our request in the earlier part of this year....' Of the refugee ship whose passage had prompted this protest, the Colonial Office wrote: 'We trust that, even if the *Sakaria* cannot be turned back, she will at least be refused all facilities at Turkish ports on her passage through.'

On December 29 the 'illegal' immigration was discussed at the Foreign Office, where Warr minuted: 'The only hope is that all the German Jews will be stuck at the mouths of the Danube for lack of ships to take them....'

Throughout the winter months of 1939 and 1940, while the British were thus fighting the 'illegal' Jewish immigration, the Germans were imposing their evil rule upon Poland. Even during the six weeks of battle the Jews, as well as the

245

Poles, had suffered considerable losses. During the bombing of Warsaw, several thousand Jewish civilians had been killed, while more than 30,000 Jewish soldiers were killed in action while fighting in the Polish army. But it was after the successful advance of their soldiers that the Jewish fate was revealed – when German units of the dreaded SS murdered, in cold blood, hundreds of leading Polish civilians, non-Jews and Jews alike – professors, lawyers, writers and politicians – and began a fierce anti-Jewish campaign. A terrible example of what was in store for Polish Jewry had taken place on September 9, at Bedzin, when German troops and SS men burned down the Great Synagogue, and, as the flames spread to the Jewish quarter, cordoned off the area, shooting anyone who tried to flee from the flames. By the time the fires had burned themselves out, more than a hundred Jews had been burned to death.

For the Jews of Palestine, war had brought a new spirit of determination. Rallying to Ben Gurion's advice, they would fight the war as if there were no White Paper, but at the same time continue to fight the White Paper as if there were no war. Recruitment and a desire to serve the Allied cause went parallel with the hope of bringing in, legally or 'illegally', as many European Jews as could escape the torment of Nazi rule.

At a meeting of the War Cabinet on 12 February 1940, Churchill, who had entered the Government as First Lord of the Admiralty on the outbreak of war, raised the question, which both Weizmann and Jabotinsky had raised with him personally, of allowing the Jews of Palestine to be armed and trained in their own defence. Churchill told his former political opponents, now his colleagues, that, as the official minutes recorded:

> ... it might have been thought a matter for satisfaction that the Jews in Palestine should possess arms, and be capable of providing for their own defence. They were the only trustworthy friends we had in that country, and they were much more under our control than the scattered Arab population.
>
> He would have thought that the sound policy for Great Britain at the beginning of the war would have been to build up, as soon as possible, a strong Jewish armed force in Palestine. In this way we should have been able to use elsewhere the large and costly British cavalry force, which was now to replace the eleven infantry battalions hitherto locked up in Palestine.
>
> It was an extraordinary position that at a time when the war was probably entering its most dangerous phase, we should station in Palestine a garrison one-quarter of the size of our garrison in India – and this for the purpose of forcing through a policy which, in his judgement, was unpopular in Palestine and in Great Britain alike.

Churchill was not successful: Lord Halifax called his proposal 'discreditable', on the grounds that the problem was 'a much wider one' than Palestine alone, 'and had repercussions throughout the Muslim world'. Chamberlain supported Halifax, telling his colleagues: 'we certainly could not give the Jews alone freedom to arm.'

This same War Cabinet of 12 February 1940 discussed the 1939 White Paper decision to limit Jewish land purchase in Palestine. Once more, Churchill put forward the Zionist arguments. It was, he said, 'a short-sighted policy', which would 'put a stop to agricultural progress in Palestine'. Such a policy would not only be bad for agriculture, but would 'cause a great outcry in American Jewry'. The Secretary of State for War, Oliver Stanley, defended the restrictions on Jewish land purchase, telling his colleagues that it would be 'a good thing' for Palestine to slow down the intensive land cultivation. 'There was a great danger', Stanley asserted, 'of over-production of citrus fruits.'

Malcolm MacDonald supported Stanley. 'It would be an error of judgment', he believed, 'to exaggerate the influence of the Jewish element in the United States.' Churchill made one further appeal on behalf of maintaining Jewish land purchase rights from the Mediterranean to the Jordan, as laid down in the Mandate, telling his colleagues,

... that he, personally, ascribed to Government encouragement very little of the credit for the great agricultural improvements which had taken place in Palestine. Broadly speaking, they were all the result of private Jewish efforts. So far as the Government of Palestine had played any part in agricultural development, it was with Jewish money wrung from the settlers by taxation.

Nor was he impressed by the political grounds on which it was attempted to justify our action in bringing this great agricultural experiment to an end. The political argument, in a word, was that we should not be able to win the war without the help of the Arabs; he did not in the least admit the validity of that argument.

Churchill's protest was unsuccessful, and the land purchase regulations were put into force. 'The effect of these regulations', Ben Gurion declared on February 28, 'is that no Jew may acquire in Palestine a plot of land, a building, or a tree, or any right in water except in towns and a very small part of the countryside. . . . They not only violate the terms of the Mandate but completely nullify its purpose.' On March 6, during a debate in the House of Commons, a Labour MP, Philip Noel Baker, protested against the new regulations:

Today the Jews are a weak and hunted race. Tens of thousands, perhaps hundreds of thousands, of them have already perished; their property has been stolen and destroyed, and it is because, in the general holocaust of civilised standards, their influence has gone, that we dare to do this shameful act, that we try to repudiate the moral contract which we made with them during the last Great War.

Despite this setback to their position in Palestine, the Jews now pressed for the creation of a specifically Jewish military force – a Jewish Division, which could

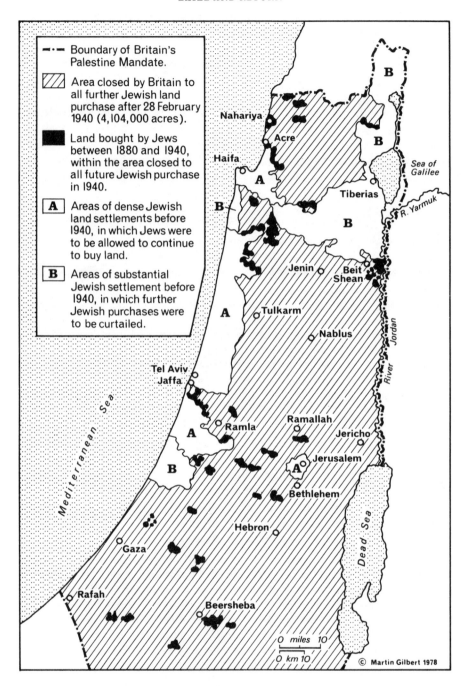

Boundary of Britain's Palestine Mandate.

Area closed by Britain to all further Jewish land purchase after 28 February 1940 (4,104,000 acres).

Land bought by Jews between 1880 and 1940, within the area closed to all future Jewish purchase in 1940.

A Areas of dense Jewish land settlements before 1940, in which Jews were to be allowed to continue to buy land.

B Areas of substantial Jewish settlement before 1940, in which further Jewish purchases were to be curtailed.

Nahariya
Acre
Haifa
A
B
Sea of Galilee
Tiberias
R. Yarmuk
B
B
Jenin
Beit Shean
Tulkarm
A
Nablus
River Jordan
Tel Aviv
Jaffa
A
Ramla
Ramallah
Jericho
Jerusalem
A
B
Bethlehem
Hebron
Dead Sea
Gaza
Rafah
Beersheba
Mediterranean Sea

0 miles 10
0 km 10

© Martin Gilbert 1978

248

fight the Germans as an integral part of the Allied armies. Churchill, who became Prime Minister in May 1940, was sympathetic to the project, and gave it his support in a personal interview with Weizmann four months later. But both the Foreign Office and the War Office opposed it, and for four years the project was delayed and postponed: four years of war during which the Jews most wished to serve, not only, as they did, in each of the Allied armies, but as a distinctly and recognizably Jewish group.

Churchill was involved in the winter of 1940 in one further Palestinian matter. Early in November 1940 two ships, the *Milos* and the *Pacific*, had reached Haifa with 1,771 'illegal' immigrants. The High Commissioner, Sir Harold MacMichael, refused to allow them to land, and they were transferred to a French liner, the *Patria*, which the British had specially chartered in order to deport them to the Indian Ocean island of Mauritius. On November 20, while the immigrants were still being transferred to the *Patria*, MacMichael broadcast a blunt communique setting out the new deportation policy. The British Government, he declared:

. . . can only regard a revival of illegal Jewish immigration at the present juncture as likely to affect the local situation most adversely, and to prove a serious menace to British interests in the Middle East. They have accordingly decided that the passengers shall not be permitted to land in Palestine but shall be deported to a British colony and shall be detained there for the duration of the war.

Their ultimate disposal will be a matter for consideration at the end of the war, but it is not proposed that they shall remain in the colony to which they are sent or that they should go to Palestine. Similar action will be taken in the case of any further parties who may succeed in reaching Palestine with a view to illegal entry.

On November 24, while the *Patria* was still at anchor off Haifa, another immigration ship, the *Atlantic*, with 1,783 refugees on board, was escorted into Haifa Bay by the Royal Navy. On the morning of November 25 the first two hundred of those 'illegals' were likewise transferred to the *Patria*, when explosives, intended by the Haganah to immobilize the ship and halt the deportation, blew up more forcefully than intended, and within fifteen minutes the *Patria* had sunk, drowning more than 250 refugees.

The scale of the *Patria* tragedy led the British Government to announce that, whereas the remaining 1,600 refugees on board the *Atlantic* would still be deported to Mauritius, the 1,900 refugees who had been on the *Patria* when it sank would be allowed to remain in Palestine. This decision led to an immediate protest from the British Commander-in-Chief in the Middle East, General Wavell, who telegraphed to the Secretary of State for War, Anthony Eden, on November 30:

Have just heard the decision re Patria immigrants. Most sincerely trust you will use all possible influence to have decision reversed. From military point of view it is disastrous. It will be spread all over Arab world that Jews have again successfully

249

challenged decision of British Government and that policy of White Paper is being reversed. This will gravely increase prospect of widespread disorders in Palestine necessitating increased military commitments, will greatly enhance influence of Mufti, will rouse mistrust of us in Syria and increase anti-British propaganda and fifth column activities in Egypt. It will again be spread abroad that only violence pays in dealing with British.

If present decision stands must withdraw recommendation in my 0/27581 of 26 Nov. to open Basra–Baghdad–Haifa Road, as certain result will be great increase of anti-British feeling and action in Iraq. Please exert all your influence. This is serious.

The reply to General Wavell came, not from the War Office or the Colonial Office, but from Churchill himself, who told the General, on December 2:

Secretary of State has shown me your telegram about Patria. Cabinet feel that, in view of the suffering of these immigrants, and perils to which they had been subjected through the sinking of their ship, that it would be necessary on compassionate grounds not to subject them again immediately to the hazards of the sea. Personally, I hold it would be an act of inhumanity unworthy of British name to force them to re-embark. On the other hand Cabinet agreed that future consignments of illegal immigrants should be sent to Mauritius provided that tolerable conditions can be arranged for them there.

Churchill's telegram continued:

I wonder whether the effect on the Arab world will be as bad as you suggest. If their attachment to our cause is so slender as to be determined by a mere act of charity of this kind it is clear that our policy of conciliating them has not borne much fruit so far. What I think would influence them much more would be any kind of British military success. I therefore suggest that you should reconsider your statement about the Basra–Baghdad–Haifa road when we see which way the compass points.

I am sorry you should be worrying yourself with such matters at this particular time and I hope at least you will believe that the views I have just expressed are not dictated by fear of violence.

Churchill's telegram was decisive, and Wavell's protest was overruled: the *Patria* deportees were allowed to remain in Palestine, first in the internment camp at Athlit, and within a year, at liberty. Nor was Churchill's judgement at fault, for on December 14 a military intelligence report on the effect of the *Patria* decision on the Arabs concluded that the effect had been 'remarkably small'.

The aftermath of this episode proved, however, a blow to the Zionists, for on December 26 the British Government suspended the quota for legal immigration for three months, thus halting all immigration until March 1941. This decision was reached despite Churchill's insistence, only two days before, that the Government, as he minuted, 'have also to consider their promises to the Zionists, and to be guided by general considerations of humanity towards those fleeing from the cruellest forms of persecution'. Having received this clear indication of Churchill's attitude, Sir John Shuckburgh minuted, that same day, in deciding not to inform Churchill of the suspension of the quota: 'Our object is to keep the business as far as possible on the normal administrative plane and outside the realms of Cabinet policy and so forth.' Subsequently, the quota for April to September 1941 was also suspended, and no immigration certificates issued for that period either.

Both Churchill and the Jewish Agency had expressed the hope that the conditions of detention of the deported immigrants in Mauritius should not be onerous. As early as 13 November 1940, Churchill's Private Secretary, John Martin, had insisted, on Churchill's instructions, that the deportees should be 'decently treated in Mauritius'. But the Government department responsible held a different view, which was expressed succinctly on 11 January 1941 by S. E. V. Luke when, in a Colonial Office minute, he laid down that the conditions of the detention of the deportees 'should be sufficiently punitive to continue to act as a deterrent to other Jews in Eastern Europe'.

As the war continued, the Zionists were appalled by the mounting campaign of terror against the Jews of Poland, and by the continuing refusal of the British Government to modify in any way the immigration or land purchase restrictions of the 1939 White Paper. In February 1940, in a book entitled *The Jewish War Front*, Jabotinsky argued that the Jews were also an integral part of the Allied war effort, and, with copious and disturbing quotations, showed that the terrible Jewish sufferings in Poland, although played down in the British Press, were well known to all those who read the news agency telegrams, and thus to all those responsible for Government policy. The Jews, Jabotinsky argued, must now work towards full statehood; and he added:

The Jewish State is a true and proper war aim. Without it, the ulcer that poisons Europe's trouble cannot be healed: for without it there can be no adequate emigration of the millions whose old homes are irretrievably condemned; without it there can be no equality; and without this, no peace.

19

Beyond the Abyss
1939-1942

FROM the moment that the Germans marched into Poland in September 1939, Nazi sadism found horrific outlets on Polish Jewry. As the American Jewish historian, Isaiah Trunk, has recorded, after a detailed study of the contemporary evidence:

Military operations were still going on when the German army and SD Einsatzkommandos undertook a campaign of bloody repression. They usually arrested a group of Jews or Poles, who were kept as hostages and eventually shot. Sometimes mock executions were staged, in which the victims stood for hours in suspense anticipating execution.

Pious Jews had their beards removed by blunt instruments, which tore their skin, or had their beards burned off. Swastikas were branded on the scalps of some victims; others were subjected to 'gymnastics', such as 'riding' on other victims' backs, crawling on all fours, singing and dancing, or staging fights with one another.

The Nazis took a special sadistic pleasure in violating religious feelings, deliberately choosing Jewish religious holidays on which to carry out their assaults. They instituted a special campaign of burning down synagogues, or, after destroying their interiors, turned them into stables, warehouses, bathhouses, or even public latrines. . . .

Any Jew who tried to enter a burning synagogue in order to save the Torah scrolls was either shot or thrown into the flames. In many places the military staged autos-da-fe of Torah scrolls, Hebrew books, and other religious articles, and forced the Jews to sing and dance around the flames and shout that the Jews were to blame for the war. The Jewish communities were also compelled to bear the cost of tearing down the remaining walls of the houses and clearing the rubble. It is estimated that several hundred synagogues were destroyed in the first two months of the occupation.

At the same time, mass arrests of Jews were carried out in which thousands of men, women, and children were interned in 'civilian prison camps' set up in synagogues, churches, movie houses, and the like, or put behind barbed-wire fences on open lots and exposed to the soldiers' cruelty and torture.

In the rampage of persecution throughout Poland, people were taken off the streets or dragged from their homes and put on forced labor. They were tortured and beaten, and deprived of their human dignity when forced to perform such acts as cleaning latrines with their bare hands or, in the case of women, washing the floor with their own underwear. Normal life was paralyzed by the arbitrary arrests for forced labor. . . .

Hundreds of civilians, Trunk wrote, 'Poles, and Jews, were slaughtered outright or imprisoned in buildings which were sealed and then set on fire or blown up, the imprisoned dying a horrible death'.

Humiliation, torture and death; this pattern was repeated during 1940 and 1941 wherever the German armies advanced. Often, among Germany's allies, local sadists emerged who needed no lessons in killing and torture; as the cruel influence of the swastika spread across Europe, the Jews found themselves set upon, ill-treated and murdered by men of many nationalities: among them fascist Austrians, Frenchmen, Belgians, Croats, Slovaks, and Rumanians, and by the psychopathic dregs of those defeated or corrupted societies for whom the Nazi example stirred the worst instincts, and made possible the most sadistic responses.

Following the German invasion of Russia on 22 June 1941, the orgy of murder against the Jews reached a terrible depth, unprecedented in the history of civilized men. Hundreds of Nazi executioners, freed from all restraint, and supported by overwhelming military strength, rounded up and slaughtered whole communities, massacring in a single day as many as five, ten and even fifteen thousand helpless, innocent, unarmed men, women and children.

The events following the German arrival in one town, Bialystok, were part of a pattern repeated in every area of Russia invaded by Germany. Bialystok was the town in which, in 1906, seventy Jews had been killed, in one of the worst of the Tsarist pogroms, a crime that had shocked liberal Europe. This same Bialystok was occupied by the Germans on 27 June 1941, five days after their invasion of the Soviet Union. On the second day of the occupation the Germans burnt down the main synagogue, burning to death at least 1,000 Jewish men, women and children who had been forced inside at gunpoint. A week later, on July 3, some 300 of the town's leading Jewish scholars were taken to a field outside the town, and murdered. On July 12, the Jewish sabbath, a further 3,000 men were killed in the same field. The scale of these killings was unprecedented; the Jews who were murdered were the victims, not of reason, however perverted, but of madness: a madness that had seized hold of groups of men, many of them in their early twenties, well-drilled, 'educated' to kill, and devoid of all pity, or sense of shame.

Among those who organized this slaughter was a German-born Nazi official, Adolf Eichmann. Thirty five years old in March 1941 – three months before the German invasion of Russia – he became the head of a special Gestapo section,

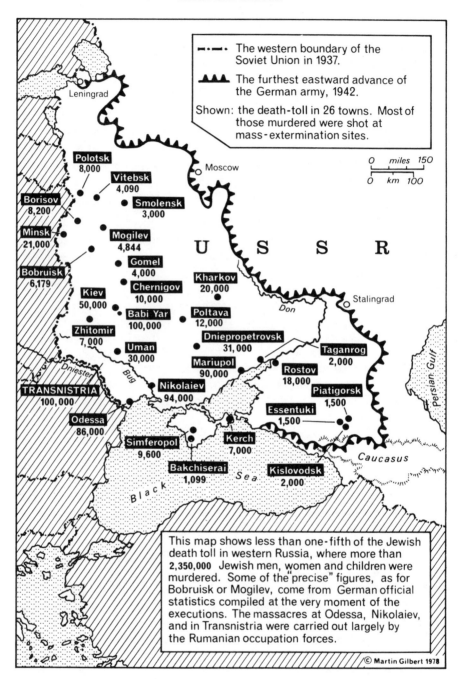

The western boundary of the Soviet Union in 1937.

The furthest eastward advance of the German army, 1942.

Shown: the death-toll in 26 towns. Most of those murdered were shot at mass-extermination sites.

Leningrad

Moscow

0   miles   150
0   km   100

Polotsk
8,000

Vitebsk
4,090

Borisov
8,200

Smolensk
3,000

Minsk
21,000

Mogilev
4,844

U   S   S   R

Bobruisk
6,179

Gomel
4,000

Kiev
50,000

Chernigov
10,000

Kharkov
20,000

Don

Stalingrad

Babi Yar
100,000

Poltava
12,000

Zhitomir
7,000

Dniepropetrovsk
31,000

Taganrog
2,000

Uman
30,000

Dniester

Mariupol
90,000

Rostov
18,000

Piatigorsk
1,500

Bug

Nikolaiev
94,000

TRANSNISTRIA
100,000

Essentuki
1,500

Persian Gulf

Odessa
86,000

Simferopol
9,600

Kerch
7,000

Caucasus

Bakchiserai
1,099

Black   Sea

Kislovodsk
2,000

This map shows less than one-fifth of the Jewish death toll in western Russia, where more than **2,350,000** Jewish men, women and children were murdered. Some of the "precise" figures, as for Bobruisk or Mogilev, come from German official statistics compiled at the very moment of the executions. The massacres at Odessa, Nikolaiev, and in Transnistria were carried out largely by the Rumanian occupation forces.

© Martin Gilbert 1978

IVB4, responsible for 'Jewish affairs', and for the expulsion of 'unwanted' populations.

In 1960 Eichmann was put on trial by the Israeli Government, and was closely cross-examined about the mass murders in the east. Not only 'cold' statistics, of hundreds and thousands killed, but many stories of individual suffering, emerged during the trial; on one occasion, Eichmann himself recalled how he had gone to inspect the work of the killer squads. Near the town of Minsk he had seen young SS men shooting into a pit already full of writhing bodies: 'I can still see,' he said in his interrogation, 'a woman with a child. She was shot and then the baby in her arms. His brains splattered all around, also over my leather overcoat.'

Another non-Jew, who witnessed the terrible killings, and later spoke about them, was a German engineer, Hermann Friedrich Graebe, a civilian employee of a building firm. Graebe was working in an office in one of the German-occupied towns, Rovno, when he heard from his assistant that Jews were being shot nearby. Curiosity led him to the site, where, as he told the Eichmann trial twenty years later:

I saw a big earth ditch, some thirty meters long and forty meters deep. Before it were several lorries from which people were being driven out by Ukrainian militiamen under the command of an SS man. The people who had got off the trucks – men, women, and children of all ages – had to undress upon the order of the SS man, who carried a riding or dog-whip, and put down their clothing in fixed places.

I saw a heap of shoes of about 800 to 1,000 pairs, great piles of underlinen and clothing. Without screaming or weeping, these people undressed, stood around in family groups, kissed each other, said farewell and waited for a sign from another SS man, who stood near the pit, also with a whip in his hand. . . .

No complaints or pleas for mercy were heard. A family of about eight persons passed by – a man and a woman, both about fifty, with their children of about one, eight and ten and two grown-up daughters of twenty and twenty-four. An old woman with snow-white hair was holding a one-year-old child in her arms, singing to it and tickling it. The child was cooing with delight. The couple were looking on with tears in their eyes. The father was holding the hand of the ten-year-old boy and speaking to him softly; the boy was fighting back his tears. The father pointed toward the sky, stroked his head and seemed to explain something to him. At that moment the SS man at the pit shouted something to his comrade. The latter counted off about twenty persons and instructed them to go behind the pit. Among them was the family I mentioned. A girl, slim, with black hair, pointed to herself as she passed by me and said 'Twenty-three years'. . . .

People were closely wedged together and lying on top of each other so that only their heads were visible. All had blood pouring from them. Some of the people shot were still moving.

Only a tiny remnant of the Jews of German-occupied Russia survived the Nazi executions. One of them, a young boy by the name of Abraham, later reached Palestine. There, in evidence at the trial of Adolf Eichmann in 1960, he told the court how in his village, near Grodno, the Nazis had entered all the Jews' houses, forced the inhabitants out into the street at gunpoint, and struck each person a heavy blow as they passed through the door. Abraham's evidence continued:

We were brought to the market place in the middle of the town, were told to kneel, heads down. Whoever did not do so was either shot right through the head or severely beaten. I was shorter than the others, so I could raise my head without being discovered, and I saw in front of me a long trench about thirty yards long. We were led to that trench. Machine-gun bursts were heard and people would fall into the trench. I saw a Jewish girl struggle. She refused to undress. They hit her and then she was shot too. All were shot – children, women, family after family.

Being small, and in the confusion, the young boy was able to slip away from the main group:

I managed to reach the edge of the road and they apparently did not notice me. Right next to me I found Zelig, the carpenter from our town – he had been employed by the Gestapo and had a labor card, a special document saying that he had to be spared. At that moment, he was approached by a German who stuck the revolver into his neck. He held out his labor card. The German shot him and his face darkened, but he still spoke for a second. He said, 'I have a card.' He was shot again and fell.

Of the thousand Jews assembled that night in that one village, nine hundred had been murdered by dawn, including Abraham's own mother and two brothers.

Another witness of these terrible events had also managed to reach Palestine after the war, and she too gave evidence at the Eichmann trial. In her village, near Pinsk, hundreds of armed SS men had surrounded the Jewish quarter, and forced the Jews out of their homes. The prosecutor's account of her evidence, published in his book *Justice in Jerusalem*, told of how the Jews of that particular village:

. . . were chased like animals to the central square of the town, where they were kept until the next morning, without food or water. Then, when they were exhausted by fear and fatigue, all were marched outside the town. They reached a huge ditch and were told to stop and undress.

'Even when I saw the naked people who had arrived before us, I still did not believe they would kill us, I hoped it would be just torture,' she said. Taking off her clothes, she stood there clinging to her six-year-old daughter. Her mother, her grandmother and her sister were all nearby. Her hopes were in vain. The SS men started shooting the Jews one by one, firing point-blank into the back of each victim's head, then kicking the body into the open pit. Yoselewska saw her father and mother disappear into the ditch. Then the Germans approached her grandmother, who was holding two little girls in her arms, comforting them and pointing to heaven, where they would soon meet all their beloved ones. In a moment all three were shot. 'Then I saw my sister embrace a girl friend; the two of them tried to cover their nakedness with each other's bodies, pleading with a uniformed SS man to spare their young lives. In reply they were both shot and went down.

As I stood there paralyzed with horror,' continued Mrs. Yoselewska, 'my little daughter, Malka, was wrung from my arms and killed'.

At that particular moment, she said, she felt nothing more. The German who shot her missed his aim, and the bullet merely grazed her head. She only felt a booted leg kicking her into the ditch to bleed to death or die of suffocation.

By a miracle, Mrs Yoselewska did not die. Alone escaping from the pit, she was looked after by partisans, and survived. After 1948, she rebuilt her shattered life in Israel, married and had two children. The world whose death-throes she witnessed was totally destroyed. By the end of 1941, one SS group was able to report – with pride in its precision – a total of 56,696 executions. Another SS group reported that it had 'so far liquidated about 80,000 people'. In only two days, 23,000 Jews were slaughtered at Kamenets-Podolsk; in two days, at Kiev, 33,771 Jews were killed. Within a year of the German invasion of Russia, 1,400,000 Jews had died, all of them in circumstances of the utmost horror and torment.

In parts of the Ukraine and the Crimea, the local populations took part in these atrocities. One SS group, reporting from a Crimean village, explained that the village elders had 'asked for permission to kill the Jews themselves'. But only six months after the German invasion of Russia, an even larger-scale, more organized and systematic murder policy was being devised, for on 20 January 1942, in the Wannsee suburb of Berlin, a group of German officials met to discuss what they described as 'the final solution' of the Jewish question. Eichmann was among those present. So too were representatives of the German Foreign Office, and the Ministry of Justice. Their decision sealed the fate of another three and a half million Jews, and was intended to cover even the Jews of as yet unconquered countries, including Britain, Spain, Sweden, Turkey and Portugal.

At the Wannsee Conference it was decided to deport all European Jewry to the eastern territories under German rule; to put them to work in road-building, 'the sexes apart'; to keep them at work while 'a large part . . . fall out through natural causes'; and to ensure that the 'surviving remnant' were, as the notes of the Conference put it, 'treated specially'. These measures must be taken, particularly against the remnant who managed to survive, in order to ensure no 're-creation of Jewry'.

Towards the end of the Conference, 'various possibilities for a solution' were discussed; at his trial Eichmann stated that what this meant was that they debated 'various methods of killing'. Drinks were then served, followed by lunch, and the Conference was over; so, too, was any hope that the Jews of any part of Europe would be allowed to pass unscathed into the post-war world.

20

Holocaust, Resistance and Flight

FOLLOWING the Wannsee Conference of January 1942, the Nazis began the systematic deportation and murder of Jews from all over Europe. Their destination was the death camps, most of which had been set up on Polish soil. Henceforth, for nearly two and a half years, from the furthest extremities of the German occupation, from France, Belgium and Holland, from Greece and Yugoslavia, from Norway, from central Europe, from the Balkans and from Italy, hundreds of thousands of Jews were taken by train to their death.

By the time of Germany's surrender in May 1945, six million Jews had been murdered, many at camps set up solely for the task of killing. Many others had died at camps where debilitating forced labour was but a temporary respite before death from starvation, torture or the gas chambers. Others had been shot dead while on the march, or left to die of hunger at the roadside. Yet others starved to death, without even water, in the sealed railway trucks that were taking them to their doom. Some even died at the hands of doctors sadistically experimenting on their bodies, often with no anaesthetic, mutilating, 'freezing' and castrating without cause or compassion. Thus, within twelve years of the Nazis coming to power in Germany, the 'Holocaust' of European Jewry was complete.

Wherever they could, the Jews fought back in their own defence. In many towns, and even in some of the concentration camps, uprisings took place against the German tyranny. In Warsaw, 800 German soldiers were killed when the Jewish population, weakened by hunger, wracked by disease, nevertheless rose up in revolt. Small groups of Jews, several thousand in all, escaped to the woods, marshes and hills, formed their own partisan groups, or joined local resistance forces. Their deeds were heroic, their bravery beyond praise. But the power of the German military machine was enormous, and its vengeance terrible.

Nor was the plight of the Jews confined to German-occupied Europe. On 21 January 1941 a vicious anti-Jewish pogrom broke out in Bucharest, the Rumanian capital, and in the course of a three-day rampage of terror, 120 Jewish men, women and children were murdered in cold blood – many shot down in the streets – while Jewish houses, shops and synagogues were looted and destroyed.

Even as the nature of the atrocities was becoming known, the British War

Cabinet resisted any suggestion that those Jews who could escape from Nazi-controlled Europe should be allowed into Palestine. On 14 February 1941, after Weizmann had appealed to the new Colonial Secretary, Lord Moyne, for a substantial and immediate allocation of immigration certificates for Rumanian Jews, Moyne had rejected his appeal with the argument that, as 'Rumania is regarded as occupied enemy territory', the 'machinery for verification of the *bona fides* of applicants' had disappeared.

On 3 April 1941 a pro-Nazi rebellion took place in Iraq. It was quickly suppressed, but not before more than 120 Jews had been murdered in the streets of Baghdad. With the suppression of the Iraq rebellion, Haj Amin, the Mufti, had gone to Berlin, where, on April 8, he expressed publicly the sympathy of the 'Arab nation' for Germany, and offered Hitler the active support of the Arabs in helping to bring about the downfall of what he called the 'English-Jewish coalition'.

The Mufti remained in Berlin, in charge of a special bureau which broadcast pro-Nazi propaganda throughout the Arab world. In June 1941, as the full force of the anti-Jewish riots in Baghdad became known, the Jewish Agency asked the British Government to allow Iraqi Jews to emigrate to Palestine. But when Lord Moyne, on July 30, suggested allowing a maximum of 750 to go to Palestine, the High Commissioner, Sir Harold Macmichael, rejected even this small number, on the grounds, as he explained to Moyne on 5 August, that there was no work for them to do, and thus no way of absorbing them into the Palestine economy; this in spite of the Jewish Agency's assertion the previous April, in a letter to Eric Mills, that there was a shortage of more than 4,000 agricultural workers on Jewish farms and settlements.

Since 1940, those Jews who had been caught trying to get to Palestine had been deported by the British, some to the island of Mauritius in the Indian Ocean and others to more distant colonies: the very same colonies, in fact, that had refused to receive them as refugees before the outbreak of war.

From Europe, the Jews continued to seek an escape from the Nazi grip. Yet not all those refugees who managed to escape towards the Mediterranean found their future in any way assured. In December 1941 a small boat of only two hundred tons, the *Struma*, had reached Istanbul with 769 Jews on board, *en route* for Palestine. In pursuance of the White Paper policy, the British authorities in Palestine had declared that these refugees would not be allowed to enter Palestine. Two months later, while negotiations were still proceeding about allowing at least the children to get to Palestine, the Turkish Government ordered the ship out of Turkish waters, and back into the Black Sea. There it was sunk, probably by a German submarine, and all but one of the passengers were drowned. In the House of Commons, the Colonial Secretary, Oliver Stanley, announced:

259

His Majesty's Government earnestly hope that such a tragedy will not occur again. It does not, however, lie in their power, amid the dangers and uncertainties of the war, to give any guarantee, nor can they be party to any measures which could undermine the existing policy regarding illegal immigration into Palestine in view of the wider issues involved.

Among the 'wider issues' was the British fear of offending the Arab States in the Middle East. On 16 February 1942 the War Cabinet discussed what should be done with those 'illegal' immigrants from Nazi-occupied Europe who, having been caught by the Mandate police, had been detained in internment camps in Palestine. The discussion took place three days after Weizmann's younger son Michael, an officer in the Royal Air Force, had been killed in action off the coast of France. Under a previous War Cabinet decision of 27 November 1940, all 'illegal' immigrants who had been detained would have to be deported to the Indian Ocean island of Mauritius as soon as shipping could be found for them, and held there until the end of the war, when they would be released, on condition that they then went elsewhere than Palestine. At the War Cabinet, Churchill suggested that the internees should not be deported to Mauritius, but released. In November 1940, he said, 'it had looked as though we might be subjected to a wave of illegal immigration. But now that the whole of South-Eastern Europe was in German hands this risk must be greatly diminished'.

Lord Moyne challenged Churchill's argument, and challenged it successfully, telling his War Cabinet colleagues, as the official minutes recorded:

... that this risk could not be ignored. He referred to a ship of 200 tons with 600 or 700 would-be immigrants which had sailed from Constansa and had recently arrived at Istanbul on the way to Palestine. On security grounds alone, any relaxation of the War Cabinet decision on this matter was open to strong objection. Further, any weakening of our attitude in this matter would afford encouragement to the very undesirable trade in illegal immigration into Palestine.

Despite Moyne's refusal to grant immigration certificates to individual Jews who escaped from Rumania, the Jews still fought to reach Palestine, and continued to be smuggled there illegally. This too provoked a firm response, and on 5 March 1942 the War Cabinet decided formally that: 'All practicable steps should be taken to discourage illegal immigration into Palestine.'

On 6 May 1942 an Extraordinary Zionist Conference was held at the Biltmore Hotel in New York. Its theme, expressed most forcefully by the Chairman of the Jewish Agency Executive, David Ben Gurion, was that the Jews could no longer depend upon Britain to establish a Jewish National Home in Palestine, and that to secure this goal the Jewish Agency should replace the British Mandate as the government of Palestine. When the conference ended on May 11, a majority of the delegates were committed to the establishment of Palestine as a 'Jewish Commonwealth', as well as an end to all immigration restrictions. By the Biltmore Programme, as it was known, the Zionists adopted for the first time since Balfour, the idea of a Jewish State as the official policy of the Zionist movement.

On 18 May 1942, after another British War Cabinet discussion on illegal immigration, it was officially decided that 'no steps whatever should be taken to facilitate the arrival of "refugees" into Palestine'. It was the War Cabinet secretariat itself that put the word 'refugees' in inverted commas. Three weeks later, in a debate in the House of Lords, Lord Moyne, who had left the Colonial Office at the end of February 1942, argued that the Jews were not really a 'race' at all. 'It is very often loosely said that the Jews are Semites,' Moyne told the House on June 9, 'but anthropologists tell us that, pure as they have kept their culture, the Jewish race has been much mixed with Gentiles since the beginning of the Diaspora,' and he added: 'During the Babylonian captivity they acquired a strong Hittite admixture, and it is obvious that the Armenoid features which are still to be found among the Sephardim have been bred out of the Ashkenazim by an admixture of Slav blood.'

To the Arabs, however, Moyne asserted, the Jews were 'not only alien in culture but also in blood'. Palestine could not absorb three million dispossessed Jews of Europe: 'immigration on this scale would be a disastrous mistake and indeed an impracticable dream'. The Arabs, he said, 'who have lived and buried their dead for fifty generations in Palestine, will not willingly surrender their land and self-government to the Jews'. Moyne had another idea for Jewish resettlement after the war, telling the House of Lords:

On May 25, at the annual dinner of the Anglo-American Palestine Committee, Dr. Weizmann again declared that Palestine alone could absorb and provide for the homeless and Stateless Jews uprooted by the war. It is to canalise all the sympathy of the world for the martyrdom of the Jews that the Zionists reject all schemes to resettle these victims elsewhere – in Germany, or Poland, or in sparsely populated regions such as Madagascar. . . .

I hope the Government will give serious consideration to the possibility of negotiations with the neighbouring States of the Levant to take part in re-settling the Jews. It is obvious that the fear of political domination will be decreased if they can be spread over a wider area and shared among different Administrations. A Federation of the Northern Arab States [Syria, Lebanon, Transjordan] might well assist such a solution. . . .

Despite the anti-British rebellion in Iraq, and the repeated pro-Nazi declarations of the Mufti, several British Cabinet Ministers still hoped to appease the Arabs by stating publicly that the 1939 Palestine White Paper would become permanent post-war policy of the British Government. Churchill was strongly opposed to any such announcement, and on 27 April 1943, in a secret War Cabinet memorandum, he informed his colleagues: 'I cannot in any circumstances contemplate an absolute cessation of immigration into Palestine at the discretion of the Arab majority.'

Churchill went on to suggest that after the war it might be possible actually to add to the area of Jewish self-government, by making two former Italian colonies, Eritrea and Tripolitania, 'into Jewish colonies, affiliated, if desired, to the National Home in Palestine'. His memorandum ended:

We have certainly treated the Arabs very well, having installed King Feisal and his descendants upon the Throne of Iraq and maintained them there; having maintained the Emir Abdullah in Transjordania and having asserted the rights of self-government for the Arabs and other inhabitants of Syria.

With the exception of Ibn Saud and the Emir Abdullah, both of whom have been good and faithful followers, the Arabs have been virtually of no use to us in the present war. They have taken no part in the fighting, except in so far as they were involved in the Iraq rebellion against us. They have created no new claims upon the Allies, should we be victorious.

Unknown to Churchill, two weeks later, on 12 May 1943, the Mufti lodged a strong personal protest with the German Government, against the proposed emigration to Palestine of 4,500 Bulgarian Jews. But the Mufti was not alone in his opposition to allowing these few Jews to escape the ever-widening net of persecution. Five months earlier, on 14 December 1942, the British War Cabinet had discussed an urgent request from the Jewish Agency to allow these same Bulgarian Jews to go to Palestine. Their immigration, it was pointed out, would fall within the existing immigration quotas. But the response of the British Government had been against any such immigration. 'This proposal', the Colonial Secretary, Lord Moyne, told his War Cabinet colleagues, 'had been rejected on security grounds'; that was to say, he explained, in accordance with an earlier Cabinet decision of 1939 concerning the 'exodus of nationals from a country with which we were at war'.

This decision was not made without some knowledge of what was happening to the Jews of Europe. Indeed, the immediately preceding item of War Cabinet business had been a report from the Foreign Secretary, Anthony Eden, who had told the War Cabinet that there were 'indications' that large-scale massacres of Jews were taking place in Poland. 'It was known', Eden added, 'that Jews were being transferred to Poland from enemy-occupied countries for example, Norway; and it might be that these transfers were being made with a view to wholesale extermination of Jews.' And six weeks earlier, on 28 September 1942, the Polish Government in exile published in London a detailed account of the killings at Auschwitz concentration camp. Among the facts revealed were the deaths of 4,000 prisoners by shooting, 2,900 by gassing and 2,000 by phenol injections. A further 1,200 people had been beaten to death, and 800 had committed suicide by walking into the camp's electric fence.

On 17 December 1942 the British House of Commons heard Anthony Eden read out an Allied declaration to the effect that the German Government were now carrying out 'Hitler's oft repeated intention to exterminate the Jewish

Among the hundreds of thousands of *non*-Jews sent by the Nazis to concentration camps were anti-Nazis, Jehovah's Witnesses, homosexuals, the mentally ill, and the chronically sick.

Vaivara

Klooga
ESTONIA

North Sea

LATVIA

LITHUANIA

USSR

Baltic Sea

Stutthof

Neuengamme   Ravensbrück

Bergen-Belsen   Sachsenhausen

Treblinka

Chelmno

Mittelbau Dora   Gross Rosen
Buchenwald

POLAND

Sobibor

GERMANY

Auschwitz   Maidanek

Flossenberg

Natzweiler

CZECHOSLOVAKIA

Plaszow   Belzec

FRANCE   Dachau

Mauthausen

AUSTRIA   HUNGARY

RUMANIA

Gospič

Jasenovač

Sajmište

ITALY

Adriatic Sea

YUGOSLAVIA

0   miles   100

0   km   100

Auschwitz concentration camp in which more than 4 *million* people were murdered between 1941 and 1944, including Jews, Gypsies, and Soviet prisoners-of-war.

Camps set up solely for the murder of Jews.

Other camps in which Jews and non-Jews were put to forced labour, starved, tortured, and murdered in conditions of the worst imaginable cruelty. Most of these camps had "satellite" labour camps nearby.

© Martin Gilbert 1978

263

people in Europe'. The declaration, which was published simultaneously in London, Moscow and Washington, continued:

From all occupied countries, Jews are being transported in conditions of appalling horror and brutality, to Eastern Europe. In Poland, which has been made the principal Nazi-slaughterhouse, the ghettoes established by the German invaders are being systematically emptied of all Jews except a few highly skilled workers required for war industries.

None of those taken away are ever heard of again. The able bodied are slowly worked to death in labour camps. The infirm are left to die of exposure and starvation or are deliberately massacred in mass executions.

The victims 'of these bloody cruelties', the Allied declaration stated, could be 'reckoned in many hundreds of thousands of innocent men, women, and children'.

On hearing this terrible account, a Labour member of Parliament, William Cluse, asked for a moment of silence, and for the only time in its long history, the House of Commons stood in silence, in recognition of the Jewish fate.

A month later, on 19 January 1943, Cluse asked the Government to 'ease the immigration arrangements' for Palestine, so that 'a large number' of Jews could enter. But the Government's answer was a negative one, explained by the Labour Party leader, Clement Attlee, who told the House of Commons, that 'efforts to save the Jews cannot be simply British efforts'.

Despite the continuing severity of the Palestine immigration restrictions, the British Mandate authorities did admit just over 10,000 Jews to Palestine in the first three years of war. A further 9,000 had succeeded in entering 'illegally'. For these immigrants, a new chance of life opened up as it did, on 18 February 1943, when a further 858 children, 269 women and 100 men reached Palestine. All of them were refugees from Poland who had fled first to the Soviet Union and then to Persia, from where they had come by sea to Egypt, and thence by train to Palestine. The children, known as 'the Teheran children', were mostly orphans whose parents had been murdered by the Nazis.

A month later, on 23 March 1943, the Archbishop of Canterbury, Cosmo Gordon Lang, moved a resolution in the House of Lords, urging 'immediate measures, on the largest and most generous scale', to give all other Jews who could escape, 'temporary asylum' in Britain. They were confronted, he said, with 'wholesale massacre'. Speaking in the same debate, Herbert Samuel said that if the immigration rules could be relaxed, 'some hundreds, and possibly a few thousands, might be enabled to escape from this holocaust'. But again, the Government declined to relax its regulations, and at the end of the debate Viscount Cranborne stated officially that if the Government did open its doors to refugees there might then arise shortages of housing accommodation and food. Indeed, he added, 'the difficulties are no less in the Colonial territories. There are not unlimited supplies.'

As news of the killings was smuggled out to neutral and Allied soil, it continued to cast a pall of horror and despair over all who understood it. An example of how this news reached the Jews elsewhere is a letter which Ehud Avriel received while he was in Istanbul, organizing the transit of immigrant ships to Palestine. The letter, dated 17 July 1943, had been sent from Bedzin, and was signed by five young Polish Jews: Aranka, Hersch, Zvi, Koziak and Shlomo. It read:

Dear Friends,

After a long wait, today we received your courier and the letter he brought from you. Unfortunately he came a little too late. For years we dreamt about an opportunity to report about our life and our struggle. During the first year and a half of the war, we established an immense network of training farms and a strong youth movement, much larger than in normal times.

But then, suddenly, all regular work was disrupted, the ovens were installed, and the systematic extermination began.

The operation began in the Warthegau and in the districts of Posen and Lodz. About 80,000 Jews were gassed. The official term for this procedure was 'Aussiedlung' [population transfer]. In the town of Lodz there remains a small, hermetically closed community: they are doomed to die of hunger and consumption. At the moment we have no news from there. The place of extermination is called Chelmno, the death camp at Kulmhof. . . .

In the *General Gouvernement* of Warsaw, Lublin, Czenstochau and Cracow, there are no Jews left. They were gassed, mostly in Treblinka. This is a notorious camp, where not only Jews from Poland but also from Belgium, Holland, and other Western countries have died.

The most beautiful chapter in our struggle was the uprising in Warsaw. Zivia and Yosef organized the defence together with many youngsters. There were terrible battles in the ghetto. To our sorrow only about 800 of the enemy fell. The result: all the Jews and the ghetto utterly annihilated.

There seem to be no more Jews in the *General Gouvernement*, once called Poland, except for about 30,000 in three forced-labour camps. In a few weeks they, too, will be gone. . . .

The letter of the five continued:

The Ukraine is '*Judenrein*'. In Bialystok there still remain some 20,000 Jews living under relatively better conditions. The district of Lublin was entirely liquidated. East Upper Silesia was the last Jewish community where something resembling human conditions prevailed. But three weeks ago, 7,000 Jews were 'transferred' from there. They are being exterminated in Auschwitz: some are shot, others gassed.

In the near future the district from which we write to you will also be '*Judenrein*'. When you receive this letter, none of us will be alive. . . .

'Our hope to reach Palestine,' the five from Bedzin wrote, 'will unfortunately never be realized.' And even the one fragment of reasonable news in their letter, about the 20,000 Jews remaining in Bialystok, proved a chimera for, within a

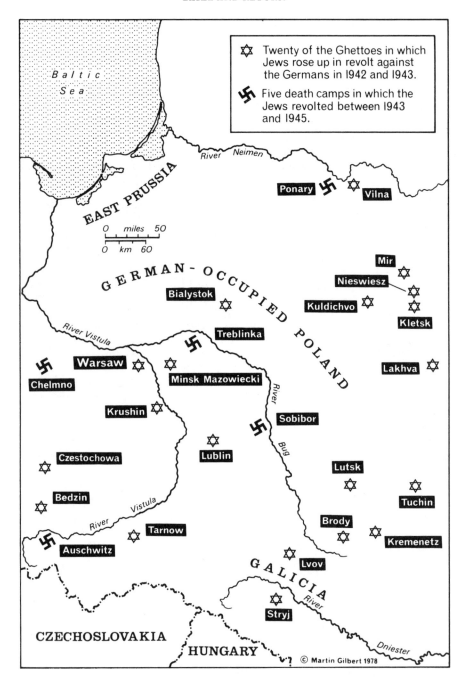

Baltic Sea

Twenty of the Ghettoes in which Jews rose up in revolt against the Germans in 1942 and 1943.

Five death camps in which the Jews revolted between 1943 and 1945.

River Neimen

EAST PRUSSIA

Ponary

Vilna

GERMAN - OCCUPIED POLAND

0 miles 50

0 km 60

Mir

Nieswiesz

Bialystok

Kuldichvo

Kletsk

River Vistula

Treblinka

Warsaw

Lakhva

Chelmno

Minsk Mazowiecki

River

Krushin

Sobibor

Bug

Czestochowa

Lublin

Lutsk

Bedzin

Tuchin

River Vistula

Brody

Tarnow

Kremenetz

Auschwitz

GALICIA

Lvov

CZECHOSLOVAKIA

HUNGARY

Stryj

River

Dniester

© Martin Gilbert 1978

266

month, the Nazis decided to transport all Bialystok Jewry to the Treblinka death camp. Brave beyond credibility, the Jews of Bialystok followed those of Warsaw in resisting their deportations; on 16 August 1943 they rebelled. But the Germans, with their overwhelming military force, crushed the revolt, and proceeded with the deportations. In all, of the 40,000 Jews who had been confined to the Bialystok ghetto in August 1941, only 260 survived the earlier mass-shootings, the previous deportations, the revolt, and the final extermination.

All over German-occupied Europe, Jewish communities like that of Bialystok were being wiped out: all of them centres of a vigorous Jewish life and culture for many centuries. Despite the heroism of individuals, and the continuing activities of Jewish partisans, the Nazi murder machine, often helped by local non-Jews, proved too powerful to break. At the same time, as German control spread to every corner of Europe, the chance of flight grew smaller and smaller: eight ships only had been able to set off on the perilous journey from the Black Sea to Palestine in 1942, two in 1943, and eight in 1944.

From the day the war began, to the day it ended, less than 9,000 Jews were successfully carried away in these 'illegal' ships from the countries that had fallen under German rule, a pitifully small number compared with those who died. Nevertheless, in the late summer of 1943 there was a change in British policy which did save several hundred more lives. Ehud Avriel has recorded in his memoirs, *Open the Gates!* that, at the end of August 1943, while he was still in Istanbul, he received an official message through the British Embassy in Ankara, to the effect that 'from now on every Jew who is able to reach the shores of Turkey under his own steam – repeat: under his own steam – is to be issued a visa to Palestine and to be sent on his way by British authorities'.

The first boat to benefit from Britain's new policy was the *Milka*, which had come from the Rumanian port of Constantsa with 240 refugees from the Bukovina. To greet them at the Haidarpasha railway station, the terminus for Asia Minor and the Middle East, were four railway cars with a notice on them saying: 'Reserved for Passengers to Palestine'. Before the end of the year a second boat, the *Maritza* also reached Turkish waters, bringing with it 224 survivors from the forced marches and concentration camps of Transnistria; they too continued unmolested from Turkey to Palestine, and to a new life.

In the British House of Commons, pressure continued to try to create an Allied open door for those refugees who did manage to escape. On 14 December 1943 the House discussed the failure of an inter-Allied conference at Bermuda to produce just such a policy, despite five months of talk. During the debate, Eleanor Rathbone, warned that the result of the Bermuda conference had been 'pitiably little'. It was not, she added, 'the way to tackle a task on which the lives of thousands of innocent people depend'. And she declared bitterly:

If it had not been for the restrictions placed on immigration to Palestine in Pre-war years, even before the Palestinian White Paper, imposed partly for economic reasons and partly to please the Arabs, tens of thousands of men, women and children who now lie in bloody graves would long ago have been among their kindred in Palestine. That is something I shall never forget, and I hope the House will never forget it either.

Despite his pre-occupations with the conduct of the war, Churchill had continued to support the idea of an eventual Jewish National Home in Palestine with a Jewish majority. But as the war progressed he had begun to accept the arguments which the Peel Commission had put forward before the war, and which many Jews had also accepted, albeit reluctantly, in favour of two separate States in Palestine, one Arab and one Jewish. On 12 January 1944 Churchill wrote to Clement Attlee and Anthony Eden: 'Some form of partition is the only solution,' and thirteen days later he informed the Chiefs of Staff Committee: 'Obviously we shall not proceed with any form of partition which the Jews do not support.'

Inside Palestine, a tiny group of desperate Jews felt unable either to trust Britain's word, or to wait until the war was over. Calling themselves the Irgun Zvai Leumi – the 'National Military Organization' – and holding Jabotinsky as their inspiration, in January 1944 they called upon the Jews of Palestine to revolt. Their demand was 'Immediate transfer of power in Eretz Israel to a Provisional Hebrew Government'. Their method, expressed succinctly by their leader, Menachem Begin in his memoirs *The Revolt*, was: 'A prolonged campaign of destruction. . . .' Yet Begin, like Ben Gurion, saw the Allied winning of the war as of paramount importance, and, while attacking several police stations in August 1944 in search of arms, the Irgun decided, as Begin wrote in his memoirs 'not to attack military installations so long as war with Nazi Germany was in progress'. This decision, Begin added, 'was punctilliously obeyed until May 1945'.

On 28 September 1944 Churchill announced in the House of Commons that a Jewish Brigade Group would be set up, to be trained and armed by Britain as a front line military unit. Five days later, on October 3, the Mufti, who was then in Berlin, wrote to the head of the SS, Heinrich Himmler, proposing the establishment of 'an Arab-Islamic army in Germany'. The German Government, Haj Amin added, 'should declare its readiness to train and arm such an army. Thus it would level a severe blow against the British plan and increase the number of fighters for a greater Germany.'

The Mufti was convinced that the setting up of an Arab army under German auspices 'would have the most favourable repercussions in the Arab-Islamic countries', and he proposed November 2, the anniversary of 'the infamous Balfour Declaration', as the date of the public announcement. A senior SS officer, General Berger, had already reported to Himmler that in a conversation on September 28 the Mufti 'noted happily that the day is nearing when he will head an army to conquer Palestine'. But no such announcement was made, and the Mufti's army remained a figment of his imagination. The Mufti himself remained in Berlin, supervizing Nazi propaganda broadcasts to the Middle East, and organizing parachute drops in British-controlled areas. A month after his letter to Himmler, four Arab parachutists were dropped into northern Iraq, where their aim was to continue sabotage work undertaken earlier by other parachutists. But the local village headman informed the police and the saboteurs were caught.

On 4 November 1944 Weizmann and Churchill met to discuss the future of Palestine. If the Jews could 'get the whole of Palestine', Churchill told Weizmann, 'it would be a good thing, but if it came to a choice between the White Paper and partition, then they should take partition'. Churchill told Weizmann that 'he too was for the inclusion of the Negev' in the future Jewish State.

During their meeting, Churchill gave Weizmann the impression that he 'did not seem to think much of the Arabs, or to their attitude in this war'. He had gone on to criticize the Jewish terrorism which had broken out against the British in Palestine, desperate acts by the Irgun and Stern Gang which the Jewish Agency had condemned; but, as Weizmann noted, 'he had not laboured the point'. Churchill went on to ask Weizmann to see the new British Minister-Resident in Cairo, Lord Moyne, who would, Churchill believed, be sympathetic. 'Lord Moyne', Churchill said, 'had changed and developed in the past two years.'

But before Weizmann could take Churchill's advice, Lord Moyne was assassinated in Cairo by two young Jews who, having witnessed the sinking of the *Patria*, and despairing of Britain's refusal to abandon the White Paper restrictions on Jewish immigration, had committed what Churchill described, in the House of Commons on 17 November 1944, as 'a shameful crime'. In his speech Churchill went on to say: 'If our dreams for Zionism are to end in the smoke of assassins' pistols, and our labours for its future to produce only a new set of gangsters worthy of Nazi Germany, many like myself would have to reconsider the position we have maintained so consistently and so long in the past.' Weizmann shared Churchill's sense of outrage. Indeed, even before Churchill's speech, the Jewish Agency Executive issued a statement calling upon the Jewish community in Palestine 'to cast out the members of this destructive band, deprive them of all refuge and shelter, to resist their threats, and render all necessary assistance to the authorities in the prevention of terrorist acts and in the eradication of the terrorist organization'.

While British and Jewish leaders expressed their horror at Lord Moyne's assassination, the deliberate murder of Europe's Jews was reaching its terrible climax, with more than five million Jews having already perished, and hundreds of thousands more being murdered each month. For the British policymakers, however, the overriding concern still seemed to remain that of the Jewish refugees seeking to reach Palestine: so much so that on 24 December 1944 the new High Commissioner to Palestine, Lord Gort, telegraphed to the Foreign

Office from Jerusalem to ask that the Soviet Government, whose troops had reached both Bucharest and Sofia, be asked to close both the Rumanian and Bulgarian frontiers on the grounds, as he put it, that 'Jewish migration from South East Europe is getting out of hand'.

From Palestine itself, despite the intense bitterness created by the anti-refugee policy, 33,000 Jews enlisted in the British Army, and many of them fought in Crete, Syria, Iraq, North Africa, Italy and Austria. Some volunteered to fight behind the German lines, and thirty-two of them were actually parachuted by the British into Nazi-occupied Europe. Among those who were parachuted was the twenty-three-year-old Hannah Senesh, who, after being captured and cruelly tortured by the Nazis, was executed in Budapest on 4 November 1944; and Enzo Sereni, who was murdered in Dachau two weeks later.

Not unnaturally, the Jews of Palestine were proud of what they had contributed to the Allied cause. 'This record', a Zionist memorandum of 1946 pointed out, 'may be compared with the total of 9,000 Arabs who enlisted in Palestine, but who hailed partly from Transjordan, Syria and the Lebanon; long before the end of the war, this total was reduced by at least one-half through desertions and discharges.'

The Jews played their part in all the Allied armies, and their losses were often heavy. Of the 500,000 Jewish soldiers who fought in the ranks of the Red Army, as many as 200,000 were killed in action. But, when the war ended on 8 May 1945, the 'victory' had a bitter, tragic taste for all Jews, and for the shattered remnant of eastern European Jewry there seemed little hope of a decent future in the lands so drenched with the blood of their loved ones.

The Jewish death toll will never be fully known. Among the million and a half children who were murdered were many whose names were never recorded. Hundreds of thousands of individuals, whose names are found before the war in lists of doctors, nurses or teachers, students or lawyers, writers or poets, disappeared without trace.

In the Nazi lists of those deported by train to the concentration camps, tens of thousands from as far away as France, Belgium, Italy or Greece, are many whose exact fate is unknown. That they were murdered is certain: but for many of them it is not known whether they died in the appalling conditions of a sealed cattle-truck, or were shot when they chanced to stumble or cough during a forced march from their homes to a camp, whether they were gassed, experimented on, or tortured to death in a concentration camp or even left while still alive to die in a pit of corpses. What is known is that in each of the German-occupied countries of Europe the Jews were either murdered where they lived, or deported hundreds of miles to their deaths. Six million is the minimum figure of those who perished.

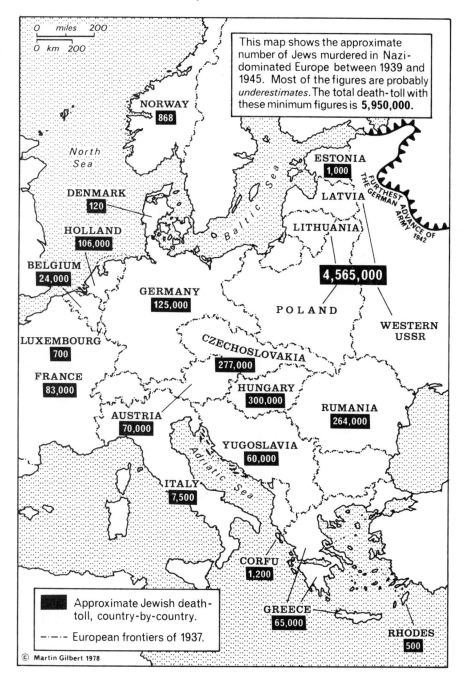

This map shows the approximate number of Jews murdered in Nazi-dominated Europe between 1939 and 1945. Most of the figures are probably *underestimates*. The total death-toll with these minimum figures is **5,950,000**.

NORWAY
868

North Sea

ESTONIA
1,000

DENMARK
120

LATVIA

HOLLAND
106,000

LITHUANIA

Baltic Sea

FURTHEST ADVANCE OF THE GERMAN ARMY OF 1942

BELGIUM
24,000

GERMANY
125,000

4,565,000

POLAND

WESTERN USSR

LUXEMBOURG
700

CZECHOSLOVAKIA
277,000

FRANCE
83,000

HUNGARY
300,000

AUSTRIA
70,000

RUMANIA
264,000

YUGOSLAVIA
60,000

Adriatic Sea

ITALY
7,500

CORFU
1,200

GREECE
65,000

RHODES
500

Approximate Jewish death-toll, country-by-country.

–·–·– European frontiers of 1937.

© Martin Gilbert 1978

0 miles 200

0 km 200

21

Closing the Door,
'Justice' and Revolt
1945-1946

WITH the end of the war in Europe on 8 May 1945, Jews all over the world hoped, and expected, that the doors of Palestine would be opened for the survivors of the holocaust. The number of people involved was not much more than 150,000; their suffering had been terrible, and their survival little short of miraculous. Neither their political views, their professions, their place of birth, their class or their diverse ways of life had played any part in their fate: only their Jewishness. The attraction of building a new life in Palestine derived almost entirely from this fact: as Jews, they had been singled out for the most evil torments devised by man; as Jews, therefore, they wished to live in dignity, protected by their own people, and not dependent upon the approval or sufferance of any non-Jewish majority.

On 22 May 1945, two weeks after the German surrender, Dr Weizmann wrote direct to Churchill, to ask that Jewish immigration be resumed. But in his reply on June 8, Churchill informed Weizmann that there could be 'no possibility of the question being effectively considered' until the proposed Peace Conference. Weizmann was appalled by this decision to delay what was, for the survivors of the holocaust, a matter of urgency. On June 13 he replied to Churchill that the contents of Churchill's letter had come 'as a great shock' to him, and he went on:

I had always understood from our various conversations that our problem would be considered as soon as the German war was over; but the phrase 'until the victorious Allies are definitely seated at the Peace table' substitutes some indefinite date in the future. I am sure that it cannot have been your intention to postpone the matter indefinitely, because I believe you realise that this would involve very grave hardship to thousands of people at present still lingering in the camps of Buchenwald, Belsen-Bergen etc., who cannot find any place to go if the White Paper is to continue for an unspecified period.

Weizmann proposed returning to the question after the British General Election, which was to be held on July 5. But when the result of the election was announced, the Conservatives had been defeated, and Churchill was no longer Prime Minister. Henceforth, the Zionists could not hope to benefit from Churchill's personal hostility to the White Paper policy. The new Labour

Government, led by Clement Attlee, and with Ernest Bevin as Foreign Secretary, decided to maintain the White Paper policy, despite the Labour Party's opposition to that policy in 1939. Indeed, Churchill, in a reply dictated on June 29, but not sent, had warned Weizmann that one solution to 'your difficulties' might be the transfer of the Mandate from Britain to the United States which, he wrote, 'with her great wealth and strength and strong Jewish elements, might be able to do more for the Zionist cause than Great Britain. I need scarcely say I shall continue to do my best for it. But, as you will know, it has few supporters, and even the Labour Party now seems to have lost its zeal.'

Sensing this new mood, on June 26 David Ben Gurion had declared, at a Press Conference in New York: 'If the British Government really intends now to maintain and enforce the White Paper, it will have to use constant and brutal force to do so.' To attempt to maintain the White Paper policy would, he warned, 'create a most dangerous situation' in Palestine. Irgun activities were also intensified: on July 13 a British Army truck carrying gelignite fuses was ambushed, and the constable on escort duty was killed in the attack, while on July 25 a railway bridge was blown up on the Lydda-Kantara railway.

On August 24 the Officer Administering the Government of Palestine, J. V. W. Shaw, wrote to the new Colonial Secretary, Arthur Creech Jones, quoting Ben Gurion's New York speech and also the words of the American Zionist leader, Abba Hillel Silver, to the effect that 'Jews will fight for their rights with whatever weapons are at their disposal'. The picture, Shaw warned, was 'a sombre one', and he went on:

The young Jewish extremists, the product of a vicious education system, know neither toleration nor compromise: they regard themselves as morally justified in violence directed against any individual or institution that impedes the complete fulfilment of their demands.

In a similar spirit their ancestors in the second century B.C. laid waste Palestine until a ravaged countryside and ruined cities marked the zenith of Hasmonaean power. The prototypes of the Stern Group and National Military Organisation are the Zealots and Assassins according to whose creed even Jews married to Gentiles were worthy of death in Roman times.

These Zealots of to-day, from Poland, Russia and the Balkans have yet to learn toleration and recognition of the rights of others. As the Foreign Secretary said recently of the Balkans, these people do not understand what we understand by the meaning of the word democracy.

The Jewish Agency may deplore terrorism; but every immoderate speech, such as those quoted at the beginning of this letter, the flagrant disregard on the one hand for the authority of Government in maintaining law and order and on the other for the Arab case, the chauvinism and intolerance of their educational system all contribute to an atmosphere in which the fanatic and the terrorist flourish.

Shaw's analysis of the situation continued:

The Jewish leaders appear to be deliberately pushing extremism to a point when an explosion can no longer be avoided and do not scruple to use the plight of the Jews in Europe as a main political excuse. There are many Jews who deplore this state of affairs, but the rigidity of the discipline imposed by the political machine effectively discourages criticism except where it has no practical effect on Zionist policy. The Jews, like so much in Europe, need education in toleration and democracy.

The Jewish Agency, and the Zionist leaders, continued to press for an end to the immigration restrictions of the White Paper. In London, a special Palestine Committee of the Cabinet reported, on October 19, that Britain would support the appointment of an Anglo-American Commission, to examine 'the situation of the Jews in Europe', and to make recommendations 'for its alleviation'. The Chairman of the Palestine Committee, Herbert Morrison – the Lord President of the Council – warned, however, in his report, of Muslim opposition to any relaxation of the immigration restrictions. President Truman's wish that the survivors of the concentration camps should be allowed into Palestine had, Morrison pointed out, already led to protests not only from the Arab States, but also from 'the Congress in India'.

On October 10 Weizmann went to see Bevin, in the hope of changing the British Government's mind, but his effort was in vain, and a month later, on November 13, Bevin announced that the White Paper policy would continue.

The Labour Government carried out the policy it had announced. Although nearly 100,000 Jews moved through Europe during 1945, in search of the routes, ports and ships for Palestine, by the end of the year only 13,100 had been allowed by the British to enter; this was 1,500 *less* than had been allowed in during 1944.

With Palestine so effectively barred to Jewish refugees, and the American quota system still rigidly enforced, it might be thought that, as compensation, the British immigration laws would be relaxed. But in a Cabinet memorandum of October 30, the Home Secretary, J. Chuter Ede, set out the principal basis of Labour's immigration policy, that it would not be 'right', as he thought, for Britain to contemplate 'any large-scale addition to our foreign population at the present time'.

Chuter Ede's memorandum set out certain 'limited' classes of refugees who would be allowed into Britain. All were dependent upon one relative at least being in Britain already, and 'willing and able to provide accommodation and maintenance'. Relative was defined as husband, wife, parent, grandparent, child or grandchild. 'If both the man and the wife are living together abroad,' he noted, 'it should not be the general practice to admit such couples.' Some children, including orphans, were already in special hostels run by voluntary organizations, but, Chuter Ede stressed, 'any large scale extension of schemes of this kind would involve unjustifiable demands on available housing accommodation', and he added:

I am clear – although on humanitarian grounds I reach the conclusion with the utmost regret – that any policy of granting these applications freely ought not to be contemplated. . . .

In addition to such considerations as the shortage of housing and of clothing and supplies of various sorts, there is the consideration that at the time when demobilisation is in the process the admission of a large number of foreigners would create apprehension as to competition in the labour market. . . .

On November 6 the Cabinet met to discuss the question of the admission of Jewish refugees to Britain. Chuter Ede, whose memorandum was before the Cabinet, warned that 'floods of applicants' could not be admitted. Many of the would-be refugees, he explained, would be 'elderly people who would be non-productive and might become a burden on the community'. There was also, he said, the problem of young people between the ages of eighteen and twenty-one, whose arrival would involve 'a permanent addition to the foreign population competing in the employment market with British subjects'.

A Minister not named in the minutes pointed out that in the past Britain had derived 'more benefit than harm' from a liberal policy towards refugees. But the minutes went on to record that:

. . . the admission of a further batch of refugees, many of whom would be Jews, might provoke strong reactions from certain sections of public opinion. There was a real risk of a wave of anti-Semitic feeling in this country. There was evidence of this in the recent protest of rate payers against the foreign colony in Hampstead.

One proposal was made by Ernest Bevin, who suggested to his Cabinet colleagues that those refugees who were admitted should be trained in agriculture, in order to spread them 'more widely', and thus prevent too many of them from seeking what Bevin described as 'openings in commerce'. The Cabinet finally accepted Chuter Ede's restrictions. It also agreed with his proposal that those new refugees 'whose relatives already in this country have been admitted on a temporary basis should be admitted on the same basis, and be expected to leave the United Kingdom when the alien who is already here departs'.

During the winter of 1945 the British Government became concerned by the exodus of the 80,000 surviving Polish Jews, many of whom sought to escape not only the evil memories all around them, but also the growing Polish anti-semitism. On 8 December 1945 the Commander-in-Chief of the British Forces in Berlin informed the Foreign Office that six thousand Polish Jews had reached Berlin from Poland in the previous month. 'As these persons are Polish citizens,' the Commander-in-Chief declared, 'they cannot be described as persons displaced from their homes by reason of the war, nor as refugees from persecution instigated by Germany or her allies. We are therefore refusing them food and accommodation in our sector of Berlin and onward transit into our Zone.'

According to a non-Jewish, and non-Zionist, report sent to the Foreign Office from Berlin on 5 January 1946, some 65 per cent of these unwelcome Polish Jews wished to go on to Palestine. Four days later the British Embassy in Warsaw reported that Polish Jewry had been 'so shockingly decimated by the Germans, and anti-Jewish feeling is still so prevalent, that they would prefer to go elsewhere. . . .' As for their ultimate destination, the Embassy noted, 'Zionism has always been strong here.' It was these facts that alarmed the British Foreign Office. On January 9 Sir George Rendel wrote, in a memorandum to the Foreign Secretary, Ernest Bevin:

If we authorise the British military authorities to admit these people we may be playing the Jewish game and facilitating a manoeuvre which is not only likely to cause us great political inconvenience and expense but is also likely to cause great hardship and suffering to the Jews themselves.

Rendel argued that 'the right policy' would be for the British Government 'to make every possible effort to prevent these people from entering the British Zone'. Those Jews who did get through, he suggested, should be sent to those camps already housing German refugees. If this were done, he wrote, 'they may well have a legitimate grievance on the ground that they are being put together with people who have persecuted them in the past, and also given treatment no more favourable than that accorded to the defeated enemy. This again may be embarrassing, but it would perhaps be the most effective deterrent to further unauthorized movement.'

Rendel went on to criticize the Zionist aim of trying 'to secure a special national status for Jews'. That same day, January 9, the British Embassy in Warsaw suggested that one way of putting pressure on the Polish Government not to allow any more Jews to flee westward would be to say to the Polish Government 'that by further increasing the chaos over the situation of displaced persons in Germany, they risk putting off the day when we can accept the German population of Poland in accordance with the Potsdam decision. . . .'

The exodus of Polish Jews did not end at Berlin. All over Europe, Zionist emissaries were organizing 'escape' routes to Palestine. One main route led through the British Zone of Austria into Italy. On 10 January 1946, in an attempt to block this route, Sir Noel Charles, the British Ambassador in Rome, proposed to the Foreign Office in London:

. . . that I be authorised officially to inform the Italian Government that we are concerned at the growing illegal emigration traffic and would welcome any measures they can take to check it. I could then suggest that the Italian Government should institute an exit visa regulation which would give them a basis for taking action against illegal emigrants.

I should also like to be able to assure the Italian Government that we are doing our utmost to check clandestine influx of refugees from Austria. . . .

Routes of the 'Illegal' Immigrants, 1945–1948

The head of the Refugees Department at the Foreign Office, Douglas Mackillop, understood more clearly the reasons for the exodus of Polish Jewry, noting on January 12 that it arose 'partly for racial & economic reasons, readily understandable since the new Poland does not offer them the same opportunities as the old, and there is a spontaneous general wish on the part of European Jewry to go to Palestine'. Mackillop added: 'Though it is magnified & artificially fostered by Zionist propaganda, it is a real aspiration.'

Despite Mackillop's understanding of the 'real aspiration' of Polish Jewry, the Foreign Office continued to examine every possible pressure to keep the Polish Jews inside Poland. Even the British Treasury was involved in these efforts. On January 18 a Treasury memorandum suggested applying pressure by means of the funds being made available by the Interim Treasury Committee on Polish Questions. According to the Treasury, some Polish Jews had already been refused funds, and the memorandum explained: 'The non-payment of allowances from ITC sources to Polish holders of Immigration Certificates was based on the assumption that they were embryonic Palestine citizens....' The Treasury memorandum continued: 'Certificate holders who wish to receive maintenance from the ITC must relinquish their claim to Palestine citizenship and revert to refugee status.'

On 25 January 1946 the Cabinet's Overseas Reconstruction Committee met in London, with Bevin as chairman. The purpose of the meeting was to discuss what Bevin described as 'the serious problem' caused by the exodus of Jews from eastern Europe into the British and American Zones of Germany and Austria, and into Italy. The Chancellor of the Duchy of Lancaster, John Burns Hynd, told his colleagues that during his own recent visit to Germany 'he had spoken with Jews at Belsen Camp, and these were all in favour of going to Palestine'. Hynd gave as his personal advice:

It would be undesirable to let it be thought that there would be an early opportunity for large numbers of Jews to go to Palestine, as this would not only encourage the present movement, but would also encourage Polish Jews forming part of the large mass of Poles who were now being repatriated from our Zone in Germany to Poland, to refuse to go home.

Bevin told the Cabinet Committee that the Foreign Office had considered sending 'an appeal' from the British to the Soviet Government 'to suspend the movement of Polish Jews from Poland', but felt that such an approach would be 'unprofitable'. They had also considered asking the Polish Government to create 'more tolerable conditions' for Jews already in Poland, but feared that if they did this, the Poles 'would resent the imputation' of anti-semitism. Bevin, however, did not believe that Polish anti-semitism was the principal cause of the Jewish desire to leave, telling his colleagues that, according to his information, 'most of the Jewish migrants from Poland were influenced by political rather than racial motives in their efforts to reach Palestine'.

According to the Chancellor of the Duchy of Lancaster, the British authorities in Germany and Austria 'were already tightening the control arrangement'; nevertheless, some Jews were still managing to cross from eastern Europe into the British Zones. The Chancellor of the Duchy wondered 'whether such persons should be treated as displaced persons'; he himself 'felt that they should not be so treated but should be dealt with on the same basis as German refugees and provided with rations on the reduced scale for Germans'.

A Jewish member of the Government, Lord Nathan, told the Cabinet Committee that:

> ... for generations Poland had been a centre of anti-semitism. Many Jews who had returned to Poland or had emerged from concealment had found their businesses and homes in the hands of others and on this account were not received with any great favour.
>
> He did not believe that there had been any organised evacuation. In the past, Jewish propaganda had sought to create a Jewish majority in Palestine by introducing one million Jews into that country out of a European pool of five million Jews. That pool had disappeared and to achieve such a majority in Palestine it would now be necessary to get almost all surviving European Jews to go to Palestine.

Lord Nathan suggested, however, that in order to halt 'the illegal departure of Jews from Italy', the British Government should concert measures with the Italian Government 'to ensure that the arrangements made to prevent illegal emigration of Jews were effective'.

The Cabinet accepted Lord Nathan's suggestion to enlist Italian support in stopping Jews leaving Italy for Palestine. They also accepted the Chancellor of the Duchy of Lancaster's proposal that Jewish refugees 'filtering through our control zones' should be 'dealt with' by a reduction in rations, so that henceforth they would be treated, not as displaced persons, but as Germans.

A struggle now began, in Palestine and in Europe, between the British Government and the Jews: a struggle marked by increasing bitterness and extremism on both sides. The British, determined to halt the now swelling tide of 'illegal' immigration from liberated Europe to Mandatory Palestine, went so far as to return captured immigrants from the waters of the eastern Mediterranean to which they had sailed, to the displaced camps in Germany from which they had fled. In Europe itself, at the frontier crossings between Austria and Italy, British troops halted concentration camp survivors who were on their way to the Adriatic, and to Palestine, and held them in former prisoner-of-war camps.

Inside Palestine, the Irgun reacted by attacking British military installations, and, as death sentences and reprisals increased the tension, acts of increasing desperation marked their efforts. Force alone, the Irgun believed, could bring an end to the White Paper, open Palestine to unimpeded Jewish immigration, and make possible a Jewish majority, and Jewish statehood. When Bevin himself

279

publicly warned the Jews not to 'push to the head of the queue', it was not only the homeless and displaced alone who saw this remark as a crude anti-semitic quip, which grossly belittled the reality of the refugee plight.

In Palestine, it was not only those who were caught carrying out acts of violence, but even teenagers caught pasting up posters, who faced the full rigour of the mounting bitterness and hatred. One such boy was Asher Tratner, a pupil at Haifa High School, who was shot and wounded in the hip one night while, unarmed, he was putting anti-British posters on walls. Menachem Begin, the Irgun commander, recalled in his memoirs how Tratner, although wounded, was neither seen by a doctor, nor sent to hospital. Instead, Begin wrote:

He was dispatched, his wound open and bleeding, to the Acre Jail. The wound festered. His jailers tied him to the bed. The boy had to wipe the blood and pus from his wound with strips torn from his shirt. The guards continued to maltreat him.

I was told by Rabbi Blum, whom the authorities had appointed prison chaplain, that he had drawn the attention of the British to the critical condition of the young prisoner. The reply was characteristic: 'Rabbis should concern themselves with the souls of the prisoners, not with their bodies. Mind your own business.'

Asher's spirit was not broken, but his body was destroyed. When at last the prison doctor was brought he diagnosed severe blood poisoning and the boy was removed to hospital. But it was too late. Even amputation of his leg did not save Asher. After weeks of suffering in the Acre Jail and the Haifa hospital, he died.

On 1 February 1946 the *Manchester Guardian* published a full report of the situation of the Jews still in Poland. The four headlines to the report read:

JEWS STILL IN FLIGHT FROM POLAND
DRIVEN ABROAD BY FEAR
POLITICAL GANGS OUT TO TERRORIZE THEM
CAMPAIGN OF MURDER AND ROBBERY

Since the beginning of 1945, the newspaper reported, some 353 Jews had been murdered by Polish thugs. 'Unfortunately,' it added, 'anti-Semitism is still prevalent in spite of the Government efforts to counteract it.' As a result of the war, this anti-semitism 'always present in Polish society', had been 'greatly aggravated by German propaganda'. Since the end of the war, ritual murder accusations had been made against Jews in Cracow and Rzeszow. In Radom, a hospital for Jewish orphans had been attacked. In Lublin, two Jews, already wounded by thugs while on a bus, had been tracked down to the local hospital and murdered there, in their hospital beds.

On the day after the publication of this detailed press report, Sir George Rendel despatched a telegram to Warsaw. Although designated 'of particular secrecy', it was deliberately not shown to Ernest Bevin until after it had been sent. Headed 'Exodus of Jews from Poland', it asked the British Ambassador, Victor Cavendish Bentinck, to inform the Polish Government that:

... large numbers of Polish Jews are in fact succeeding in leaving Poland, their objective being the British and American Zones in Germany and Austria en route for Italy and thence by illegal means to Palestine. These movements are entirely illegal and constitute a difficult and embarrassing administrative problem for us, and we should consequently be glad if the Polish Government would take further and energetic steps to prevent further illegal emigration of this kind.

In a second telegram to Warsaw that same day, the Foreign Office accepted that the Poles were doing their utmost to stop '*illegal* emigration', but went on:

We are no less concerned, however, at exodus of Polish Jews *with Polish visas*, and you should take any opportunity you can to make it plain that our objection is not to illegal emigration only but to all emigration of this kind.

The Foreign Office telegram continued:

... it is difficult to avoid conclusion that exodus is due to external political motives, and His Majesty's Government feel they are entitled to ask the Polish Government to co-operate to the best of their power with a view to checking a movement so clearly calculated to increase our difficulties in Palestine and elsewhere.

The motives of Polish Jewry did not go undefended, nor did their desperate desire to leave Poland go unexplained. On February 20 Victor Cavendish Bentinck explained, in a despatch to the Foreign Office, that the Jews of Poland 'do not wish to continue residence in what is for them one huge cemetery'. Cavendish Bentinck also forwarded the views of the Chief Rabbi of Warsaw, views which provided an eloquent testimony to Jewish aspirations. According to the Chief Rabbi:

The great majority of the Jews wanted to leave Poland: they looked upon Palestine as their traditional home, the cradle of their race and the centre of their faith.
They did not care whether Palestine was a Jewish State, a British Dominion, a bi-partite Arab Jewish State, so long as they could go there. They could not believe that it could not take them in.
Their 'Zionism', if such it could be called, was not a political movement but the result of terror, the need to emigrate, and the hope at last to fulfil the age-old aspirations of the Diaspora.
Had the Jews not wandered long enough? This yearning for Palestine was a basic human instinct and had nothing political in it, at any rate so far as the 'Grey' Jews of Poland was concerned, the homeless, starving, wandering, terrified, individual Jew.

Despite British efforts to prevent the Polish Jews from setting out on the hazardous road to Palestine, the situation inside Poland itself made flight inevitable. The facts were known to the Foreign Office: on March 14 Cavendish Bentinck reported from Warsaw that food supplies belonging to the Chief Rabbi's Emergency Council had been allowed to proceed in a car flying the Union

Jack. Yet even with this protection, the car had been stopped 'and four Polish Jews, one of whom was a woman, travelling in it, were taken out and shot by the roadside for being Jews'. The Ambassador added that anyone with a Jewish appearance was in 'danger', and on March 28 the Foreign Office learned that a group of Jewish leaders travelling from Cracow to Lodz had been seized, tortured, and murdered. But the Foreign Office reaction was, as an official minute expressed it, 'to abstain from adding, by interference, to the many points at issue between H.M.G. and members of the Slav bloc'.

Just as had happened before the war, alternate havens to Palestine were now sought for homeless Jews. But the post-war response was as negative as the pre-war response had been. On 6 April 1946 the British Consulate-General in Madagascar reported to the Foreign Office that Madagascar might be suitable for 200 colonists 'of the peasant class', but went on to warn that 'stress should be laid on providing the right type of colonist in the first instance, and not city bred Jews who were worn and emaciated through long confinement in concentration camps. . . .'

On April 11 the World Jewish Congress explained to the Foreign Office why the 'uprooted Jews' did not wish to remain in Europe, or to be repatriated to the European states in which they had lived before the war. The principal reasons were 'the annihilation of family and friends, the destruction of the social and economic basis of existence', and the continuing hostility 'of large sections of the local population which for many years have been under the influence of anti-semitic propaganda'. According to the World Jewish Congress, all the available evidence 'shows conclusively that the majority desire to settle in Palestine'. But on April 27 Sir George Rendel minuted on this appeal:

The Jews have had a *ghastly* time, but
(i) They are *not* a separate nationality.
(ii) There *is* room for them in Europe, they are needed in Europe.
(iii) There are other groups who deserve just as much consideration.

It was against such arguments that the Jews were to pit their efforts month by month. Yet the Zionists were concerned, not only with the fate of Polish Jewry, but also with the condition of tens of thousands of other Jews in Displaced Persons camps in the British Zones of Germany and Austria. On 3 January 1946 Sir George Rendel had recorded in the Foreign Office a complaint made four days before by a United Nations refugee official, Miss A. E. Wood, who told him:

. . . that by virtually prohibiting 'out relief' and insisting on all Jewish Displaced Persons coming into camps in order to get any kind of relief, the military authorities were creating extremely bad feeling against themselves on the part of the Jews and their supporters. Moreover, the way in which this policy was being enforced was causing great bitterness, as Jews were often instructed to move into camps at 24 hours' notice or less, and were treated almost as though they were criminals.

Miss Wood showed Rendel a letter from a British Major to a Jewish Rabbi which, as Rendel noted, 'was certainly expressed in the most unhappy terms'.

In the DP camps in the British Zone of Austria there was likewise much unease throughout the spring and summer of 1946, especially when Austrian police were used by the British to punish Jews who were protesting at conditions in the camps and demanding to be allowed to go to Palestine. In one such camp, Jewish women, survivors of the concentration camps, were stripped, and searched by Austrian guards: a humiliating moment which revived terrible and recent memories. On 20 March 1946 Henry Mack, the United Kingdom Political Representative informed the Foreign Office of 1,350 Jewish survivors of the Polish concentration camps who were being held in a DP camp in the American Zone of Austria, at Bad Gastein. 'Almost all want to go to Palestine,' Mack wrote, and only thirty-two of them had expressed a wish to go to the United States. Mack added: 'The Zionist flag is prominently displayed.'

There were other Jews also, beyond Europe, for whom Palestine offered the hope of a freer existence. On 18 April 1946 the World Jewish Congress informed the British Foreign Office of the plight of the Jews of Afghanistan: their status was 'tantamount to slavery, and they are the victims of a cruel racial policy largely the result of German propaganda before and during the early years of the war'.

Since the end of 1945, the specially appointed Anglo-American Committee had been pursuing its enquiries in the United States, Europe and Palestine, in search of a solution. On 12 February 1946 the Committee members reached Vienna, where they took their enquiries into the Displaced Persons camps. One of the Committee members, Richard Crossman, recalled, in his book *Palestine Mission*:

Policies which seemed sane enough in the White House or in Downing Street struck these wretched people as sadistic brutality. Measures which made sense to them appeared to busy British and American politicians downright unreasonable. Mr. Bevin, in his famous Press conference, when he announced the formation of the Anglo-American Committee, had jocularly remarked that the Jew should not push to the head of the queue. That might go down in Britain; in Belsen it sounded like the mouthing of a sadistic anti-Semite.

Two of us had seen a Polish Jew tear up the document which promised him emigration to America, saying that he could never trust a Christian again; he would not go to America because what happened in Germany might happen there. In Washington that must sound like the raving of a lunatic: in a Bavarian Assembly Centre where the huddled survivors were still cooped up behind barbed wire nine months after the day of liberation, it was the considered view of many sober and intelligent Jews.

One of the tasks of the Anglo-American Committee was to find out the true aims of the remnant of European Jewry. In the secrecy of the Cabinet Committee, three weeks before, Bevin had described their motives as 'political rather than racial', and this was very much the Foreign Office view. 'Did they *really* want to go to Palestine?' Crossman had asked himself. 'Or was this idea the result of Zionist propaganda?' There was no doubt that Zionist emissaries had been to all the Displaced Persons camps, and had taken charge of much of the educational and social work in the camps. These Zionists had already shown themselves to be a powerful force: they had even successfully prevented a United Nations plan to send unaccompanied Jewish orphans to care in Switzerland. This action had greatly angered the policymakers in London, and even Washington. But, as Crossman recalled:

Even if there had not been a single foreign Zionist or a trace of Zionist propaganda in the camps these people would have opted for Palestine. Nine months had passed since V-E day and their British and American liberators had made no move to accept them in their own countries. They had gathered them into centres in Germany, fed them and clothed them, and then apparently believed that their Christian duty had been accomplished.

For nine months, huddled together, these Jews had had nothing to do but to discuss the future. They knew that they were not wanted by the western democracies, and they had heard Mr Attlee's plan that they should help to rebuild their countries. This sounded to them pure hypocrisy. They were not Poles any more; but, as Hitler had taught them, members of the Jewish nation, despised and rejected by 'civilized Europe'. They knew that far away in Palestine there was a national home willing and eager to receive them and to give them a chance of rebuilding their lives, not as aliens in a foreign state but as Hebrews in their own country. How absurd to attribute their longing for Palestine to organized propaganda! Judged by sober realities, their only hope of an early release was Palestine.

The Anglo-American Committee visited the camps amid much hostility. This was not surprising, for, as Crossman recalled, the inmates 'regarded the British officials as prison warders', and had no appreciation for a statesman, Bevin, 'who forebade them to go to Palestine and offered them no other homeland'. At a camp near Villach the Committee came across several hundred Polish Jews – men, women and children – who had been prevented by the British from crossing into Italy, and who had been held for seven months in a disused prisoner-of-war camp, guarded, and confined, by British troops. As Crossman recalled:

The camp policeman, elected by the inmates, was a Polish boy of sixteen who had spent six years of his life in concentration camps. His had been the survival of the fittest, of the personality able to cajole, outwit or bribe. I asked him if he had relatives in America and he replied that his mother was there. I asked him whether he wrote to her and his handsome face contorted with passion: 'I have cut her off, root and branch. She has betrayed the destiny of my nation.' I asked him what he meant, and he replied: 'She has sold out to the Goy. She has run away to America. It is the destiny of my nation to be the lords of Palestine.' I asked him how he knew this was the Jewish destiny and he replied: 'It is written in the Balfour Declaration.'

Crossman commented: 'It was useless to argue with that boy or to tell him that the Balfour Declaration had promised no such thing. He was the product of his environment, of six years under the SS in concentration camps and nine months under the British at Villach.'

The Anglo-American Committee proceeded from Europe to Palestine, where it continued to take evidence. Among the Zionist leaders who appeared before it was Golda Meyerson, who told the Committee that the 160,000 members of the Histadrut – the General Federation of Jewish Labour – were willing to receive 'large masses of Jewish immigrants, with no limitations and no conditions whatsoever'. Mrs Meyerson went on to try to explain to the Committee 'what it means to be the member of a people whose every right to exist is constantly being questioned', and she went on:

Together with the young and the old survivors of the D.P. camps, the Jewish workers in this country have decided to do away with this helplessness and dependence upon others within our generation. We want only that which is given naturally to all people of the world, to be masters of our own fate – *only* of our fate, not of the destiny of others; to live as of right and not on sufferance, to have the chance to bring the surviving Jewish children, of whom not so many are left in the world now, to this country so that they may grow up like our youngsters who were born here, free of fear, with heads high.

'Our children here', Mrs Meyerson told the Committee, 'don't understand why the very existence of the Jewish people as such is threatened. For them at last, it is natural to be a Jew.'

In April 1946, while the Anglo-American Committee had been preparing its report, which included the recommendation of an immediate grant of 100,000 immigration certificates to the Jews of the D.P. camps, British pressure on the Italian Government grew. As had been suggested by the British Ambassador, a diplomatic protest had led to the Italians refusing to allow two 'illegal' immigrant ships, called by the Jews the *Dov Hos* and the *Eliahu Golomb*, to leave the port of La Spezia, on the Italian Riviera. For their part the 1,014 refugees, most of whom were from Poland and central Europe, refused to leave the ships, and declared a hunger strike. If force were used against them, they declared, they would commit mass suicide, and sink the ships. In Palestine, Golda Meyerson proposed a hunger strike by fifteen Zionist leaders, as a gesture of support with the refugees, and as a means of forcing the British to allow the ships to sail. Before starting the strike, the leaders went to see the Chief Secretary of the Palestine Government, Henry Gurney. In her memoirs Mrs Meyerson recalled how:

He listened, then he turned to me and said: 'Mrs. Meyerson, do you think for a moment that His Majesty's Government will change its policy because *you* are not going to eat?' I said, 'No, I have no such illusions. If the death of six million didn't change government policy, I don't expect that my not eating will do so. But it will at least be a mark of solidarity.'

The hunger strike was, in fact, successful, and on May 8 the *Dov Hos* and the *Eliahu Golomb* sailed for Palestine, their 1,014 passengers having been granted immigration certificates from the next month's quota.

The Anglo-American Committee published its Report on 1 May 1946. Among its recommendations were the end to the land purchase restrictions of the 1939 White Paper, and the immediate grant of 100,000 immigration certificates to the Jewish survivors. The Jews of Palestine were bitterly disappointed that their hope of statehood was not endorsed by the Committee, which recommended a continuation of the Mandate. The Arabs of Palestine, opposed to the entry of a further 100,000 Jews, rejected the Report and declared a general strike.

On June 12, at the Labour Party Conference at Bournemouth, Ernest Bevin rejected even the 100,000 extra certificates, and declared that the reason why the Americans had wanted Palestine to take 100,000 Jewish refugees was that they did not want 'to have too many of them in New York'. Bevin also claimed that it would cost £200 million to finance the transfer and settlement of the 100,000, and involve the despatch to Palestine of another Division of British troops: both burdens that the British taxpayer ought not to have to bear.

Frustration now overcame, and indeed almost overwhelmed, the Jews of Palestine. On June 16 the military arm of the Jewish Agency, the Haganah, blew up nine bridges, and damaged the Haifa railway workshops. On June 29 the British retaliated by sealing the Jewish Agency buildings, and arresting three thousand Jews throughout Palestine, including most of the senior members of the Zionist Executive. Two days later, Richard Crossman told a hostile House of Commons:

I must say frankly to the House that what we are trying to impose on the Jewish Community is a reimposition of the White Paper, something which no Jew in Palestine accepts as either law or order. This affects not only the extremists of the Left or the Centre. No Jew anywhere, least of all Dr. Weizmann or the Haganah, can be won over to support the Government by the arrests of thousands of their brothers.

'It is impossible to crush a resistance movement', Crossman added, 'which has the passive toleration of the mass of the population.'

Meanwhile, the pogroms in Poland continued, and on 4 July 1946 the two hundred survivors of the once flourishing Jewish community of Kielce, in Poland, were confronted with one of the oldest forms of anti-semitic hatred, a ritual murder charge. As in Tsarist days, the local mob attacked the Jews in the streets and in their homes, and forty-two Jews were killed.

Within twenty-four hours of the Kielce pogrom, more than five thousand Jews fled from all over Poland, and crossed the frontier into Czechoslovakia. But they were harassed wherever they went: in Bratislava, on the Danube, there were further anti-Jewish demonstrations. These new refugees also turned towards Palestine, despite the difficulties of the journey across unfriendly frontiers. But now one avenue of hope was emerging, for, as a result of pressure from the United States, the British Cabinet had begun to discuss the possibility of allowing 100,000 European Jews to enter Palestine.

In Palestine itself the arrest of the Zionist leaders had created a ferment of discontent. On July 9 Weizmann, as President of the Jewish Agency, issued a statement on behalf of those who had been imprisoned. The excuse for these arrests, for the seizure of the Jewish Agency archives, and for the countrywide searches and arrests, had been, he said, the 'deplorable and tragic' acts of Jewish terrorism of recent months. Yet these acts, he added, 'have sprung from despair of ever securing, through peaceful means, justice for the Jewish people'.

Within three weeks that despair reached a climax with, on July 22, the blowing up of the King David Hotel in Jerusalem by members of the Irgun. Ninety-one people were killed: British administrators working in the hotel, Arabs and Jews.

The Cabinet met on July 23, and at once considered a request from the Government of Palestine for a wholesale arms search 'with a view to breaking up the Jewish resistance movement'. But Attlee advised a more moderate policy: 'although there was evidence that the Hagana had been implicated in some of the earlier acts of violence', he said, 'there was no reason to believe that any but the most extreme advocates of violence were involved in this latest outrage.' It would Attlee urged, 'be a mistake to rush in to a widespread search for arms, which would be taken as a measure directed against all the Jews of Palestine. . . . Such action would have the effect of alienating all sections of Jewish opinion in Palestine.'

At a further Cabinet two days later, a suggestion was made to stop immigration altogether, but this punitive measure was also rejected. Such an action, the Cabinet minutes of July 25 recorded, 'would cause hardship to innocent and suffering people'. In addition, the minutes recorded, it was 'hardly consistent with the announcement in a few days of a policy which would provide (among other things) for the immigration of 100,000 Jews in the fairly near future'. Any measures taken 'in respect of this latest outrage' should, it was agreed, 'be directed only to that section of the Jewish community which had been responsible for it'.

The Cabinet of July 29 discussed an American request to begin the movement of the 100,000 Jews to Palestine within one month, but Attlee argued that the movement should not begin until plans for Jewish and Arab 'provincial autonomy' had been further developed. The Cabinet's attitude was one of compromise and hope for a reasonable solution. At a further Cabinet meeting on July 30 Sir John Shaw, the Chief Secretary to the Government of Palestine, stressed that 'The majority of Jews disliked bloodshed and the Jewish community were, as a whole, shocked by the King David outrage'; so much so, he explained, that the Haganah had offered to help the British to track down those responsible.

During the Cabinet's discussion of 'illegal' immigration, on July 30, it was agreed, despite Attlee's own doubts as to the wisdom of the measure, to deport to Cyprus all 'illegal' refugees who were caught trying to enter Palestine. At the same time, it was suggested that Dr Weizmann be asked to use his influence 'to persuade illegal immigrants not to resist transfer to staging camps in Cyprus', on the understanding that they would soon be transferred to Palestine as part of the 100,000. But Jewish fears were now too roused to trust such a proposal, which both Weizmann himself, and the Jewish Agency, were unwilling to accept. For them, immediate and unimpeded immigration to Palestine itself was the dominant need, on which no compromise was possible.

A serious blow to Zionist hopes of Labour Government support had come on July 24, with the publication of a plan drawn up by yet another Cabinet Committee on Palestine, and announced in the House of Commons on July 30 by Herbert Morrison, the Lord President of the Council and Deputy Prime Minister. Under this new plan, Palestine was to be divided into three areas. The first area, constituting 43 per cent of the Mandate area, and including Jerusalem, was to remain under British control. The second area, making up 40 per cent of the country, was to become an area of Arab provincial autonomy. The third area, the remaining 17 per cent of Palestine, was to become the area of Jewish provincial autonomy: all three areas to be under British rule.

Only if the Jews accepted this plan, Morrison announced, would the 100,000 refugees of the Anglo-American Committee recommendation be allowed into Palestine. Even so, those allowed in would have to be refugees primarily from Germany, Austria and Italy. Adult refugees from Poland, Rumania and eastern Europe would not be included in the total, only orphan children from these areas. Nor would Britain agree to receive these refugees, even under these restrictions, unless the United States Government agreed in advance to undertake 'sole responsibility for the sea transport of these refugees', as well as providing them 'with food for the first two months after their arrival in Palestine'.

Speaking in the House of Lords on July 31, a distinguished British Jew, Victor Rothschild – a scientist of repute, and a grandson of the first Lord Rothschild – while deploring the King David explosion and stressing that he himself had never been a Zionist, or even connected with any Zionist organizations, went on in moving terms to explain the effect of the continuing refugee restrictions on 'the Jewish mentality'. All the young Jews in Palestine, he pointed out, 'have had fathers, mothers and relations who were among the six million Jews tortured and gassed to death by Hitler'. Lord Rothschild's own family had also suffered. 'It is

288

a strange feeling to have had relations put to death in some terrible way,' he said, and he added:

> I wonder how many of your Lordships are in the same position that I am, of having had an aunt whom one loved dearly – she was seventy-five years old and quite blind – clubbed to death by the SS on the railway station outside an extermination camp.
>
> She had kept a small farm in Hungary for many years, and was much liked by the other farmers in the district.
>
> Please do not think that by telling this story I am trying to evoke any personal sympathy. I tell it quite objectively, because I believe such episodes help one to understand the despair and desperation which have led to the unforgettable events of the last few months.

Lord Rothschild went on to speak of how the maintenance of the 1939 White Paper restrictions was regarded by Jews as 'a betrayal of previous promises', to be contrasted with the way in which the Mufti, Hitler's wartime ally, had been welcomed recently by the King of Egypt. Likewise, Rothschild added, 'the Palestinian Jews could not help but notice the Arab record in the war; the Rashid Ali revolt in Iraq, in which a member of the Irgun lost his life while on a special mission for the British. He is now a captain – in the Habbaniyah cemetery.' Lord Rothschild continued:

> How fortunate it is that human beings find it so difficult to appreciate the horrors and miseries that go on in the world. We hear that millions of Indians have starved to death, or that countless Chinese have been drowned in floods. We say, and perhaps even feel for a short time, 'How terrible,' and then we go about our business. It is lucky that we can do this because if we could really feel what has happened we should perhaps be unable to go on living.
>
> The same applies about the Jew who was skinned alive, or his six million coreligionists who were gassed, tortured, and experimented on by Hitler. We say 'How terrible,' then we forget and go about our business. But, and this is the thing I find so difficult to keep in my mind, not one Jew in Palestine forgets one of these episodes – forgets that the woman in the next settlement had her one-year-old daughter roasted alive in front of her eyes.
>
> And when the scales seemed once more to be weighted against them, the last tenuous threads snapped and they said, 'There is no hope; therefore let us die fighting.'

In a debate in the House of Commons on August 1, nine days after the King David explosion, Winston Churchill himself went so far as to attribute the prewar Arab riots to the fact that 'the Jew was, in many cases, allowed to go far beyond the strict limits of the interpretation which was placed upon the Mandate'. As for the desire of the survivors to go to Palestine, he said, the President of the Board of Trade, Sir Stafford Cripps, had already said that there was no room for the Polish Jews in Palestine and, in his own speech, Churchill expressed his specific support on this issue with Labour Party policy, telling the House of Commons:

I agree entirely with what the President of the Board of Trade said on this point – no one can imagine that there is room in Palestine for the great masses of Jews who wish to leave Europe, or that they could be absorbed in any period which it is now useful to contemplate.

The idea that the Jewish problem could be solved or even helped by a vast dumping of the Jews of Europe into Palestine is really too silly to consume our time in the House this afternoon.

Britain, said Churchill, should not be 'in too great a hurry' to give up the idea that European Jews 'may live in the countries where they belong' and he continued:

I must say that I had no idea, when the war came to an end, of the horrible massacres which had occurred; the millions and millions that have been slaughtered. That dawned on us gradually after the struggle was over. But if all these immense millions have been killed and slaughtered, there must be a certain amount of living room for the survivors, and there must be inheritance and properties to which they can lay claim.

Are we not to hope that some tolerance will be established in racial matters in Europe, and that there will be some law reigning by which, at any rate, a portion of the property of these great numbers will not be taken away from them? It is quite clear, however, that this crude idea of letting all the Jews of Europe go into Palestine has no relation either to the problem of Europe or to the problem which arises in Palestine.

Churchill then referred to the King David Hotel explosion. 'It is perfectly clear', he told the Commons, 'that Jewish warfare directed against the British in Palestine will, if protracted, automatically release us from all obligations to persevere, as well as destroy the inclination to make further efforts in British hearts.' And yet, Churchill added, 'we must not be in a hurry to turn aside from large causes which we have carried far'.

For many Jews, Churchill's speech, and in particular his remark about the absurdity of allowing the holocaust survivors to go to Palestine, was a bitter disappointment. Did even the one English statesman in whom they had faith not see the desperation of their current predicament? Was it really possible that the 1939 White Paper had survived intact all the disasters and horrors that war had brought, even in the mind of one of its fiercest and most outspoken opponents? At least the Jews believed that they could rely on Britain to carry out one of the Allied wartime pledges, that of bringing the Nazi criminals to trial, a pledge which Churchill himself had publicly endorsed on several occasions.

Yet, despite Churchill's pledges, even the Jewish hope of securing justice against their murderers had become increasingly remote by the summer of 1946.

The history of British hesitations with regard to the war crimes trials reveals the extent to which the Jews, despite the enormity of their sufferings, were not considered either a nation, or a people who, having suffered as such, deserved the support of the existing Allied states. On 17 July 1944, while the war was still being fought, an official British Foreign Office memorandum stated: 'The Allies cannot undertake responsibility for enforcing universal retrospective justice in Germany,' and added, with reference to the various Allied declarations about bringing war criminals to justice: 'None of these declarations appears to involve His Majesty's Government in an inescapable commitment to bring to trial the perpetrators of crimes against Jews and others in enemy countries.'

Thought was also given, while the war was still in progress, to Britain's relations with any post-war Government in Germany. Here too, the question of bringing war criminals to trial appeared not as a necessity, but as a future obstacle. On 7 February 1945 a member of the Reconstruction Department of the Foreign Office, Paul Falla, minuted that future Governments in Germany 'will be unpopular enough already without having to appear as champions and avengers of the Jews and other more or less disliked minority groups'.

For the Jews, it seemed self-evident that as many as possible of those tens of thousands of individuals who had taken part in destroying one third of all world Jewry, and who had done so in circumstances of revolting brutality, should be brought to trial, even if the process of collecting the evidence, and finding the criminals, were a long and complex one. For the British, no such sense of injustice existed. Indeed, on 8 January 1946 a member of the German Department of the Foreign Office, Con O'Neill, cast doubt upon the need for a further trial of major war criminals after the Nuremberg proceedings were over, on the grounds that 'we don't want war crimes trials to become a universal bore'. But the extent of the actual crimes committed was well known; indeed, on 30 July 1946 Patrick Dean, the Assistant Legal Adviser at the Foreign Office, informed his superiors, from Nuremberg, that 'some of the evidence was too nauseating to be read to the Court'.

Even after the first of the war trials – the Belsen trial – had begun, at Luneberg in the autumn of 1945, the British attitude, as far as the Jews were concerned, was not such as to give confidence to the Jews themselves that the terrible consequences of their tragedy were really understood. On 24 October 1945 the Palestine Government had asked if a former prisoner at Auschwitz, Isabella Rubinstein, could go from Tel Aviv to Luneberg to give what was described as her 'unusually clear evidence', about one particularly sadistic woman overseer at Belsen. But David Scott Fox, a member of the War Crimes Section of the German Department of the Foreign Office, minuted: 'It is a matter of indifference whether the lady goes to Luneberg from this section's point of view.' At Nuremberg itself, Jewish representation was not considered of major importance. Indeed, on 16 January 1946, after the Board of Deputies of British Jews had asked to attend the Nuremberg Trials, the British representatives at Nuremberg informed the Foreign Office that, 'No Jewish organisations are permanently represented by observers at the trials.'

During 1946 all the States previously occupied by Germany were encouraged by Britain to send investigating teams in pursuit of war criminals, following which these criminals were to be tried for crimes against particular nationals – Czechs, Poles, Yugoslavs, etc. For their part, the British investigations focussed increasingly on crimes against British nationals. Crimes against Jews as such were not the specific concern of any nation. Hence many murderers of Jews were not sought out.

On 23 February 1946 a War Office internal minute explained that the war trials would have to be restricted for yet another reason, the danger of 'uniting a large number of Germans of the less democratic type'. Those who received heavy sentences, the minute explained, 'would become martyrs, and those who were given small punishments might come to regard them as an honour'. Certainly, for some Jewish observers, the sentences often seemed ludicrously light: thus in March 1946, at the first trial held by a German court – in the Soviet sector of Berlin – a former Nazi, Paul Heinen, was found guilty of 'a crime against humanity', and sentenced, as the British authorities in Berlin reported to the Foreign Office on March 11, 'to two years and one month's penal servitude and three years loss of all civil rights'.

As the trials progressed, it became clear that many of those found guilty of crimes would receive light sentences, and that others, for want of a thorough enough search for evidence, would be released altogether. On June 12, Richard Beaumont, of the War Crimes Section of the German Department of the Foreign Office, noted officially, about the Sachsenhausen concentration camp trial: 'experience seems to show that the British Military Courts in awarding sentences are inclined to give the accused the fullest benefit of any doubt which may exist.' A month later, on July 16, the Secretary of State for War was provided with a 'brief' for the Cabinet, in which it was argued by the War Office that 'work on cases concerning concentration camps which are not in the British Zone, but whose camp staffs are in British hands, should be stopped, even where small numbers of British victims were involved, and that the alleged criminals should be handed over to the Nation territorially concerned'.

The Jews, of course, did not constitute a 'Nation', and were thus unable to secure justice on their own behalf.

Within British Government circles, from the hundreds of minutes and memoranda written on the subject, one of the few sympathetic voices, as far as the crimes committed against the Jews were concerned, was that of Patrick Dean, who had understood the enormity of the crimes that had been committed against the Jewish people. On June 18 Dean commented critically on the low sentences, often of 'a few months only', being given to those found guilty of 'peculiarly atrocious murder'. The Belsen trial, he noted, had resulted 'in a very small number of death sentences'. The existing basis of many of the trials was, he wrote, absurd, whereby 'if a man is implicated in the murder of more than, say, a hundred persons, he is worthy of death, whereas if he has only murdered two or three or four he should get off with a prison sentence'. Dean commented: 'ridiculous sentences imposed after lengthy and over-legalistic hearings merely confirm the view which is held by so many Germans that the British are fools and not that they are the living embodiments of justice.'

Dean made one further protest, on June 24, pointing out that the War Office was insisting, in concentration camp cases, on trying to prove 'that each of the accused was personally responsible for at least one murder'. Dean added:

This is a ridiculous method of procedure, since the victims or potential victims who could have proved the necessary facts are themselves dead or vanished long ago.

It seems worse than ridiculous to anyone who has any knowledge whatever of the calculated cruelty with which the concentration camps staff carried out millions of murders all over Europe.

Dean's arguments were of no avail, either in the War Office, or in the Foreign Office, where the Legal Adviser, Sir William Beckett, noted on June 25: 'Orders to courts to impose sentences of a severe nature are contrary to our system and what in the long run we stand for,' while Sir Basil Newton, who had been British Minister in Prague at the time of the German occupation in March 1939, added, on June 27: 'If sentences err on the side of leniency that is a fault on the right side.'

Not only leniency, but also early release from custody, became the theme of the war crimes trial procedures. On 24 September 1946, Frederick Garner, of the Foreign Office, minuted: 'I really think that July 31st 1947 should be made the outside limit. For us to keep people in custody without trial for more than two years would be to expose us to the criticism that we were doing the very thing for which we condemn the Nazis.' On November 4, ten days after Garner wrote this minute, the question of the war crimes trials was discussed by the Cabinet, when it was made clear, as the official Cabinet minutes recorded, that Britain 'should advocate a policy of discontinuing trials for war crimes'. A month later, on December 5, Garner noted, in a Foreign Office minute: 'I think the correct interpretation of the Cabinet's view is that they would like to see war crimes trials everywhere wound up as quickly as possible and that they would like us to take the lead in bringing this about.'

As a result of the twelve trials held by the Military Tribunals at Nuremberg, 177 Nazi criminals were found guilty of crimes against humanity. Twelve were sentenced to death. Most of the others were the beneficiaries of the Clemency Act of January 1951 passed by the United States High Commissioner in

Germany, John J. McCloy. In the United States Occupation Zone, which included Dachau concentration camp, 1,941 Nazis were found guilty of war crimes, and 462 were sentenced to death. In the British Occupation Zone, which included Belsen, 1,085 were found guilty, and 240 sentenced to death. In the French Zone the ratio was even smaller: 2,107 tried and 104 sentenced to death. But even of these 806 death sentences passed by the three Allied courts, only 486 of the sentences were actually carried out.

After 1951 more trials were held throughout the areas of former German rule. But the penalty for the proven murder of tens, and even hundreds of innocent civilians was often limited to two or three years in prison. In addition many known war criminals were living in countries, particularly in South America, from which they could not be extradited: or even in Europe.

During 1946 the position even of the surviving Jews in Germany became subject to the dictates of a harsh policy, illustrated by a Foreign Office confidential note sent to the Control Office for Germany and Austria on 5 July 1946. The note stated, tersely, 'We must have . . . a clear definition of the term German JEW and must prevent German JEWS from emigrating to PALESTINE.'

As before the war, the British Government's pressure against the 'illegal' Jewish immigrants was intense. But with each month the organizers of the 'Bricha', or 'Flight', as it was called, were able to mobilize their resources, driven forward by the determination of the survivors to reach Palestine, whatever the hardships of the journey. For most of them, there could never be a peril so foul as that from which they, the mere remnant of European Jewry had escaped. Between August 1945 and May 1946, sixty-four ships set off, from ports in France, Italy, Yugoslavia, Greece, Bulgaria and Rumania, bearing more than 73,000 men, women and children to Palestine.

Some Jews found refuge elsewhere than Palestine. More than 15,000 went to Latin America; nearly 13,000 reached the United States; 7,000 went to Canada; and 6,000 went to Australia. But the majority wanted to go to Palestine, where, despite British opposition, the groundwork of Jewish statehood was being laid with deliberation and careful planning.

In October 1946 eleven new Jewish settlements were established in the Negev in a single night, aimed at ensuring that the Negev would be included within the boundaries of the State. Two weeks earlier, on October 1, Weizmann had gone to see Bevin at the Foreign Office, to ask Bevin to agree to some form of partition, as first put forward ten years earlier by the Peel Commissioners. But Bevin replied: 'The Arabs would not accept partition. Was he to force it on them with British bayonets?' Bevin also spoke of the growing anti-semitic feeling in Britain, telling Weizmann that 'he had never seen so much anti-semitism under the skin as there exists now'.

Bevin told Weizmann that he wanted 'to work out a plan for a unitary state', but this plan, already announced in outline by Herbert Morrison in the House of Commons, involved setting up a tiny Jewish enclave in Palestine, under British, not Jewish sovereignty. The Arabs had already denounced it, and on October 4 President Truman also rejected it. The Zionists did not know how to respond. There were 'a few', Ben Gurion wrote to Weizmann from Paris on October 28, 'who believe that we should resign ourselves to the Morrison plan, since it gives us a possibility of immigration and constructive work and may in the future lead to a State'. Ben Gurion himself was sceptical of such an outcome, and the Morrison plan was rejected. Yet Ben Gurion, like Weizmann, was willing to accept some form of partition, provided it gave the Jews full statehood in whatever area was allocated to them. 'We should, in my opinion,' Ben Gurion told Weizmann in his letter of October 28, 'be ready for an enlightened compromise even if it gives us less in practice than we have a right to in theory, but only so long as what is granted to us is really in our hands. That is why I was in favour of the principle of the Peel Report in 1937 and would even now accept a Jewish State in an adequate part of the country. . . .' Ben Gurion's letter ended:

We are the generation which came after you, and which has been tried, perhaps, by crueller and greater sufferings; and we sometimes, for this reason, see things differently. But fundamentally we draw from the same reservoir of inspiration – that of sorely tried Russian Jewry – the qualities of tenacity, faith, and persistent striving which yields to no adversity or foe.

The 22nd Zionist Congress opened in Basle on 9 December 1946. The new Negev settlements, Weizmann told the delegates, 'have, in my deepest conviction, a far greater weight than a hundred speeches about resistance – especially when the speeches are made in New York, while the proposed resistance is to be made in Tel-Aviv and Jerusalem'. Weizmann did not minimize the cause of Jewish bitterness. Indeed, his speech contained a powerful reproach of Britain's White Paper policy, for, as he told the delegates, in bitter tones:

Whenever a new country was about to come under Gestapo rule, we asked that the gates of the National Home be opened for saving as many as possible of our people from the gas-chambers. Our entreaties fell on deaf ears; it seemed that the White Paper was more sacred for some people than life itself.

Sometimes we were told that our exclusion from Palestine was necessary in order to do justice to a nation endowed with seven independent territories, covering a million square miles; at other times we were informed that the admission of our refugees might endanger military security during the war.

It was easier to doom the Jews of Europe to a certain death than to evolve a technique for overcoming such difficulties. When human need, the instinct of self-preservation, collided with the White Paper, the result was the 'Struma', the 'Patria' and Mauritius.

These were stern words, describing a situation which many of the delegates regarded as a justification for armed resistance. But Weizmann urged the delegates to demand a halt to all anti-British acts of terror and violence. What was needed, he said, was 'the courage of endurance and the heroism of super-human restraint'. Terrorism, he declared, was 'a cancer in the body politic' of Palestinian Jewry. Accused of being a demagogue, Weizmann cried out in anger to his critics: 'If you think of bringing the redemption nearer by un-Jewish methods, if you lose faith in hard work and better days, then you commit idolatry and endanger what we have built.'

Weizmann ended his appeal for moderation with one final, anguished out-burst, telling the delegates: 'Would that I had a tongue of flame, the strength of prophets, to warn you against the paths of Babylon and Egypt. "Zion shall be redeemed in judgement", and not by any other means.'

Weizmann's appeal was unsuccessful: it was narrowly defeated, by 171 votes to 154, but it was defeated nevertheless. 'Perhaps it was in the nature of things that the Congress should be what it was,' he reflected in his memoirs, 'for not only were the old giants of the movement gone . . . but the in-between generation had been simply wiped out; the great fountains of European Jewry had been dried up. We seemed to be standing at the nadir of our fortunes.' And to the Congress itself he declared, in his final address: 'The Jewish people, especially those waiting in the camps, look to you to open the gates.'

Epilogue:
The Coming of
Jewish Statehood
1947-1948

FOR six years, from 1939 to 1945, the Jews had been caught between the evil designs of those who sought to destroy them, and the indifference of those who had no special desire to help them. Six million had been murdered; not only Jewish lives, but Jewish life, had been blotted out. Traditions, possessions, culture, the natural evolution of future generations of many more millions: all had been destroyed, more than one third of the whole of world Jewry. No longer could the Jews entrust their fate to others; the Holocaust was a bitter, final culmination of two thousand years of persecution. By the winter of 1946 the arguments in favour of Jewish statehood were, for the Jews, of overwhelming clarity.

In Palestine itself, the British remained vigilant in their search for hidden Jewish arms. Jews caught in possession of arms were arrested, imprisoned, and even flogged. Following one such flogging, on 29 December 1946 the Irgun seized a British major and three sergeants, and flogged them in retaliation. With the opening weeks of 1947 the violence increased: on January 1 an Irgun group, in attacking a British police post, killed a policemen. The British Press began to urge partition, and a British withdrawal.

The British Government was coming close to the end of both its patience and its self-confidence. On 1 January 1947, at a meeting of the Cabinet's Defence Committee, it was agreed 'that to continue this policy in Palestine in present circumstances placed the Armed Forces in an impossible position'. Three days later the Secretary-General of the Arab League, General Azzam Pasha, announced that the Arabs would vote against any partition scheme that might be put forward, and they would continue to oppose any further Jewish immigration.

Such Arab hostility was well known. But on the morning of January 7 a new factor was introduced into the Middle East discussion, which made Arab goodwill even more essential. For on that day a 'Top Secret' memorandum, written four days before, was circulated to the Cabinet, entitled 'Middle East Oil'. Its authors were Ernest Bevin, the Foreign Secretary, and Emanuel Shinwell, the Minister of Fuel and Power, and they submitted facts and charts to illustrate what they called 'the vital importance for Great Britain and the British Empire of the oil resources of this area'. The Middle East, they stressed, was likely to provide 'a greater proportion of the total world increase of production than any other oil-bearing region'. By 1950, the 'centre of gravity' would shift from Persia 'to the Arab lands', with Saudi Arabia, Bahrain, Kuwait and Iraq being the main oil producers.

Bevin and Shinwell went on to warn of the grave risks involved in offending the Arabs 'by appearing to encourage Jewish settlement and to endorse the Jewish aspiration for a separate State'.

Bevin himself now favoured a plan put forward by the Arab States for a 'unitary' State in Palestine, and in a further 'Top Secret' memorandum on January 14, he made one last attempt to warn his colleagues against partition. 'The certainty of Arab hostility to partition is so clear,' he wrote, 'and the consequences of permanently alienating the Arabs would be so serious, that partition must on this ground alone be regarded as a desperate remedy.' Such a decision, he wrote, would 'contribute to the elimination of British influence from the vast Moslem area between Greece and India', and would have consequences even beyond strategy. 'It would also', he wrote, 'jeopardize the security of our interests in the increasingly important oil production in the Middle East.'

Bevin told his colleagues that he favoured 'an independent unitary State' in Palestine, with special rights for the Jewish minority, but incorporating 'as much as possible of the Arab plan'. He went on to explain that he did not accept Arab demands to halt Jewish immigration altogether, although, he wrote, 'steps must be taken to prevent a real flooding of the country by Jewish immigrants'.

Bevin argued that 'a Jewish Government' would not accept the partition lines as final, but would eventually seek to expand its frontiers. 'If Jewish irredentism is likely to develop after an interval,' he commented, 'Arab irredentism is certain from the outset. Thus the existence of a Jewish state might prove a constant factor of unrest in the Middle East.'

When the Cabinet met on the morning of January 15, Bevin stated that if a 'bi-national unitary State' could be set up in Palestine, with an Arab and a Jewish province each with 'a right of secession' after a number of years, then 'pressure for the creation of a separate Jewish State would subside'. It would be helpful, he added, if the United States 'could be persuaded to admit a number of Jewish immigrants from Europe', and he had already instituted enquiries in Washington to this end.

Bevin was answered by the Colonial Secretary, Arthur Creech Jones, who told the Cabinet that he could see 'no solution on the lines of the Arab plan for a unitary State, for illegal immigration of Jews would continue and the present state of tension would be perpetuated' while Britain remained responsible for law and order. The Jews, Creech Jones added, 'would not accept as satisfactory any scheme which did not provide for a Jewish national State, whose nationals would have a Jewish nationality'.

During the ensuing discussion, Hugh Dalton, the Chancellor of the Exchequer, supported partition, and a 'mini' Jewish State. It was clear, he said, that the Zionists were determined 'to insist on the right of the Jews to enter as immigrants, subject only to the control of a purely Jewish authority, some purely Jewish area in Palestine, however small it might be'. This determination, he added, 'ruled out all solutions other than Partition'. This view was supported by Aneurin Bevan, the Minister of Health, who warned of 'a general outbreak of anti-Semitism' in Britain if the Government had to repress the continuing disorders in Palestine by force. For the Jews, Bevan noted, partition was already 'a compromise solution', and if this opportunity to put it forward were lost, 'it was likely that the leadership of the Jews would pass to men who would advocate more extreme solutions and more violent courses'. Bevan had a further point to make. The official minutes recorded:

The Minister also challenged the view that, from the angle of our strategic interest, it must be our objective to avoid estranging the Arab States. In his view, a friendly Jewish State in Palestine would give us a safer military base than any we should find in an Arab State. The Jews were under the continuing influence of countries friendly to ourselves. If, however, India and other Muslim countries passed under Russian influence, for how long could we expect to retain a secure military base in an Arab Palestine?

A. V. Alexander, the Minister of Defence, disagreed. If Britain could not satisfy both Arabs and Jews, he said, 'there could be no doubt', from a defence point of view, 'that it was vital for us to retain the goodwill of the Arab world'.

The arguments in favour of making Palestine a 'unitary' State, and of rejecting a separate Jewish State, were challenged by the Colonial Secretary, Arthur Creech Jones. 'In my opinion,' he wrote in a secret Cabinet memorandum on January 16, 'the cost of enforcing this plan would be disorder and bloodshed on a scale which we could never contemplate.' It would also, he argued, be 'a gross betrayal' of the Jews, who would be 'handed over to the mercy' of an Arab state 'run by the Mufti'. Creech Jones recommended partition into an Arab and a Jewish State. 'This solution', he believed, 'possesses an element of finality which is elsewhere absent.'

The Cabinet met again on January 22. While some Arab States 'would no doubt oppose Partition', Creech Jones commented, 'he was by no means certain that they would all be united in that policy for long'. Both Transjordan and Saudi Arabia might, he believed, support partition in the end. The next speaker, Emanuel Shinwell, stressed that if Britain had to choose 'between the friendship of the Jews and of the Arab world, he felt that on a long view the friendship of the Jews was more valuable to us than that of the Arabs'. Recent experience in both Egypt and India, he pointed out, suggested that if a 'unitary' State were set up in Palestine with an Arab majority, 'it would not necessarily remain friendly towards us or willing to allow us to maintain a strategic base in Palestine'.

The Cabinet now came to a decision which marked a turning point in the history of the British Mandate. Failing 'an agreed settlement' between Jews and Arabs, the Cabinet minute recorded, 'any solution of this problem would have to come before the United Nations'.

One last attempt was made by Britain to find an agreed solution, but in a further 'Top Secret' memorandum of February 6, Bevin and Creech Jones jointly reported to the Cabinet that the Arabs were 'implacably opposed to the creation of a Jewish State in any part of Palestine, and they will go to any lengths to prevent it': indeed, it was clear that the 'younger generation' of Arabs would 'take up arms to resist the imposition of Partition'. At the same time, the Arabs insisted on receiving some 'satisfactory assurance' from Britain that it would not be possible for the Jews, by continuing immigration, 'to secure a majority in Palestine'. The Jews, for their part, still interpreted the Balfour Declaration and the Mandate 'as implying a promise that a Jewish State will be established in the whole of Palestine': they would accept partition as a compromise, but they would not give up their 'essential point of principle', the establishment, somewhere in Palestine, of 'a sovereign Jewish State'.

In view of the deadlock, Creech Jones and Bevin proposed that Britain 'submit the problem to the United Nations', and at a Cabinet meeting on February 14 this proposal was accepted. That same day, Bevin announced that Britain would hand the whole problem to the United Nations.

For the next nine months the future of Palestine was argued over with much passion on all sides. For the Jews, it was at last an opportunity to put their case to an international body, and they did so fully aware of all that was at stake, not only for the 630,000 Jews already in Palestine, but for the hundreds of thousands who still hoped to go there. On 8 May 1947 a leading American Zionist, Rabbi Abba Hillel Silver, told a special session of the United Nations set up to hear the arguments about the future of Palestine:

The Jewish people belongs in this society of nations. Surely the Jewish people is no less deserving than other peoples whose national freedom and independence have been established and whose representatives are now seated here.

The Jews were your allies in the war, and joined their sacrifices to yours to achieve a common victory. The representatives of the Jewish people of Palestine should sit in your midst. We hope that the representatives of the people which gave to mankind spiritual and ethical values, inspiring human personalities and sacred texts which are your treasured possessions, and which is now rebuilding its national life in its ancient homeland, will be welcomed before long by you to this noble fellowship of the United Nations.

The Arabs also put their case; that same day the representative of Iraq, Dr Fadhil Jamail, insisted that the Arabs of Palestine should not, as he put it, 'suffer for the crimes of Hitler'. But on May 12 David Ben Gurion pointed out, in answer to this line of argument, that the homeless Jewish refugees were being brought to 'our own country', to Jewish towns and villages, and not to Arab inhabited areas. The Jews who had returned, he said, 'are settled in Petah Tikvah, Rishon le-Zion, Tel Aviv, Haifa, Jerusalem, Deganiya, the region of the Negev, and other Jewish towns and villages built by us'.

On May 15 the United Nations set up a Special Committee on Palestine, known popularly by its initials as UNSCOP. That same day, in Palestine itself, two British officers were killed dismantling a mine on the railway. Two weeks later, 400 Jews from French North Africa reached Palestine: the first Jews to come from Arab lands as 'illegals'. As with all those caught by the Royal Navy, they were taken to Cyprus and interned: the *New York Times* of June 1 called it the Haganah's 'first non-European rescue bid'.

On June 2 UNSCOP elected its Chairman, Emil Sandstrom, a Swedish Supreme Court Judge. As UNSCOP set off for Palestine, the Arab Higher Committee declared a complete boycott throughout Palestine of all UNSCOP proceedings, giving as its reason that UNSCOP's terms of reference included a study of the problem of the Jewish Displaced Persons who, leaving Europe in a series of 'illegal' ships, were still being intercepted by the British and deported to Cyprus.

Even before UNSCOP began its work, it was clear that the fate of the DPs would be a predominant issue. On April 14, 2,552 'illegal' immigrants had reached Haifa on board the *Guardian*, and three Jews had been killed while unsuccessfully resisting a Royal Navy boarding party which was in the process of transporting the 'illegals' to Cyprus. On April 22 a further 769 'illegals', arriving on board the *Galata*, had likewise been transhipped, followed by 1442, who arrived on board the *Trade Winds* on May 17, 1,457 on board the *Orletta* on May 24, and a further 399 on board the *Anal* on May 31.

The UNSCOP members were already in Palestine when, in July, another 'illegal' ship, named by the Jews *Exodus 1947*, reached Palestine waters from Genoa, with many German and Polish refugees on board. After three Jews had been killed in a skirmish with the Royal Navy, the ship was brought into Haifa under British naval escort. But its 4,500 refugee passengers were ordered by Bevin to go, not to Cyprus, but back to Europe, and they were at once forcibly transferred to another ship, the *Empire Rival*.

Among those who recalled the impact of the transfer of the refugees on the members of UNSCOP was one of the two Jewish liaison officers to the Committee, Aubrey Eban, who persuaded four of the eleven Committee members, including the Chairman, to go to Haifa to see for themselves what was happening. There, Eban wrote in his autobiography, the four members watched 'a gruesome operation', for, as he explained:

The Jewish refugees had decided not to accept banishment with docility. If any one had wanted to know what Churchill meant by a 'squalid war', he would have found out by watching British soldiers using rifle butts, hose pipes and tear gas against the survivors of the death camps. Men, women and children were forcibly taken off to prison ships, locked in cages below decks and sent out of Palestine waters.

When the four members of UNSCOP came back to Jerusalem, Eban recalled, 'they were pale with shock', and he added: 'I could see that they were preoccupied with one point alone: if this was the only way that the British Mandate could continue, it would be better not to continue it at all.'

A few days before the refugees began their journey back to Europe, Golda Meyerson had declared, in a speech in Tel Aviv: 'to Britain we must say: it is a great illusion to believe us weak. Let Great Britain with her mighty fleet and her many guns and planes know that this people is not so weak, and that its strength will yet stand it in good stead.'

On Bevin's orders, the *Empire Rival* was sent first to Port de Bouc, in southern France, where the refugees refused to land, and then to Hamburg. Forced by British troops to disembark on the hated German soil from which they had already fled, these 'illegals' were sent to a Displaced Persons Camp at Pöppendorf. According to the Yugoslav member of UNSCOP, the *Exodus 1947* saga 'is the best possible evidence we have'.

On July 4 David Ben Gurion appeared before UNSCOP. His evidence opened with a survey of Jewish history since biblical times: 'With an indomitable obstinacy,' he said, 'we always preserved our identity. Our entire history is a history of continuous resistance to superior physical forces which tried to wipe out our Jewish image and to uproot our connections with our country and with the teaching of our prophets.' At the same time, he added, 'An unbroken tie between our people and our land has persisted through all these centuries in full force,' strengthened in each generation through 'Jewish homelessness and insecurity' in the Diaspora. Ben Gurion continued:

The homelessness and minority position make the Jews always dependent on the mercy of others. The 'others' may be good and may be bad, and the Jews may sometimes be treated more or less decently, but they are never masters of their own destiny; they are entirely defenceless when the majority of people turn against them.

What happened to our people in this war is merely a climax to the uninterrupted persecution to which we have been subjected for centuries by almost all the Christian and Moslem peoples in the old world.

There were and there are many Jews who could not stand it, and they deserted us. They could not stand the massacres and expulsions, the humiliation and discrimination, and they gave it up in despair. But the Jewish people as a whole did not give way, did not despair or renounce its hope and faith in a better future, national as well as universal.

Ben Gurion also paid tribute to Britain: 'It will be to the everlasting credit of the British people,' he said, 'that is was the first in modern times to undertake the restoration of Palestine to the Jewish people,' while at the same time, in Britain itself, Jews 'were and are treated as equals. A British Jew can be and has been a member of the Cabinet, a Chief Justice, a Viceroy. . . .'

Speaking of the fate of European Jewry, Ben Gurion noted that in a recent Gallup Poll taken in the American Zone of Germany, 14 per cent of the Germans questioned had condemned Hitler's massacre of the Jews, 26 per cent had been 'neutral', and 60 per cent had approved the killings. And he went on to tell the Committee:

The Jews do not want to stay where they are. They want to regain their human dignity, their homeland, they want a reunion with their kin in Palestine after having lost their dearest relations. To them, the countries of their birth are a graveyard of their people. They do not wish to return there and they cannot. They want to go back to their national home, and they use Dunkirk boats.

Were a Jewish State to be established, Ben Gurion said, it would mean the settlement 'of the first million Jews' in the 'shortest possible' time.

On July 8 Dr Weizmann gave evidence before UNSCOP. The Jews, he said, had 'an abnormal position' in the world: one that had beset them throughout their history. It was characterized by one thing above all, 'the homelessness of the Jewish people'. There were, of course, many individual Jews who had 'very comfortable homes', particularly in America, western Europe, Scandinavia and 'formerly in Germany', but, as an ethnic group, as a 'collectivity', they were homeless. Weizmann continued:

They are a people, and they lack the props of a people. They are a disembodied ghost. There they are with a great many typical characteristics, many strong characteristics which have not disappeared throughout centuries, thousands of years of martyrdom and wandering, and at the same time they lack the props which characterise every nation.

We ask to-day: 'What are the Poles? What are the French? What are the Swiss?' When that is asked, everyone points to a country, to certain institutions, to parliamentary institutions, and the man in the street will know exactly what it is. He has a passport.

If you ask what a Jew is – well, he is a man who has to offer a long explanation for his existence. And any person who has to offer an explanation as to what he is, is always suspect – and from suspicion there is only one step to hatred or contempt.

It was now his duty, Weizmann went on, although in the past he had never thought it would be necessary, 'to try to explain: "Why Palestine?",' and he went on to ask:

Why not Kamchatka, Alaska, Mexico, or Texas? There are a great many empty countries. Why should the Jews choose a country which has a population that does not want to receive them in a particularly friendly way; a small country; a country which has been neglected and derelict for centuries. It seems unusual on the part of a practical and shrewd people like the Jews to sink their effort, their sweat and blood, their substance, into the sands, rocks and marshes of Palestine.

Well, I could, if I wished to be facetious, say it was not our responsibility – not the responsibility of the Jews who sit here – it was the responsibility of Moses, who acted from divine inspiration. He might have brought us to the United States, and instead of the Jordan we might have had the Mississippi. It would have been an easier task. But he chose to stop here. We are an ancient people with an old history, and you cannot deny your history and begin afresh.

For the establishment of the Jewish National Home, Weizmann told the Committee, the Jews owed the British 'a sincere tribute', but the time had come for the 'Home' to evolve. Partition would, he believed, be the best evolution in the current circumstances. 'If it is final,' he said, 'the Arabs will know, and the Jews will know, that they cannot encroach upon each other's domain.' Partition would represent 'a new and great sacrifice on the part of the Jewish people', but its advantage would be that it could not be 'whittled down' further, or 'bargained down'. Yet the area of Palestine which the Jews would have after partition: '. . . must be something in which Jews could live and into which we could bring a million and a half people in a comparatively short time. It must not be a place for graves only, or graveyards, or, as you sometimes see on very full trains, "standing room only".' Whatever was done, Weizmann asked the Committee, 'do it quickly. Do not let it drag on. Do not prolong our agony. It has lasted long enough and has caused a great deal of blood and sorrow on many sides.'

The UNSCOP deliberations continued to a background of violence. Three months earlier, on May 4, the Irgun and Stern gangs had attacked Acre gaol, releasing forty-one prisoners. Three of those involved in the attack had been captured, and on July 29 the British hanged them at Acre gaol. Two days later, on July 31, as a reprisal against these executions, the Irgun murdered two British sergeants, and booby-trapped the ground underneath their bodies. In Britain, individual Jews felt the full force of anti-semitic hostility, while the British public demanded that the troops be brought home. In Palestine several Jews were murdered by British soldiers as a counter-reprisal. Bitterness poisoned all hope of a return to any form of normal relations while British rule continued.

UNSCOP held its last meeting on August 31. Its majority report, signed by the representatives of Canada, Czechoslovakia, Guatemala, the Netherlands, Peru, Sweden and Uruguay, proposed the creation of two separate and independent States, one Arab and one Jewish, with the city of Jerusalem under international trusteeship. Under these proposals, the Jewish State would contain 498,000 Jews and 407,000 Arabs; the Arab State would contain 725,000 Arabs and 10,000 Jews; and the city of Jerusalem and its environs, including the Arab towns of Bethlehem and Beit Jalla, would contain 105,000 Arabs and 100,000 Jews. The Negev was to be part of the Jewish State, western Galilee a part of the Arab State.

The Arab Higher Committee rejected even the proposal for a 'mini' Jewish

The United Nations Partition Plan of November 1947

State, just as the Arabs had rejected the Peel Commission's similar proposal ten years before. Subject to further discussions on the actual boundary lines, the Jewish Agency accepted the UNSCOP proposals, even though they would keep a quarter of the Jews of Palestine outside the area of Jewish statehood. Acceptance would involve a sacrifice, Abba Hillel Silver declared on October 2, but this sacrifice 'will be the Jewish contribution to a painful problem and will bear witness to my people's international spirit and desire for peace'.

On 29 November 1947 the General Assembly of the United Nations voted on the UNSCOP proposals, which were accepted by thirty-three votes to thirteen, with ten abstentions. Britain was among those States which abstained. All six independent Arab States voted against the plan, as did Afghanistan, Cuba, Greece, India, Iran, Pakistan and Turkey. Among those in favour of partition were the United States, the Soviet Union, Australia, Canada, France, the Netherlands, New Zealand, Poland and Sweden.

For the Jews of the Diaspora, the news that there was to be a Jewish State in Palestine represented, as the American Zionist Emergency Council declared, 'a milestone in the history of the world', which had 'ended 2,000 years of homelessness for the Jewish people'. For the Jews of Palestine, the news that they were to have a State, albeit a 'mini' one, led to rejoicing in the streets. Among those who rejoiced was a young Palestinian born soldier, Moshe Dayan, who later recalled in his memoirs:

I felt in my bones the victory of Judaism, which for two thousand years of exile from the Land of Israel had withstood persecutions, the Spanish Inquisition, pogroms, anti-Jewish decrees, restrictions, and the mass slaughter by the Nazis in our own generation, and had reached the fulfillment of its age-old yearning – the return to a free and independent Zion.

We were happy that night, and we danced, and our hearts went out to every nation whose U.N. representative had voted in favor of the resolution. We had heard them utter the magic word 'yes' as we followed their voices over the airwaves from thousands of miles away. We danced – but we knew that ahead of us lay the battlefield.

Among those who were to die on that battlefield in the months ahead was Dayan's own younger brother Zorik, for the Arabs, both inside Palestine and beyond it, turned violently against the United Nations decision. Even the 'mini' Arab State which they were offered was of no interest to their leaders and propagandists: their hatred was towards Jewish statehood, and, from the moment of the United Nations vote, Arab terrorists and armed bands attacked Jewish men, women and children all over the country, killing eighty Jews in the twelve days following the vote, looting Jewish shops, and attacking Jewish civilian buses on all the highways.

For the Arabs outside Palestine, a similar wave of anti-Jewish hatred led to violence against Jews in almost every Arab city: in British-ruled Aden, scene of a savage attack on Jewish life and property, eighty-two Jews were killed on December 9. In Beirut, Cairo, Alexandria and Aleppo Jewish houses were looted, and synagogues attacked. In Tripolitania more than 130 Jews were murdered by Arab mobs.

There followed, in Palestine, five and a half months of terrorism and violence. 'Jews will take all measures to protect themselves,' the Jewish National Council declared on December 3, and the Jewish instinct for moderation was a strong one. On December 13 the Jewish Agency, representing a majority of Palestinian Jewry, denounced the mounting tide of Irgun reprisals, calling them 'spectacular acts to gratify popular feeling'. Nevertheless, as the Arab attacks rose in viciousness during the first four months of 1948, as Jewish Jerusalem was besieged and its water supply cut off, the battles and the reprisals gained a cruel momentum: the death of 250 Arabs in the village of Deir Yassin on April 9, and of seventy-seven Jewish doctors and nurses four days later, while on their way to the Hadassah hospital on Mount Scopus, were but the most widely publicized episodes in a series of attacks and counter-attacks, random killings and military operations, which claimed several thousand lives on both sides.

The British announced that they would withdraw from Palestine altogether on May 15. During the six weeks before they did so, the Arabs did everything in their power to break communication between the Jewish settlements, to prevent Jews from reaching Jerusalem, and to disrupt all Jewish life within the city itself. Many of the Arabs involved in these military acts, and in the sniping and killing of Jewish civilians, were regular soldiers from outside Palestine, from Syria, and even from Iraq. It was these Iraqi troops who had cut off Jerusalem's water supply.

During April and early May, every isolated Jewish village was subjected to a massive attack: on April 13 four hundred Arab troops attacked Kfar Etzion, just south of Bethlehem. Beaten off, they attacked again on May 12, when a hundred Jews were killed, and only four survived. Fifteen Jews captured at Kfar Etzion were machine-gunned to death after they had surrendered, while being photographed by their captors.

Despite the Arab attacks, the Jews were determined not to be driven out of their promised 'mini' State. In the full scale battles that developed during April between the Arab and Jewish armed forces, Tiberias, Haifa, Acre, Safed and Jaffa were occupied by Jewish forces between April 19 and May 14, while in Jerusalem, Arab troops were driven from several suburbs. Between November 1947 and May 1948, more than 4,000 Jewish soldiers and 2,000 Jewish civilians had been killed, nearly 1 per cent of the total Jewish population.

As May 15, the day of the British withdrawal, drew near, the Jewish situation, despite the capture of the main towns, was still precarious; especially as four well armed Arab armies, those of Egypt, Transjordan, Syria and the Lebanon were massing on the southern, western and northern borders, preparing to invade at the very moment of the British withdrawal. At the last moment, the British advanced the withdrawal date, by twenty-four hours, to May 14. On May 12, the Chief of Operations of the Haganah, Yigael Yadin – who was married to Arthur Ruppin's daughter Carmella – told Ben Gurion and the other Jewish political leaders: 'The regular forces of the neighbouring countries, with their equipment and their armaments, enjoy superiority at this time.' However, Yadin added, the future of the Jews in Palestine 'cannot be merely a military consideration of arms against arms and units against units, since we do not have those arms and that armoured force. The problem is to what extent our men will be able to overcome enemy forces by virtue of their fighting spirit, of our planning and our tactics.'

For the first time since the defeat of Bar Kokhba by the Roman forces more than 1800 years before, the Jews were preparing to defend their sovereign rights. On the morning of May 14 the last British High Commissioner left Jerusalem. Britain's thirty year rule was at an end. That same afternoon, in Tel Aviv, Ben Gurion declared the independence of the Jewish State, to be called 'the State of Israel'.

One of those who was present during the independence ceremony was Golda Meyerson, who later recalled how, when Ben Gurion spoke the words 'the State of Israel':

My eyes filled with tears and my hands shook. We had done it. We had brought the Jewish state into existence – and I, Golda Mabovitch Meyerson, had lived to see the day. Whatever price any of us would have to pay for it, we had recreated the Jewish national home.

The long exile was over. From this day on, we would no longer live on sufferance in the land of our forefathers. Now we were a nation like other nations, masters – for the first time in twenty centuries – of our own destiny. The dream had come true – too late to save those who had perished in the Holocaust, but not too late for the generations to come.

The coming into existence of the State of Israel was opposed by every Arab State, and in the war that followed, the Jews – Israelis now – suffered considerable losses. But their State survived, forming a small but viable entity on the eastern shore of the Mediterranean. More than 550,000 Palestinian Arabs had fled from the area which became Israel; more than two-thirds of them fled to other areas of Palestine – the West Bank and the Gaza Strip – which had been allocated under the United Nations Partition Plan to Arab sovereignty, areas which were at once occupied by Transjordan and Egypt respectively.

For Jews, not only in Israel, but throughout the Diaspora, the establishment of their State was the culmination of centuries of longing, of decades of struggle, and of five years of horror. Since the end of the war in 1945 non-Zionists as well as Zionists, had been forced to ask themselves: if we had had a State in 1939, how many Jews might we have saved from the Holocaust?

Since the establishment of the State of Israel in 1948, whenever antisemitism threatened Jews in the Diaspora, they had somewhere to which they could turn. Henceforth, to uproot themselves ceased to be either so difficult or so uncertain. Between 1948 and 1952, more than half a million Jews from Arab lands as far apart as Morocco and the Yemen, flocked to Israel, and rebuilt their lives without the stigma of second-class citizenship. It was not always easy; but the challenge of being one's own master was one which drew forth great reserves of energy and courage. Similar problems were faced and similar courage was shown by more than 120,000 Jews who, in the decade after 1967, reached Israel from the Soviet Union.

Jews such as those from Arab lands or from the Soviet Union did not necessarily turn to Palestine because they were Zionists whose basic creed was a Jewish homeland in the land of the Patriarchs, but because they were Jews whom some corner of the world had rejected, persecuted, humiliated yet again, and whom Israel had welcomed.

On 19 May 1948, five days after the establishment of the State of Israel, its first Prime Minister, David Ben Gurion, spoke of how Jewish statehood had been achieved, and of how it should be maintained. 'We know', he declared, 'that not by the grace of nations was our freedom won, not upon their bounty will its continuance depend.' The Jewish community in Palestine had been built 'with our own flesh and blood: so too we build, so too we shall guard the State'; and he continued:

Never have we lost faith in the conscience of mankind. Always we shall demand of the world what is justly ours. But morning and evening, day in and day out, we must remind ourselves that our existence, our freedom and our future are in our own hands. Our own exertions, our own capacity, our own will, they are the key.

Careers after 1948

of some of the diplomats and politicians quoted in the text

EHUD AVRIEL: subsequently Israeli Consul-General in Chicago, 1974–76, and Ambassador-at-Large, 1977–

PHILIP NOEL BAKER: subsequently Minister of Fuel and Power, 1950–51; Nobel Peace Prize, 1959; Chairman, Labour Party Foreign Affairs Group, 1964–70.

RICHARD BEAUMONT: subsequently British Ambassador to Morocco, 1961–65; to Iraq, 1965–67; to Egypt, 1969–72. Director-General of the Middle East Association, 1973–

MENACHEM BEGIN: subsequently Prime Minister of Israel, 1977–

DAVID BEN GURION: subsequently Prime Minister of Israel, 1948–53 and 1955–63.

TERENCE BRENAN: subsequently Director of Middle East Centre for Arab Studies, Beirut, 1948–53.

R. A. BUTLER: subsequently Home Secretary, 1957–62; Deputy Prime Minister, 1962–63, and Foreign Secretary, 1963–64.

RONALD CAMPBELL: subsequently British Ambassador to Egypt, 1946–50.

SIR NOEL CHARLES: subsequently British Ambassador to Turkey, 1949–51.

LORD CRANBORNE: subsequently (as Lord Salisbury) Leader of the House of Lords, 1951–57; Secretary of State for Commonwealth Relations, 1952, and Lord President of the Council, 1952–57.

RICHARD CROSSMAN: subsequently Chairman of the Labour Party, 1960–61; Minister of Housing and Local Government, 1964–66, and Lord President of the Council, 1966–68.

MOSHE DAYAN: subsequently Defence Minister of Israel, 1967–74, and Foreign Minister, 1977–

PATRICK DEAN: subsequently Permanent U.K. Representative at the United Nations, 1960–64, and Ambassador to Washington, 1965–69.

AUBREY EBAN: subsequently (as Abba Eban) Deputy Prime Minister of Israel, 1963–66, and Foreign Minister, 1966–74.

ANTHONY EDEN: subsequently Prime Minister of Britain, 1955–57.

ELIAHU EPSTEIN: subsequently (as Eliahu Elath) Israeli Ambassador to Washington, 1949–50; to London, 1950–59.

PAUL FALLA: subsequently Deputy Director of Research at the Foreign Office, 1958–67.

FREDERICK GARNER: subsequently Head of the Consular Department, Foreign Office, 1956–58; Ambassador to Costa Rica, 1961–67.

THOMAS HODGKIN: subsequently Research Associate, Institute of Islamic Studies, McGill University, Montreal, 1958–61, and Director of the Institute of African Studies, University of Ghana, 1962–65.

DAVID KELLY: subsequently Ambassador to the USSR, 1949–51, and Chairman of the British Council, 1955.

TEDDY KOLLEK: subsequently Mayor of Jerusalem, 1966–

MALCOLM MACDONALD: subsequently U.K. Commissioner General in South East Asia, 1948–55; High Commissioner in India, 1955–60; in Kenya, 1964–65, and H.M. Special Representative in Africa, 1966–69.

HENRY MACK: subsequently Ambassador to Iraq, 1948–51, and to Argentina, 1951–54.

ROGER MAKINS: subsequently Ambassador to the United States, 1953–56, and Chairman of the U.K. Atomic Energy Authority, 1960–64.

JOHN MARTIN: subsequently Deputy Under-Secretary of State, Colonial Office, 1956–65.

GOLDA MEIR: subsequently Foreign Minister of Israel, 1956–65, and Prime Minister, 1969–74.

ERIC MILLS: subsequently on Special Colonial Office duties in the Sudan, 1950–51, and British Guiana, 1952–56.

HERBERT MORRISON: subsequently Foreign Secretary, 1951.

CLIFFORD NORTON: subsequently U.K. Delegate to the United Nations Assembly, 1952–53.

CON O'NEILL: subsequently Ambassador to Finland, 1961–63; to the European Communities in Brussels, 1963–65; Deputy Under-Secretary of State, Foreign and Commonwealth Office, 1969–72.

A. W. G. RANDALL: subsequently a British Delegate to the International Conference on the Law of the Sea, 1958.

PATRICK REILLY: subsequently Ambassador to the USSR, 1957–60, and to France, 1965–68.

ISRAEL ROKACH: subsequently Israeli Minister of the Interior, 1953–55, and Deputy Speaker of the Knesset, 1957–59.

VICTOR ROTHSCHILD: subsequently Permanent Under-Secretary, Central Policy Review Staff, Cabinet Office, 1970–74.

DAVID SCOTT FOX: subsequently Minister to Rumania, 1959–61; Ambassador to Chile, 1961–66, and to Finland, 1966–69.

MOSHE SHERTOK: subsequently (as Moshe Sharett) Foreign Minister of Israel, 1948–54, and 1955–60; Prime Minister, 1954–55.

G. M. WARR: subsequently British Ambassador to Nicaragua, 1967–70.

CHAIM WEIZMANN: subsequently the first President of the State of Israel, 1948–52.

YIGAEL YADIN: subsequently Professor of Archaeology at the Hebrew University of Jerusalem, and Deputy Prime Minister of Israel, 1977–

List of Archival Sources

1915

22 January	Samuel memorandum: Foreign Office papers, 800/100
13 March	Asquith to a friend: Montagu papers
16 March	Barrow memorandum: Cabinet papers, 27/1
16 March	Montagu memorandum: Lloyd George papers
19 March	Asquith to a friend: Montagu papers
27 March	Harcourt memorandum: Harcourt papers
17 April	Foreign Office meeting: Cabinet papers, 27/1
14 July	Sherif Hussein to British authorities Cairo: Foreign Office papers, 371/2767
30 August	Wingate to British authorities Cairo: Wingate papers
30 August	McMahon to Sherif Hussein: Foreign Office papers, 371/2767
11 October	Cabinet minutes: Cabinet papers, 2/86
12 October	Clayton to Maxwell: Foreign Office papers, 371/2486
12 October	Maxwell to Kitchener: Foreign Office papers, 371/2486
24 October	McMahon to Sherif Hussein: Foreign Office papers, 371/2767
14 December	McMahon to Sherif Hussein: Foreign Office papers, 371/2767

1917

15 January	Lord Drogheda's note: Foreign Office papers, 371/3043
7 February	Sykes discussion with Zionists: Central Zionist Archive
28 February	Sykes to Picot: Sykes papers
23 March	Weizmann to Scott: Weizmann papers
25 March	Jabotinsky to the Foreign Office: Foreign Office papers, 371/3101
3 April	Lloyd George–Sykes discussion: Cabinet papers, 24/9
4 April	Weizmann to Sokolow: Central Zionist Archive

14 April	Ormsby Gore memorandum: Cabinet papers, 24/10
20 April	Jabotinsky to the Foreign Office: Foreign Office papers, 371/3101
27 April	Weizmann to Sokolow: Weizmann papers
5 May	Kerr to Graham: Foreign Office papers, 371/3101
6 May	Jabotinsky to Graham: Foreign Office papers, 371/3101
11 May	Wingate to Graham: Foreign Office papers, 371/3055
13 June	Weizmann–Graham discussion: Foreign Office papers, 371/3058
20 June	Weizmann to Sacher: Weizmann papers
2 July	Sacher draft: Weizmann papers
10 July	Sokolow to Sacher: Central Zionist Archive
11 July	Sidebotham memorandum: Central Zionist Archive
11 July	Sacher to Sokolow: Central Zionist Archive
18 July	Sacher note: Central Zionist Archive
18 August	Ormsby Gore minute: Cabinet papers, 21/58
23 August	Montagu memorandum: Foreign Office papers, 371/3083
3 September	War Cabinet minutes: Foreign Office papers, 371/3083
18 September	Amery diary: Amery papers
24 September	Graham minute: Foreign Office papers, 371/3083
3 October	Weizmann–Rothschild memorandum: Foreign Office papers, 371/3083
4 October	War Cabinet minutes: Cabinet papers, 23/4
6 October	Balfour to House: Foreign Office papers, 371/3083
8 October	Goodhart to Foreign Office: Foreign Office papers, 371/3083
16 October	Sir W. Wiseman to Balfour: Foreign Office papers, 371/3083
17 October	Zionist replies to the Foreign Office: Foreign Office papers, 371/3083
17 October	Foreign Office memorandum: Foreign Office papers, 371/3083
17 October	McNeill memorandum: Foreign Office papers, 371/3083
24 October	Graham minute: Foreign Office papers, 371/3083
26 October	Curzon memorandum: Cabinet papers, 24/30
30 October	Sykes memorandum: Foreign Office papers, 371/3083
31 October	War Cabinet minutes: Cabinet papers, 23/4
31 October	Amery diary: Amery papers
1 November	Graham minute: Foreign Office papers, 371/3083
3 November	Graham note: Foreign Office papers, 371/3083
3 November	Hardinge note: Foreign Office papers, 371/3054
4 November	Rothschild to Balfour: Foreign Office papers, 371/3083
26 November	Barker to War Office: Foreign Office papers, 371/3054
26 November	Graham note: Foreign Office papers, 371/3054

19 December   Toynbee–Namier memorandum: Foreign Office papers,
               371/3054

1918

14 January   Clayton to War Cabinet: Cabinet papers, 27/23
19 January   War Cabinet Middle East Committee minute: Cabinet
               papers, 27/23
21 February   Amery diary: Amery papers
2 March   Balfour to Allenby: Foreign Office papers, 371/23237
3 March   Sykes to Feisal: Foreign Office papers, 800/221
30 May   Weizmann to Balfour: Balfour papers
18 June   Clayton to Sykes: Foreign Office papers, 800/221
18 July   Feisal to Sykes: Foreign Office papers, 800/221
9 August   Storrs to Sykes: Foreign Office papers, 800/221
29 October   War Cabinet Eastern Committee: Cabinet papers, 27/24
2 December   Toynbee minute: Foreign Office papers, 371/3398
12 December   Palestinian Arab petition: Foreign Office papers, 371/4153
17 December   Weizmann to Zionist Commission: Weizmann papers

1919

2 January   Clark Kerr minute: Foreign Office papers, 371/4153
16 January   Curzon to Balfour: India Office Library, Curzon papers
19 January   Balfour to Curzon: India Office Library, Curzon papers
21 January   Sir Henry Wilson diary: Imperial War Museum archive
3 February   Gregory minute: Foreign Office papers, 371/3937
4 February   Sir Henry Wilson diary: Imperial War Museum archive
1 March   Feisal to Frankfurter: Foreign Office papers, 371/13749
22 March   Ormsby Gore to the Foreign Office: Foreign Office papers,
               371/4167
25 March   Curzon to Balfour: India Office Library, Curzon papers
19 June   Clayton to Foreign Office: Foreign Office papers, 371/4171
5 July   Balfour to Clayton: Foreign Office papers, 371/4171
9 August   Curzon to Balfour: India Office Library, Curzon papers
20 August   Fisher diary: Fisher papers
19 September   Weizmann to Churchill: War Office papers, 32/5732
22 September   Weizmann to Churchill: Weizmann papers
27 September   Lawrence to Curzon: Lawrence papers
27 September   Young to Curzon: Foreign Office papers, 371/4183
28 September   Curzon minute: Foreign Office papers, 371/4183
12 October   Wardrop to Curzon:Foreign Office papers, 371/3663

25 October	Churchill memorandum: Churchill papers, 16/18
27 November	Gwynne to Churchill: Churchill papers, 16/13
18 December	Wright to Foreign Office: Rumbold papers
31 December	Forbes Adam memorandum: Foreign Office papers, 371/4215

1920

19 April	Congreve to Allenby: India Office Library, Curzon papers
	Allenby to Curzon: India Office Library, Curzon papers
24 April	Sir Henry Wilson diary: Imperial War Museum archive
16 July	Curzon to Allenby: India Office Library, Curzon papers
2 August	Fisher diary: Fisher papers
20 August	Curzon to Balfour: India Office Library, Curzon papers

1921

17 January	Lawrence to Churchill: Churchill papers, 17/14
14 March	Palestinian Arab petition: Churchill papers, 17/20
11 May	Captain Seymour to Admiralty: Colonial Office papers, 733/9
14 May	Young to Samuel: Colonial Office papers, 733/3
15 August	Churchill to Palestinian Arab delegation: Central Zionist archive
22 June	Imperial Cabinet minutes: Lloyd George papers
22 July	Meeting at Balfour's house: Weizmann papers
1 August	Young to Churchill: Colonial Office papers, 733/14
5 August	Young to Churchill: Colonial Office papers, 733/10
10 August	Weizmann to Tulin: Weizmann papers
12 August	Palestinian Arab memorandum: Central Zionist archive
15 August	Palestinian Arab deputation: Central Zionist archive
17 August	Fisher diary: Fisher papers
	Cabinet minutes: Cabinet papers, 23/26
22 August	Palestinian Arab deputation: Central Zionist archive
23 August	Young to Sacher: Weizmann papers
31 August	Weizmann to Deedes: Weizmann papers
29 October	Congreve order: Churchill papers, 17/11
2 November	Samuel to Colonial Office: Colonial Office papers, 733/7
3 November	Clauson minute: Colonial Office papers, 733/7
	Meinertzhagen minute: Colonial Office papers, 733/7
1 December	Shuckburgh minute: Colonial Office papers, 733/7
13 December	Weizmann to Deedes: Weizmann papers
29 December	Foreign Office to Washington: Command paper 2559 of 1926

1922

17 January	Shuckburgh minute: Colonial Office papers, 733/29
3 March	Shuckburgh report: Colonial Office papers, 733/37
24 May	Samuel draft memorandum: Colonial Office papers, 733/34
12 June	Mills minute: Colonial Office papers, 733/22
22 June	Young to Churchill: Colonial Office papers, 733/22
5 July	Churchill to Deedes: Colonial Office papers, 733/35

1927

10 January	Wedgwood to Irwin: India Office papers, Irwin collection

1928

21 January	Weizmann note: Churchill papers, 22/194
5 March	Balfour memorandum: Churchill papers, 2/193

1929

5 September	Telegram to the War Office: Cabinet papers, 24/205
29 September	Chancellor to the Colonial Office: Cabinet papers, 24/206
	Musa Kazim Pasha warning: Cabinet papers, 24/206
12 October	Chancellor to the Colonial Office: Cabinet papers, 24/207
26 October	Palestine police report: Cabinet papers, 24/207
18 December	Sacher to Shaw Commission: Sacher papers

1930

1 May	Cabinet Palestine Committee minutes: Cabinet papers, 27/423
17 November	Weizmann to Passfield and Henderson: Cabinet papers, 27/433
18 November	Weizmann to Passfield and Henderson: Cabinet papers, 27/433

1932

9 April	Wauchope to Colonial Office: Cabinet papers, 27/486
12 April	Cabinet Palestine Committee: Cabinet papers, 27/486

1933

21 March	Rumbold to Simon: Rumbold papers
22 March	Lady Rumbold to her mother: Rumbold papers

28 March	Rumbold to Simon: Rumbold papers
30 March	Rumbold to Simon: Rumbold papers
2 April	Lady Rumbold to her mother: Rumbold papers
5 April	Lady Rumbold to her mother: Rumbold papers
	Rumbold to Simon: Rumbold papers
7 April	Cabinet Committee on Refugees: Cabinet papers, 96/33
18 August	Hoare to Willingdon: India Office Library, Hoare papers
28 August	Willingdon to Hoare: India Office Library, Hoare papers
23 November	Hoare note: Home Office papers, 45/15882

1934

28 March	Cunliffe-Lister memorandum: Cabinet papers, 24/248

1935

12 November	Mills to Chief Secretary: Foreign Office papers, 371/19919

1936

4 September	Wauchope to Ormsby Gore: Cabinet papers, 24/264
26 November	Vera Weizmann diary: Weizmann papers
15 December	Wauchope to Ormsby Gore: Cabinet papers, 24/267

1937

4 January	Clark Kerr to the Foreign Office: Foreign Office papers, 371/20804
6 January	Lady Rumbold to her mother: Rumbold papers
	Rendel minute: Foreign Office papers, 371/20804
9 January	Rendel minute: Foreign Office papers, 371/20804
19 January	Weizmann to the Peel Commission: Colonial Office papers, 733/342
13 February	Baggallay minute: Foreign Office papers, 371/20804
18 February	Vansittart note: Foreign Office papers, 371/20804
12 March	Churchill evidence to the Peel Commission: Churchill papers, 2/317
22 April	Baggallay minute: Foreign Office papers, 371/20806
30 April	Hull to Eden: Foreign Office papers, 371/20806
31 May	Rendel note: Foreign Office papers, 371/20806
5 June	Ormsby Gore to Eden: Foreign Office papers, 371/20807
8 June	Rendel–Selzam discussion: Foreign Office papers, 371/20807

15 June	Weizmann to Ormsby Gore: Churchill papers, 2/315
25 June	Ormsby Gore memorandum: Cabinet papers, 24/166
29 June	General Dill telegram: Cabinet papers, 24/166
16 July	Jabotinsky to Churchill: Churchill papers, 2/316
26 July	Lampson to Foreign Office: Foreign Office papers, 371/20810
	Rendel note: Foreign Office papers, 371/20810
29 September	Cabinet minutes: Cabinet papers, 23/89
6 October	Cabinet minutes: Cabinet papers, 23/89
8 October	Cabinet minutes: Cabinet papers, 23/89
10 October	Muslim protest to Viceroy: Foreign Office papers, 371/20820
12 October	Battershill to Shuckburgh: Foreign Office papers, 371/20819
15 October	Ormsby Gore to Eden: Foreign Office papers, 371/20819
	Campbell minute: Foreign Office papers, 371/20816
	Rendel minute: Foreign Office papers, 371/20816
20 October	Rendel note: Foreign Office papers, 371/20818
25 October	Mackereth to Eden: Foreign Office papers, 371/20818
27 October	Kelly to Foreign Office: Foreign Office papers, 371/20819
	Rendel memorandum: Foreign Office papers, 371/20818
28 October	Rendel note: Foreign Office papers, 371/20819
	Brenan note: Foreign Office papers, 371/20818
29 October	Rendel report: Foreign Office papers, 371/20818
30 October	Mackereth to Eden: Foreign Office papers, 371/20819
2 November	Bullard minute: Foreign Office papers, 371/20818
3 November	Rendel minute: Foreign Office papers, 371/20818
5 November	Rendel note: Foreign Office papers, 371/20818
9 November	Ormsby Gore memorandum: Cabinet papers, 24/272
11 November	Rendel memorandum: Foreign Office papers, 371/20820
12 November	Makins memorandum: Foreign Office papers, 371/20820
13 November	Vansittart minute: Foreign Office papers, 371/20820
15 November	Mackereth to Rendel: Foreign Office papers, 371/20821
	Rendel minute: Foreign Office papers, 371/20820
	Eden minute: Foreign Office papers, 371/20820
19 November	Foreign Office memorandum: Cabinet papers, 24/273
26 November	Eden to Lindsay: Foreign Office papers, 371/20821
31 December	Weizmann to Shuckburgh: Churchill papers, 2/315

1938

9 January	Ormsby Gore to Chamberlain: Foreign Office papers, 371/21862
11 January	Amery to Churchill: Churchill papers, 2/348
9 March	Ormsby Gore note: Foreign Office papers, 800/321

10 March	Colonial Office to MacMichael: Foreign Office papers, 371/21887
30 May	Amery to MacDonald: Amery papers
31 May	Garner to Henderson: Foreign Office papers, 371/21635
18 June	Governor of Kenya to Colonial Office: Foreign Office papers, 371/22534
29 June	Orde to Foreign Office: Foreign Office papers, 371/21888
4 July	Weizmann–MacDonald discussion: Cabinet papers, 24/278
20 July	Cabinet Committee on Refugees: Cabinet papers, 23/94
21 July	Waterlow to Foreign Office: Foreign Office papers, 371/21888
24 July	MacMichael to Colonial Office: Colonial Office papers, 733/358
25 July	Downie to Foreign Office: Foreign Office papers, 371/21888
6 August	MacDonald–Wauchope–Haining discussions: Cabinet papers, 24/278
9 August	Consul-General Munich to Foreign Office: Foreign Office papers, 371/21706
12 August	MacDonald–Tannous discussion: Cabinet papers, 24/278
21 August	MacDonald Cabinet memorandum: Cabinet papers, 24/278
11 October	Amery diary: Amery papers
19 October	Cabinet minutes: Cabinet papers, 23/96
	Egyptian Prime Minister to Chamberlain: Cabinet papers, 27/651
24 October	Cabinet Committee minutes: Cabinet papers, 27/651
1 November	Criminal Investigation Department report: Colonial Office papers, 733/359
9 November	MacDonald-Tannous discussion: Cabinet papers, 24/652
11 November	MacDonald to High Commissioner: Cabinet papers, 24/652
	Ogilvie Forbes to Foreign Office: Foreign Office papers, 371/21637
12 November	Smallbones to Foreign Office: Foreign Office papers, 371/21637
13 November	Ogilvie Forbes to Foreign Office: Foreign Office papers, 371/21637
14 November	Cabinet minutes: Cabinet papers, 27/651
	MacDonald–Weizmann discussion: Cabinet papers, 24/652
15 November	Makins note: Foreign Office papers, 371/22536
	Chamberlain to Council for German Jewry: Foreign Office papers, 371/22536
	Cresswell note: Foreign Office papers, 371/21637
16 November	Smallbones to Foreign Office: Foreign Office papers, 371/21638

20 November   Kennard to Halifax: Foreign Office papers, 371/21638
                Weizmann to Sinclair: Thurso papers
28 November   MacDonald–Rutenberg discussion: Cabinet papers, 24/652

1939

14 January   Carvell to Foreign Office: Foreign Office papers, 371/23052
16 January   Smuts to Amery: Amery papers
18 January   MacDonald memorandum: Foreign Office papers, 371/23221
21 January   Consul-General Moscow to Lord Halifax: Foreign Office
                papers, 371/24097
24 January   Foreign Office to Sofia Legation: Foreign Office papers,
                371/23246
                Baxter to MacDonald: Foreign Office papers, 371/23221
                Halifax–Weizmann discussion: Foreign Office papers,
                371/23221
26 January   Halifax minute: Foreign Office papers, 371/23221
27 January   Cabinet minutes: Cabinet papers, 27/651
30 January   Simon to MacDonald: Foreign Office papers, 371/24087
2 February   Shepherd to British Embassy Berlin: Foreign Office papers,
                371/23052
8 February   Jewish Settlers to Foreign Office: Foreign Office papers,
                371/23245
                Cadogan to Halifax: Foreign Office papers, 371/23222
                Baggallay minute: Foreign Office papers, 371/23222
14 February   Palestine Round Table Conference minutes: Foreign Office
                papers, 371/23224
18 February   Palestine Round Table Conference minutes: Foreign Office
                papers, 371/23224
24 February   Hoare to MacDonald: Foreign Office papers, 371/24088
28 February   Hardinge to Halifax: Foreign Office papers, 371/24085
2 March   Foreign Office to Henderson: Treasury papers, 188/226
3 March   India Office note: Foreign Office papers, 371/24088
6 March   Cabinet Committee minutes: Cabinet papers, 27/651
8 March   Randall minute: Foreign Office papers, 371/24081
                Cabinet minutes: Cabinet papers, 23/97
13 March   Governor of Southern Rhodesia despatch: Foreign Office
                papers, 371/24091
22 March   Cabinet minutes: Cabinet papers, 23/98
24 March   Weizmann to Chamberlain: Premier papers, 1/352
3 April   Kendall to Foreign Office: Foreign Office papers, 371/24089
11 April   Rathbone to Churchill: Churchill papers, 2/374

20 April   Cabinet Committee minutes: Cabinet papers, 24/285
23 April   MacMichael to MacDonald: Foreign Office papers, 371/24089
25 April   Waterlow to Foreign Office: Foreign Office papers, 371/24089
26 April   Reilly minute: Foreign Office papers, 371/24083
28 April   Levy report: Foreign Office papers, 371/24089
 1 May   Cabinet minutes: Cabinet papers, 23/99
 8 May   Waterlow to Foreign Office: Foreign Office papers, 371/24089
 9 May   Foreign Office to Hoare: Foreign Office papers, 371/24089
                Cabinet Committee on Refugees, minutes: Foreign Office
                  papers, 371/24090
                Reilly note: Foreign Office papers, 371/24089
                Randall note: Foreign Office papers, 371/24089
10 May   Waterlow to Foreign Office: Foreign Office papers, 371/24090
19 May   Warr minute: Foreign Office papers, 371/24099
26 May   Inter-Departmental Conference minutes: Foreign Office
                  papers, 371/24090
27 May   Winterton to Foreign Office: Foreign Office papers,
                  371/24090
                Campbell to Yugoslav Government: Foreign Office papers,
                  371/24091
30 May   Campbell *aide memoire*: Foreign Office papers, 371/24091
 1 June   Randall memorandum: Foreign Office papers, 371/24090
 3 June   Minutes relating to Socotra: Foreign Office papers,
                  371/24091
 9 June   Reilly minute: Foreign Office papers, 371/24083
14 June   Randall minute: Foreign Office papers, 371/24091
15 June   Randall note: Foreign Office papers, 371/24086
                Maybin to Foreign Office: Foreign Office papers, 371/24091
23 June   Sargent note: Foreign Office papers, 371/24091
 6 July   Norton to Foreign Office: Foreign Office papers, 371/24084
 7 July   Cabinet Committee: Treasury papers, 188/226
22 July   Colonial Office note: Foreign Office papers, 371/24091
24 July   Reilly minute: Foreign Office papers, 371/24100
31 July   Foreign Office note: Foreign Office papers, 371/24084
 2 August   All-Party deputation: Foreign Office papers, 371/24100
 4 August   Cabinet Committee minutes: Cabinet papers, 27/651
17 August   Report on Slovak Jewry: Foreign Office papers, 371/24085
18 August   Reilly minute: Foreign Office papers, 371/24085
 1 September   Halifax to Knatchbull-Hugesson: Foreign Office papers,
                  371/24094
 8 September   American Ambassador in Berlin to Foreign Office: Foreign
                  Office papers, 371/24100

18 September	Foreign Office note: Foreign Office papers, 371/24100
	Weizmann to MacDonald: Foreign Office papers, 371/23251
	Colonial Office discussion: Foreign Office papers, 371/23251
20 September	Shuckburgh minute: Foreign office papers, 371/24094
25 September	War Cabinet Committee on Refugees, minutes: Foreign Office papers, 371/24078
	Italian refugee transit offer: Foreign Office papers, 371/24095
26 September	Warr minute: Foreign Office papers, 371/24101
30 September	Colonial Office statistics: Foreign Office papers, 371/24097
10 October	Downie minute: Colonial Office papers, 733/395
14 October	MacDonald minute: Colonial Office papers, 733/395
24 October	Bennett minute: Colonial Office papers, 733/395
29 December	Warr minute: Foreign Office papers, 371/24097

1940

12 February	War Cabinet minutes: Cabinet papers, 65/5
13 November	Churchill instruction: Premier papers, 4/51/1
30 November	Wavell telegram: Premier papers, 4/51/2
2 December	Churchill to Wavell: Premier papers, 4/51/2
14 December	Military Intelligence Report: Colonial Office papers, 732/86
24 December	Churchill minute: Colonial Office papers, 733/430
	Shuckburgh minute: Colonial Office papers, 733/419

1941

11 January	Luke minute: Colonial Office papers, 733/445
14 February	Moyne to Weizmann: Weizmann papers
24 April	Jewish Agency to Mills: Colonial Office papers, 733/438
30 July	Moyne to MacMichael: Colonial Office papers, 733/438
5 August	MacMichael to Moyne: Colonial Office papers, 733/438

1942

16 February	War Cabinet minutes: Cabinet papers, 65/25
5 March	War Cabinet minutes: Cabinet papers, 65/25
18 May	War Cabinet minutes: Cabinet papers, 65/26
14 December	War Cabinet minutes: Cabinet papers, 65/28

1944

17 July	Foreign Office minute: Foreign Office papers, 371/2976

4 November	Churchill–Weizmann discussion: Weizmann papers
24 December	Gort to Foreign Office: Foreign Office papers, 371/51110

1945

7 February	Falla minute: Foreign Office papers, 371/51011
22 May	Weizmann to Churchill: Weizmann papers
8 June	Churchill to Weizmann: Weizmann papers
13 June	Weizmann to Churchill: Weizmann papers
25 August	Shaw to Creech Jones: Cabinet papers, 129/2
10 October	Cabinet Palestine Committee report: Cabinet papers, 129/3
24 October	Scott Fox minute: Foreign Office papers, 371/50992
30 October	Chuter Ede memorandum: Cabinet papers, 129/4
6 November	Cabinet minutes: Cabinet papers, 128/2
8 December	Commander-in-Chief Berlin to Foreign Office: Foreign Office papers, 371/57686

1946

3 January	Rendel note: Foreign Office papers, 371/57684
5 January	British Embassy Warsaw to Foreign Office: Foreign Office papers, 371/57684
8 January	O'Neill minute: Foreign Office papers, 371/57583
9 January	Rendel to Bevin: Foreign Office papers, 371/57689
	British Embassy Warsaw to Foreign Office: Foreign Office papers, 371/57684
10 January	British Ambassador Rome to Foreign Office: Foreign Office papers, 371/57686
12 January	Mackillop minute: Foreign Office papers, 371/57685
16 January	British representatives Nuremberg to Foreign Office: Foreign Office papers, 371/57529
18 January	Treasury memorandum: Foreign Office papers, 371/57685
25 January	Cabinet Overseas Reconstruction Committee minutes: Foreign Office papers, 371/55784
2 February	Rendel to British Embassy Warsaw: Foreign Office papers, 371/57686
20 February	Cavendish Bentinck to Foreign Office: Foreign Office papers, 371/57688
23 February	War Office minute: War Office papers, 32/12208
11 March	Foreign Office report: Foreign Office papers, 371/55771
14 March	Cavendish Bentinck to Foreign Office: Foreign Office papers, 371/57689

20 March	Mack to Foreign Office: Foreign Office papers, 371/57689
28 March	Foreign Office minute: Foreign Office papers, 371/57689
6 April	Consul-General Madagascar to Foreign Office: Foreign Office papers, 371/57690
11 April	World Jewish Congress to Foreign Office: Foreign Office papers, 371/57690
18 April	World Jewish Congress to Foreign Office: Foreign Office papers, 371/57689
27 April	Rendel minute: Foreign Office papers, 371/57690
12 June	Beaumont note: Foreign Office papers, 371/57647
18 June	Dean note: Foreign Office papers, 371/57671
24 June	Dean note: Foreign Office papers, 371/57548
25 June	Beckett note: Foreign Office papers, 371/57548
27 June	Newton note: Foreign Office papers, 371/57548
5 July	Foreign Office confidential note: Foreign Office papers, 371/57597
16 July	Secretary of State for War, brief: War Office papers, 32/12208
23 July	Cabinet minutes: Cabinet papers, 128/6, Cabinet 72
25 July	Cabinet minutes: Cabinet papers, 128/6, Cabinet 73
29 July	Cabinet minutes: Cabinet papers, 128/6, Cabinet 74
30 July	Cabinet minutes: Cabinet papers, 128/6, Cabinet 75
	Dean to Foreign Office: Foreign Office papers, 371/57597
24 September	Garner minute: Foreign Office papers, 371/57429
28 October	Ben Gurion to Weizmann: Weizmann papers
4 November	Cabinet minutes: Cabinet papers, 128/6, Cabinet 94
5 December	Garner minute: Foreign Office papers, 371/57587

1947

1 January	Cabinet Defence Committee: Cabinet papers, 129/16
7 January	Bevin–Shinwell memorandum: Cabinet papers, 129/16
14 January	Bevin memorandum: Cabinet papers, 129/16
15 January	Cabinet minutes: Cabinet papers, 128/11
16 January	Creech Jones memorandum: Cabinet papers, 129/16
22 January	Cabinet minutes: Cabinet papers, 128/11
6 February	Bevin–Creech Jones memorandum: Cabinet papers, 129/16
14 February	Cabinet minutes: Cabinet papers, 128/9

Bibliography

In this bibliography I list those historical works, pamphlets and official reports which I have consulted during the preparation of this book, and from which the material, not in the list of archival sources, has been drawn.

PART ONE: Official Reports (in chronological order)

1903 *Royal Commission on Alien Immigration*, 4 volumes, Command papers 1741, 1742 and 1743 of 1903, London

1922 *Establishment of a National Home in Palestine: Hearings before the Committee on Foreign Affairs, House of Representatives* (18–21 April 1922), Washington

1922 *Statement of British Policy in Palestine* (the Churchill White Paper), Command Paper 1700 of 1922, London

1924 *League of Nations Permanent Mandates Commission, Minutes*, annual volumes, Geneva, 1924–1939

1930 *Report of the Commission on the Palestine Disturbances of August, 1929* (the Shaw Report), Command paper 3530 of 1930, London

1930 Leonard Stein, *Memorandum on the Palestine White Paper of October, 1930*, London

1930 Sir John Hope Simpson, *Palestine: Report on Immigration, Land Settlement and Development*, Command paper 3686 of 1930, London

1936 *Memorandum Submitted to the Palestine Royal Commission on Behalf of the Jewish Agency for Palestine*, London, November 1936

1937 *Palestine Royal Commission Report* (the Peel Report), Command paper 5479 of 1937, London

1937 *Palestine Royal Commission: Minutes of Evidence Heard at Public Sessions*, Colonial No. 134 of 1937, London

1938 *Palestine Partition Commission Report* (the Woodhead Commission), Command paper 5854 of 1938, London

1938 *Palestine: Statement by His Majesty's Government in the United Kingdom*, Command paper 5893 of 1938, London

1939 *Palestine: A Statement of Policy* (the MacDonald White Paper), Command paper 6019 of 1939, London

1944 *The Jewish National Home in Palestine: Hearings Before the Committee on Foreign Affairs, House of Representatives* (hearings of 8, 9, 15 and 16 February 1944), Washington
1947 *The Jewish Case Before the Anglo-American Committee of Enquiry on Palestine: Statements and Memoranda*, Jerusalem
1947 *The Jewish Plan for Palestine: Memoranda and Statements Presented by the Jewish Agency for Palestine to the United Nations Special Committee on Palestine*, Jerusalem
1947 *United Nations Special Committee on Palestine: Report to the General Assembly*. volume III, Annex A (Oral Evidence Presented at Public Meetings), Lake Success

PART TWO: Diaries, Letters and Speeches

C. R. Ashbee, *A Palestine Notebook*, London, 1923
The Earl of Balfour, *Speeches on Zionism*, London 1928
Norman H. Baynes, *The Speeches of Adolf Hitler, April 1922–August 1939*, 2 volumes, London, 1942
David Ben Gurion, *Rebirth and Destiny of Israel*, New York, 1954
David Ben Gurion, *Letters to Paula*, London, 1971
Izhak Ben-Zvi, *The Hebrew Battalions: Letters*, Jerusalem, 1969
Eliahu Elath, *Zionism at the UN: A Diary of First Days*, Philadelphia, 1976
Albert M. Hyamson, *The British Consulate in Jerusalem, in Relation to the Jews of Palestine*, London, part I, 1939; part II, 1941
Martin Gilbert, *Winston S. Churchill*, volume IV, 'Companion Documents', (in three parts), London, 1977
Lady Algernon Gordon Lennox (editor), *The Diary of Lord Bertie of Thame 1914–1918*, 2 volumes, London, 1924
James G. McDonald, *Where can The Refugees Go?* (a speech delivered on 19 November 1944), London, 1944
Colonel R. Meinertzhagen, *Middle East Diary 1917–1956*, London, 1959
Raphael Patai (editor), *The Complete Diaries of Theodor Herzl*, 5 volumes, New York, 1960
N. A. Rose (editor), *Baffy: The Diaries of Blanche Dugdale 1936–1947*, London, 1973
Arthur Ruppin, *Three Decades of Palestine*, Jerusalem, 1936
Hannah Senesh, *Her Life and Diary*, London, 1971
Maurice Simon (editor), *Speeches Articles and Letters of Israel Zangwill*, London, 1937
Meyer W. Weisgal (General Editor), *The Letters and Papers of Chaim Weizmann*, several volumes, London, 1968–

PART THREE: Memoirs and Biographies

Ehud Avriel, *Open the Gates! A Personal Story of 'Illegal' Immigration to Israel*, London, 1975

Menachem Begin, *The Revolt*, London, 1951

Menachem Begin, *White Nights*, London, 1978

Mendel Beilis, *The Story of My Sufferings*, New York, 1926

Alex Bein (editor), *Arthur Ruppin: Memoirs, Diaries, Letters*, London, 1971

Winston S. Churchill, *The Second World War*, volume 5, with documentary appendix, London, 1952

Richard Crossman, *Palestine Mission: A Personal Record*, London, 1946

Moshe Dayan, *Story of My Life*, London, 1976

Abba Eban, *An Autobiography*, London, 1978

Martin Gilbert, *Sir Horace Rumbold: Portrait of a Diplomat, 1869–1941*, London, 1973

Lieutenant-Colonel F. H. Kisch, *Palestine Diary*, London, 1938

Teddy Kollek, *For Jerusalem*, London, 1978

Shmarya Levin, *Youth in Revolt*, New York, 1930

David Lloyd George, *The Truth About the Peace Treaties*, 2 volumes, London, 1938

Shane Leslie, *Mark Sykes: His Life and Letters*, London, 1923

M. A. Novomeysky, *Given to Salt: The Struggle for the Dead Sea Concession*, London, 1958

Lord Rothschild, *Meditations of a Broomstick*, London, 1977

Harry Sacher, *Zionist Portraits and Other Essays*, London, 1959

Joseph B. Schechtman, *The Mufti and the Feuhrer: The Rise and Fall of Haj Amin el-Husseini*, New York, 1965

Leon Simon, *Ahad Ha-am: A biography*, London, 1960

Fritz Stern, *Gold and Iron: Bismarck, Bleichröder, and the Building of the German Empire*, London, 1977

Ronald Storrs, *Orientations*, London, 1939

Meyer W. Weisgal and Joel Carmichael (editors), *Chaim Weizmann: A Biography by Several Hands*, London, 1962

Chaim Weizmann, *Trial and Error: The Autobiography of Chaim Weizmann*, New York, 1949

Vera Weizmann, *The Impossible Takes Longer*, London, 1967

PART FOUR: Historical Works

Rev. Michael Adler, *The Jews of the Empire and the Great War*, London, 1919

Ahad Ha'am, *Ten Essays on Zionism and Judaism*, London, 1922

Reuben Ainsztein, *Jewish Resistance in Nazi-Occupied Eastern Europe*, London, 1974

Norman Angell and Dorothy Frances Buxton, *You and the Refugee: The Morals and Economics of the Problem*, London, 1939

George Antonius, *The Arab Awakening: The Story of the Arab National Movement*, London, 1938

Dan Bahat (editor), *Twenty Centuries of Jewish Life in the Holy Land: The Forgotten Generations*, Jerusalem, 1975

Salo W. Baron, *A Social and Religious History of the Jews*, New York, 1952

Salo W. Baron, *The Russian Jew under Tsars and Soviets*, 2nd edition, New York, 1976

Yehuda Bauer, *Flight and Rescue: Brichah, The Organized Escape of the Jewish Survivors of Eastern Europe, 1944–1948*, New York, 1970

Yehuda Bauer, *From Diplomacy to Resistance*, New York, 1973

Dr Alex Bein, *Theodore Herzl: A Biography*, Philadelphia, 1941

Dr Alex Bein, *The Return To The Soil: A History of Jewish Settlement in Israel*, Jerusalem, 1952

H. H. Ben-Sasson and S. Ettinger (editors), *Jewish Society through the Ages*, London, 1971

Norman Bentwich, *England in Palestine*, London, 1932

Jacob Billikopf and Dr Maurice B. Hexter, *The Jewish Situation in Eastern Europe including Russia*, Chicago, 1926

Herbert Ivan Bloom, *The Economic Activities of the Jews of Amsterdam*, Williamsport, 1937

The Rev. Hugh Callan, *The Story of Jerusalem*, London, 1891

Daniel Carpi and Gedalia Yogev, *Zionism: Studies in the History of the Zionist Movement and of the Jewish Community in Palestine*, volume 1, Tel Aviv, 1975

Gavriel Cohen, *Churchill and Palestine 1939–1942*, Jerusalem, 1976

Israel Cohen, *My Mission to Poland 1918–1919*, London, 1951

Israel Cohen, *A Short History of Zionism*, London, 1951

Norman Cohn, *Warrant for Genocide: The Myth of the Jewish World-conspiracy and the Protocols of the Elders of Zion*, London, 1967

Joan Comay, *Who's Who in Jewish History: After the Period of the Old Testament*, London, 1974

Lucy Dawidowicz, *The War Against the Jews*, London, 1975

Simon Dubnow, *History of the Jews*, 4 volumes, New York, 1967–1971

Simon Dubnow, *History of the Jews in Russia and Poland: From the Earliest Times Until the Present Day*, 3 volumes, Philadelphia, 1916–20

Abba Eban, *My People: The Story of the Jews*, New York, 1968

Walter J. Fischel, *Jews in the Economic and Political Life of Mediaeval Islam*, London, 1937

Isaiah Friedman, *The Question of Palestine, 1914–1918: British-Jewish-Arab Relations*, London, 1973

Isaiah Friedman, *Germany, Turkey and Zionism 1897–1918*, London, 1977

Lloyd P. Gartner, *The Jewish Immigrant in England, 1870–1914*, London, 1960

Martin Gilbert, *The Arab–Israeli Conflict: Its History in Maps*, London, 1974

Martin Gilbert, *Winston S. Churchill*, volume III, 1914–1916; volume IV, 1917–1922; volume V, 1923–1939, London, 1971, 1975, 1977

Victor Gollancz, *'Nowhere to Lay Their Heads': the Jewish Tragedy in Europe and Its Solution*, London, 1945

Paul Goodman (editor), *Chaim Weizmann: A Tribute on His Seventieth Birthday*, London, 1945

Solomon Grayzel, *The Church and the Jews in the Thirteenth Century*, New York, 1966

Louis Greenberg, *The Jews in Russia: The Struggle for Emancipation*, New Haven, 1944 and 1951

Philip Guedalla, *Napoleon and Palestine*, London, 1925

Gideon Hausner, *Justice in Jerusalem*, New York, 1966

Irving Howe, *The Immigrant Jews of New York: 1881 to the Present*, London, 1976

J. C. Hurewitz, *The Struggle for Palestine*, New York, 1950

Albert M. Hyamson, *Palestine: The Rebirth of An Ancient People*, London, 1917

V. Jabotinsky, *The Jewish War Front*, London, 1940

V. Jabotinsky, *The Story of the Jewish Legion*, New York, 1954

Samuel Katz, *Battleground: Fact and Fantasy in Palestine*, New York, 1973

Elie Kedourie, *In the Anglo-Arab Labyrinth: The McMahon–Husayn Correspondence and Its Interpretations 1914–1939*, Cambridge, England, 1976

Lionel Kochan, *Pogrom: 10 November 1938*, London, 1957

Walter Laqueur, *A History of Zionism*, London, 1972

Neville Laski, *Jewish Rights and Jewish Wrongs*, London, 1936

Lieutenant-Colonel Netanel Lorch, *The Edge of the Sword: Israel's War of Independence*, 2nd revised edition, Jerusalem, 1968

Raphael Mahler, *A History of Modern Jewry 1780–1815*, London, 1971

Jacob R. Marcus, *The Jew in the Medieval World: A Source Book 315–1791*, New York, 1938

Arthur D. Morse, *While Six Million Died*, London, 1968

Abraham A. Neuman, *The Jews in Spain*, Philadelphia, 1944

James Parkes, *The Emergence of the Jewish Problem 1878–1939*, London, 1946

Lieutenant-Colonel J. H. Patterson, *With the Zionists in Gallipoli*, London, 1916

Lieutenant-Colonel J. H. Patterson, *With the Judaeans in the Palestine Campaign*, London, 1922

Lieutenant-Colonel Pirie-Gordon (military editor), *A Brief Record of the Advance of the Egyptian Expeditionary Forces*, Cairo, 1918

Léon Poliakov, *The History of Anti-Semitism*, 3 volumes, London, 1974

Y. Porath, *The Emergence of the Palestinian-Arab National Movement, 1918–1929*, London, 1974

Peter George J. Pulzer, *The Rise of Political Anti-Semitism in Germany and Austria*, New York, 1964

Gerald Reitlinger, *The Final Solution*, London, 1953

Emmanuel Ringelblum, *Polish-Jewish Relations during the Second World War*, Jerusalem, 1974

N. A. Rose, *The Gentile Zionists: A Study in Anglo-Zionist Diplomacy, 1929–1939*, London, 1973

Cecil Roth, *A History of the Marranos*, second revised edition, Philadelphia, 1959

Cecil Roth, *A Short History of the Jewish People*, revised and enlarged edition, London, 1959

Cecil Roth, *The History of the Jews in Italy*, Philadelphia, 1946

Arthur Ruppin, *The Jewish Fate and Future*, London, 1940

H. Sacher, *A Hebrew University for Jerusalem*, London, 1915

H. Sacher, *Israel: The Establishment of a State*, London, 1952

Gershom Scholem, *Sabbatai Sevi: The Mystical Messiah 1626–1676*, London, 1973

A. J. Sherman, *Island Refuge: Britain and Refugees from the Third Reich*, London, 1973

Herbert Sidebotham, *Great Britain and Palestine*, London, 1937

Leon Simon and Leonard Stein (editors), *Awakening Palestine*, London, 1923

Sir John Hope Simpson, *The Refugee Problem*, London, 1939

Nahum Sokolow, *Hibbath Zion*, Jerusalem, 1934

Nahum Sokolow, *History of Zionism*, 2 volumes, London, 1919

Joshua Starr, *Jews in the Byzantine Empire 641–1204*, Athens, 1939

Joshua Starr, *Romania, the Jews of the Levant After the Fourth Crusade*, Paris, 1949

Leonard Stein, *Zionism*, 2nd edition, London, 1932

Leonard Stein, *The Balfour Declaration*, London, 1961

Christopher Sykes, *Cross Roads to Israel*, London, 1965

Zosa Szajkowski, *Jews, Wars, and Communism*, volume 1, New York, 1972

Arieh Tartakower and Kurt R. Grossman, *The Jewish Refugee*, New York, 1944

David Vital, *The Origins of Zionism*, London, 1975

Josiah C. Wedgwood, *The Seventh Dominion*, London, 1928

BIBLIOGRAPHY

Yigael Yadin, *Masada: Herod's Fortress and the Zealots' Last Stand*,
    London, 1966

In addition to the works cited above, the sixteen volumes of the *Encyclopaedia
Judaica*, Jerusalem 1972, provide an indispensable background for any student
of the emergence of Jewish statehood: Isaiah Trunk's article on the German
occupation of Poland in 1939, from which I quote in chapter nineteen, is from
volume thirteen of this encyclopaedia.

Index

compiled by the author

Aaronsohn, Aaron: founds an experimental farm in Palestine (1910), 71, 91; gives important intelligence to the British (1916), 92, 106; influences Sykes (1917), 93; influences Ormsby Gore (1917), 96; 'a real Palestinian', 107–8; to go to the United States, 109

Aaronsohn, Samuel: 109

Aaronsohn, Sarah: spies for Britain (1917), 96; her death, 102

Abdul Hamid, Turkish Sultan: Herzl contacts (1896), 48; his sovereignty to be recognized, 53; Herzl advocates a Jewish University in Palestine to (1902), 58

Abdullah, Emir of Transjordan: 179, 262

Abyssinia: Italian invasion of, 171

Acre: beseiged by Napoleon, 25; its future discussed (1916), 89; anti-Zionist petition of Arabs from (1918), 115; occupied by Jewish forces (1948), 307

Aden: Arabs kill Jews in (1947), 307

Adriatic Sea: and Jewish refugees, 234

Afghanistan: plight of Jews in (1946), 283; votes against Jewish and Arab States in Palestine (1947), 306

Africa: Jewish traders in, 21, 22; bleak Jewish future in, as seen by Chaim Weizmann (in 1885), 42

Ahad Ha'am: wants a Jewish 'spiritual centre' in Palestine, 45–6, 50, 58; and the coming of war (in 1914), 79

Akaba: Feisal meets Weizmann near (1918), 114; Saudi Arabian claims to (1937), 193

Al Aksa Mosque: Arabs allow Mendel Beilis to visit (1914), 73; Haj-Amin accuses Jews of wishing to take possession of (1928), 151

Aleppo: Jewish community in, 8, 12; its future discussed (in 1915), 87, 89; prosperous future of, foreseen (1917), 111; Arabs attack Jews in (1947), 307

Alexander II, Tsar of Russia: and the Jews of Russia, 36

Alexander, A. V.: 'vital' for Britain to retain 'the goodwill of the Arab world', 299

Alexander, D. L.: an anti-Zionist Jew (1917), 97

Alexandria (Egypt): Jews find refuge in, 17; Arabs attack Jews in (1947), 307

Algiers: Jews find refuge in, 17; Jews of, seek refuge in Jerusalem, 27; Arabs of, emigrate to Palestine (1930s), 230

Alien Immigration, Royal Commission on: hears evidence (1902), 55–6, 58, 61

Alkalai, Rabbi Judah: an advocate of Jewish 'national' unity, he settles in Jerusalem (1874), 33–4

Allenby, General: advances against Turks (1917), 110, 111; in control of Jerusalem, 112; five thousand Jews serve in army of (1918), 114; enters Damascus, 115; and Zionism, 119, 128, 129–30

Alliance Israelite: its school in Jerusalem, 32; its work in the nineteenth century, 33; Jews of Rumania appeal to (1881), 38

Allon, Yigal: 197

Almohades: anti-Jewish violence of, 9

America: Jews settle in, 17, 22

Amery, Leopold: and the

evolution of the Balfour Declaration, 100, 107–8, 112; supports a British Government loan to Zionists (1928), 151; his reaction to Arab terrorism (1938), 195; writes of 'the agony of the Jews' of central Europe (1938), 200; critical of British appeasement (1938), 209, 210; critical of Palestine White Paper (1939), 229–30; critical of British policy to Jewish refugees (1939), 239

Amsterdam: Jewish traders of, in the seventeenth century, 21

Anal: 'illegal' immigrants reach Palestine on (1947), 301

Ancona: shipowners of, forbidden to take Jews to Palestine, 20

Andrews, Lewis: gives evidence to Peel Commission (1936), 165–6; murdered by Arabs (1937), 186; his murderers defended, 190

Anglo-American Committee: examines the Palestine and displaced persons problem (1945–6), 274, 283, 284; its report published, 286; acceptance of its recommendations made dependent upon certain conditions, 288

Angola: possible Jewish settlement in (1939), 221

Antwerp: anti-Jewish riots in, 13

Arab Federation: Jewish attitude towards (in 1937), 171, 184; Lord Moyne advocates Jewish settlement in (1942), 261

Arab Higher Committee: boycotts work of United Nations in Palestine (June 1947), 301; rejects proposals of the United Nations Special Committee on Palestine (August 1947), 304

Arabia: the Arab war potential in (1915), 87

Arabs: conquest of Palestine by, 8; and the crusaders, 11, 12; seize a synagogue in Jerusalem (1720), 24; protest against influx of Jews to Palestine (1891), 43; not willing to 'yield their place easily' in Palestine (1891), 45; and the growing number of Jews in Palestine, 66, 68; employed on a Jewish experimental farm (1910), 71; welcome Mendel Beilis as one of the 'great Jewish heroes' (1914), 73; anti-Jewish violence of, in Palestine (1913), 74; and a possible Jewish State in Palestine (1914), 82; and the coming of war (in 1914), 86–7, 89; and the possibility of cooperation with the Jews, 93; and the evolution of the Balfour Declaration, 95, 98, 106, 110–11; their hostility to Zionism, 112, 113–14, 119; and the Weizmann-Feisal Agreement (of 1919), 116, 118; their continuing opposition to Zionism (1919–22), 124, 129–33, 137, 140; Churchill's rebukes to, 137–9; Ruppin's desire for Jewish friendship with, 148; Lloyd George's low opinion of, 137;

Churchill's low opinion of, 145–6, 176–7; their opposition to Zionism championed by several British Lords (1921), 143–4; Ruppin sees danger in estrangement from, 149; boycott Balfour in Jerusalem (1925), 150; their continuing hostility to Zionism (1928–33), 151–7, 160, 161, 164; refuse to cooperate with Peel Commission (1936), 165; Britain 'cannot afford' to quarrel with, 167; immigrate to Palestine, 168–9; gain from Jewish enterprise, 169; agree to give evidence to the Peel Commission, 174–5; unwilling to accept even the existing 400,000 Jews of Palestine (in 1936), 175; opposed to the partition of Palestine (1937), 180, 182; British proposal to transfer them eastwards across the Jordan, 185–6; 'not a mere handful of aborigines', 192; and the price of peace, for Britain, 193; and the continuing terror campaign in Palestine (1938), 195; 'the only nation in the world with at least three kings', 196; and the continuing violence in Palestine (1938), 197, 201, 204–5; Jewish reprisals against, 204–5; 'restless and anti-Jew', 205; the moderates powerless, 205–6; attack a Jewish village (1938), 207; and Jewish land purchase (1938), 209; and British possibility of obtaining 'goodwill' of, throughout the Arab world (1938), 210; warnings against 'capitulation to pressure' of (1938), 217; and the persecutions of European Jewry (1939), 218–19; British policy towards (1939), 218–19, 220–3, 225, 226, 228, 229–30; attitude towards 'illegal' Jewish refugees, 227, 238; and the refusal by Britain of visas for 20,000 Polish Jewish children (18 September 1939), 243, 244; and Jewish self-defence (1940), 246–7; their attitude to the Jews, as described by Lord Moyne (1942), 261; declare a general strike, in protest against increased Jewish immigration (1946), 286; Bevin voices anti-partition views of (October 1946), 294; and the oil of, as a factor in British policy (January 1947), 297–8; 'goodwill' of, a further factor in British policy, 299; declare a boycott throughout Palestine of all United Nations' enquiry work (June 1947), 301; react with violence to the United Nations' vote giving a State to both the Jews and the Arabs in a partitioned Palestine (November 1947), 306–7

Argentine, The: Russian Jews immigrate to (1881–1914), 44; Jewish agricultural colonies in, 45, 57, 68; open to Jews,

156; tightens regulations against Jewish immigration, 240

Armenians: massacred during the First World War, 96, 163

Ashbee, C. R.: and Zionism (1919), 119–20

Ashkelon: Jewish synagogue in, 7

Ashtory Ha-Parhi: a Jewish geographer, settles in Palestine, 17

Asia: 'misery' of Jews in (1897), 51

Asquith, H. H.: and the possibility of Jewish 'Home Rule' (1915), 83, 84

Assimi: takes 'illegal' Jewish refugees to Palestine (1939), 227

Assyria: conquest of Jewish kingdom by, 3

Astir: 'illegal' Jewish refugees seek to reach Palestine on board (1939), 223, 227–8

Athlit: Jewish agricultural farm established at, 71; Jewish refugees interned at, 245, 250

Atlantic: 'illegal' immigrants transferred to Patria from, 249

Attlee, Clement: and British policy towards the Jews during the Second World War, 264, 268; and Britain's post-war policy towards Palestine and the Jews, 273, 284, 287, 288

Auschwitz: news of killings in, reaches London (28 September 1942), 262; further news of killings in, reaches Istanbul (1943), 265

Australia: 'not desirous' of

receiving Jewish refugees (1938), 203; Jewish survivors find refuge in (1945–8), 294; votes in favour of a Jewish and an Arab State in Palestine (1947), 306

Austria: Jews of, 10; anti-Jewish violence in (1819), 29; Rothschilds of, 30; Jewish participation in national life of, 45; Herzl fears for future of Jews in, 47; blood-libel accusation in Bohemian province of (1899), 53; occupied by Nazi Germany (1938), 198, 199, 211, 212; Jews fight in ranks of allied forces in (1939–45), 270; Jewish refugees seek to reach Palestine through (1946), 276, 278, 279, 281, 283

Auto-Emancipation: published (1882), 41

Awni Bey: his evidence to the Peel Commission, 175

Azerbaijan: Jewish governor of, 8

Azzam Pasha, General: voices Arab opposition to any further Jewish immigration into Palestine (January 1947), 297

Ba'al Shem Tov: Hassidic leader, 24

Babylon: and the conquest of Jerusalem, 3; Jewish exiles in, 6; Jewish religious life in, 7

Bad Gastein: Jews in D.P. camp at (1946), 283

Baggallay, Lacy: and Arab attitudes to Palestine, 178, 179; contrasts Jewish 'hot air' with potential

Arab action (1939), 222; takes notes of reasons for refusing visas to 20,000 Polish Jewish children, after outbreak of war (1939), 243–4

Baghdad: aid to the Jews of, 32; British forces advance towards, 87; prosperous future of, foreseen (1917), 111; captured by the British, 112; Jews murdered in (1941), 259

Bahamas: only a few Jewish refugees accepted (1939), 244

Bahrain: its oil, and British policy (1947), 298

Balfour, A. J. (later Lord Balfour): critical of Rumanian anti-semitism (1914), 76; and the evolution of the Balfour Declaration (1917), 93, 97–8, 100, 102, 103, 106–7; and British support for the Zionists (1917–20), 109, 111, 112–13, 122, 135–6; supports Zionism in the House of Lords (1922), 144; boycotted by Arabs in Jerusalem (1925), 150; supports a British Government loan to the Zionists (1928), 150–1; quoted, on the 'great enterprise' in which Britain and the Jews were partners, 226

Balfour Declaration, the: evolution of (1914–17), 92–108; Arab leaders seek annullment of, 132–3, 175; the partition of Palestine 'compatible' with (1938), 197; the possible repudiation of (1938), 208; and 'Arab

detestation of the Jewish invasion' (1939), 218; Churchill denounces betrayal of (1939), 230; 'infamous', according to Mufti, 268

Balkans: Jews find refuge in, 22

Balta: anti-Jewish violence at (1882), 39–40

Baltic Sea: Jews settle by, 10

Barbados: refuses to take a single Jewish refugee in six months (1939), 244

Bar Kokhba, Simeon: leads Jewish revolt against Romans, 6; and the revival of Jewish sovereignty in Palestine in 1948, 308

Barker, General: wants immediate promise of Palestine to the Jews (1917), 110

Barnett, Zerah: a British Jew, active in Palestine (1870s), 41; and the founding of Tel Aviv, 70

Barrow, General Sir Edmund: and Palestine (1915), 83

Barsky, Moshe: murdered by Arabs (1913), 74, 197

Basel: first Zionist Congress opens at (1897), 50; later Zionist Congresses held at, 52, 60, 62

Basra: 87

Battershill, W. D.: describes Arab 'gunmen' (1937), 187

Bavaria: Jews of, 10; anti-Jewish violence in (1819), 29; gives a decoration to a Jew, 31; anti-semitism in (1919), 126; eastern European Jews expelled from (1923), 149

Baxter, C. W.: on the dangers of 'sending more

and more Jews into Palestine' (1939), 218–19

Beaumont, Richard: and Nazi war crimes, 292

Beaverbrook, Lord, 240

Beckett, Sir William: and the trial of Nazi war criminals, 293

Bedzin: murder of Jews at (1939), 246; a letter from five surviving Jews of, reaches Istanbul (1943), 265

Beersheba: and the First World War, 87, 92, 106, 109

Begin, Menachem: describes Irgun wartime policy, 268; describes the death of Asher Tratner, 280

Beilis, Mendel: accused of ritual murder (1911), 72–3; mentioned, 80; his son serves in Allenby's army (1918), 114

Beirut: crusaders massacre Jews of, 11; its future discussed (1915–16), 89; Arabs attack Jews in (1947), 307

Beisan: 210

Belgium: tightens regulations towards refugees (1939), 240; Nazis murder Jews of, 258, 265, 270

Belkind, Israel: advocates 'a political centre for the Jewish people' in Palestine (1882), 38

Belkind, Naaman: executed by the Turks (1917), 111

Belloc, Hilaire: 143

Belon, Dr: and the Jews of the Galilee in the sixteenth century, 19

Belsen: Jewish displaced persons 'still lingering in' (1945), 272; Jews in, 'all in favour of going to Palestine' (1946), 278; attitude to Bevin in (1946), 283; trial of war criminals of, 291, 294

Ben Gurion, David: his evidence to the Peel Commission (1936), 174; denounces Jewish terrorism (1938), 205; discusses Britain's reaction to Arab terrorism, 207; and the validity of 'treaties and pledges', 208; and Zionist policy during the Second World War, 246, 247, 260, 268; warns against post-war maintenance of White Paper (June 1945), 273; willing to accept Partition (October 1946), 295; points out that Jewish survivors of the Holocaust will not displace Arabs in Palestine, 301; explains that the Jews are determined never to be 'defenceless' again (July 1947), 302–3; and the coming of Jewish Statehood (May 1948), 308; 'our freedom and our future are in our own hands', 309

Ben Josef, Slomo: sentenced to death, 200; executed, 201

Ben Yehuda, Eliezer: and the revival of the Hebrew language, 54, 71; and the British Mandate for Palestine (1922), 148

Ben Zvi, Izhak: a pioneer of Jewish self-defence (1905), 64; denounces Jewish terrorism (1938), 205

Benedict XIII, Pope: censors the Talmud, 19

Bennett, J. S.: on Jewish immigration and British policy (1939), 244–5

Berger, General: and the Mufti, 268–70

Berlin: Nazi boycott of Jews in (1933), 158; Mufti visits (1941), 259; Mufti remains in (1944), 268–9; British seek to halt arrival of Polish Jews in (1945–6), 275

Bermuda Conference: does 'pitiably little' (1943), 267

Berthelot, Philippe: at San Remo Conference, 130

Bet Alfa: synagogue in, 7

Beth Saida (Galilee): Jews of, 19

Bethlehem: a possible Russian administration for (1915), 85

Bevan, Aneurin: argues importance to Britain of 'a friendly Jewish State' in Palestine (January 1947), 299

Bevin, Ernest: and Britain's post-war Palestine policy (1945–8), 273, 274, 275, 276, 278; warns Jews not to 'push to the head of the queue' (1946), 279–80, 283; describes Jewish desire to go to Palestine as 'political' (1946), 284; rejects conclusions of Anglo-American Committee, 286; rejects Weizmann's appeal for partition, 294–5; stresses importance of Arab oil for Britain (January 1947), 297–8; and the abandonment of Britain's Palestine Mandate, 300

Bialystok: anti-Jewish violence in (1906), 66; anti-Jewish pogrom in (1914), 81; fate of Jews

in, after Nazi occupation (1941), 253, 265, 267

Biltmore Programme: 260

B.I.L.U.: urges Jews to go to Palestine (1882), 38

Bismarck, Herbert: critical of 'the filthy Jew' Bleichröder, 31

Bismarck, Otto von: and the Jews, 31; Herzl contacts, 48

Black Death: Jews blamed for, 13

Black Hundreds: incite anti-Jewish violence in Russia (1905), 62

'Black Paper', The: causes distress to Jews (1939), 232

Black Sea: Jews settle by, 3, 4, 6; Jews travel as 'illegals' to Palestine from (1934), 161, 207; Jews continue to try to reach Palestine from (1934–40), 223, 245; 'illegal' immigrants on board *Struma* forced back to (1942), 259; only a few immigrant ships able to escape across, after outbreak of war, 267

Blech, E. C.: reports on the Jews of Palestine (1907), 68

Bleichröder, Gerson: and the Jews of Germany in the nineteenth century, 31–2

Blum, Rabbi: told to 'mind your own business', 280

Board of Deputies of British Jews: Jews of Rumania appeal to (1881), 38; wishes to attend the Nuremberg Trials (1946), 291–2

Bohemia: blood-libel accusation in (1899), 53; Nazi occupation of, makes Jews second-class citizens (1939), 225

Bolshevik Party (in Russia): some Jews support, 71–2; anti-war propaganda of (1917), 100; come to power in Russia (1917), 110 (see henceforth index entry for Soviet Union)

Boston: Russian Jews settle in, 44

Bratislava: Jews harrassed in (1946), 287

Brazil: open to Jews (1930), 156; possible Jewish 'settlement' in (1938), 214; tightens regulations against Jewish refugees (1939), 240

Brenan, Terence: 188, 190

Breslau: anti-Jewish riots in, 13

Brest-Litovsk: Jews protected in, 13; Bolsheviks made peace with Germans at, 112

Brit Shalom: seeks Arab-Jewish reconciliation, 150

British Guiana: possible Jewish 'settlement' in (1938), 214, 217, 220, 228, 237; few Jewish refugees accepted (1939), 244

British Honduras: few Jewish refugees accepted (1939), 244

Brooke-Popham, Sir Henry: worried about a Jewish 'enclave' in Kenya (1938), 200

Buber, Martin: wants 'a Jewish University in Palestine' (1902), 58

Bucharest: anti-Jewish riots in (1936), 198; murder of Jews in (1941), 258

Buchenwald: ill-treatment of Jews at, reported in some detail (1939), 220;

Jewish displaced persons 'still lingering in' (1945), 272

Bulgaria: British pressure on, against 'illegal' Jewish refugees seeking to reach Palestine (1939), 218; Lord Moyne rejects immigration of Jews to Palestine from (1942), 262; Lord Gort seeks to prevent Jewish refugees reaching Palestine from (1944), 270; Jews set off for Palestine from (1945–8), 294

Bullard, Sir Reader: 191

Bund, the: founded (1897), 52; active, 71, 73

Burke, Haviland: warns against Jews (1904), 61–2

Burma: not suitable for Jewish refugees, owing to 'strong objections' of Burmese (1939), 225

Butler, R. A.: 241

Byron, Lord George: and the Jews, 26

Byzantium: Jews of, 7, 9

Cadogan, Sir Alexander: and the problems of finding an 'Arab solution' for Palestine (1939), 221–2

Caesarea: Jews of, persecuted by Christians, 7

Cairo: anti-semitic book published in (1899), 53; Lord Moyne assassinated by two young Jews in (1944), 269; Arabs attack Jews in (1947), 307

Callan, Hugh: describes Jews as 'the only patriots' in Jerusalem (1891), 43

Campbell, Ronald: warns of Egyptian opinion

(1937), 188; urges Yugoslav Government to halt movement of 'illegal' Jewish refugees towards Palestine (1939), 234

Canaan: Jewish life in, 3

Canada: Jews of, 29; Russian Jews immigrate to, 44, 68; Jews of, support Zionism (1917), 97; restrictions on Jewish immigration to (1930), 155; Jews find refuge in (1945–8), 294; supports a Jewish State in Palestine (1947), 304; votes in favour of Jewish and Arab statehood in Palestine, 306

Cape Town: Jews of, 22

Caporetto: Italian defeat at (1917), 105

Caribbean: Jews of, 21

Carpathians: Jewish traders cross, in Roman times, 5; the Hassidic movement crosses, in the eighteenth century, 24

Cartagena (South America): Jews burnt at stake in, 19

Carthage: Jews settle in, 3

Carvell, J. E. M.: reports on new German concentration camp (1938), 208, 217

Casimir the Great: protects Jews, 13

Caspian Sea: Jews settle by, 3

Cavendish Bentinck, Victor: and the Jews of Poland after the Second World War, 280–2

Cecil, Lord Robert: and the Balfour Declaration, 100; and Jabotinsky's imprisonment, 129

Ceylon: Jewish traders and, in the seventeenth

century, 22; only a few Jewish refugees accepted (1939), 244

Chamberlain, Houston Stewart: describes the Jews as the universal corruptors (1899), 53

Chamberlain, Joseph: and a possible Jewish 'home' in Africa (1903), 60

Chamberlain, Neville: and British policy in Palestine (1938–9), 195, 210, 225, 226, 232, 247; and British policy towards Jewish refugees (1938–9), 214, 241; 'Jews aren't a loveable people', 239

Chancellor, Sir John: reports on 'deep-seated hatred of the Arabs for the Jews' (1929), 153

Charles, Sir Noel: proposes measures to check the 'clandestine influx' of Jewish refugees (1946), 276, 285

Chelmno: Nazi death camp at, 265

Chicago: Jews of, 30; Russian-born Jews settle in, 44; appeal on behalf of Jewish refugees made in (1938), 199

China: Jewish traders and, 22

Chrzanow: pogrom at (1919), 121

Churchill, Colonel Charles: wants Jews to promote regeneration of Palestine (1842), 28

Churchill, (Sir) Winston S.: denounces anti-Jewish violence in Tsarist Russia (1905), 64–5; 'Jerusalem must be the only ultimate goal', 69;

and British military attitudes to Zionism (in 1919), 124–5; his own views on Jews, Bolshevism and Zionism (1920), 127–9; as Colonial Secretary, is the British Cabinet Minister responsible for Palestine (1921–22), 132–48; supports a British Government loan to Zionists (1928), 151; condemns German anti-semitism (1935), 162; re-iterates his condemnation (1936), 163–4; his evidence to the Peel Commission (1937), 176–7; and the Peel Commission Report, 182, 185; speaks against the Palestine White Paper (1939), 230, 232; supports Jewish armed units for self-defence (1940), 246–7; opposes restrictions on Jewish land-purchase in Palestine (1940), 247; favours Jewish military force with the allied armies, but overruled, 249; urges upholding of 'general considerations of humanity' towards Jewish refugees (1940), 250–1; suggests release of Jewish detainees in Mauritius, but overruled (1942), 260; rejects idea of Arab veto on Jewish immigration (1943), 261; in favour of partition of Palestine (1944), 268, 269; and Weizmann's appeal to end the Palestine immigration restrictions (1945), 272–3; and the fate of the Jewish

survivors of Central Europe (1946), 289–90

Chuter Ede, J.: opposes 'large-scale' Jewish immigration to Britain (1945), 274–5

Clark Kerr, (Sir) Archibald: 116, 178

Clauson, Gerard: 140

Clayton, Colonel Gilbert: and the Arab war potential (in 1915), 87; and Arab unease at Zionism (1918), 112; and Jewish land purchase (1919), 122

Clemenceau, Georges: 117

Clerk, Sir George: critical of Zionism (1917), 95

Cluse, William: urges Government to allow more Jews into Palestine (1943), 264

Cochin: 'black Jews' of, 84

Cohen, Arthur: encourages Pinsker to publish Auto-Emancipation (1882), 41

Cohen, Israel: witnesses effect of pogrom (1919), 121

Cologne: Jewish self-defence in, 13

Colombia: suspends Jewish immigration (1939), 236, 240

Congreve, General William: and British military attitudes to Zionism, 129, 130, 141

Constantinople: Jews find refuge in, 17; Napoleon advances towards, 25

Cordova: 11

Cossacks: torment Jews, 22

Coupland, Professor: and the partition of Palestine (1936), 172, 174–5; critical of Palestine White Paper (1939), 229

Cracow: Jews of, murdered in Second World War, 265; ritual murder charge against Jews of, after the Second World War, 280

Cranborne, Viscount: and Government refusal to relax immigration restrictions (1943), 264

Creech Jones, Arthur: and Britain's Palestine policy (1945-8), 273; supports a 'Jewish national state' (January 1947), 298, 299; and the abandonment of Britain's Palestine Mandate, 300

Cresswell, (Sir) Michael: on Nazi 'barbarities' (1938), 214

Crete: Jewish refugees stranded on (1939), 238; Jewish soldiers fight in ranks of allied armies in, 270

Crimea: Jews of, 10; slaughter of Jews of, during the Second World War, 257

Cripps, Sir Stafford: and the future of the surviving Jews of Poland (1946), 289, 290

Cromer, Lord: in Egypt, 173

Crossman, Richard: recalls the desire of Jewish survivors to go to Palestine (1946), 283-5; critical of arrest of Jews inside Palestine (1946), 286

Crusaders: persecute Jews, 9-10, 11; Jewish refugees from, 13, 17

Cuba: votes against Jewish and Arab States in Palestine (1947), 306

Cunliffe-Lister, Sir Philip (later Lord Swinton):

and Arab hostility to Jewish immigration (1934), 161-2

Curzon, Lord: an opponent of the Balfour Declaration, 105-6, 119, 120-1; his continuing opposition to Zionism (1919), 122, 123; clashes with T. E. Lawrence, 123-4; and British military hostility to Zionism, 129; believes Jews to be 'the best judges of what they wanted', 130; reverts to his criticisms of the Balfour Declaration, 131

Cyprus: Jewish revolt against Romans in, 6; Jewish refugees not wanted by (1939), 235; takes 291 Jewish refugees (1939), 244; Jewish 'illegal' refugees deported to (1946), 288, 301

Czechoslovakia: Jews flee to (1938), 198; some Jews refused refuge in, 199; successful Nazi German pressure against, 208-9; Jewish refugees from 'need not leave', according to British experts, 227; Jews flee from Poland into (1946), 287; supports a Jewish State in Palestine (1947), 304

Czenstochau: Jews of, murdered in Second World War, 265

Dachau: concentration camp set up at (1933), 158; Austrian Jews sent to (1938), 198; account of 'brutal treatment' in (1939), 217; Enzo Sereni, a Jewish Palestinian parachutist, murdered in

(1944), 270; war crimes trials and, 294

Daily Chronicle: advocates a 'Zionist State' (1917), 93

Daily Express: declares there is 'no room for the Jews in Britain' (1938), 208; opposes any British Government expenditure on behalf of Jewish refugees (1939), 240

Daily Telegraph: publishes letter from Jabotinsky (1937), 184

Dalton, Hugh: supports 'some purely Jewish area in Palestine' (January 1947), 298-9

Damascus: Jewish community in, 8, 12; Jews find refuge in, 17; false accusation against Jews of (February 1840), 27, 32, 33; its future discussed (1915-16), 87; prosperous future of, foreseen (1917), 111; two Jewish spies executed in (1917), 111; Arab aspirations for, 112; entered by British troops (1918), 115; Syrian General Congress meets in (1919), 121-2; Arab meeting in, calls Palestine 'an integral part of the Arabian homeland' (1937), 186; said to be the centre of the recruitment of Palestinian 'gunmen', 187

Danube: and Jewish settlers in Roman times, 5; and Jewish persecutions at the time of the crusades, 9, 10; Jews refused refuge in region of (1938), 199; British pressure against Jewish refugees seeking escape along (1939), 234,

236, 245

Danzig: Jewish refugees from (1939), 238

Dardanelles: naval and military campaign at (1915), 82–3, 85, 89

Darwin, Charles: his theory held up for emulation by the Jews, 46

Davar: denounces Jewish terrorism, 205

Dawson of Penn, Lord: and Jewish refugee doctors (1933), 159

Dayan, Moshe: recalls first day of Hanita settlement, 197; recalls declaration of Jewish Statehood, 306

Dayan, Zorik: killed in action, 306

Dean, (Sir) Patrick: and the post-war trials of Nazi war criminals, 291, 292–3

Deedes, Sir Wyndham: Weizmann confides in, 139–40, 141; in Palestine, 146

Deganya: Jewish farm founded at (1909), 71; mentioned, 85; Holocaust survivors settle in, 301

Deir Yassin: 307

Demnate (Morocco): anti-Jewish violence in (1885), 42

Denmark: Jews reach Cabinet rank in (1911), 29; Austrian Jews flee to (1938), 199; Jews welcomed (1938), 203

Dill, Lietuenant-General: and Jewish objections to partition (1937), 180

Djerba Island: Jews of, 4

Dov Hos: Jewish refugees seek to reach Palestine on (1946), 285–6

Downie, H. F.: and Jewish 'illegal' immigration to Palestine, 207, 245

Dreyfus, Captain: his trial, 47

Drogheda, Lord: and Jewish 'rights' in Palestine (1916), 92

Dubnow, Ze'ev: 'We want to conquer Palestine' (1882), 39

Dubossary: blood-libel accusation in (1903), 59

Duff Cooper, Alfred: appeals to Government not to close Palestine to Jewish refugees (1939), 239–40

Dulberg, George: and Jewish solidarity, 53–4

East Indies: Jews of, 21, 22

East Prussia: anti-Jewish violence in (1819), 29

Eban, Aubrey: describes impact of deportation of 'illegal' refugees (1947), 301–2

Eden, Anthony: and Palestine, 179, 187, 192, 193–4; resigns as Foreign Secretary (1938), 203; Secretary of State for War (1940), 249, 250; informs the War Cabinet of the Nazi murder of Jews throughout Europe (14 December 1942), 262; informs House of Commons of Nazi atrocities (17 December 1942), 262, 264

Education: and the Jewish desire to be free from discrimination, 57–8; considered by the Jews 'a primary need', 173

Egypt: Jews settle in, 3; Jewish revolt against Romans in, 6; the Jewish traders of, 7; Jewish public figures in,

9; Maimonides settles in, 11; and the crusaders, 11; and the Mamluk rulers of Palestine, 17; and the 'false' messiah, 22; Napoleon in, 25; Jews deported to (December 1914), 82; and the future of Palestine, 85; Lord Cromer in, 173; achieves independence, 174; seeks to apply pressure against the Jewish National Home in Palestine, 178; opposed to any 'independent Jewish State' as her neighbour (1937), 182, 188, 189; her possible opposition to Britain feared, 192, 201; 'profound effect' on, of British policy against 'illegal' Jewish refugees (1939), 228; her armies prepare to attack the Jewish State at birth (1948), 307–8; occupies the Gaza Strip, 308

Eichmann, Adolf: his trial, and testimony, 253, 255, 256; present at the Wannsee Conference (1942), 257

Ein Gev: founded (1937), 179–80

Ekaterinoslav: murder of Jews in (1905), 62

Elath, Gulf of: early Jewish community of, 8

Eleazar: and the suicide of the Jews of Masada, 5

Eliahu Golomb: Jewish refugees seek to reach Palestine on (1946), 285–6

Elijah of Ferrara: settles in Jerusalem, 17

Elijah de Vides: a Jewish philosopher from the Galilee, 21

Elizavetgrad: anti-Jewish

violence in (1881), 36, 59

Elliot, Walter: does not consider Arabia more important that the United States (1939), 219

Emerson, Sir Herbert: a Jewish State 'utopian in the extreme' (1939), 237

Empire Rival: 'illegal' Jewish refugees returned to Germany on (1947), 301–2

England: Jews of, 10; and the 'false' messiah, 22; and the Hassidic movement, 24; Meshed Jews migrate to, 27; and the fate of Damascus Jewry (1840), 27. *See also under index entry for Great Britain*

Epstein, Eliahu: evidence to Peel Commission, 168–9

Eritrea: suggested by Churchill as a Jewish colony (1943), 262

Euphrates River: possible Jewish refugee haven on (1938), 214

Everybody's: opposes entry of Jewish refugee doctors and dentists to Britain (1938), 208

Evian Conference: 202–3, 234

Exodus 1947: 'illegal' immigrants reach Palestine on (1947), 301, 302

Extraordinary Zionist Conference: held in New York (1942), 260

Fadhil Jamail, Dr: does not want Palestine Arabs to 'suffer for the crimes of Hitler', 300

Falla, Paul: and War Crimes trials, 291

Faro: Jewish printing press in, 16

Farouk, King of Egypt: welcomes Mufti (1946), 289

Feinberg, Avshalom: spies for Britain (1915–17), 89, 91, 95

Feisal, Emir: and Zionism, 113–14; meets Weizmann (June 1918), 114; enters Damascus (October 1918), 115; meets Weizmann (December 1918), 116; at the Paris Peace Conference (1919), 118; his views challenged in Damascus, 121–2; to be financed by the Zionists, 123; agrees to 'abandon' claims to Palestine (1921), 132; King of Iraq, 262

Feldman, Dayan Asher: on the Zionist ideal (1903), 61

Ferrant Martinez: preaches against Jews, 15

Feuchtwanger, Lion: his manuscripts seized (1933), 157

Fez: Jews of, 8; Jews massacred by Muslims in, 9; Maimonides in, 11; Jews killed in (1864), 27

Fiji: only three Jewish refugees accepted in six months (1939), 244

Fisher, H. A. L.: 122, 123, 131; proposes offering Palestine Mandate to the United States (1921), 137

Flanders: Jews of, and Palestine, 12

Flossenburg: German concentration camp set up at (1938), 208

Focsani: 'Lovers of Zion' meet at (1881), 38

Forbes Adam, Eric: and

Zionism (1919), 127

Forbes, Sir George Ogilvy: reports on anti-Jewish measures in Germany (1938), 212, 214

Formosa: Jewish traders and, 22

France: Jews of, 4, 10; Jews find refuge in, 17; and the 'false' messiah, 22; and the fate of Damascus Jewry (1840), 27; Jews reach Cabinet rank in (1848), 29; Rothschilds of, 30; Jewish delegates from, at 'Lovers of Zion' conference (1884), 41; Russian Jews immigrate to, 44; Jews participate in national life of, 45; Herzl fears anti-Jewish 'victims' in, 47; and the coming of war (in 1914), 80; and the future of Palestine (1914–18), 83; and the Zionist Movement (1917), 102; a possible Mandatory in Palestine (1919), 123; opposes Balfour Declaration (1920), 130; her dwindling influence over Syria (1937), 184; tightens refugee restrictions (1939), 240; Nazis murder Jews of, 258, 270; Jews set off for Palestine from (1945–7), 294; votes in favour of a Jewish and an Arab State in Palestine (November 1947), 306

Frankfurt: Jewish self-defence in, 13; restrictions on Jews lifted in, 25; Rothschilds of, 29; Nazi ill-treatment of Jews in (1938), 212, 214

Frankfurter, Felix: Feisal's letter to (1919), 118

Freer, Miss: finds Jerusalem 'virtually a Jewish city' (1907), 68

Galata, 'illegal' immigrants reach Palestine on (1947), 301
Galatz: 223
Galicia: Jews obtain autonomy in, 15; Russian armies enter (1914), 79, 81; anti-Jewish violence in (1917), 116
Galilee: Romans suppress Jewish revolt in, 6; Jewish communities in, 7, 8; and the crusaders, 11; Jews from Spain and Portugal settle in, 17, 19; Jewish life in, in the sixteenth century, 21; Hassidic leader settles in, 24; Jewish land-purchase in, 28; and the proposed partition of Palestine, 179, 180; Jews killed in (1938), 205; Jews to be excluded from most of (1938), 210; to be part of an Arab State (1947), 304
Garner, Frederick: and Nazi war crimes, 293
Gaster, Rabbi Moses: 89; wants Jews in Palestine recognized as a 'nation' (1917), 93
Gawler, George: advocates Jewish settlement in Palestine (1845), 28
Gaza: early Jewish community of, 7, 17, 21; British battles for (1916–17), 92, 93, 95, 106, 109, 110; anti-Zionist petition from Arabs of (1918), 115; Arabs flee to (1948), 308
Gaza, Mufti of: hanged by the Turks, 96

Gederah: Russian Jews establish a Palestinian settlement at (1884), 39; and the First World War, 87, 91
Genoa: Jews expelled from, 20
George VI, King: his view of 'illegal' Jewish immigration to Palestine (1939), 223
Germany: Jews of, 9; Jews find refuge in, 22; anti-Jewish riots in (1819 and 1830), 29–30; anti-semitism in, in the nineteenth century, 31–2; Jewish delegates from, at 'Lovers of Zion' conference (1884), 41; Jews participate in national life of, 45; Herzl fears for future of Jews in, 47; and the Zionist movement in the First World War, 102, 103, 105; and Hitler's early anti-semitic activities in (1919–20), 125–6, 129; further anti-semitism in (1923), 149; Hitler comes to power in (1933), 157–9; anti-Jewish legislation in (1935), 162; fate of Jews in (1935), 162–3; annexation of Austria by (1938), 198, 199; annexation of Sudetenland by (1938), 208–9; expulsion of Polish-born Jews from (1938), 211; Kristallnacht pogrom against the Jews (1938), 211–12; British pressure on, to halt flow of Jewish refugees to Palestine (1939), 223; fate of Jews of Poland after occupation by (1939), 252–3; fate of

Jews of Russia after invasion by (1941), 253; Jewish survivors seek to reach Palestine from (1946), 278, 281; Gallup Poll in, shows majority approval of Hitler's policies (1947), 303
Gerona: 12
Ghetto: established in Venice (1516 AD), 20; to be avoided in Palestine (1937), 194
Gibraltar: Jews reach Straits of, 6; accepts only a single Jewish refugee in six months (1939), 244
Golan heights: Jewish synagogue in shadow of, 7
Gold Coast: only a few Jewish refugees accepted (1939), 244
Goldman, Emma: 127
Gomel: anti-Jewish violence in (1903), 60
Goodhart, Heron: and German support for Zionism (1917), 103
Gort, Lord: and 'illegal' Jewish refugees seeking to reach Palestine (1939), 223; warns against 'Jewish migration from South East Europe' (1944), 270
Graebe, Hermann Friedrich: his testimony about Nazi atrocities in German-occupied Russia, 255
Graham, (Sir) Ronald: and Zionism (in 1917), 96, 97; and the evolution of the Balfour Declaration, 101, 105, 106, 108, 109, 110
Graham, Stephen: anti-Jewish allegations of (1914), 73–4
Granada: Jews massacred by Muslims in, 9

Great Britain: a baptised
Jew becomes Prime
Minister of (1868), 29;
Jewish delegates from, at
'Lovers of Zion'
conference (1884), 41;
Russian Jews immigrate
to, 44; Jews participate in
national life of, 45; Ahad
Ha'am's criticism of Jews
of (1893), 46; Royal
Commission on Alien
Immigration to (1902),
55–6; and the coming of
war (in 1914), 79–80; and
the future of Palestine
(1914–18), 82–91; and the
evolution of the Balfour
Declaration (1917),
92–108. For subsequent
references, see the index
entry for *Palestine*, and
the list of chapter
headings.
Greece: Jews settle in, 3;
the Jews of, during its
struggle against the
Turks, 26; British
pressure on, against
'illegal' Jewish
immigration (1938–9),
207, 226–7, 233, 234, 241,
244, 245; Nazis murder
Jews of, 258, 270; Jews
set off to Palestine from
(1945–8), 294; votes
against a Jewish and an
Arab State in Palestine
(1947), 306
Greenberg, Leopold:
asserts dangers of Jewish
assimilation (1903), 58;
and the offer of a possible
Jewish 'home' in Africa
(1903), 60; describes the
aim of Jewish settlement
in Palestine (1913), 74
Gregory, J. D.: 'the Jews
deserve all they get', 120
Grodno: anti-Jewish

pogrom in (1914), 81
Grynszpan, Herschel:
shoots a German diplomat
(1938), 211
Guadalajara: Jewish
printing press in, 16
Guardian: 'illegal' refugees
reach Palestine on (1947),
301
Guatemala: supports a
Jewish State in Palestine
(1947), 304
Güdemann, Chief Rabbi
Moritz: supports the
continuing dispersal of
the Jews (1897), 50
Gurney, Henry: and Jewish
hunger strike on behalf of
refugees from Europe
(1946), 285–6
Gwynne, H. A.: 126

Haaretz: denounces Jewish
terrorism, 205
Haganah: Jewish Agency's
defence force, 197, 249,
286, 287, 288, 301
Haidamaks: persecute
Jews, 24
Haifa: Jews join Arabs in
defence of, 11; captured
by Napoleon, 25; its
future discussed (1916),
89; anti-Zionist petition
from Arabs of (1918),
115; Palestinian Arab
Congress in, demands
end to Jewish immigration
(1921), 132–3; Arab
gangs formed in (1929),
153; Arab employment
rises in, 161; Arab
'gunmen' near (1937),
187; terror and counter-
terror at (1938), 205;
Holocaust survivors settle
in, 301; occupied by
Jewish forces (1948), 307
Haig, Sir Douglas: 101

Hailey, Lord: critical of
'Polish and German
colonists' in Palestine
(1937), 186
Haining, General: 205, 206
Haj Amin el-Husseini:
appointed Mufti of
Jerusalem (1921), 132;
and the disturbances of
1928–9, 151–2; in London
(1930), 154; orders
boycott of Jewish goods
in Palestine (1933), 160;
gives evidence to the Peel
Commission (1936), 175;
opposed to partition
(1937), 180; his 'black
list', 186; evades arrest,
186; 'sitting just across
the border' (1938), 205–6;
consolidates his position
(1938), 211; opposes the
Palestine White Paper
(1939), 229; criticisms of,
230; would-be
appeasement of (1940),
250; offers Hitler Arab
support against the
'English-Jewish' coalition
(1941), 259; opposes
emigration of Bulgarian
Jews to Palestine (1943),
262; wants to set up an
'Arab-Islamic army' in
Germany (1944), 268;
welcomed by the King of
Egypt (1946), 289; his
influence criticized
(1947), 299
Halifax, Lord: 196, 203;
praises attitude of
Egyptian Government
during Munich crisis
(1938), 210; and the
formulation of British
policy towards 'the
Arabs' (1938), 212, 222,
223, 226, 228–9; urges
Turkish Government to
halt flow of 'illegal'

Jewish refugees
(1 September 1939), 242;
opposes Jewish armed
units for self-defence in
Palestine (1940), 246–7
Hammat-Gader: synagogue
in, 7
Hampstead (London):
protest against 'foreign
colony' in (1945), 275
Hanita: founded (1938), 197
Harcourt, Lewis: and the
future of Palestine (1915),
84
Hardinge, Sir Alexander:
reports King's view of
'illegal' Jewish
immigration (1939), 223
Hardinge, Lord: and the
Jews of Russia (in 1917),
109–10
Hassidism: 24, 126
Hebron: Jews of, in the
fifteenth century AD, 17;
in the sixteenth century,
21; anti-Zionist petition
of Arabs from (1918),
115; Arabs kill Jews in
(1929), 151, 162
Hedjaz: Palestine Arabs
receive arms from (1929),
153
Heine, Heinrich: 29
Heinen, Paul: sentenced for
'a crime against
humanity', 292
Helsingfors Programme:
urges active Jewish
settlement in Palestine
(1906), 66
Henderson, Arthur: 155
Henderson, Sir Nevile:
223, 242
Herzl, Theodor: favours
assimilation of the Jews
(1893), 46; confronted by
anti-semitism, 46–7;
argues in favour of 'a
Jewish exodus' to
Palestine (1895), 47; his

diplomatic efforts (1896),
48; publishes *The Jewish
State* (1896), 49–50;
organizes the first Zionist
Congress (1897), 50–1;
visits Palestine (1898),
52–3; speaks to Royal
Commission on Alien
Immigration (1902),
55–6; and the proposal
for a specifically Jewish
university (1902), 57–8;
visits Russia (1903),
59–60; opposes a Jewish
'homeland' in Uganda
(1904), 61; dies (1904),
62; mentioned, 74, 76
Hess, Moses: urges Jews to
return to the Land of
Israel (1862), 32–3; his
influence, 40
Hexter, Dr Maurice:
evidence to Peel
Commission, 170
Hill, Sir John Gray: his
house in Jerusalem
bought by Jews (1914), 76
Himmler, Heinrich: and
the Mufti, 268, 269
Hirsch, Baron Maurice de:
and Jewish agricultural
settlements in the
Argentine, 45; meets
Herzl (1895), 47; Herzl's
criticism of settlements
of (1902), 57
Hitler, Adolf: influenced by
a British-born anti-
semitic writer, 53;
absorbs anti-semitism in
Vienna (from 1908),
69–70; his early anti-
semitic speeches in
Munich (in 1919), 125–6;
his anti-semitic
programme (1920), 129,
131–2; comes to power in
Germany (1933), 157–9,
162; enters Vienna (1938),
198, 199; annexes

Sudetenland (1938),
208–9; threatens
'annihilation of the
Jewish race in Europe'
(January 1939), 220;
demands removal of
'Jewish bacillus' (April
1939), 225; the Mufti
offers Arab support to,
against Britain and the
Jews (1941), 259; teaches
Jews of Poland that they
are not Poles, but
'members of the Jewish
nation', 284
Hoare, Sir Reginald: on
need to take measures
against Jewish 'illegal'
immigrants (1939), 223,
228
Hoare, Sir Samuel: and the
question of German
Jewish refugees seeking
entry to Britain, 159, 203,
216–17; and the decision
not to assist refugees
financially (1938–9), 237
Hodgkin, Thomas: defends
murder of Lewis
Andrews, 190
Holland: Jews reach, from
Spain, 17; Jews protected
by, in the seventeenth
century, 21–2; Jews
reach Cabinet rank in, 29;
Jews flee to (1938), 199;
Jews welcomed (1938),
203; regulations towards
Jewish refugees tightened
(1939), 240; Nazis
murder Jews of, 258, 265;
supports a Jewish State
in Palestine (1947), 304,
306
Hong Kong: a few Jewish
refugees accepted (1939),
244
Hope-Simpson, Sir John:
his report on land-
availability in Palestine

(1930), 155
Hos, Dov: his evidence to the Peel Commission, 173
House, Colonel: and Zionism (in 1917), 103
Huldah: attacked by Arabs (1929), 153–4
Hull, Cordell: 179
Hungary: Jews of, 10; Jews flee to (1938), 198; some Jews refused refuge in (1938), 199; British pressure on (1939), 226, 233, 234; fate of a 75-year-old Jewish lady from (1944), 289
Hussein, Sherif of Mecca: his correspondence with the British (1915–16), 86, 87, 89
Hynd, John Burns: and the desire of Jewish survivors to reach Palestine (1946), 278, 279

Ibn Saud: 191, 193, 262
Illustrated Sunday Herald: article on Jews, Bolshevism and Zionism in (1920), 127–9
India: Jews reach border of, 6; Meshed Jews migrate to, 27; Muslims of, intervene to oppose the partition of Palestine (1937), 184, 187–8, 196; Britain afraid of arousing 'hostility' of Muslims of (1938), 201, 222; votes against Jewish Statehood (1947), 306
Indus, River: Jews settle by, 6
Iraq: British Mandate over, 123, 132, 171; achieves independence, 174, 184; applies pressure on Palestine (1937–8), 178, 192, 193, 225; Britain

afraid of losing 'friendship' of, 201; 'Holy War' preached in (1938), 211; Weizmann proposes Jewish land purchase in, as alternative for Jewish refugees not allowed to go to Palestine (1938), 214; fear of anti-British rebellion in (1940), 250; rebellion in, crushed (1941), 259; Arab saboteurs parachuted behind British lines in (1944), 269; Jewish soldiers fight in ranks of allied armies in, 270; Jewish soldiers help suppress pro-Nazi revolt in, 289; future importance of oil of, as a factor in British policy (1947), 298; troops of, seek to crush Jewish State at birth (1948), 307–8
Irgun Zvai Leumi: demands a 'Hebrew Government' in Palestine (1944), 268; Churchill critical of acts of terror of (1944), 269; its activities against the British Army in Palestine intensified (July 1945), 273; its attacks continued (1946), 279, 287, 297; its attacks reach a climax (1947), 304; Jewish Agency condemns attacks of (1947), 307; a member of, loses his life while on a special mission for the British, 289
Irwin, Lord: 150 (for subsequent index entry see Halifax, Lord)
Isaiah: his promise of the restoration of Israel recalled (in 1882), 39
Islam: and the Jews, 9, 15;

Jews forcibly converted to, 26–7; its 'hordes' criticized by Churchill, 177
Islington, Lord: an opponent of Zionism, 143
Israel, State of: and the Hassidic movement, 24
Istanbul: arrival of 'illegal' Jewish immigrants at (1942), 260; news of fate of Polish Jewry reaches (1943), 265
Italy: the Jews of, 7; Jews find refuge in, 17; Jews persecuted in, 19–20; Jews reach Tiberias from, 21; and the 'false' messiah, 22; Jews reach Cabinet rank in (1870), 29; Rothschilds of, 30; Jews participate in national life of, 45; Jews of, support Zionism (1917), 97; clashes with Britain over movement of Jewish refugees to Palestine (1939), 245; Jews fight in ranks of allied forces in (1943–5), 270; British pressure on, to halt flow of 'clandestine' Jewish refugees (1946), 276, 278, 279, 281, 285; Jews set off to Palestine from (1946–8), 294

Jabneh: Jewish scholars at, 7
Jabotinsky, Vladimir: organizes Jewish self-defence (1903), 59; urges vigorous Jewish settlement in Palestine (1906), 66; and the coming of war (in 1914), 79; advocates a Jewish military force (in 1914), 80, 85, 92, 93, 95; his

scheme supported (1917), 96; to go to Russia (in 1917), 109, 110; organizes Jewish self-defence in Jerusalem (1920), 129; and the Revisionist movement, 161; his criticisms of the Peel Commission Report (1937), 182, 184, 185; and the Revisionist congress in Prague (1938), 195; urges Jewish self-defence by armed units, and wins Churchill's support (1939), 246; urges a Jewish State as 'a true and proper war aim' (1940), 251; the Irgun inspired by, 268

Jacob: 'that mean fellow', 120

Jacobstadt: 101

Jacques of Verona: recommends Jewish guides, 17

Jaffa: Jews settle near, 7; Jews buy agricultural land near (1856), 28; a Jewish agricultural school set up near (1870), 33; Jewish pioneers arrive from Russia to (1882), 39; Jewish population of, increasing (1907), 68; Jewish land purchase near, 70–1; a possible Russian administration for (1915), 85; and the First World War, 87, 97; anti-Jewish violence in (1921), 133; Arabs attack British police in (1933), 160; Arab employment rises in, 161

Jamaica: only five Jewish refugees accepted in six months (1939), 244

Jassy: persecution of Jews of (1867), 31

Jeddah: Arab forces enter, 113

Jemal Pasha: 'his will was law' (1916), 91

Jericho: Jewish synagogue in, 7

Jerusalem: the capital of Judaea, 3; the Temple a centre of Jewish pilgrimage, 4–5; and the Romans, 6, 7; 'next year in', 7; Jewish academy in, in the tenth century, 8; and Judah Halevi's longing for, 11; and the crusaders, 12; and the Jews, in the fifteenth century, 17, 19; and the 'false' messiah, 22; Arabs seize a Jewish synagogue in (in 1720), 24; and Napoleon, 25; North African Jews seek refuge in, 27; Jews buy agricultural land near (1856), 28; Alliance Israelite school in, 32; a girls school founded in (1864), 33; Rabbi Alkalai settles in (1874), 34; Jewish quarter built outside the walls of (1871), 41; Arabs of, protest against Jewish immigration (1891), 43; visited by the Kaiser (1898), 52–3; growing number of Jews in (1905), 68; its future under discussion (1915), 83, 85, 87, 89; the British conquest of (1917), 106, 109, 111, 123; 'is become a burdensome stone' (1919), 125; anti-Jewish riot in (1920), 129; Lloyd George's attachment to, 131; Hebrew University inaugurated in (1925), 150; Arab-Jewish tension

in (1928–9), 151–2; Arabs attack British police in (1933), 160; Arabs protest against any further Jewish immigration in (1936), 164; and the proposed partition of Palestine, 179; Muslims of India opposed to 'Jewish rule' in, 196; Jews killed in (1938), 205; Arab control of criticized (1939), 232; Holocaust survivors settle in, 301; to be excluded from the Jewish State (1947), 304; beseiged by Arab forces (1948), 307

Jewish Agency: Weizmann resigns from (1930), 155; employs only Jewish labour in Palestine, 161; urges Jews to exercise restraint in face of Arab attack (1936), 164; evidence given to Peel Commission by senior members of, 168–71, 172, 174; Arab objections to, 175; its defence force, the Haganah, 197; a 'cloud' hangs over its relations with British Cabinet ministers (1939), 226; and 'illegal' immigrants detained in Mauritius (1940), 251; seeks visas for Iraqi Jews, after Baghdad pogrom (1941), 259; seeks to replace British Mandate as the government of Palestine (1942), 260; condemns terror acts of Irgun and Stern Gangs (1944), 269; its condemnation of terrorism seen as ineffective (1945), 273; urges end to White Paper immigration restrictions

(1945), 274; clashes with British authorities (1946), 286, 287; accepts UNSCOP partition plan (1947), 306; condemns Jewish terrorist attacks (1947), 307

Jewish Agency Executive: condemns all acts of terror by Jews (1944), 269

Jewish Brigade Group: Churchill announces formation of (1944), 268

Jewish Chronicle: letter to, urges Jewish settlement in Palestine (1860), 28; letter to, explains Jewish solidarity (1900), 53-4; letter to, on Zionist ideals (1903), 61; describes a 'remarkable' meeting in Manchester (1905), 64

Jewish Guardian: Lawrence of Arabia's message to, (1918), 115

Jewish State, the: Herzl claims 'foundation' of (1897), 51

Jezreel valley: 17

Job: would have been exasperated by Zionists, 131

Josephus: comments on Jewish pilgrims to Jerusalem, 5; describes the reasons for the Jewish mass-suicide on Masada, 5

Judaea: Jewish kingdom in, 3; Jewish revolt in, 5, 6; and the crusaders, 11; Russian Jews purchase land in foothills of (1884), 39

Judah Halevi: his longing for Jerusalem, 11

Justinian, Emperor: anti-Jewish measures of, 7

Kabtanik, Martin: and the

Jews of Palestine in 1491, 19

Kalischer, Rabbi: urges the return of the Jews to the Land of Israel (1860), 32, 33; land given to 'Lovers of Zion' by son of (1884), 41

Kamenets-Podolsk: slaughter of Jews at, 257

Kattowitz: 'Lovers of Zion' conference at (1884), 41; details of anti-Jewish measures in (1939), 241

Katznelson, Dr Avraham: evidence to Peel Commission, 172

Kelly, David: his report from Egypt (1937), 189

Kendall, Anthony: and 'illegal' Jewish refugees (1939), 227

Kennard, Sir Howard: reports on Polish attitude to Jews (1938), 215

Kennedy, Joseph: tells Britain 'not to over-estimate' power of Jewish lobby in the United States (1939), 226

Kenya: possible Jewish immigration to (1938), 200, 234; some Jewish refugees reach (1939), 244

Kerr, Philip (later Lord Lothian): and Zionism, 96; and Indian Muslim opposition to 'any Jewish state', 196

Kfar Etzion: 307

Kharkov: Jews leave for Palestine from (1881), 38; Russian Zionists meet in (1903), 60

Khatzman, Vera: letters from Chaim Weizmann to, 54, 62, 64, 66; records Weizmann's secret meeting with the Peel

Commission (1936), 167-8

Kielce: Polish attack on Jews in (1946), 286-7

Kiev: Jews expelled from (1910), 72; ritual murder trial in (1913), 72-3; anti-semitic newspaper appeal in (1917), 100; Nazi slaughter of Jews at (1941), 257

King-Crane Commission: critical of Zionist programme (1919), 124, 125

King David Hotel (Jerusalem): blown up, 287-8; debate on destruction of, in the British Parliament, 288-90

Kiryat Haroshet: attacked by Arabs (1938), 207

Kishinev: anti-Jewish violence in (1903), 59; further violence in (1905), 62; anti-Jewish violence in, under Rumanian rule (1938), 198

Kitchener, Lord: has 'a very poor opinion' of Palestine (1915), 83; and the Arab war potential, 87

Kollek, Teddy: recalls foundation of Ein Gev (1937), 179-80

Korazim (Galilee): Jews of, 19

Korets (Russia): Jews murdered at (1881), 39

Kremenchug: Jews leave for Palestine from (1881), 38

Kristallnacht: a German pogrom (1938), 211-12, 214-15, 216

Krushevan, Pavolaki: anti-semitic provocations of (1903), 59

Kun, Bela: 127, 128

Kunavina: Jews killed in (1884), 41
Kurds: 171
Kursk: anti-Jewish measures in (1905), 62
Kutais: blood libel charge against Jews of (1878), 36
Kuwait: its oil, and British policy (1947), 298

La Spezia: Jewish 'illegal' immigrant ships to be detained at, 285
Lampson, Sir Miles (later Lord Killearn): 182
Lang, Cosmo Gordon: urges Government to give Jews 'temporary asylum' in Britain (1943), 264
Lansing, Robert: 117
Latvia: Jews of, 166
Lawrence, T. E. ('Lawrence of Arabia'): enters Damascus, 115; and the Weizmann-Feisal Agreement (of 1919), 116; and the role of the Jews in the Middle East, 123; and Arab claims to Palestine, 132
Lazarus, Emma: her poem of welcome (1883), 44
League of Nations: and the Palestine Mandate, 117, 132, 146, 148, 149, 176, 192, 228
Lebanon: French control over (1919), 123; Arab attacks into Palestine, from (1938), 204; Arab soldiers from, enlist in British army, 270; troops from, gather to cross into northern Palestine (1948), 307–8
Leeward Islands: accepts only a single Jewish refugee in six months

(1939), 244
Legislative Council (in Palestine): Jewish objections to (1932), 156
Lenin, Vladimir: some Jews support, 72; enters Petrograd (1917), 110
Levin, Shmarya: 79, 80
Levontin, Zalman David: leads a group of Russian Jews to Palestine (1882), 38
Levy, Joseph: describes plight of 'illegal' Jewish refugees (1939), 227, 237–8
Lewis, Councillor: critical of Jewish immigrants to London (1902), 55
Libya: Jews of, 27
Liesel: carries Jewish refugees to Palestine (1939), 238
Lima: Jews burnt at stake in, 19
Lindsay, Lord: urges Jews to return to Palestine (1847), 28
Lisbon: anti-Jewish riots in, 15, 16
Lishansky, Yosef: spies for Britain (1917), 95; executed by the Turks, 111
Litani River: 124
Lithuania: Jews of, 10, 13, 22, 35, 166
Lloyd George, David: and the future of Palestine (1915), 83; opposes a withdrawal from Gallipoli (1915), 86; and the Jewish Legion (1917), 92; and the evolution of the Balfour Declaration (1917), 93, 95, 100; and Britain's decision to acquire the Palestine Mandate (1919–20), 122–3, 130, 131; his

continuing support for Zionism (after 1920), 135–6, 137
Lodz: fate of Jews in (1943), 265; Jews murdered while on their way to (1946), 282
Logan, Alderman: appeals on behalf of Jewish refugees (1938), 216
Loire, River: Jews settle by, 6
London: and the Damascus affair (of 1840), 27; and the Russian pogroms (1881–2), 39; visited by Pinsker (1882), 41; 'Lovers of Zion' society established in (1884), 41; criticisms of Jewish immigrants in (1902), 55–6; news of Nazi atrocities against Jews made public in (1942), 264
Lopez de Ayala: portrays Jews as bloodsuckers, 15
Los Angeles: 'cinema business' of a cause for censure, 174
'Lovers of Zion': founded (1881), 38; Kattowitz conference of (1884), 41; supported by the ten-year-old Chaim Weizmann (1885), 42; criticized (1891), 45; supported (1895), 48; support the Zionist Congress (1897), 50; support a Jewish university in Jerusalem (1914), 76
Lublin: murder of Jews of, in Second World War, 265; murder of two Jews of, in hospital, after the Second World War, 280
Lucius Quietus: suppresses Jewish revolt, 6
Lueger, Karl: success of

anti-semitic party of, 48; and Hitler, 70

Luke, S. E. V.: urges 'punitive' conditions for Jewish detainees in Mauritius (1941), 251

Luther, Martin: his advice on the Jewish question, 20–1

Luxembourg, Rosa: 127

Maccabee, Judah: leads revolt againt Syrians, 5; mentioned, 41, 49, 111

McCloy, John J.: and clemency towards Nazi war criminals, 293–4

MacDonald, Malcolm: and Britain's Palestine policy (1938–40), 200, 201–2; in Jerusalem (August 1938), 205–6; and the evolution of the St James Conference, 206, 211, 212, 214, 217, 218, 219, 220, 221; and the decision to impose permanent minority status on the Jews of Palestine (1939), 222–3, 225–6, 228; and the fear of Jewish refugees acquiring 'the right to migrate' to Britain (1939), 228; warns against 'Zionist' influence on League of Nations (1939), 229; Churchill critical of, 232; and measures to halt flow of Jewish refugees to Palestine (1939), 241, 242; answers Weizmann's appeal to grant visas to 20,000 Polish Jewish children (1939), 243–4; and Jewish 'illegal' immigration, 245; opposes exaggeration of strength of Jewish lobby

in the United States (1940), 247

MacDonald, Ramsay: 156

McGregor, P. J. C.: reports on Jewish 'nationalist spirit' in Palestine (1914), 76

Mack, (Sir) Henry: on desire of Jewish survivors to go to Palestine (1946), 283

Mackereth, Gilbert: reports from Damascus on 'Palestinian terrorists' (1937), 187, 190

Mackillop, Douglas: on reasons for exodus of Polish Jewry (1946), 278

McMahon, Sir Henry: letters of (1915–16), 86, 87, 89

MacMichael, Sir Harold: and Jewish immigration to Palestine (1938), 196; and Arab fears of Arab terrorism, 205; and an Arab attack on a Jewish village, 207; and the capture of 'illegal' Jewish refugees (1939), 227; and the deportation of 'illegal' refugees (1940), 249; rejects appeal on behalf of Iraqi Jews, after Baghdad pogrom (1941), 259

McNeill, Ronald: and Jewish nationalism (in 1917), 104

Madagascar: Lord Moyne critical of Jewish refusal to settle in, 261; not suitable for settlement of 'emaciated' Jews (1946), 282

Mahmoud Pasha: 206, 210

Maimonides: Jewish philosopher, 11

Main, River: Jews of, 9

Mainz: Jewish self-defence

in, 13; restrictions on Jews lifted in, 25

Majorca: Jews of, 4; massacre of Jews in, 15

Makins, (Sir) Roger (later Lord Sherfield): warns of possible hostility of Middle East States (1937), 192; doubts desirability of German Jewish refugees as immigrants (1938), 214

Malaya: some Jewish refugees reach (1939), 244

Malta: Jews of, 4; only a few Jewish refugees accepted (1939), 244

Manchester Guardian: reports on Nazi terror (1933), 158; appeals for clemency on behalf of two Jews sentenced to death (1933), 200; publishes full report on Polish anti-semitic activities (1946), 280

Manchuria: possible Jewish 'territory' in, 69

Manhattan: Jews in slums of (1900), 44

Manning, Cardinal: protests against Russian persecution of the Jews (1882), 39

Mantua: anti-Jewish riots in, 13

Maritza: brings Jewish refugees to safety (1943), 267

Marrakesh: Jews killed in (1864), 27

Martin, (Sir) John: in Palestine (1936), 165, 174; on need for Jewish deportees to be 'decently treated' in Mauritius (1940), 251

Marx, Karl: 29, 32, 127

Masada: Jewish defence of, 5

Masaryk, Jan: tells a cautionary tale (1938), 209
Massey, William: 135
Mauritius: Jewish traders of, in the seventeenth century, 22; refuses to take a single Jewish refugee in six months (1939), 244; Jewish 'illegal' immigrants deported to (1940), 249, 251, 259, 260, 295
Maxwell, General: and the Arab war potential (in 1915), 87
'May Laws': impose disabilities on Russian Jewry, 40
Maybin, Sir John: opposes Jewish immigration to Northern Rhodesia (1939), 236–7
Mea Shearim: founded outside Jerusalem (1871), 41
Mecca: pilgrimage of 'New Muslims' to, 27; Turks driven from (in 1918), 114
Medina: pilgrimage of 'New Muslims' to, 27
Meighen, Arthur: 135
Mein Kampf: quoted, 70
Meinertzhagen, Colonel: opposes British military hostility to Zionism (1920), 129, 130; on Arab intimidation (1921), 135, 140–1, 146, 148; calls the Jews 'a nation without a home' (1938), 196
Melitopol: anti-Jewish violence in (1905), 62
Menachem Mendel of Vitebsk: settles in the Galilee, 24
Meshed: forcible conversion of Jews in (March 1839), 26–7

Mesopotamia: Jewish revolt against Romans in, 6; Jewish farmers in, 7; the Arab war potential in (in 1915), 87; Emir Feisal to become ruler of, 132
Metz: Jews expelled from (1871), 31
Mexico: restrictions on Jewish immigration to (1930), 155
Mexico City: Jews burnt at stake in, 19
Meyerson, Golda (later Mrs Meir): gives evidence to the Peel Commission (1936), 173; rebels against 'expressions of sympathy' for the Jews (1938), 203; describes desire of the Jews 'to be masters of our own fate' (1946), 285; hunger-strike of (1946), 285–6; tells the British 'it is a great illusion to believe us weak' (1947), 302; recalls her emotions on hearing the Jewish State proclaimed (1948), 308
Mikveh Israel: founded (1870), 33; 'amazing' (1918), 114
Milan: Jews expelled from, 20
Milka: brings Jewish refugees to safety (1943), 267
Mills, Eric: 143; warns of fate of German Jews (1935), 162–3; gives evidence to Peel Commission (1936), 165; Jewish Agency letter to, on shortage of agricultural workers in Palestine (1941), 259
Milos: immigrants on, to be deported, 249

Minsk: anti-Jewish violence in (1881), 39; Russian Zionist conference in (1902), 58; Nazi atrocities near (1941), 255
Mogilev: Jews driven from (1824), 35
Mohammed: Jews accused of poisoning, 152
Money, Sir Alfred: and Zionism (1919), 119
Montagu, Edwin: an anti-Zionist Jew, 83–4, 98–100, 103, 106, 122, 123
Monte Carlo: 'the horrible crowd of Jews', 130
Montefiore, C. G.: an anti-Zionist Jew (1917), 97, 103
Montefiore, Moses: devotes life to the cause of the Jews, 28; his philanthropic work in Jerusalem, 33; visits Russia to protest against Jewish disabilities (1846), 36; his hundredth birthday (1884), 41; protests against anti-Jewish violence in Morocco (1885), 42
Morocco: Jews of, 8; Jews persecuted in, 13; Jews find refuge in, 17; and the 'false' messiah, 22; aid to the Jews of, 32; anti-Jewish violence in (1885), 42; 'inarticulate' Jews of, 166; Arabs of, emigrate to Palestine (1930s), 230; Jews from, emigrate to the State of Israel (after 1948), 309
Morrison, Herbert: and Muslim opposition to greater Jewish immigration (1945), 274; and a new British plan for Palestine (1946), 288, 295
Moscow: intolerant of

Jews, 22; the Jews of, 36; Jews expelled from (1891), 45; Jews killed in (1903), 59; Jewish students refused entry to (1905), 62; news of Nazi atrocities on Jews made public in (1942), 264

Moselle, River: Jews of, 9

Moser, Alderman: 69

Moses: 'might have brought us to the United States' (Weizmann), 304

Moses, Mayer: 29

Mosul: Jewish governor of, 8

Motza: Arabs kill Jews in (1929), 151, 162

Mount of Olives: English aspirations for (1915–17), 83, 99; first British High Commissioner welcomed on (1920), 130–1

Mount Scopus: Jewish land purchase on (1914), 76; Jewish doctors and nurses murdered on their way to (1948), 307

Mount Zion: Jewish community of, 17

Moyne, Lord: 'sceptical' of possible Jewish settlement in British Guiana (1939), 228; rejects immigration certificates for Rumanian Jews, after Bucharest pogrom (1941), 259; agrees to allow 750 Iraqi Jews to go to Palestine, after Baghdad pogrom (1941), 259; rejects Churchill's argument in favour of releasing Jewish detainees in Mauritius (1942), 260; gives his views in the House of Lords about the Jewish race, Jewish immigration to Palestine, and Arab attitudes to Jews (1942), 261; opposes immigration

of Bulgarian Jews to Palestine (1942), 262; assassinated by two young Jews in Cairo (1944), 269

Munich: Hitler's anti-semitic speeches in (1919), 126; anti-semitic programme formulated in (1920), 129, 131; Nazi concentration camp set up near (1933), 158

Musa Kazim Pasha: refuses to see Weizmann (1921), 137, 141; warns of Arab uprising (1929), 153; in London (1930), 154; demands halt to all Jewish immigration to Palestine (1933), 160

Mussolini, Benito: 157, 171, 189

Nablus: Arab gangs formed in (1929), 153; Arabs attack British police in (1933), 160

Nahalal: Weizmann meets Coupland at, 174–5

Nahmanides: Jewish philosopher, and Palestine, 12

Namier, (Sir) Lewis: and the future of the Jews in Palestine (1917), 111–12

Napoleon Bonaparte: and the Jews, 25; his defeat, 26, 35

Nasi, Don Joseph: rebuilds Tiberias, 21

Nathan, Lord: on the fate of the Jews in post-war Europe (1946), 279

Nazi-Soviet Pact: impact of news of, on Zionist Congress, 242

Negev desert: and the proposed partition of Palestine, 179, 180, 269;

eleven new Jewish settlements in (October 1946), 294, 295; to be part of a Jewish State (1947), 304

Netter, Charles: sets up a Jewish agricultural school near Jaffa (1870), 33, 39

New Europe: advocates a 'Jewish Palestine' (1917), 95

New Statesman and Nation: murder of Lewis Andrews defended in, 190

Newton, Sir Basil: on need for 'leniency' in the trial of Nazi war criminals, 293

New York: Jews settle in, 25; and the Damascus affair (of 1840), 27; 'Lovers of Zion' society established in (1884), 41; Russian Jews settle in, 44; a Jewess from, at the first Zionist Congress (1897), 50; a million Jews reported in (1907), 68; Bevin alleges anti-Jewish attitude in (1946), 286

New York Times: reports on plight of 'illegal' Jewish refugees (1939), 227, 237; and the arrival of Jews from North Africa to Palestine (1947), 301

New Zealand: votes in favour of an Arab and a Jewish State in Palestine (1947), 306

Nicaragua: tightens immigration restrictions (1939), 240

Nicholas I, Tsar of Russia: and the Jews, 35–6

Nicholas II, Tsar of Russia: 'it was the Jews who crucified our Lord', 45

Nigeria: refuses to take a

single Jewish refugee in six months (1939), 244

NILI: Jewish spies active on behalf of Britain (1915–17), 89, 91, 95–6, 102, 111

Noah, Mordecai M.: 25

Noel Baker, Philip: opposes land-purchase restrictions on Jews of Palestine (1940), 247

Nordau, Max: supports Herzl, 48, 50–1

North Africa: 'misery' of Jews in (1897), 51; Jewish educational disabilities in, 57; Jews fight in ranks of allied forces in (1939–45), 270; Jews reach Palestine from (1947), 301

North America: Jews of, 21

Northern Rhodesia: possible Jewish settlement in (1939), 222, 236–7; some Jewish refugees reach (1939), 244

Norton, (Sir) Clifford: reports on ill-treatment of Jews from Bohemia and Moravia (1939), 239, 241

Norway: Nazis murder Jews of, 258, 262

Novomeysky, Moses: supports Jewish university in Palestine (1903), 61; visits Palestine (1910), 71

Nuremberg Laws: discriminate against Jews (1935), 162; extended to Austria (1938), 198; extended to Bohemia and Moravia (1939), 225

Nuremberg Trials: 291–4

Oder River: anti-Jewish riots on, 13

Odessa: anti-Jewish violence in (1871), 36; Jewish pioneers set off for Palestine from (1882), 39; Pinsker influenced by pogrom in, 40; 'Lovers of Zion' committee founded in (1884), 41; Jewish self-defence group in (1903), 59; anti-Jewish measures in (1905), 62; three hundred Jews murdered in (1905), 62; Jews of, help buy land in Jerusalem for a Jewish university (1914), 76

Ohio: the Jews of, 25

Oil: Arab control of (foreseen in 1917), 111; becomes a factor of political importance (1937), 193; its importance stressed, in connection with Anglo-Arab relations (1947), 297

O'Neill, (Sir) Con: and the Nuremberg trials, 291

Orde, (Sir) Charles: in Riga, 200

Orletta: 'illegal' immigrants reach Palestine on (1947), 301

Ormsby Gore, William: on Zionism (1917), 96, 98; on the NILI spies (1917), 102–3; Colonial Secretary (1936–8), 165, 170; supports the partition of Palestine, 179, 180, 184–6; orders campaign against Arab terrorism (1937), 186, 187, warns of 'Arab intransigence', 191; Palestine as 'a place of refuge' for persecuted Jewry (1938), 195; and Indian Muslim opposition to 'any Jewish State',
196; resigns, 203–4

Ottolenghi, Joseph: an American Jew in the eighteenth century, 25

Ottoman Turks: rulers of Palestine from 1517 to 1917, 19, 21; and the 'false' messiah, 22; impose a 'head tax' on all Jews, 24; and the Jews of Greece, 26; receive Arab protest against Jewish immigration to Palestine (1891), 43; their power to obstruct Jewish settlement (1891), 45; and possible Russian intervention, on behalf of the Jews of Palestine (1903), 60; and Jewish land purchase in Palestine (1914), 76; and the coming of war (in 1914), 79–80, 81, 83, 84, 87; at war, 95–6; and the British conquest of Palestine (1917–18), 101, 105–7, 111

Pacific: immigrants on, to be deported, 249

Pakistan: votes against Jewish Statehood (1947), 306

Palestine: receives its name from the Romans, after the suppression of the Jewish revolt, 6; synagogue building in, in biblical times, 7; and the Arab conquest of, 8, 9; and the Tartar invasion, 12; and the expulsion of the Jews from Spain and Portugal, 17; and the 'false' messiah, 22; Meshed Jews settle in, 27; North African Jews seek refuge in, 27; British non-Jews advocate Jewish settlement in (in the 1840s), 28; a Jewish agricultural school set up in (1870), 33; a British explorer's view of the future of (1874), 34; Jews from Tsarist Russia argue in favour of settlement in, 36; Jewish settlement in (1870s), 41; Edmond de Rothschild's first visit to (1887), 42–3; visited by Ahad Ha'am (1891), 45; the Jewish charity system in, criticized (1893), 46; Herzl urges 'the return of the Jews to' (1896), 48, 49; the Basle Programme advocates Jewish 'systematic settlement' in (1897), 51; the Kaisers' visit to (1898), 52–3; Hebrew language to be revived in (1901), 54; return of Jews to (in 1900s), 55, 57; the call for a Hebrew university in (1902), 57–8; growing number of Jews in (1907), 68; Jewish farms founded in (1909), 71; Mendel Beilis reaches (1913), 73; and the coming of war (in 1914), 82; its future under discussion (1915–16), 83–7, 89, 91, 106; Arabs protest against Jewish immigration to, 149–50; Arab violence against Jews in (1929), 151–5; continual Arab protests against Zionist settlement in, 156, 160; Arab violence against Jews in (1936), 164; the Jewish achievement in, praised by Weizmann (1936),

167; Royal Commission examines situation in (1936–7), 164–77; and British policy towards (1937–9), 178–242; and British policy towards, during the Second World War, 242–51, 259–64, 267–70; and the emergence of Jewish statehood (1945–8), 272–309

Panama: bows to British pressure on Jewish 'illegal' immigration (1939), 245

Papal States: Jews expelled from, 20

Pappenheim, Bertha: her fate under the Nazis (1936), 163

Paris: and the Damascus affair (of 1840), 27; 'Lovers of Zion' society established in (1884), 41; Dreyfus trial in (1894), 47; effect of anti-semitism in, on Max Nordau, 48

Paris Peace Conference, of 1919: 116, 117

Passchendaele: battle for (1917), 101, 103

Passfield, Lord: meets Palestine Arab deputation (1930), 154–5; meets Weizmann (1930), 155

Passover: Jewish celebration of, 7; anti-Jewish violence in Russia during festival of (in 1882), 39; Jews expelled from Moscow during festival of (in 1891), 45; anti-Jewish violence in Kishinev during (in 1903), 59; Jews expelled by the Turks from Jaffa during (in 1917), 97

Patria: 'illegal' refugees

transferred to (1940), 249; their fate a subject of dispute between Wavell and Churchill, 249–50; Weizmann recalls fate of, 295

Patterson, Lieutenant-Colonel J. H.: 85

Peel, Lord: heads Royal Commission (1936), 160, 164–5, 168, 174, 177

Peel Commission Report: quoted, 160; its proposal for the partition of Palestine, 178–9, 180, 182, 184, 191–3

Pell, Robert: reports on British policy towards Jewish refugees (1939), 237

Peloponnese (Greece): Jews massacred in, 26

Permanent Mandates Commission: Arabs protest to (1924), 149, 184–6; regards Palestine as 'a place of refuge' for persecuted Jewry (1938), 195

Persia: Jews of, 26–7, 33, 166; possible opposition to Britain's Palestine policy feared, 192; votes against Jewish statehood (1947), 306

Persian Gulf: Jews settle by, 3; a Jewish governor of, 9; Jewish traders in, 22

Peru: justifies restrictions on Jewish immigration (1938), 203; supports a Jewish State in Palestine (1947), 304

Petah Tikvah: Jewish village in Palestine (founded 1878), 41, 87; Holocaust survivors settle in, 301

Philadelphia: Jews settle in, 25, 44

Philo of Alexander: comments on Jewish pilgrims to Jerusalem, 4

Picot, Georges: 93

Pinsk: Weizmann criticizes Jews of (1895), 47–8; weakness of Zionism in (1898), 52; evidence of Nazi atrocities near, after the German invasion of Russia (1941), 256–7

Pinsker, Leon: urges a national centre for the Jews, 40–1

Pirie-Gordon, Major: and British conquest of Jerusalem, 111

Plehve: Herzl appeals to (1903), 59–60

Po, River: 13

Poland: the Jews of, 22, 29, 126, 155, 159, 166, 168, 171, 189; Britain's assessment of policy of (1937), 192; anti-Jewish attacks in (1935–8), 198, 200; hostility to Jews in (November 1938), 215; British pressure on, to halt flow of refugees towards Palestine (1939), 233, 234, 241; plight of Jewish refugees from Czechoslovakia in (1939), 239, 241; German invasion of (1 September 1939), 242; visas for 20,000 Jewish children from, refused by Britain (18 September 1939), 243–4; fate of Jews in, under Nazi occupation (1939–45), 245–6, 252–3, 265; fate of Jewish survivors in, after the Second World War (1945–6), 275–6, 278, 280–2, 286–7; votes in favour of a Jewish and an

Arab State in Palestine (1947), 306

Poltava: Jewish self-defence in (1905), 64

Pöppendorf Camp: Jewish 'illegal' refugees deported from Palestine to (1947), 302

Port Said: cries of 'Down with the Jews' at (1937), 189

Portugal: anti-Jewish feeling in, 15, 16; Jews expelled from, 17; Nazi plans to kill off Jews, 257

Posen: fate of Jews in (1943), 265

Prague: Zionist Congress in (1933), 160; Revisionists hold a World Congress in (1938), 195; German occupation of (1939), 225, 233; fate of Jews in (1939), 239

Protocols of the Elders of Zion: circulates in Russia (1903), 59; publicized in Russia (1913), 73; circulated in Britain (1919), 126, 128; circulated by the Arabs in Palestine (1929), 152

Provence: Jews of, and Palestine, 12

Pumbeditha: Jewish academy of, 7, 57

Rachel's Tomb: Jewish land-purchase near, 41

Radom: Jewish orphans attacked in (1946), 280

Rafah: Avshalom Feinberg killed near (1917), 95

Ramla: Jewish community in, 8, 17; and the First World War, 87

Randall, A. W. G.: and 'illegal' Jewish refugees (1939), 223, 227, 234–5;

and South American opposition to Jewish refugees, 236; learns of ill-treatment of Jews in Prague (1939), 239

Rashi: a Jewish scholar of the eleventh century AD, 11

Rathbone, Eleanor: critical of British diplomats (1939), 226; critical of war-time immigration policies (1943), 267–8

Razvet: anti-semitic appeal in (1917), 100

Red Army: Jewish soldiers fight in ranks of (1941–5), 270

Red Sea: Jews settle by, 6

Reggio (Italy): 19

Rehovot: 172, 194, 210, 227

Reilly, (Sir) Patrick: and Jewish refugees, some of whom 'are definitely criminals or spies' (1939), 227; critical of 'scandalous traffic' of Jewish 'illegal' refugees (1939), 236; critical of Czech Jews 'who panicked unnecessarily', and left Czechoslovakia as refugees (1939), 239; suggests pressure on Slovak Government to prevent Jews going to Palestine (1939), 242

Rendel (Sir) George: on the 'tragic position' of the Jews (in 1936), 171–2; on Iraqi attacks on Iraqi Jews, 178; and the Peel Commission proposal for the partition of Palestine, 179, 182; and Indian Muslim reaction to Britain's Palestine policy, 188; opposes a Jewish State in Palestine, 188; reports on Arab hostility

to a Jewish State in
Palestine (1937), 189–90;
proposes the
abandonment of
partition, 191, 192–3; and
the future of Polish Jews
seeking to leave Poland
(1946), 276, 280–1, 282
Revisionists: 161, 195; and
'illegal' immigration of
Jews to Palestine, 161,
205, 238; anti-Arab
reprisals by, 201
Rhine: Jews settle along, 5,
9, 10; fate of the Jews to
the east of (in 1936), 166
Rhineland: anti-Jewish
violence in (1819), 29
Riga: 100
Rishon-le-Zion: Russian
Jews purchase land at
(1882), 38; and the First
World War, 87; Holocaust
survivors settle in, 301
Rohlings, August: anti-
semitic book by (1899), 53
Rokach, Israel: evidence to
Peel Commission, 173–4
Roman Empire: and the
Jews, 5–7, 9
Rome: restrictions on Jews
lifted in, 25
Rome and Jerusalem:
published (1862), 32
Roosevelt, President
Franklin Delano: and the
Evian Conference (1938),
202; refuses to lessen
anti-refugee restrictions
(1939), 240
Rothschild, Baron Albert:
Theodor Herzl appeals
to (1895), 47
Rothschild, Baron Edmond
de: praised by the ten-
year-old Chaim
Weizmann (1885), 42;
his first visit to Palestine
(1887), 42–3
Rothschild, Evelina de:

founds a girls' school in
Jerusalem (1864), 33
Rothschild, Mayer Amschel:
founder of a dynasty, 29,
30
Rothschild, Nathaniel: the
first Jew to receive a
British peerage (1885), 29
Rothschild, Lord (Victor):
his appeal in the House of
Lords on behalf of
persecuted Jewry (1946),
288–9
Rothschild, Lord (Walter
Lionel Rothschild): and
the evolution of the
Balfour Declaration
(1917), 97–8, 100, 101–2,
103, 108, 109
Rovno: Nazi atrocities at,
255
Rozanof: anti-semitic
pamphleteer, 74
Rubinstein, Isabella: her
'unusually clear evidence'
about Nazi war crimes,
291
Rumania: and the Jews, in
the nineteenth century,
31, 36–7, 38; Jewish
delegates from, at 'Lovers
of Zion' conference
(1884), 41; anti-Jewish
riots in (1907), 66; further
anti-Jewish riots (1914),
76; attacks on Jewish
property in (1926), 150;
anti-semitism in (1930s),
155, 159, 166; British
assessment of policy of
(1937), 192; anti-Jewish
riots in (1935–7), 198;
anti-semitism continues
rife in (1938), 200;
rebuked by Britain, for
allowing Jewish refugees
to travel towards Palestine
(1939), 223, 227–8, 233,
234–5, 236, 241, 244;
Jews of, refused

immigration certificates
to Palestine (1941), 259;
Jews continue to seek to
escape from (1942), 260;
General Gort seeks to
prevent Jewish refugees
going to Palestine from
(1944), 270; Jews set off
to Palestine from
(1945–8), 294
Rumbold, Sir Horace:
reports from Berlin, on
Nazi excesses (1933), 157,
158; a member of the Peel
Commission (1936–7),
164–5, 168, 169, 170, 172,
173, 174, 175, 176–7;
critical of Palestine
White Paper (1939), 229
Rumbold, Lady: witnesses
Nazi boycott of Jewish
shops (1933), 157–8; her
reflections on Tel Aviv
and the Jews (1936), 174
Ruppin, Arthur: reaches
Palestine (1907), 68;
and the founding of Tel
Aviv (1909), 71; and Arab
hostility to Jews (1913),
74; buys land for a Jewish
university in Jerusalem
(1914), 76; and the
position of the Jews of
Palestine on the coming
of war (in 1914), 82;
forced to leave Palestine
(1916), 91; witnesses
arrival of the first High
Commissioner to
Palestine (1920), 130–1;
stresses need for 'practical
accomplishments' in
Palestine (1921), 134;
his fears for the future
(1922), 148; witnesses
anti-semitism in Bavaria
(1923), 149; seeks Arab-
Jewish conciliation
(1925), 150; sees Jewish
village destroyed by Arabs

(1929), 153–4; gives
evidence to Shaw
Commission, 154; warns
of Arab hostility to the
Jews (1931), 156; on
'frightful' situation of the
Jews of Germany (1933),
157; on need for large-
scale Jewish immigration
to Palestine (1933), 159;
gives evidence to the Peel
Commission (1936),
169–70; reports 'a
general mood of
uneasiness' (1937), 184;
and the news of the
Nazi-Soviet pact (1939),
242
Russell, Sir Alison:
impressed by Jewish land
reclamation (1938), 209
Russia: and the Hassidic
movement, 24; and
Jewish misfortunes under
Tsarist rule, 24, 35–43;
exodus of Jews from
(1881–1914), 44–6; Jews
support socialism in
(1897), 52; Jews 'the
scapegoat' in (1902), 56;
anti-Jewish laws increase
in (1901), 57; renewal of
anti-Jewish violence in
(1903), 59–60; anti-
Jewish measures in
(1905), 62; anti-Jewish
violence in (1905), 62, 64;
Winston Churchill
denounces anti-Jewish
violence in (1905), 64–5;
anti-Jewish violence
continues in (1907), 66;
anti-Jewish measures in
(1911), 72; and the
coming of war (in 1914),
79; revolution in (1917),
96; and the best 'battle
cry' for the Jews of (in
1917), 97; anti-semitism
in (1917), 100; defeatism

in, 105; and the would-be
impact of the Balfour
Declaration on (in 1917),
109–10; the Bolsheviks
come to power in (1917),
110
Rutenberg, Pinhas:
advocates a Jewish
military unit (in 1914),
79–80, 85; his scheme for
the electrification of
Palestine (1921–22),
141–6; speaks to British
Colonial Secretary (1933),
161–2; his concession
area and British plans for
Palestine, 180, 210; his
appeal for Jewish
immigration to Palestine
(1938), 217
Rzeszow: ritual murder
charge against Jews in
(1946), 280

Sacher, Harry: edits
Palestine (1917), 92–3;
wants a 'Jewish State' in
Palestine (1917), 93,
97–8; fears future Arab
veto on Jewish
immigration (1921), 139;
gives evidence to Shaw
Commission (1929), 154
Sachsenhausen: trial of Nazi
war criminals from, 292
Sadeh, Yizhak: 197
Safed: a Jewish centre, 17,
19, 21; Jewish land-
purchase near, 28; anti-
Zionist petition of Arabs
from (1918), 115; Arabs
kill Jews in (1929), 151–2,
162; occupied by Jewish
forces (1948), 307
Sakaria: British pressure
against passage of, to
Palestine (1939), 245
Salonica: Jews find refuge
in, 17

Salzmann, Joseph:
murdered by Arabs
(1913), 74
Samaria: Jewish kingdom in,
3; Jewish revolt against
Romans in, 6; and the
crusaders, 11
Samuel, (Sir) Herbert
(later Lord Samuel): his
ideas for Jewish
settlement in Palestine
(1914–15), 82, 83; and the
future of Palestine (1917),
103; Britain's first High
Commissioner in
Palestine (1920–5),
130–1, 132, 133, 136, 137;
and the future of Jewish
immigration to Palestine,
142–3; protests against
the Palestine White
Paper (1939), 228; urges
Government to relax
immigration restrictions
(1943), 264
San Francisco: Russian-
born Jews settle in, 44;
and the British conquest of
Jerusalem, 123
San Remo Conference: 130,
131
Sandstrom, Emil: 301
Sandu: takes 'illegal'
refugees to Palestine
(1939), 227
Santo Domingo: Jewish
refugees welcomed
(1938), 203
Sarawak: only three Jewish
refugees accepted in six
months (1939), 244
Sardinia: Jews of, 4
Sargent, Sir Orme: 237
Saudi Arabia: 171, 178, 191,
193; the importance of
its 'friendship' to
Britain (1938), 201; to be
invited by Britain to
discuss the future of
Palestine (1938), 210;

influence of, over British
policy (1939), 219, 225–6;
future importance of oil
of (1947), 298; a possible
supporter of partition, 299
Saxony: Jews of, 10
Scheldt, River: 13
Scots: Lloyd George places
'second' among nations,
after Jews, 131
Scott, C. P.: 93
Scott Fox, (Sir) David: and
the war crimes trials, 291
Sedlits: Jews killed in
(1906), 66
Sein, Abraham: sentenced
to death, 200
Selassie, Haile: 209
Senesh, Hannah: executed
by Nazis (1944), 270
Sereni, Enzo: murdered in
Dachau (1944), 270
Seville: Jewish community
in, 8; anti-Jewish
preaching in, 15
Seychelles: refuses to take
a single Jewish refugee in
six months (1939), 244
Seymour, Captain: reports
Arabs satisfied by halt to
Jewish immigration
(1921), 133
Shabtai Zevi: his messianic
appeal, 22
Shaw, J. V. W. (later Sir
John Shaw): critical of
'young Jewish extremists'
(August 1945), 273–4;
says majority of Jews in
Palestine 'dislike
bloodshed' (July 1946),
288
Shaw, Sir Walter: his report
on the 1929 disturbances,
151–4
Shechem (Nablus): and the
Tartar invasion of
Palestine, 12
Sheikh Yussuf: opposes
partition of Palestine, 179

Shepherd, F. M.: reports
on Buchenwald
concentration camp
(1939), 220
Shertok, Moshe: evidence
to Peel Commission, 168,
169
Shibly al-Jamal: protests
against Balfour
Declaration (1921), 137;
reported to have spoken
of the need for 'killing'
Jews, 142
Shimshelevich, Izhak (see
Ben Zvi, Izhak)
Shinwell, Emanuel (later
Lord Shinwell): and
Britain's future
dependence on Arab oil
(January 1947), 297–8;
believes Jewish friendship
'more valuable' to Britain
than Arab friendship, 299
Shuckburgh, (Sir) John:
136, 141, 142, 187, 194;
alarmed at 'illegal'
Jewish immigration
(1939), 245; and the
keeping of immigration
decisions 'outside the
realm of Cabinet policy'
(1940), 251
Sicily: Jews of, 4
Sidebotham, Herbert: on
the meaning of 'a Jewish
State' (1917), 98
Silesia: Jews of, 10
Silver, Abba Hillel: warns
that 'Jews will fight for
their rights' (1945), 273;
urges United Nations to
give the Jews their
'national freedom' (1947),
300; accepts UNSCOP
partition plan as evidence
of Jewish 'desire for
peace', 306
Silver, Alderman James:
opposes Jewish
immigration to Britain

(1902), 55
Simon, Sir John: 157, 220,
240
Sinclair, Sir Archibald: his
criticisms of the proposed
partition of Palestine
(1937), 182; Weizmann
confides in (1938), 215
Siraf: Jewish governor of, 9
Skopje: 115
Slovakia: fate of Jews in
(1939), 241–2
Smallbones, R. T.: reports
on arrest of Jews in
Germany (1938), 212, 214
Smuts, J. C.: envisages 'a
great Jewish State' in
Palestine (1919), 127;
wants Palestine to take
'its fair share' of Jews
(1938), 217
Smyrna: Jews find refuge
in, 17
Socotra: would accept
Christian, but not Jewish,
refugees (1939), 236
Sokolow, Nahum: proposes
industrial development in
Palestine (1884), 41; and
the Sykes-Picot agreement
(of 1916), 89; wants 'a
Jewish society' in
Palestine (1917), 93;
and the evolution of the
Balfour Declaration, 95,
96, 98, 101, 109, 110; at
the Paris Peace
Conference (1919), 117;
Arab leader refuses to
meet (1921), 137; talks to
British Colonial
Secretary (1933), 161–2
Solomon ben Judah: a
religious leader in
Jerusalem in the tenth
century AD, 8
Somaliland: refuses to take
a single Jewish refugee in
six months (1939), 244
Sonnenschein, Rosa: an

American Jewess, at the first Zionist Congress (1897), 50

South Africa: Jews of, support Zionism (1917), 97; restrictions on Jewish immigration to (1930), 155

South America: Jews of, 19, 21; Jewish refugees made increasingly unwelcome in (1939), 236; Jews find refuge in (1945–8), 294

Southern Rhodesia: unable to accept sixteen German Jewish refugees (1939), 225

Soviet Union: concludes peace with Germany (1918), 112; role of Jews in (1919), 120; criticism of Jewish Commissars in, 126, 127–8; Jewish disabilities in (in the 1920s), 149; Jewish culture suppressed in (in the 1930s), 201; execution of Jews in (in the 1930s), 218; fate of Jews in, after Nazi invasion of (22 June 1941), 253; votes in favour of a Jewish and an Arab State in Palestine (1947), 306; Jews from, emigrate to the State of Israel (after 1967), 309

Spain: Jews of, 4, 8; Maimonides born in, 11; expulsion of the Jews from, 15–16, 17, 19, 21; Arab influence in, criticized, 177; Nazi plans to kill Jews of, 257

St Clair, Garner: reports on Jewish 'distress' in Vienna (1938), 199

St Louis: Russian-born Jews settle in, 44

St Petersburg: Jewish book burnt in (1836), 35; the Jews of, 36

Stanley, Oliver: defends restrictions on Jewish land-purchase in Palestine (1940), 247; refuses to 'undermine' British restrictions on immigration to Palestine (1942), 259–60

Stern Gang: Churchill critical of terror acts of (1944), 269; compared to the Zealots who rebelled against Roman rule, 273; and the attack on Acre prison (1947), 304

Storrs, Ronald: on Zionist achievements (1918), 114; critical of rate of Jewish immigration into Palestine (1937), 191

Strand Magazine: Churchill article in, condemns German anti-semitism (1935), 162

Strasbourg: Jews massacred in, 13; Jews find refuge in, 22

Struma: tragic fate of 'illegal' refugees on (1941–2), 259, 295

Sudetenland: 208–9, 211, 212, 215

Suleiman I, Sultan: encourages Jews to return to Palestine, 21

Sunday Chronicle: calls Zionism 'a source of pride' (1917), 95

Sunday Express: opposed to entry of 'foreign Jews' into Britain (1938), 200

Sura: Jewish academy of, 7, 57

Surinam: possible Jewish 'homeland' in (1905), 62

Swaziland: only a few Jewish refugees accepted (1939), 244

Sweden: Nazi plans to kill Jews of, 257; supports a Jewish State in Palestine (1947), 304, 306

Switzerland: Jews flee to (1938), 198; regulations towards refugees made more strict (1939), 240

Sydenham, Lord: an opponent of Zionism, 144

Sykes, Sir Mark: and the future of Palestine, 85, 89, 92, 93, 106, 110–11; and Arab fears of Zionism, 112, 113–14

Sykes-Picot Agreement (of 1916): 89

Syria: conquers the Land of Israel, 5; the Arab war potential in (1915), 87; to be 'the granary of Europe' (1917), 111; 'room' for Jews and Arabs in (1919), 118; French control over (1919), 123; Palestine Arabs receive arms from (1929), 153; weakening French influence in (1937), 184; Palestinian Arab 'bandits' recruited in, 187; hostility to Britain's Palestine policy of, 193; Britain afraid of losing 'friendship' of (1938), 201; 'Holy War' preached in (1938), 211; Jews fight in ranks of allied forces in (1939–45), 270; Arab soldiers from, enlist in British army, 270; troops of, seek to crush Jewish State (1948), 307–8

Szold, Henrietta: evidence to Peel Commission, 172

Tanganyika: refuses to take a single Jewish refugee in

six months (1939), 244

Tannous, Dr Izzet: urges
return of Mufti to
Palestine (1938), 206, 211

Tartars: devastate
Jerusalem, 12; seize Jews
as slaves, 22

Tchlenow, Yehiel: 109, 110

'Teheran children': reach
safety in Palestine (1943),
264

Tel Aviv: founded (1909),
71; Mendel Beilis settles
in (1914), 73; and the
First World War, 87;
Peel Commission visits
(1936), 165; Peel
Commission discusses,
173–4; ugly but
impressive, 174;
refugees from Germany
and Austria in, 220–1;
Holocaust survivors
settle in, 301; Jewish
Statehood declared in
(May 1948), 308

Thame, Lord Bertie of: and
the dangers of a Jewish
State (1919), 121

The Times: reports on
plight of Rumanian Jews
(in 1878), 31; comments
on the 'war of liberation'
in Palestine (1917), 95;
publishes letter from two
anti-Zionist Jews (1917),
97; wishes to rally Jewish
influence (1917), 105; on
the frontiers of Palestine
(1919), 124; Zangwill
appeals for a Jewish
'solid, surveyable
territory' in a letter to
(1922), 143; rebuked for
describing the
assassination of Lewis
Andrews as a 'dastardly
murder', 190; publishes
letter describing Jews as
'a nation without a home'

(1938), 196; publishes
letter criticizing
Palestine White Paper
(1939), 229

Theodosiya: anti-Jewish
violence in (1905), 62

Tiberias: rebuilt by the Jews
in 1561, 21; Jewish land-
purchase near, 28; a
Jewish wedding party
attacked at (1938), 205;
Jews murdered at (1939),
223; occupied by Jewish
forces (1948), 307

Toledo: Jews of, welcome
Muslims, 8; Christian
massacre of Jews in, 15

Tortosa: Jews forced to
defend their religion in,
15

Toynbee, Arnold: and the
future of the Jews in
Palestine (1917), 111–12,
115

Trade Winds: 'illegal'
immigrants reach
Palestine on (1947), 301

Transjordan: British
Mandate over, 123, 132;
Arabs of Palestine receive
arms from (1929), 153;
closed to Jewish
settlement (since 1922),
172; proposed transfer of
Palestinian Arabs to
(1937), 185–6; to discuss
the future of Palestine
(1938), 210; pressure on
Britain from (1939),
225–6; Arab soldiers
from, enlist in British
army, 270; a possible
supporter of partition,
299; its troops seek to
crush the Jewish State
(1948), 307–8; occupies
the West Bank, 308

Tratner, Asher: his death
recalled, 280

Treblinka: Jews murdered

at, 265, 267

Trent (Italy): Jews of,
accused of ritual murder,
20

Tripoli: Arabs from,
emigrate to Palestine
(1930s), 230; Arab
protests against the
proposed partition of
Palestine (1937), 188–9

Tripolitania: suggested by
Churchill as a Jewish
colony (1943), 262; Arabs
attack Jews in (1947), 307

Trotsky: 127

Truman, Harry S.: wants
concentration camp
survivors allowed into
Palestine (1945), 274;
rejects British plan to
retain overall British
control of Palestine (1946)
295

Trumpeldor, Captain
Joseph: fights at
Dardanelles (1915),
85–6; advocates a Jewish
Legion (1917), 92

Trunk, Isaiah: on fate of
Polish Jewry under the
Nazis, 252–3

Tunis: a Jew serves as
United States consul in
(1813–16), 25; Jews killed
in (1869), 27

Tunisia: Jews persecuted
in, 13

Turkey, Republic of:
possible opposition to
Britain's Palestine policy
from (1937), 192; British
pressure on, to halt flow
of Jewish refugees towards
Palestine (1939), 242,
244, 245; Nazi plans to
kill Jews of, 257; orders
'illegal' immigrant ship
Struma out of Turkish
waters (1942), 259; Jewish
refugees able to pass

through, on way to
Palestine (1943–5), 267;
votes against Jewish
Statehood (1947), 306
Tustar: Jewish carpet
industry at, 9
Tyre: Jewish community in,
8

Ueberall, Ehud (later
Avriel): describes fate of
Jews in Austria (1938),
198–9; learns of fate of
Jews of Poland (1943),
265; learns of relaxation
of British immigration
restrictions (1943), 267
Uganda: a possible Jewish
'homeland' in (1903),
60–1, 69; only three
Jewish refugees accepted
in six months (1939), 244
Ukraine: persecution of the
Jews in, 22, 24; the Jews
of, under Tsarist rule, 35;
anti-Jewish violence in
(1917–20), 116, 117, 120,
121, 126, 140; slaughter
of Jews in, during the
Second World War, 257,
265
Uman (Ukraine): Jewish
self-defence in, 24
United Nations: 284, 300;
sets up a special
committee on Palestine
(UNSCOP), 301
United States of America,
the: and the Hassidic
movement, 24; and the
strength of early Jewish
life in, 25; and the fate of
Damascus Jewry (1840),
27; Jews from Germany
find refuge in (after 1830),
30; Jews from Tsarist
Russia seek refuge in, 36,
44–5; protests against
Russian pogroms in

(1903), 59; its continuing
appeal to the Jews of
Russia (1907), 66; Jews
of, support a Jewish
experimental farm in
Palestine (1910), 71; and
the coming of war (in
1914), 80; and the future
of Palestine (1915), 84;
enters the First World
War (1916), 96; and the
evolution of the Balfour
Declaration (1917), 102,
105, 106–7; and a possible
mandate over Palestine
for (1917–20), 112, 122–3,
137; Feisal wants help
from Zionist Jews of
(1918), 115; introduces
Quota Act which restricts
Jewish immigration
(1924), 149, 155; and
Britain's Palestine policy
(1937), 179; and the Evian
Conference (1938), 203;
British pressure on, 203;
importance of, compared
with that of 'Arabia'
(1939), 219; Jewish
influence in, belittled
(1939), 221, 222, 226;
reported 'embarrassment'
over German Jewish
refugees (1939), 223; and
support for the idea of a
Jewish State (1939), 237;
sympathy for Jewish
refugees in, to be
combatted by the British
Foreign Office (1939),
237–8; maintains strict
refugee quotas (1939),
240; seeks clarification of
British policy towards
German Jewish refugees
(1939), 242–3, 244;
Churchill on possible
'outcry' among Jews of
(1940), 247; Churchill
suggests transfer of

Britain's Palestine
Mandate to (July 1945),
273; British policy
clashes with (1946), 286;
Jews find refuge in
(1946–8), 294; votes in
favour of Jewish and Arab
Statehood (29 November
1947), 306
UNSCOP: and the future of
Palestine (1947), 301–2,
303, 304
Uruguay: supports a Jewish
State in Palestine (1947),
304

Valencia: anti-Jewish riots
in, 13
Vansittart, Sir Robert:
opposes arming the Jews
of Palestine for self-
defence (1937), 178;
opposes a Jewish
majority in Palestine, 192
Venice: shipowners of,
forbidden to take Jews to
Palestine, 20; restrictions
on Jews lifted in, 25
Vergani, Ernst: anti-
semitism of, in Vienna,
68–9; and Hitler, 70
Vienna: Herzl's experiences
in (1893), 46–7; Herzl
fears for future of Jews in,
47; election of anti-
semitic mayor in (1895),
48; anti-semitism in
(since 1888), 68–9;
Hitler's reflections on,
69–70; Hitler enters, and
annexes to Germany
(1938), 198, 199, 225
Vienna, Congress of: and
the Jews (1878), 31, 38
Vilna: Jewish socialists in
(1897), 52; Herzl visits
(1903), 59; anti-Jewish
pogrom in (1914), 81;
the Jews of, during the

First World War, 104

Vitebsk: Jews driven from (1824), 35

Vitovt, Grand Duke: protects Jews in Lithuania, 13

Vladimir, Grand Duke, of Russia: Herzl writes to, 48

von Breidenbach, Bernhard: and the Jews of Palestine in the fifteenth century AD, 17

von Selzam: and German fears of a Jewish State in Palestine (1937), 188

von Treitschke: 'the Jews are our misfortune', 80, 81

Wagner, Richard: 53

Walter, Bruno: 157

Wannsee Conference: fate of European Jews discussed at (1942), 257, 258

War Crimes Trials (1945–6): 290–4

Wardrop, John: and the danger of 'Jewish intrigues' (1919), 125

Warr, G. M.: on Jewish and other refugees, a question of priorities (1939), 233; on Jewish refugees from Germany (1939), 245

Warren, Charles (Sir): advocates widespread Jewish rural settlement in Palestine (1874), 34

Warsaw: German bombardment of (1939), 242, 246; Jewish uprising against the Germans in (1942), 258; murder of Jews of (reported in 1943), 265; report of situation of Jewish survivors in, after

the Second World War (1946), 276

Washington: news of Nazi atrocities against Jews made public in (1942), 264

Waterlow, Sir Sidney: and 'illegal' Jewish immigration to Palestine, 207, 226–7, 228

Watson, Cathcart: opposes a Jewish 'homeland' in Uganda (1904), 61

Wauchope, Sir Arthur: on Arab hostility to Zionism (1932), 156, 165; his private talk with Weizmann (1936), 170–1; proposes armed units of Jews, for self-defence (1937), 178

Wavell, General: warns of Arab unrest (1940), 249–50; his warnings challenged by Churchill, 250

Wedgwood, Josiah: criticizes British officials in Palestine, 150; criticizes 'unjust law' of Arab control of Jerusalem, 232; criticizes 'conduct worthy of the Middle Ages' pursued by Britain towards Jewish refugees, 235, 239

Weimar Republic: Jewish life in (1919–33), 163

Weizmann, Chaim: 'to Zion! let us go' (1885), 42; criticizes the Jews of Pinsk as 'creatures devoid of personality' (1895), 47–8; at second Zionist Congress (1898), 52; 'Israel is awaiting its children' (1900), 54; wants 'a Jewish University in Palestine' (1902), 58, 61; 'ours is such a feeble

generation' (1904), 62; 'Our fate is to prepare. . . .' (1905), 64; 'When shall we have a single calm day?' (1906), 66; and the Mendel Beilis blood libel charge (1913), 73; explains Zionism to Arthur Balfour, 76; and the impact of the coming of war (in 1914), 79–81; and the evolution of the Balfour Declaration (1916–17), 89, 93, 95, 96, 97–108; and the early years of British rule in Palestine (1917–22), 112, 114, 116, 122, 124, 125, 135–6; addresses Paris Peace Conference (1919), 117–18, 121; his 'fiery energy' praised (1920), 128; Arab leader refuses to meet (1921), 137; his fears for the future (1921), 139–40, 141; seeks a British Government loan (1928), 150–1; resigns as President of Zionist Organization (1930), 155; speaks of Jewish disabilities throughout the world, 155–6; defends Jewish employment of all-Jewish labour in Palestine, 161–2; his evidence to the Peel Commission (1936), 166–8; his private talk with Wauchope (1936), 170–1; his private talks with Coupland, 172, 174–5; his letter to the Peel Commission (1937), 175–6; and the proposed partition of Palestine, 179, 180, 194; rejects 'permanent minority status' for Jews of Palestine, 196; on the

Arab psychology, 201–2; not allowed to address the Evian Conference (1938), 202; 'very despairing' (November 1938), 214; distressed by British policy of 'dangling false hopes before the eyes of a tortured people' (November 1938), 215; sees British Government about to 'undermine' basis of Jewish presence in Palestine (1939), 219; told of 'vital' need to Britain of Arab support (1939), 222; and the Palestine White Paper (1939), 226; at the 21st Zionist Congress (1939), 242; appeals to Britain for visas for 20,000 Polish-Jewish children (1939), 243–4; urges Britain to allow Jewish armed units for self-defence (1940), 246; seeks a Jewish military force to join allied armies (1940), 249–50; death of his son on active service, 260; wants Palestine to absorb 'homeless and Stateless' Jews (1942), 261; Churchill's discussion with (1944), 269; urges end to Palestine immigration restrictions (1945), 272, 274; on Jewish people's 'despair' (1946), 287; appeals in vain to Bevin, for partition (October 1946), 294; condemns Britain's war-time policy towards the Jews (December 1946), 295; condemns Jewish terrorism as 'a cancer in the body politic' (December

1946), 296; explains why the Jews wish to live in Palestine (July 1947), 303–4; accepts partition as 'a great sacrifice', 304
Wertheimer: Nazi boycott of (1933), 158
Western Australia: possible Jewish 'settlement' in (1938), 214
White Russia: the Jews of, 22
William II, German Kaiser: Herzl seeks to influence (1895), 48; in Palestine (1898), 52–3
Willingdon, Lord: 'little use' German Jewish doctors going to India (1933), 159
Wilson, Sir Henry: and Weizmann, 120; and the San Remo Conference, 130
Wilson, President Woodrow: and Zionism, 102, 103
Wingate, Captain Orde: and Jewish self-defence in Palestine, 197
Wingate, Sir Reginald: and 'Arab union', 86; and Turkish ill-treatment of the Jews of Jaffa (1917), 97
Winterton, Lord: 203, 233–4, 240
Wiseman, Sir William: 103
Wood, Miss A. E.: reports on plight of Jewish displaced persons (1946), 282–3
Woodhead, Sir John: and Arab fears of Jewish land-purchase (1938), 209
Woodhead Report: 209–10
World Jewish Congress: explains why 'uprooted' Jews do not wish to stay in Europe (1946), 282;

describes plight of Jews in Afghanistan (1946), 283
World Zionist Organization: 53; to use 'its best efforts' to help the Arab States (1918), 116
Wortsmann, Ezekiel: on need to revive Hebrew language (1901), 54
Wright, P.: his description of Jews in Poland (in 1919), 126
Würzburg: anti-Jewish violence in (1819), 29; fate of Jewish boys from (1939), 217

Yadin, Yigael: and the role of the Jewish 'fighting spirit', 308
Yemen: opposes Britain's Palestine policy (1937), 193; to discuss the future of Palestine (1938), 210; applies pressure on Britain (1939), 225–6; Arabs from, emigrate to Palestine (1930s), 230; Jews from, emigrate to the State of Israel (after 1948), 309
Yesud ha-Ma'alah: Jewish village in Palestine, 41
Yoselewska, Mrs: gives evidence of Nazi atrocities near Pinsk, 256–7
Young, Major H.: upholds Zionist aspirations (1921), 133, 136, 139, 144–5; proposes Jewish settlement in Northern Rhodesia (1939), 236
Yugoslavia: British pressure on, towards 'illegal' Jewish immigrants to Palestine (1939), 226, 233, 234; Nazis murder

Jews of, 258; Jews set off to Palestine from (1945–8), 294

Yushinsky, Andrei: murdered (1911), 72–4

Zangwill, Israel: supports Jewish 'home' in Uganda (1903), 61, 62; supports Jewish 'home' in Manchuria (1908), 69; warned about the Jews being 'a force ... going to waste' (1914), 81; Edwin Montagu scathing towards (1915), 84; wants Jews to have 'a solid, surveyable territory' (1922), 143

Zar, Mordekhai: and the 'secret' Jews of Meshed, 27

Zealots: Jewish terrorists of the 1940s compared to, 273

Zelig the carpenter: murdered, 256

Zetland, Lord: and Indian Muslim hostility to 'any Jewish sovereignty' in Palestine (1938), 210; seeks permanent Jewish minority in Palestine (1939), 219–20

Zhitomir: anti-Jewish violence in (1905), 62; three hundred Jews murdered in (1919), 121

Zion Mule Corps: 85

Zion's Greeting: published (1860), 32

Zionist Commission: sponsored by British Cabinet (1918), 112–13; and Weizmann's meeting with Feisal (of December 1918), 116; (for subsequent index entries see: Jewish Agency)

Zionist Congress: opens in Basel (1897), 50; advocates 'systematic settlement' of Jews in Palestine, 51; meets for the second time (1898), 52; meets in Vienna (1902), 58; meets in Basel (1903), 60; meets in Basel (1905), 62; meets in Prague (1933), 160; meets in Zurich (1937), 182; meets in Geneva (1939), 242; meets in Basel (1946), 295